This book truly is revolutionary—and so beautiful because of the inclusiveness and expansiveness of genre and what defines spirituality. . . . It's a colossal work, a peak in the valley of books. But most of all, it is visionary—truly the vision that takes music to the next level of being.

—Sarah Takagi, Piano faculty, New England Conservatory of Music, Extension Division; Piano faculty, Wellesley College

Music and the Soul is a breakthrough work that weaves the powers of music with the potentials of consciousness. Kurt Leland's visionary contribution brings the art of great music to the magical inner journey of transcendence.

—Don Campbell, author of *The Mozart Effect* and *Music, Physician for Times to Come*

MUSIC
and the
SOUL

A Listener's Guide
to Achieving Transcendent
Musical Experiences

My dear sister Naomi,
May your radiant Soul
illumine the world through
your music.
Lou, Aaron 2/14/05

KURT LELAND

HAMPTON ROADS
PUBLISHING COMPANY, INC.

HR
for the evolving human spirit

Cover design by Marjoram Productions
Cover digital imagery © 2004 PictureQuest/Digital Vision
and PictureQuest/Stockbyte

Hampton Roads Publishing Company, Inc.
1125 Stoney Ridge Road
Charlottesville, VA 22902

434-296-2772
fax: 434-296-5096
e-mail: hrpc@hrpub.com
www.hrpub.com

If you are unable to order this book from your local
bookseller, you may order directly from the publisher.
Call 1-800-766-8009, toll-free.

Library of Congress Cataloging-in-Publication Data

Leland, Kurt.
  Music and the soul : a listener's guide to achieving transcendent musical
experiences / Kurt Leland.
      p. cm.
  Includes bibliographical references and index.
  ISBN 1-57174-367-7 (6 x 9 tp : alk. paper)
  1. Music, Influence of. 2. Music--Psychological aspects. 3. Spiritual
life. I. Title.
  ML3920.L45 2004
  781'.11--dc22
                              2004020566

10 9 8 7 6 5 4 3 2 1
Printed on acid-free paper in the United States

You use a glass mirror to see your face;
you use works of art to see your soul.
—**George Bernard Shaw**

Contents

Finale

Preface

In the year 2000, just after Hampton Roads Publishing decided to publish *Otherwhere: A Field Guide to Nonphysical Reality for the Out-of-Body Traveler*, I was invited by senior editor Richard Leviton to write a sequel to that book. He wanted me to tackle the question of whether near-death experiences were an accurate prediction of what the Afterlife was like. Leviton's invitation led to the 2002 publication of my second book with Hampton Roads, *The Unanswered Question: Death, Near-Death, and the Afterlife.*

During the same conversation, Leviton mentioned that he had several other book concepts for which he hoped to find authors. One concerned music.

His idea was to update an esoteric classic, first published in 1933, and kept in print for much of the next fifty years: *Music: Its Secret Influence throughout the Ages*, by British composer and esotericist Cyril Scott (1879–1970). Scott himself had published a revised version of the book in 1958, but it barely mentioned composers who came into prominence after the death of the Russian mystic Alexander Scriabin in 1915.

Leviton wanted me to produce a sequel to Scott's book that would cover the rest of the twentieth century. He also wanted me to address what he considered to be a flaw in that book: Scott's claim that jazz and rock music had been "'put through' by the Dark Forces" and were inherently evil.[1]

Leviton's problem had been finding an author with the proper musical *and* spiritual training. Since I was a composer as well as a practicing psychic, he thought I might be qualified to write the sequel he had in mind.

I'd known of Scott's book for years, but had never read it. Before committing myself to updating *Music: Its Secret Influence*, I wanted to find out more about its author.

Cyril Scott was not only a composer and esotericist, but also a poet and prolific writer. His subjects ranged from music to the effects of dietary change on health and illness, including cancer, long before such ideas had gained the currency they have today in the alternative medical community.

Early in his career as a composer, Scott was considered an *enfant terrible*. His music was dubbed ultradiscordant by staid English critics. As a personal friend of French musical impressionist Claude Debussy, however, Scott eventually developed his own attractive, yet idiosyncratic form of impressionism.

Scott paid the bills by publishing a large number of songs and solo piano ditties, which damaged his reputation as a serious composer. Further damage was done when he went public about his personal philosophy, influenced by contemporary esoteric teachings, ancient yoga traditions, and his involvement with trance mediums and alternative health practitioners.

By 1950, it was difficult for Scott to get his music played. He even considered giving up composing, but a message from Beyond encouraged him to keep going. To this day, despite a modest revival of interest in his music in the 1970s, much of Scott's later output has never been performed.

Yet Cyril Scott is still a well-known name in esoteric circles, thanks to his famous trilogy of semiautobiographical literary works: *The Initiate: Some Impressions of a Great Soul*, *The Initiate in the New World*, and *The Initiate in the Dark Cycle*. Published anonymously in 1920, 1927, and 1931, respectively, these books have remained in print ever since. They purport to record the doings of an English spiritual savant by the name of Justin Moreword Haig (JMH). In the books, Scott identified himself as a poet rather than a composer.

Though Scott confessed to the authorship of the Initiate Series in his 1971 autobiography, *Bone of Contention*, speculation about the identity of the mysterious and magical JMH continues to the present day. While researching Scott on the Internet, I encountered a German website dedicated to solving this mystery.

After completing *The Unanswered Question*, I found myself sufficiently intrigued by Cyril Scott and his ideas that I assented to Leviton's proposal to write a sequel to *Music: Its Secret Influence*. I had some ideas of my own about the relationship between music and spirituality that I'd wanted to write about for years.

In the early 1980s, I attended graduate school at the University of Illinois, where I studied music composition. Concurrently with my academic work, I'd begun to experiment with receiving channeled communications, at first through a Ouija board, then by means of automatic writing. After several months of such experiments, I began to speak in trance. Eventually, I made contact with a nonphysical teacher by the name of Charles who seemed to be a clear source of information. Charles has been with me ever since.[2]

Over the years, I've received a great deal of information from Charles about how composing, performing, and listening to music can promote one's spiritual growth. Despite his apparent nonphysicality, Charles has been the best music teacher I've ever had. What I've learned from him lies behind everything I've written in this book.

In *Music and the Soul: A Listener's Guide to Achieving Transcendent Musical Experiences*, I introduce the idea of *transcendent musical experiences* (TMEs), a term I've invented to describe the extraordinary emotional, spiritual, or mystical reactions we can sometimes have when composing, performing, or listening to music.

TMEs run the gamut from chills along the spine to apparent physical paralysis. They often result in tears and feelings of being deeply moved. They can include sudden realizations about how the music is constructed or what the composer was thinking or experiencing at the time it was written. They can also produce spontaneous and ecstatic insights into life, the universe, or God. Some TMEs induce inner visions of odd colors and geometric forms impossible to duplicate in physical reality or scenes with the hyperreality of lucid dreams.

TMEs appear to be messages from our souls that guide us toward developing a greater awareness of our potentials as human beings in the physical, emotional, intellectual, and spiritual realms. Some TMEs have the power to transform or change the direction of our lives.

What brings about TMEs? Are there particular composers, genres, pieces of music, or recordings that are more likely to produce them? What can listeners, composers, and performers do to increase the likelihood of generating TMEs in themselves or an audience?

Music and the Soul attempts to answer these questions. Not only is it a *listener's* guide to achieving transcendent musical experiences, but also a handbook on how the soul guides us, through music, to increase our satisfaction and happiness in life, and become more deeply and truly ourselves. My goal has been to develop a vocabulary for discussing music in terms that *anyone* can understand, based on intuitions that we all have about the music that moves us, but perhaps have never had the words for—until now.

My focus is on classical music, because that's what I know best. But interviews with friends whose TMEs have been induced by listening to jazz and rock, from Brubeck to Led Zeppelin, demonstrate that the phenomenon is not limited to classical music. The techniques and principles for achieving TMEs that I reveal here will work just as well in other genres of music. TMEs seem to be more common than other types of mystical experiences, such as out-of-body experiences or near-death experiences. Nearly everyone I've spoken to has had at least one TME.

As I describe my TMEs and those of others, providing hints about how listeners, performers, and composers may be able to replicate such experiences themselves, I hope you'll be reminded of your own TMEs. The internal and external conditions that induced them can be important clues about how to achieve future TMEs.

In part 1, "Music and the Soul," I define what I mean by transcendent musical experiences, giving a number of examples from my own life and from interviews with friends. I then relate TMEs to mystical experiences, as defined by William James in *The Varieties of Religious Experience*, and the transient states of ecstasy or illumination that psychologist Abraham H. Maslow called peak experiences.

Maslow believed that peak experiences lead us toward ever higher levels of psychological integration and functionality. TMEs serve a similar purpose, guiding us into a closer relationship with the soul.

Charles says that the soul is our true self, a consciousness that exists beyond the physical reality with which we're familiar. The soul has certain plans for our growth, which it encourages us to realize by increasing or withdrawing the life force available to us.

Increases in life force result in feelings of satisfaction, happiness, and ecstasy; decreases result in feelings of dissatisfaction, unhappiness, and depression. As ecstatic experiences, TMEs result from higher levels of life force and are therefore a means by which the soul guides us to realize its plans for our growth.

The idea that music can be used to guide our spiritual and moral development is a key theme of Cyril Scott's book *Music: Its Secret Influence throughout the Ages*. After summarizing and commenting on the contents of Scott's book, I come to an important question: What did Scott mean when he differentiated between what he called *human* music and *ethereal* music?

Scott further divided ethereal music into two types, *deva music*, which is inspired in human composers by nonphysical (or ethereal) beings such as nature spirits and angels, and *buddhic music*, which comes from a higher realm, and portrays "that love which *is* God."[3]

Scott's descriptions of deva music and buddhic music and their effects on listeners resemble those of TMEs. But what he meant by these terms is not at all clear. The attempt to figure out how human music, devic music, and buddhic music differ from each other and how to use those differences to achieve TMEs is one of the driving forces behind this book.

Scott studied the ancient Hindu spiritual practice called *yoga* (Sanskrit for "union with the divine"). The word *deva* (Sanskrit for "shining one," meaning a god) plays an important role in that tradition. Perhaps I would find the clues I needed to discover what Scott meant by devic music in the yoga tradition.

My long-standing interest in yoga had already led me to explore a variety called *Tantra*, one branch of which deals with a spiritual energy called *kundalini* (also known as the "serpent power"), said to reside at the base of the spine. As this energy rises from that point to the crown of the head, it passes through a number of psychic energy centers called *chakras* (Sanskrit for "wheels"). Each chakra, or center, deals with a different aspect of human experience and produces a particular state of consciousness. Transcendence, the ecstatic goal of Tantra, results when each of the chakras has been activated and integrated with the others.

Kundalini resembles what Charles calls life force, and may also be used by the soul to guide us toward realizing the soul's plans for our growth. In looking into another branch of Tantra called *nada yoga* (Sanskrit for "yoga of sound"), I discovered a few more clues about how to relate TMEs, life force, yoga, kundalini, ancient and modern notions of the chakras, and music.

It then became possible for me to build what I call a *continuum of human potential*, based on the feelings that listening to certain kinds of music produce in me, from sensual pleasure or opening the heart to a sense of expanded consciousness. This continuum outlines the relationships between life force, the chakras, and elements of music, such as rhythm, harmony, melody, and form.

Maslow said that "Man is a hierarchy of needs, with the biological needs at the bottom and the spiritual needs at the top."[4] That's the basic outline of the continuum of human potential. The chakras also involve a hierarchy of needs, from physical and emotional to intellectual and spiritual. These needs form the backbone of the continuum of human potential.

In the process of creating this continuum, I was surprised to discover a type of transcendent music more powerful than any I'd heard before. This discovery not only necessitated that I add an eighth chakra to the seven that are present in most chakra systems, but also allowed me to differentiate between the music that produces expanded consciousness (corresponding to Scott's deva music), and that which produces cosmic consciousness (corresponding to Scott's buddhic music).

Throughout part 1, at the end of each chapter, I present exercises intended to prepare you for the yoga of listening described in part 2. These exercises involve an imaginary interview, in which I ask questions similar to those that elicited my friends' descriptions of their TMEs. They also encourage you to think of music in new ways by introducing the concept of *playlist*, derived from the software used to manage and play collections of music stored on a computer or portable listening device.

Playlists allow you to group songs or pieces by any criteria you wish. The criteria I suggest, based on how the music makes you feel, can allow you to begin building your own continuum of human potential, based on your favorite music.

In part 2, "The Yoga of Listening," I lay down the principles of a new kind of yoga, which involves listening to music in a meditative way. The goal of the yoga of listening, like that of Tantra, is to achieve transcendence, which I define as a direct connection with the soul or God, the source of all consciousness. The ecstasy that accompanies such a connection is momentarily experienced in TMEs. But it may become our ordinary state of being, as it is for the adepts of traditional yoga, if we're able to heal, develop, and integrate the eight centers along the continuum of human potential.

In the next eight chapters, I describe each of the chakras as centers along this continuum, detailing their characteristics, the lessons they have to teach, and the kinds of music that activate them. I also give examples of TMEs induced in myself and my interviewees by listening to music that targets each of these centers.

At the end of each chapter on the centers, I summarize its contents in tabular form and provide playlists of rock, jazz, and classical music that targets the featured center. I also suggest a number of possible musical tours of that center, which listeners may use to explore its characteristics.

Undertaking these tours will activate the center in question and help you identify other music that targets it. Such tours involve either a single piece that covers most, if not all, of the characteristics of the center or a playlist of several pieces or genres that does so. The software that manages a computer or portable listening device can also allow you to create and experience cross-genre playlists that target the center in question.

To round out part 2, I explain how the continuum of human potential can deepen your experience of a piece of music and lead to a direct connection with your soul, and beyond that to the source of all consciousness. I demonstrate how *thought forms* or *music forms*—internally perceived associations of colors and shapes produced by listening to music, as described by esotericists such as Annie Besant, C. W. Leadbeater, and Geoffrey Hodson—can become the bridge between music and the soul.

In part 3, "Music of the Soul," I explain how you can use the yoga of listening as a spiritual practice, whether you're a listener, performer, or composer. I also address the question that my editor wanted me to focus on: whether jazz and rock are products of the "Dark Forces" mentioned by Cyril Scott and are therefore evil.

Sufi mystic and musician Hazrat Inayat Khan said: "Every leaf of the tree becomes a page of sacred scripture once the soul has learned to read."[5] My conclusion is that *any* music, even jazz and rock, has value if we know how to listen to it.

The continuum of human potential and the yoga of listening can teach us how to listen to any rock song or jazz instrumental, as well as any piece of classical music, as if it were sacred scripture. In this section, I draw upon interviews with two of my friends, both deeply spiritual, one of whom views the music of the hard rock band Led Zeppelin and the other the music of the progressive rock band Yes as pages of sacred scripture.

The next question I consider is: Who are the best spiritual teachers in music? Some types of music—what I call *music of the soul*—may be more useful in the yoga of listening and achieving TMEs than others. Such music has a quality that I call *radiance*, a product of how close its composers or performers have come to God.

Radiance appears in the performances or compositions of what I call *musical adepts*, the most spiritually advanced musicians. Radiance increases as these adepts progress through levels of consciousness beyond those available to most performers and composers. Some of the greatest composers of Western classical music, including Bach, Mozart, Beethoven, and Schubert, have achieved these higher states of consciousness.

Throughout this section, at the end of each chapter, I provide an example of this radiant music of the soul, analyzing the centers that it targets and hinting at the purpose it can serve in the yoga of listening. These examples include John Coltrane's 1965 album *A Love Supreme*, a Yes song, Wagner's opera *Parsifal*, symphonies by Bruckner and Mahler, and music by several twentieth-century composers, whom I classify according to the level of radiance present in their music. I see such composers as *would-be mystics* (e.g., Schoenberg), *sometime mystics* (e.g., Bartók), and *achieved mystics* (e.g., Scriabin).

The final chapter of part 3 concerns *evolving mystics*, two living composers whose music contains a high quality of radiance, Karlheinz Stockhausen of Germany and Einojuhani Rautavaara of Finland, each of whom has composed a series of pieces about angels. The chapters on twentieth-century composers fulfill my editor's request to update Scott's book so that it covers the spiritual aspects of classical music after Scriabin.

In the concluding chapter of the book, which I call a Finale, I weave together many of the themes presented earlier, just as a composer might do in the last movement of a symphony. I also talk about a special state of consciousness that I call *inner equals outer*, in which a strong resonance develops between one's surroundings and inner being.

This state of consciousness is often present in TMEs, and may actually cause them. I give advice on how listeners, performers, and composers can create the state of inner equals outer and use it to achieve TMEs. In this final chapter, I also relate the TME of a composer friend who may be what Scott called a deva-inspired composer, one who works to relay healing messages of peace, hope, and love from realms beyond the physical through her music.

The book closes with an invitation to create a soundtrack for changing your life, using what you've learned about the yoga of listening to target any or all of the centers on the continuum of human potential. In healing, developing, and integrating these centers through listening to music, you may achieve not only transcendent musical experiences, but also the more lasting experience of transcendence that they're meant to lead you toward: the ecstatic sense of union with the soul and God that is the goal of all yoga.

Acknowledgments

I'm grateful to Richard Leviton, my editor at Hampton Roads Publishing, for the suggestion that led to the writing of this book—the second time his visionary ideas have moved my career as a writer in a direction I might never have considered without his support.

I would also like to thank Gerd and Linde Steyer, of Heidelberg, Germany, for their hospitality over the last ten years. The opportunities they've provided for making, listening to, and talking about music have contributed much to the concepts presented here. In September 2001, the Steyers invited me to join them in the Swiss Alps for a week, while I was revising the manuscript of *The Unanswered Question* for the last time before publication. For this much-needed retreat, I'm deeply grateful.

Other friends in Germany have showered me with similar kindness and hospitality over the years. I would especially like to thank Eva Gross, Franz-Hubert and Benigna Robling, and Richard and Gudrun Dvorak—as well as Regina Hornberger, Ronald Ivarsson, and New-Age composer Edwin Klotz—for the ongoing spiritual and cross-cultural dialogue that has emerged from my visits to Germany, and the deep and abiding love that has built up on both sides of this dialogue.

I owe a considerable debt of gratitude to the Charles Group, here in Boston—the many people who, over the last twenty years, have attended monthly meetings, asked questions of my nonphysical teacher, Charles, and transcribed the tapes of his responses. Without their friendship and support, the metaphysical system that underlies this book might never have come into existence.

One of the joys of working on *Music and the Soul* has been interviewing my friends about their transcendent musical experiences. I would like to thank

Sue Ellen Beers, George Corbett, Deanna Devaney, Beth Fairservis, Alan Goodwin, Jennifer Gistrak, Marjie Harrison, Kevin Johnson, Stephen Katz, Pamela Kristan, Elizabeth Locke, Ruth Mendelson, Carl Schroeder, and Deb Stavin for answering my questions so willingly and allowing me to publish what they said.

I'm also grateful to Alan for making his home available for the Charles Group meetings. Sue Ellen has been a great help in organizing, indexing, and proofreading the reams of Charles material that I've collected over the years. Carl has spent many hours helping me design and update my website. George, Alan, Kevin, and Stephen have provided much-needed support and enthusiasm for the book project from its inception. Our conversations have been instrumental in shaping the ideas presented here. Deb's humor has kept me sane throughout the writing process.

I deeply appreciate my friends Brian and Judy Galford for the many ways in which they've contributed to my emotional and spiritual well-being over the years. For his knowledge of rock and jazz, I'm especially indebted to Brian, at one time a disk jockey at a college radio station. I also wish to thank him, in his role as a professional photographer, for the photographs of me that appear in this and my previous book, *The Unanswered Question.*

I'm grateful for all the work that Diane Biello has done over the last several years in transcribing the tapes of the monthly Charles Group meetings. In the summer of 2002, she and her husband, John, invited me to Vermont for a few days when I was working on the galleys of *The Unanswered Question.* The pleasures of their company and the beautiful scenery were a great help in counterbalancing the demands of that task.

I've enjoyed my e-mail correspondence with several musicians who read my earlier books, especially Kristian Stout, who provided me with a playlist of rock music that moves him spiritually, and Roland Pier, who did the same with jazz. Roland also gave me permission to use a quip he made about the term *cosmic normative balance,* which I first introduced in *The Unanswered Question,* and which gets more play here.

While I was working on the final version of this book, my housemate, Kevin, was given a computer by his best friend from high school. It contained a library of 350 hours of popular music from the last thirty years—a gold mine of possible musical examples that have added depth to the playlists included here. I'm grateful to both of them for making this boon available to me.

The Borromeo String Quartet has been a constant source of musical and spiritual inspiration to me ever since I first heard them about ten years ago. I wish to thank them—and especially founding members Nicholas Kitchen and Yeesun Kim—for the many transcendent musical experiences that their playing has provided me and so many others in the Boston area and throughout the world. It would not be an exaggeration for me to say that much of this book has come from trying to figure out what makes their performances so emotionally, intellectually, and spiritually captivating.[1]

I would like to dedicate *Music and the Soul: A Listener's Guide to Achieving Transcendent Musical Experiences* to composer and cellist Stephen Katz, a constant musical and spiritual companion since 1981. Who I am as a composer, performer, and writer on music would be inconceivable without the time we've spent together, in person and on the phone, keeping ourselves true to the Musician within each of us, the deepest part of our souls.

PART 1

Music and the Soul

1

Transcendent Musical Experiences

The violinist had just finished playing the last note of his twenty-five-minute odyssey through the Violin Concerto of early-twentieth-century Austrian composer Alban Berg (1885–1935). Completed in the year of Berg's death, the concerto was dedicated "To the memory of an angel." This angel was the daughter of a family friend who had died in her teens. The violinist lifted his bow. Total silence. No applause.

The musicians of the Cincinnati Symphony Orchestra, as if having played beyond their expectations of themselves, audibly took in a breath, gasping as if they were a single individual. The audience seemed to be in shock. How could a piece of music so dissonant and strange at the same time be so hauntingly beautiful?

The violinist, seated on a high platform, remained motionless for what seemed like an eternal sacred moment. When at last he moved, the applause came thundering from all sides. He struggled to his feet, standing with the aid of crutches required since a childhood bout with polio. How could he *not* know what suffering and mortality meant? Somehow, he'd conveyed those lessons to us in the audience through the voice-like richness of his Stradivarius.

The year was 1978; the player, Itzhak Perlman, was well on his way to superstardom.

I was a sophomore in college, a music major, studying for degrees in clarinet performance and music composition at Ohio Wesleyan University (OWU). I'd come back to my parents' home in Dayton for spring break with a musician friend. Together we'd driven an hour south to hear the Cincinnati Symphony, a first-rate regional orchestra.

That performance still stands as one of the highlights of my concertgoing life. Judging by the reaction of the audience and the orchestra, this twenty-five-minute rapture of self-transcendence was not mine alone. We had had what I call a *transcendent musical experience* (TME).

An *ordinary* musical experience is usually relatively passive. We're exposed to music in some way and react to it with anything from indifference, if it happens to be playing in the background, to mild interest, if we happen to be humming along or tapping our feet. Ordinary musical experiences can also be more active. Our attention is fully engaged by the music, and we may enjoy it in a sensual, emotional, or intellectual way. Even ordinary musical experiences can have a spiritual component, for example, when we're singing hymns or listening to sacred music in church.

Transcendent musical experiences, however, lie beyond the range of these ordinary reactions to music. The distinguishing feature of TMEs is a sense of being deeply moved: that one's relationship with some aspect of life—physical, emotional, intellectual, or spiritual—has been immeasurably enriched or enhanced.

Anyone who enjoys or works with music—from nonprofessional listeners to composers, performers, and musical amateurs—can have a TME. Under the proper conditions, any genre of music, from classical to jazz to the many forms of popular music, is capable of producing a TME. Anyone who has a favorite group, album, song, composer, piece, or soundtrack has probably had a TME.

TMEs can range from intense pleasure to chills running along the spine or a spontaneous flow of tears. During a TME, a listener may feel taken over by the music, unable to move, or have an uncontrollable urge to dance. One's inner state may be serene, or may rise gradually from well-being, through bliss, to a sense of barely containable ecstasy.

TMEs can develop at a live concert or in church; in a car, while driving and listening to tapes, CDs, or the radio; at home, in front of the living-room sound system; or anywhere one hears piped-in music or can carry a portable listening device with headphones. They can occur when a listener is alone or with others. In a live concert, they may even be shared, as in the example of the Cincinnati Symphony performance.

Less commonly, TMEs produce a sense of illumination or mystical revelation. A listener may then experience sudden realizations about how the music is constructed, or what the composer was thinking or living through at the time it was written. Spontaneous insights into life, the universe, or God may suddenly present themselves, as may odd inner visions, as realistic as a lucid dream. Listeners may even perceive colors and geometric forms that seem to have no equivalents in physical reality.

Here's an example of a mystical TME. It involved a live concert that took place a couple of years after the symphony experience I just described, and included the work of the avant-garde American composer George Crumb (b. 1929). I knew Crumb's music from recordings, drawn to it by the mysticism implicit in works such as *Makrokosmos*, two sets of twelve preludes for amplified piano, based on the signs of the zodiac.

I'd driven the half hour from Delaware, Ohio, where I was going to school, to the Ohio State University campus in Columbus to hear the Twentieth Century Consort, a group based in Washington, D.C., play Crumb's *Vox Balanae* (Latin for "Voice of the Whale"). I was excited to witness Crumb's music in concert, since I'd read that an irreproducible element of theater and ritual was involved in any live performance of his works.

Three instruments were required to play *Vox Balanae*: flute, cello, and piano. They were electronically amplified, which allowed them to produce unusual sounds that Crumb intended to resemble the songs of humpback whales.

To further the sense of mystery, the composer had requested that the three players wear simple black face masks to obscure their features. The stage was bathed in blue light, as if the performance were taking place underwater. The masked musicians seemed like a trio of fates or minor divinities of the sea.

The piece itself was in the form of a theme with variations. Each variation represented a geologic age, because the male humpback whales' song, while seeming to be the same in each individual, slowly evolves from one generation to the next.

At times the cello sounded like a seagull, the flute like the wind. Glass rods were laid on the strings of the grand piano to produce a surreal jangling that heightened the sense of unreality. These features came together to produce the sense that I was witnessing a multidimensional cosmic drama, taking place at the center of the universe.

No one in the audience dared to move, sneeze, cough, or whisper. The music was so fragile and oddly beautiful that it seemed as if the slightest distraction would not only ruin its effect, but also cause some earthly catastrophe.

As my TME deepened, I came to feel that our involvement in the Earth's webwork of ecological interrelations was so delicate and vital that the shuffling of a single human foot could cause the extinction of a whole species—even one as magnificent in size as the humpback whale. Through the music, in a moment of mystical illumination, I could sense the existence of this webwork and my place in it, as well as that of the whales.

More recently, I've had several TMEs involving members of the Borromeo String Quartet, which is in residence in Boston at the New England Conservatory of Music. The first time I heard them play, they performed a piece written by the nineteenth-century composer Felix Mendelssohn (1809–1847) when he was eighteen years old.

Mendelssohn was a child prodigy. I considered his Quartet in A Minor, Op. 13, to be a little masterpiece of compositional integration, as well as emotional and spiritual precocity.[1]

I was familiar with the piece, having listened to it often on CD, played by a world-famous string quartet. I was looking forward to my first live hearing of the work, but was unprepared for the effect that the Borromeo's performance had on me.

There's always a danger of disappointment when listening to another interpretation of a work one knows and loves. Hearing the same recorded performance over and over again tends to etch the structural details of the work into one's musical memory, along with every nuance of feeling. Another group's ideas about such nuances can seem like a revelation or an outrage.

The Borromeo's performance was a revelation. The group made my beloved CD version of the piece seem like a half-inflated basketball. I was in ecstasy.

On another occasion, I heard the Borromeo Quartet play the so-called "Rosamunde" Quartet (No. 13 in A Minor, D. 804) by Franz Schubert (1797–1828).[2] The slow movement of this four-movement work is a set of variations on a theme from the incidental music Schubert had written for a long-forgotten play called *Rosamunde*.

Once again, as in the performance of Crumb's *Vox Balanae*, the audience was enthralled. No one dared to move, cough, or whisper.

At one point, I relaxed my concentration on the music and looked around the hall. It seemed as if everyone present was in exactly the same rapt mood. I couldn't help but feel that this was a sacred moment, that the music had placed people in a mood that was little different from prayer or worship. Somehow we'd all been lifted up out of ourselves and made one.

I have a great love for the music of Schubert. When the two-hundredth anniversary of his birth came in 1997, many of his works were performed in Boston. One involved the principal violinist of the Borromeo Quartet and his wife, the cellist. They were joined by a well-known local pianist to play Schubert's Piano Trio No. 2 in E-flat Major, D. 929. This was a late work of Schubert, composed in the year of his death.

I'd brought my housemate, Kevin, with me, eager to share with him not only the playing of these marvelous musicians, but also this piece, a favorite of mine. During the performance, I occasionally cast a sidelong glance at Kevin to see how it was affecting him. He sat with his hands gripping both arms of his seat, eyes wide, jaw hanging open. Never before had he experienced such intense music-making.

For me, too, the performance was astounding. It was as if a window had opened on the Afterlife and a strong wind were blowing through from the other side, full of longing, pain, joy, love. Everything that makes us human was there, as well as all that Schubert himself had experienced in life, and all that he was leaving behind or would never enjoy, knowing that he would soon die of syphilis.

Like many musicians, and most music listeners, I live for ecstatic moments like these, transcendent performances of transcendent music.

While the TMEs I've described aren't the only ones I've encountered in thirty-five years of concertgoing and listening to recordings of classical music, such experiences are relatively rare.

I've often considered the question of what induces TMEs, wondering whether it's possible for listeners, performers, or composers to have them more regularly. This book is the result of such musings.

I invented the term *transcendent musical experiences* in the aftermath of completing my last book, *The Unanswered Question: Death, Near-Death, and the Afterlife*. I was reading William James's classic investigation of religious and mystical experiences, *The Varieties of Religious Experience*, in which I encountered James's description of four qualities that are present in most mystical experiences. I recognized them immediately from listening experiences like those I've described.

According to James, the first defining quality of a mystical experience is *ineffability*. Such an experience is resistant to being adequately expressed in words. Though even ordinary musical experiences are difficult to describe in words, TMEs are more so.

My friend Deb, a graphic designer who grew up listening to jazz standards played by her parents on the phonograph, reports that she had a TME when she was in seventh grade. The school music teacher had put on a recording of "Take Five," a famous piece played by the Dave Brubeck Quartet. Deb tells me that she'd "never heard anything like it before," and had never felt the way she felt while listening to it. She wanted to hear it over and over.

When I asked her to be more specific about how the music made her feel, Deb, who is usually highly articulate, had to work to find the right words. Eventually, she said that the irregular rhythm "excited," "enthralled," and "moved" her. Something about the music seemed "witty," "lively," and "sophisticated." When I asked her what she thought her TME might have meant to her, she said that the music seemed like "a picture of who I was and didn't know it yet."

While the words *witty*, *lively*, and *sophisticated* aren't usually associated with mystical experiences, they nevertheless express the fascination that a TME has for the listener, as well as the listener's struggle to find words to describe that fascination adequately.

For James, the second defining quality of a mystical experience is described by the adjective *noetic*. Such an experience involves illumination, revelation, or what James calls "states of knowledge" that are "full of significance and importance."[3]

My friend Ruth, a film composer, had a TME that involved this noetic quality when she first heard a piece for strings called *Cantus in Memory of Benjamin Britten* by the Estonian composer Ärvo Pärt (b. 1935). Ruth was in her car, listening to the radio, and had to pull off the road. She told me that the music seemed to be a perfect synthesis of all the beauty and lamentation in the world. For Ruth, it was a revelation that a piece of music could so completely fuse these usually contradictory elements.

According to James, the third defining quality of mystical experiences is *transience.* Such experiences tend to be brief, lasting, "except in rare instances, half an hour, or at most an hour or two." TMEs are necessarily transient. They rarely outlast the length of the musical work that produces them. Thus the half-hour to two-hour time frame that James mentions certainly applies to TMEs. Brubeck's "Take Five" lasts a mere five and a half minutes; Pärt's *Cantus* is about seven minutes long.

For James, the fourth defining quality of mystical experiences is *passivity.* Such experiences are not the result of an act of will, although they may be preceded by physical or spiritual practices intended to facilitate them.[4]

TMEs, too, have a passive element. I know that I'm more likely to have a TME at a concert by the Borromeo Quartet than that of certain other well-known groups in Boston. But even that knowledge is no guarantee of a TME.

TMEs may have triggers. But just as spiritual practices designed to facilitate the production of out-of-body experiences or other mystical states may not work on demand, even the best intentions of composers, performers, and a receptive audience may result in a merely satisfying, rather than an ecstatic, performance.

There are three basic categories of transcendent musical experiences: those triggered in composers while composing, in performers while performing, and in listeners while listening. While composers and performers can have TMEs while listening to music, nonmusicians, of course, are limited to those produced by listening.

TMEs induced by listening are the most common. Although this book is primarily about TMEs induced by listening, I provide examples of the other two categories when applicable.

TMEs Induced by Composing

The first category of TMEs, those induced by composing, often involves remarkable feats of writing music of the highest quality in short periods of time. Composers sometimes attribute their extraordinary inspiration during such TMEs to a source outside or beyond themselves, including the divine. Some even feel that they're taking dictation from this source, as if the music were being channeled through them.

George Frideric Handel (1685–1759), for example, produced his famous oratorio *Messiah*, which lasts two and a half hours in performance, in a period of twenty-four days. In a famous anecdote, Handel is said to have reported that, while working, he "did see all Heaven before me, and the great God Himself."[5]

My friend Ruth, the film composer I mentioned previously, often has the sense of being a musical channel. She sometimes wonders why she's always getting jobs writing for national television, which she hardly ever watches. Once, while she was meditating, an inner voice told her that "Spirit also uses the broadcast medium of television, for those attuned to it," and that one purpose of her music is to counteract all the fear that comes through in the news and programs about police, crime, and murder.

The twentieth-century German composer Paul Hindemith (1895–1963) describes the kind of TME that occurs when he composes as follows:

> We all know the impression of a very heavy flash of lightning in the night. Within a second's time we see a broad landscape, not only in its general outlines but with every detail. Although we could never describe each single component of the picture, we feel that not even the smallest leaf of grass escapes our attention. We experience a view, immensely comprehensive and at the same time immensely detailed, that we never could under ordinary daylight conditions, and perhaps not during the night either, if our senses and nerves were not strained by the extraordinary suddenness of the event.[6]

Musical compositions, Hindemith says, may be "conceived in the same way," in other words, "in the flash of a single moment."[7] For Hindemith, inspiration comes as a sudden moment of illumination, rather than a sense of the divine, or some other spiritual force, working through him.

TMEs Induced by Performing

The second category of TMEs, those induced in performers while performing, may occur in practice or rehearsal sessions, or a concert or recital. The result is often a "performance high," in which the music seems to play itself. I can remember instances during clarinet recitals in college when I was so absorbed in the music that I seemed to be standing outside myself watching myself play.

The literal meaning of the word *ecstasy* is "to stand outside oneself." But the word is commonly used to describe an experience of pleasure so intense that it expands the sense of self beyond its usual limitations. During onstage TMEs, I've felt not only an ecstatic pleasure, but also a sense of liberation from doubts about my talent, fears about the playability of certain passages, or concerns with pleasing the audience, my family, or my teacher. There was no room in my consciousness for such things, only a transcendent, godlike control over the act of shaping the sounds coming out of my instrument.

My friend Stephen, the multitalented musician to whom I've dedicated this book, experienced a dramatic onstage TME during a graduate recital at the University of Cincinnati. Backstage, before the beginning of the recital, Stephen felt out of touch with the music, unfocused, and nervous.

When he came onstage to perform the Third Suite in C Major for solo cello, by Johann Sebastian Bach (1685–1750), Stephen decided to let go of all expectations and see what would happen. He sat down, arranged his cello, picked up his bow—and suddenly felt a force like a huge hand coming at him from behind. The hand, he says, "scooped me up, propelled me forward into musical space and time, and played the music through me."

As he played, Stephen felt as if he were in an airplane that someone else was flying. It was an "ecstatic and shocking experience," which made him feel both "glad and afraid," since nothing like it had ever happened to him before. The effect lasted for somewhat longer than twenty minutes, the duration of the suite.

One of Stephen's cello teachers in graduate school, a world-famous concert artist, later told him that the reason she continued to perform on the cello was to achieve a similar state. Years earlier, while playing a concerto with orchestra in a live concert, she suddenly found herself floating ten feet above the stage, looking down at her physical body as her hands continued to play. During this spontaneous out-of-body experience, she felt a sense of serenity and ecstasy that she always hoped to reproduce in subsequent performances.

A performance-induced TME that occurred during rehearsal happened during my junior year in high school. I was the principal clarinetist of the Dayton Philharmonic Youth Orchestra. The first-chair players of the wind section had formed a woodwind quintet: flute, oboe, clarinet, French horn, and bassoon. Whenever we rehearsed, we needed little discussion about how the music should be played. We simply knew, as if we could read each other's minds, or our minds could effortlessly merge.

My friend Alan, who played electric bass in a rock-blues trio in college, spoke to me of a similar TME that occurred when his group was performing at a dance marathon. Alan's trio, which included an electric guitarist and drummer, was the last in the lineup of bands to perform that night.

During their act, each member of Alan's trio was so completely on top of his part and the group's timing was so together—even when they were doing things they'd never tried before—that Alan felt an ecstatic performer's high. Their rapport was such that nothing could disturb it, not even the moment when the school authorities tried to shut the performance down, because of the lateness of the hour, by turning out the lights in the dance hall. They just kept playing in the dark, completely in sync with each other.

Another performance-induced TME involved a mystical, yet terrifying, sense of revelation. I was playing in the OWU Wind Ensemble. During my senior year, we went on a tour of several nearby towns, ranging as far north as Cleveland. On the program was a contemporary piece by a Czech composer who had emigrated to America, Karel Husa (b. 1921), *Music for Prague 1968.*

The piece had been written in protest of the 1968 Soviet annexation of Husa's homeland, Czechoslovakia. It involves an ancient Hussar melody that symbolizes the resistance of the Czech people to subjugation by a foreign power. The third of its three movements is urgent, fast, often strident.

As we played the piece in a high school gymnasium in Cleveland, I felt caught up in its emotional energy in a way that I never had before. It was as if I'd entered an emotional reality in which the military invasion was still going on: People were panicking, fleeing from the tanks rolling into Prague, while trying to gather up their loved ones; distress signals were being sent around the world, full of fear and outrage. I felt overwhelmed by the force and magnitude of the Hussar theme trying to push itself through all of this chaos and triumph over it.

I could barely keep my attention on the notes in front of me. After the performance ended, I wept in reaction to so much intensity of feeling, which seemed to have come into me from outside. It was as if the events that Husa's piece was attempting to commemorate and condemn had happened all over again—or were still happening, on some other plane, twelve years later.

TMEs Induced by Listening

The third category of TMEs, those induced in listeners while listening to music, occurs in connection with a live or recorded performance, either passively (as in most concert or home-listening environments) or actively (as when one moves along to the music in an exercise class or a dance hall).

Some listening-induced TMEs that occur during a public concert are private in content—for example, my impressions of being called to witness a multidimensional cosmic drama while listening to Crumb's *Vox Balanae*. Others may resemble the melding I experienced with my high school woodwind quintet: a shared sense of oneness with the other members of the audience. I've often felt that oneness during performances by the Borromeo Quartet.

Another type of listening-induced TME may occur when one is listening to music while alone. Such a TME usually involves recorded music and a playback system of some sort. In this book, I primarily concern myself with listening-induced TMEs of this kind.

Psychotherapist and musician Lane Arye describes such a TME in his book *Unintentional Music.* It was the result of listening to a recording of a gospel singer's rendition of the spiritual "Someone's Knocking at Your Door":

> The song peaks in long, fervent, high notes, a heart-wrenching plea. The choir, the band, it seems the air itself, is supporting this awesome singer, echoing him, loving him, praising him, somehow joining his song while still letting him sing it alone. In my living room I'm laughing, screaming, crying. Not only because his singing fills my heart to the bursting point. Not only because the song reminds me to open up whenever the divine knocks at my door. But also because I love listening to a community that supports its members in their deepest expression, their most passionate creativity, and their most honest spirituality.[8]

Arye's TME includes physical, or quasi-physical, sensations (the music "fills my heart to the bursting point"); emotional reactions that result in behavioral responses ("laughing, screaming, crying"); and a sense of the spiritual that includes both the desire to open up to the divine, and gratitude for the feeling of loving community that the music projects. Because of these physical, behavioral, emotional, and spiritual aspects, Arye's TME lends itself to explanation not only on the basis of the body or the brain but also the mind or the soul. The same thing could be said of any of the other TMEs previously described. In the next chapter, I'll consider each of these possible explanations of transcendent musical experiences.

An Imaginary Interview

I've enjoyed the process of asking my friends about their TMEs. Almost everyone I've spoken to—musicians and nonmusicians alike—has had a story to tell, sometimes several.

People love to talk about their favorite music. While it's possible to learn a lot about them from their musical tastes, I've learned far more when they've spoken to me about their TMEs. Something about these experiences goes to the very core of who we are, both as individuals and as human beings.

I've been surprised at how grateful my friends were that I asked about their TMEs, and I've often felt deeply moved by their answers. No matter how long or how well I've known them, I've found that their TMEs revealed them in a new light that brought us closer together—as if they'd given me a glimpse of their inmost depths, or the soul. Now it's your turn.

I'd like you to pretend that I'm interviewing you about your own TMEs. If you like, you can write down, or think about, answers to the following questions. Or have someone else read them aloud, pausing for your responses.

How old were you when the TME occurred? What was going on in your life at the time?

Was your TME induced by composing, performing, or listening to music? What kind of music triggered it (genre, composer, group, piece, song)? Under what conditions did it occur—for example, were you attending a concert, or listening to music while alone or with friends?

What were the physical sensations that accompanied your TME? What were your emotional reactions, both during your TME and afterward? Was your TME attended by an intellectual or spiritual component, such as sudden realizations or mystical revelations?

Did your TME seem to have some special significance for you, either then or now?

When you've finished answering these questions, you may want to share what you've written, or the stories that have developed in your mind, with someone else. If you wish, switch roles and become the interviewer, asking that person about his or her own TMEs. Like me, you may find yourself surprised and moved by what you hear.

2

Music and the Soul

How and why music affects us as deeply as it does has been a constant source of speculation from ancient times to the present. For example, fifteen hundred years ago, the Greek philosopher Plato wrote in Timaeus that music exists for the purpose of creating harmony between the various aspects of ourselves.

According to Plato, the rhythm and the harmony of music have "motions akin to the revolutions of our souls." Their purpose is not to provide "irrational pleasure," though many people seem to think so. Rather, the purpose of rhythm and harmony is "to correct any discord which may have arisen in the courses of the soul." Thus music may become "our ally," helping us to bring the soul "into harmony and agreement with herself."[1]

In recent years, neurologic research on the brain's cognitive abilities has begun to suggest that purely biophysical processes, rather than a spiritual entity such as Plato's soul, are responsible for the effects that music has on us. Such research has focused on magnetic resonance imaging (MRI) scans, which allow for the noninvasive study of healthy brains, including those of trained musicians.

Through using MRIs, a team of brain researchers at the Montreal Neurological Institute at McGill University has discovered that when we listen to music, blood rushes away from areas of the brain linked to fear or depression and toward areas associated with intense pleasure: the same areas aroused by sex, chocolate, coffee, alcohol, and illicit drugs, such as cocaine.

The leader of this team, Robert Zatorre, who is also an organist, states that music recruits neural systems of reward and emotion similar to those known to respond specifically to biologically relevant stimuli, such as food and sex, and those artificially activated by drugs of abuse. . . . This is quite remarkable, because music is neither strictly necessary for biological survival or reproduction, nor is it a pharmacological substance.[2]

Journalist Paul McKay, writing about Zatorre's research in the *Ottawa Citizen* in 2002, summarizes it as follows:

Music acts as a specialized fuel to fire millions of brain nerves that otherwise remain dormant or undeveloped. As the brain burns musical fuel, it creates chemicals that produce contentment and even ecstasy. Recent studies of choir singers show elevated levels of these after performances.[3]

Gaps remain in our knowledge of how the brain processes music. When asked about what parts of the brain are specifically responsible for such processing, Zatorre quipped, "Everything from the neck up."[4]

Yet TMEs could be a product of the *mind*, as opposed to the brain. In this view, the word *mind* would refer not to the physical brain, but to the invisible hierarchies of information processing, storing, and retrieval made possible by the interconnections and interactions of one part of the brain with another.

Such hierarchies enable us to gather and sort sensory information so that we may better understand and respond to the world around us, including our sonic environment. One example of such a hierarchy is memory, which does not appear to be localized in a specific part of the brain.

Psychologist Anthony Storr believes that the pleasure we experience in listening to music is the result of the information-processing capacities of the brain. In his view, the brain works by "scanning, sorting, and making of patterns," a process that goes on in every moment, beneath consciousness, whether we're awake or asleep. Even dreams, according to Storr, are what we can consciously recall of this sorting process. The purpose of this process is to generate or "discern an unexpected linkage, a new pattern." The action of doing so tends to produce "intense satisfaction."[5]

Journalist and composer Robert Jourdain, who wrote a book called *Music, the Brain, and Ecstasy*, believes that music provides the brain with a nonphysical maze, "an artificial environment," while at the same time forcing our awareness "through that environment in controlled ways."[6] In the process, we take pleasure in being exposed to the relations that a composer creates between his internal and external experience, his ordering process, and how he makes musical sense of his feelings about himself and the world.

As we witness the ways in which a composer transforms rhythms, melodies, and harmonies, as well as their associated personal or universal meanings, we may experience "relations far deeper than we encounter in our everyday lives."[7] These deeper relations can allow us to attain, even if only for the duration of the music, "a greater grasp of the world," as if we had risen up "from the ground to look down upon the confining maze of ordinary existence."[8] Such a perspective would probably be accompanied by Storr's "intense satisfaction" at fresh perceptions, if not also the blood and brain-chemical surges associated with ecstasy.

Progress in identifying portions of the brain that respond to certain musical situations continues to be made. Theoretical explanations of a biophysical (brain-oriented) or psychological (mind-oriented) nature are constantly being developed on the basis of new research. As yet, none of this research is conclusive. Much still remains to be learned about the relations of brain to mind, and of both to consciousness or the soul.

If transcendent musical experiences seem to be explainable on the basis of the brain, whether in physiological or psychological terms, does it make sense to associate them with philosophical, spiritual, or religious concepts such as consciousness, God, or the soul?

Peak Experiences

A pioneering psychologist active during the middle of the twentieth century, Abraham H. Maslow, believed that it *did* make sense to include philosophical, spiritual, and religious concepts within the explanatory framework of psychology. In the 1960s, Maslow invented the term *peak experience* to describe "small mystical experiences"[9]—those that didn't seem dramatic enough to fit the criteria outlined in William James's *The Varieties of Religious Experience.*

When I coined the term *transcendent musical experience*, I was thinking not only of near-death experiences (NDEs), the subject of my previous book, but also of Maslow's notion of peak experiences. Much of what Maslow had to say about the latter pertains to TMEs as well.

For Maslow, "the peak experience contains two components—an emotional one of ecstasy and an intellectual one of illumination." He went on to say that these two factors "need not be present simultaneously."[10] TMEs are peak experiences in which the component of ecstasy is usually present, and the component of illumination varies widely, or may be entirely absent.

For example, my friend Carl, a computer programmer who also composes music, has often had TMEs while listening to a recording of a piece for violin and orchestra called *The Lark Ascending,* by British composer Ralph Vaughan Williams (1872–1958). As the piece moves toward its climax, Carl feels a "huge uplift" and "soaring emotion." He has "an ecstatic, elated feeling." But, as far as illumination is concerned, all he can say afterward is that Vaughan Williams's piece seems like "the key that fits the lock."

Maslow had the radical idea of basing a new branch of psychology on the study of peak experiences. He believed that such experiences were an ordinary part of being human. Previous psychologies, which had been developed through the study of human psychopathology, hadn't dealt with them. Maslow wondered what type of psychology might develop from doing research on people who were mentally and physically healthy.

In studying such people over the course of several decades, Maslow came to the conclusion that most of them were *self-actualizing.* Maslow invented this term to describe a strong motivation to improve oneself and realize one's talents and abilities in as many ways as possible.

Maslow found that self-actualizing individuals often described transient moments of ecstasy that would occur while they were striving to realize their abilities. These ecstatic moments were frequently called the "peak" experiences of their lives—hence the term.

During further research into peak experiences, Maslow found that they were most easily triggered by dancing, sex, and "what we might term 'classical music.'" He also found that the chance-based, often random-sounding music of American avant-gardist John Cage (1912–1992), the equally chaotic surfaces of abstract-expressionist painting, and the narrative incoherence of Andy Warhol movies were never mentioned as triggers for peak experiences by the self-actualizing individuals he interviewed—even though the works of these artists represented the leading edge of the avant-garde at the time he was writing. According to Maslow, "The peak experience that has reported the great joy, the ecstasy, the visions of another world, or another level of living, has come from classical music—the great classics."[11]

All of my own TMEs have been produced in connection with classical music. But we've already seen, in the cases of my friends Deb and Alan, that jazz and rock too can produce TMEs. Under the right conditions, *any* genre of music can produce a TME.

In his book *The Secret Power of Music,* David Tame, a British esotericist, describes a peak experience that includes not only the great joy and ecstasy mentioned by Maslow in connection with listening to classical music, but also a visionary component that involves "another level of living." Tame was attending a concert in London where Bach's Fifth Brandenburg Concerto was about to be played.

Tame's peak experience began with the first notes from the orchestra. He immediately entered a "timeless moment." The musical sounds became "a tangible, living filigree lattice-work of mathematical precision which I could almost reach out and touch." In the meantime, he lost all awareness of his body, except for a flow of "silent tears."

As the music continued, Tame perceived it as waves of goodness emanating from the instruments and passing through the performance hall. They even seemed to go through the walls of the hall and out into the surrounding city.

Tame's consciousness rose to a vantage point beyond and above the concert hall, as if he were looking down at the city and seeing not only the "urban spread," but also the "underlying, causative forces which shaped and moulded it." The music seemed to be filling the area surrounding the concert hall with a nourishing and sustaining force, turning it into a "glowing light amid a great, chaotic sea of darkness."[12]

Tame's TME can furnish us with a basic template for transcendent musical experiences. TMEs often include, but aren't limited to, the following elements: timelessness; being so absorbed in the experience that awareness of anything else is pushed out; inward illumination, including perceptions of inner light or knowledge; hyperreal sense impressions that border on the synesthetic (for Tame, the sounds of the music seemed both visible and palpable); a trancelike physical immobility; an overwhelming sense of beauty that erases one's consciousness of self and lies beyond the power of language to describe; an expansion of consciousness (in Tame's case, this expansion encompassed not only the concert hall, but the surrounding urban landscape as well); and a profound impression of significance, of the spiritual meaning and import of all that has been experienced in this way.

Conversion Experiences

One aftereffect of a TME that includes any of the above-mentioned elements may be a sense of mission. Thus TMEs resemble what William James calls *conversion experiences*: mystical experiences that result in dramatic changes in one's values and the direction of one's life.

The following conversion experience comes from the writings of Amy Clampitt, a poet with whom I studied back in the early 1990s. The location is New York. The museum that Clampitt mentions, the Cloisters, is the building that houses the Metropolitan Museum's collection of medieval art. A *motet* is a choral composition for unaccompanied voices, usually based on a sacred Latin text.

On a Sunday afternoon I had wandered into the museum famil-
iarly known as The Cloisters, where in the midst of listening to a
piped-in motet, for an unasked-for moment all habitual concerns gave
way to a serenity so perfect that it amounted to a lapse of consciousness—or perhaps it is clinically more accurate to speak of a lapse so
complete that it amounted to perfect serenity.[13]

Subsequently, Clampitt felt that this was an experience of spiritual grace,
which grew over the course of a week until, "With the enthusiasm of a typical
convert, I was a churchgoer."[14] Thus Clampitt's TME involved a conversion in
the religious sphere—that to which James's term explicitly refers.

TMEs may often have the force of a conversion experience. But the
changes in values or lifestyle effected by TMEs are not limited to one's spiritual or religious practice.

We've all heard music that so captivates us that we become instant converts
to the style, genre, composer, or band that produced it. We may even emulate
the lifestyle of the musicians in question—a practice that has had a deep influence on pop culture in ways that run the gamut from harmless (clothing and
hairstyles) to potentially harmful (sexual promiscuity and drug use).

In the case of musicians, both amateur and professional, TMEs with the
force of a conversion experience are often responsible for their sense of mission.
Such TMEs sound the call to their vocation and sustain their commitment to it.

My friend Deb, whom we met in chapter 1, became a Dave Brubeck
Quartet convert after hearing "Take Five" in seventh grade. A year earlier, however, she'd had a TME with the force of a conversion experience strong enough
to determine not only a lifelong liking for a certain kind of music, but also a
commitment to becoming a highly skilled nonprofessional musician.

Deb was listening to phonograph records in a friend's basement in a northern
suburb of Chicago, where she grew up. When she heard the group Peter, Paul, and
Mary sing "500 Miles," which Deb describes as "a lonely folk ballad," she was completely captivated. The music seemed to be a perfect reflection of what she called
the "preteen angst" she was feeling at the time. Deb decided that she would learn
how to play folk guitar. Fifteen years later, she won first place in the folksinging
division of the Fiddling and Picking Contest in Douglas County, Kansas.

The High-Plateau Experience

According to Maslow, peak experiences that lead to self-actualization often
involve a sense of contemplation of, or fusion with, one or more of what he
called *values of Being* (or *B-values*). These values include, but are not limited to:

truth, beauty, goodness, perfection, justice (or fairness), simplicity, orderliness (or necessity), lawfulness (or consistency), aliveness (or being in process), comprehensiveness (or richness), unitariness (or wholeness), transcendence (e.g., of dichotomies such as good and evil), self-sufficiency, uniqueness, effortlessness, significance, and playfulness or humor.[15]

David Tame's Bach-inspired TME, described previously, contains references to a number of these values of Being—not just goodness. For example, he mentions a "living filigree lattice-work of mathematical precision." This statement implies that Tame was experiencing the B-values of aliveness ("living"), beauty ("filigree"), orderliness ("lattice-work"), lawfulness ("mathematical"), and perfection ("precision").

According to Maslow, contemplation of, or fusing with, the B-values in a peak experience "gives the greatest joy that a human being is capable of."[16] Having had such a moment of transcendent ecstasy, or "small mystical experience," people will do whatever they can to repeat it. They are, in Maslow's terminology, "meta-motivated" to realize the values of Being within themselves. The result is a peak-experience-fueled process of self-actualization.

In the case of TMEs, such meta-motivation is the reason we keep coming back to our favorite composers, groups, and pieces. It drives us to buy recordings and concert tickets, to become jazz fans, rock groupies, or opera fanatics.

Some music allows us to realize the values of Being on the physical or emotional plane; other music allows the same on the intellectual or spiritual plane. Thus it may be possible to speak of physical, emotional, intellectual, or spiritual ecstasies—or mystical experiences that have their origin in the body, heart, mind, or soul.

For Maslow, peak experiences are "transient moments of self-actualization."[17] In the same way, TMEs are moments in which we've glimpsed or realized some hitherto unknown or less familiar aspect of our human potential—or, as my friend Deb put it, "a picture of who I was and didn't know it yet."

According to Maslow, people who are motivated to repeat their peak experiences may become engaged in a process that leads not only to self-actualization, but also to what he called the *high-plateau experience:*

> After the insight or the great conversion, or the great mystic experience, or the great illumination, or the great full awakening, one can calm down as the novelty disappears, and as one gets used to good things or even great things, live casually in heaven and be on easy terms with the eternal and the infinite.[18]

The high-plateau experience is like a prolonged peak experience, in which one is constantly in touch with and sustained by the values of Being. Unlike the peak experience, the high-plateau experience "can be meaningfully aspired to," though not without "long hard work." Even though most people prefer the "peaky" quality of the peak experience—"like a moment on top of Mount Everest"—Maslow believed that in the high-plateau experience, "one can *stay* 'turned on.'"[19]

People tend to value the peak experience for this turned-on quality. But, for Maslow, it's only a "transient glimpse" of the calm and serenity of the high-plateau state of being, which is the true goal of the process of self-actualization.[20] I believe that TMEs have the same goal.

The Yoga of Listening

The high-plateau experience involves a more or less constant ability to perceive the world in terms of what Maslow called the *unitive vision:* the ability "to see the temporal and the eternal simultaneously, the sacred and the profane in the same object."[21] We've already seen a hint of this unitive vision in my friend Ruth's TME, described in the previous chapter, in which "the beauty and lamentation of the world" seemed to be fused in the music of Ärvo Pärt.

The achievement of the unitive vision is the goal of many spiritual teachings, including yoga, Taoism, and Zen Buddhism. I believe that music, too, is an encoded spiritual teaching designed to lead us into the same realms of being and self-transcendence.

The process begins with a TME that has the force of a conversion experience—one that turns us into listeners, composers, or performers. Subsequent TMEs carry us further into what it means to be a listener, composer, or performer. Music then becomes an essential tool in our process of self-actualization, often without our conscious awareness.

With conscious awareness, however, we could use music to accelerate this process, eventually leading us to the high-plateau experience to which so many spiritual practices aspire. Music itself could become a spiritual practice, a *yoga of listening.*

The Sanskrit word *yoga* means "union," and refers to spiritual practices that lead to the unitive state. The yoga of listening would be a means of using music to achieve that state.

The yoga of listening would involve, first, figuring out which music is most likely to create transcendent experiences, and under what conditions. Then, through listening to, performing, or composing such music, we could trigger TMEs more regularly, further the process of self-actualization, and end up with the unitive vision, the sustained serenity and bliss of the high-plateau experience. The purpose of this book is to lay the groundwork for such a yoga.

Defining the Soul

Through the terms *peak* and *plateau experience, self-actualization,* and *values of Being,* Maslow attempted to redefine the spiritual or religious yearning for transcendence in psychological terms. His project was to generate a vocabulary for a psychologically based mysticism that would exclude ideas like God or the soul, while at the same time honoring the subjective reality of, and perpetual human craving for, transcendent experiences.

Storr seems to be involved in a similar project when he states:

> Great music . . . depends on an inner ordering process which is largely unconscious and therefore not deliberately willed by the composer. The ordering process is something to be wooed, encouraged, waited for, or prayed for. The greatest creative achievements of human beings are a product of the human brain; but this does not mean that they are entirely voluntary constructions. The brain operates in mysterious ways which are not under voluntary control.[22]

Note the way in which Storr echoes the phrase, "The Lord works in mysterious ways." He seems to imply that modern composers should pray to their own unconscious for inspiration, in the same way that composers of previous centuries prayed to God. Like Maslow, Storr has substituted a neutral, scientifically and psychologically acceptable term—in his case, *unconscious*—for a highly charged and much-disputed religious one (*the Lord*).

In drawing attention to this verbal sleight of hand, I do not intend to champion the religious term over the psychological one. Both terms refer to a reality that many people sense as true: that there is a force within us—call it God, the soul, or the unconscious—that guides us toward the greater internal wholeness and psychological health that Maslow called self-actualization.

Whatever this part of us may be, it seems to exist beyond the ordinary sense of ourselves *as* ourselves—our egos or personalities. It also seems to be responsible for granting or withholding peak or transcendent experiences, such as those of listeners, performers, and composers of music. Yet we all try, in Storr's terms, to woo, encourage, wait, or pray for them.

If TMEs have a spiritual source, arising not (or not merely) from the body, brain, or mind, but rather from the soul, then the question is: Does the word *soul* refer to an actual entity separable from the body and capable of maintaining some kind of existence beyond it, as out-of-body experiences seem to indicate? Does the soul have access not only to various states of consciousness, but also nonphysical planes of being? Or is the word just a metaphor that stands for the most comprehensive hierarchy of organizing information that the brain is capable of supporting?

The scientific view may be that the soul is a product of consciousness, which is a product of the mind's ability to categorize and classify information, which in turn rests on the physical and mechanical abilities of brain and body. Indeed, according to Storr:

> great music can be distinguished from music which is cerebral and lacking in inspiration; but this does not mean that great music necessarily originates from some ethereal limbo. Access to one's own inner psychological depths is difficult enough without postulating another form of reality outside the human psyche.[23]

Perhaps. But I'd like to keep my options open. Science has not yet taught us which combination of elements in the brain or the mind creates our most comprehensive hierarchies of information-processing or their products, such as great works of art.

That the brain is capable of thinking in words may be demonstrated in waking life by our internal monologues. That it's equally capable of wordlessly thinking in images may be demonstrated every night in our dreams. Musicians know that it's also capable of wordless thinking in melodies and chords. And there may be levels of information processing that lie so deep in the brain that their products rise into ordinary waking consciousness as nameless, imageless waves of emotional intensity or feeling-toned energy.

Perhaps all art is an attempt to translate these waves into words, images, or music, so that the artist can share them with others—or, especially in the case of music, *invoke* them in others. Such waves seem to be the basis of my own musical imagery, before I've found the right notes to embody it.

I could call the source of these waves and the transcendent feelings that sometimes accompany them God, the soul, or the unconscious. They're all words for the same thing: some kind of inner source. But each is attached to a different set of beliefs, a way of viewing the world that posits certain experiences and denies others, while providing a vocabulary for communicating that worldview to other people.

Many belief systems of this nature exist in the world today, each purporting to present the whole and only truth. They vary widely, from those that support fundamentalist religious worldviews to those based on materialistic science.

There are many alternative perspectives as well, such as the worldviews based on yogic, spiritualistic, or New-Age beliefs. Which of them is more true than the others?

I believe that the truth or validity of concepts, beliefs, and worldviews often lies in their usefulness. Thus, whether or not there's a soul that has an existence separate from the physical body, the concept of soul is useful to me when I want to talk about certain kinds of subjective experiences. Therein lies its truth or validity for me.

So, for the purposes of this book, I'm going to call the part of us that seems to be responsible for transcendent experiences, musical and otherwise, the soul. By "otherwise," I mean mystical experiences in general, from those investigated by William James in *The Varieties of Religious Experience* to Maslow's peak experiences, and including out-of-body and near-death experiences.

I've had hundreds of mystical experiences, of all kinds, for more than thirty years. Accounts of them appear in my two previous books: *Otherwhere*, which deals with out-of-body experiences; and *The Unanswered Question*, which deals with near-death experiences and the Afterlife. As a result of these experiences, I've come to believe that the soul has an existence separate from that of the body; that another, essentially nonphysical, reality exists, in addition to the physical world we're familiar with; and that the soul's true home is this nonphysical reality.

Some religions define the soul as something we have and could easily lose, like a possession. According to my spiritual guide, Charles, whom I've been channeling for over twenty years, it would be more pertinent to say that the soul has *us*, and we could lose *ourselves* if we're not careful.

Charles defines the soul as the nonphysical portion of ourselves, a form of consciousness that resides in nonphysical reality and extends itself into physical reality through the body. He often uses the analogy of a glove to describe the relationship of the soul and the body. The body is the glove; the ego, or personality, is the hand inside the glove; and the soul is the larger, nonphysical being from which this "hand" originates.

According to Charles, the soul has a master plan for our growth. It guides us to realize that plan through managing the level of life force available to us in any given moment. That level increases when we're following the soul's master plan and decreases when we're not.

Satisfaction, happiness, and ecstasy are the result of an increase in life-force flow from the soul. Dissatisfaction, unhappiness, and depression are the result of a decrease in life-force flow.

Note the word *ecstasy* in the previous paragraph. I've already pointed out that a sense of ecstasy often accompanies TMEs, as well as Maslow's peak and high-plateau experiences. According to Charles, all such experiences result from larger than normal increases in life-force flow.

Please also note that Charles's description of the soul is not exclusive of the notions of the brain's or the mind's responsibility for producing such states. It may be, as I have hinted, that the word *soul* is simply a metaphor for the highest possible organization of the brain's or the mind's capacities. Charles, too, could be my way of accessing and personalizing such an organization.

The happiness, or ecstasy, and the unhappiness, or depression, that result from fluctuations in what Charles calls life-force flow may be explainable in terms of the release or withholding of hormones, or blood surges in the brain. Still, the question remains: What aspect of ourselves produces these ecstatic rushes or depressive slumps? Furthermore, why do they manifest themselves under some circumstances and not others?

Although, as we've seen, Maslow used the term *peak experience* for these ecstatic rushes and explained their function, he refrained from identifying their source or speculating on why they exist, other than as one manifestation of a psychological drive to achieve a greater sense of wholeness and satisfaction in life. Charles's explanation that the soul has a master plan for our growth and uses rushes and slumps in life-force flow to guide us toward realizing it seems to supply what was missing from Maslow's theory.

As Maslow pointed out, music is a major trigger for peak experiences and the process of self-actualization. In light of what Charles has said about the soul's master plan for our growth, this fact would make music a means by which the soul guides us to achieve our full potential.

In this book, I hope to provide a guide not only for achieving transcendent musical experiences, but also for helping listeners, performers, and composers realize more of the soul's master plan for their growth.

The Imaginary Interview Continues

Perhaps, as a result of the questions I posed at the end of the previous chapter, you've either written down, or mentally collected, one or more stories about your own TMEs, and possibly those of others. Now I would like you to examine these stories more closely. Once again, you may write down your answers, make mental note of them, or share them with others.

How did you respond to the questions about the physical, emotional, intellectual, or spiritual aspects of your TMEs?

Did your physical sensations include a trancelike physical immobility or hyperreal sense impressions, such as the colors in your surroundings growing more vivid?

Did your emotional reactions include a sense of overwhelming emotional intensity or indescribable beauty?

Did your TME include any mental effects, such as timelessness, complete absorption (lack of awareness of anything but the music), or no consciousness of self?

Did your TME include any spiritual components, such as illumination (experienced as inner light or knowledge), an ecstatic expansion of consciousness, or a feeling of profound importance or spiritual significance?

I believe that TMEs that produce any of these effects have their origin in the soul, and are intended to guide us toward realizing its plans for our growth. It may be useful to distinguish such TMEs from those that involve little more than chills or an enhanced sense of pleasure.

Furthermore, I believe that soul-induced TMEs are especially likely to involve the B-values described by Maslow: a sense of truth, beauty, goodness, perfection, justice (or fairness), simplicity, orderliness (or necessity), lawfulness (or consistency), aliveness (or being in process), comprehensiveness (or richness), unitariness (or wholeness), transcendence (e.g., of dichotomies such as good and evil), self-sufficiency, uniqueness, effortlessness, significance, or playfulness and humor. Did any of these values show up in your TME?

Finally, did your TME have the force of a conversion experience? If so, what did it convert you to—a new style or genre of music, a new group or band, a new composer? A new lifestyle or vocation? A new form of spiritual or religious practice? Conversion experiences, too, are often intended by the soul to guide us toward realizing its plans for our growth.

3

The Secret Influences of Music

According to Charles, the soul rarely comes right out and tells us what to do. Few of us are led to realize its plans by means of clear, inwardly stated, verbal commands. The soul guides us indirectly, by means of hidden or secret influences: a hunch, a dream, the strangely meaningful lyrics of a song that keeps repeating in our heads—and the quiet but insistent urging of rising and falling life-force flow.

Sometimes the soul communicates with us in a more dramatic, though nonverbal, way, escalating the flow of life force until we have a peak, or some other type of mystical, experience. When composing, performing, or listening to music is the trigger for such a rise in life-force flow, the result is a TME.

How does the soul guide us by means of TMEs? Here are three instances of such guidance, drawn from my own life. In each case, I was deeply affected by a TME, and the direction of my later life was determined by its secret influence.

The first occurred in elementary school, when I was in the fourth grade. At that time, in music class, we usually sang patriotic, folk, and other traditional songs, which I, like most of my peers, found boring. But once, a substitute teacher played some classical music for us on a portable phonograph.

I was enthralled by one of the pieces that she played: *Danse Macabre* by Camille Saint-Saëns (1835–1921). The music portrayed a ghostly dance in the graveyard after midnight, with Death playing an out-of-tune fiddle, and a xylophone that sounded like bones struck together.

I couldn't stop talking about the piece when I got home. My father had a recording of it in his LP collection, which he played for me. On the same recording was the Overture to *Prince Igor* by Alexander Borodin (1834–1887) and the March from *The Love of Three Oranges* by Sergei Prokofiev (1891–1953).

The deep pleasure that I felt while listening to such pieces indicated that my soul was increasing the life force available to me. Naturally, I wanted to hear them over and over.

Not long after I was introduced to *Danse Macabre*, the whole fourth grade of my school went on a field trip to hear the Dayton Philharmonic Orchestra play a children's concert. *Danse Macabre* was on the program.

On the day of the concert, I was beside myself with excitement. But when *Danse Macabre* came up, I was shocked and disappointed. The kids around me wouldn't stop talking. They were pushing and shoving each other in their seats. I couldn't understand why they weren't as enthralled as I was.

When I got home, my mother asked me how I enjoyed the concert. I couldn't answer. I burst into tears. She was surprised, since I'd been so excited about going. I tried to explain that the experience was both wonderful and awful—wonderful to hear the music live, awful to be surrounded by an unappreciative audience of noisy and rambunctious kids.

I still remember how I felt that day. I was full of an indescribable feeling that wasn't just disappointment. There didn't seem to be any way to let it out but to cry.

Crying wasn't encouraged in my household, so I was a little embarrassed that I couldn't prevent myself from doing so. Many years later, Charles would tell me that the soul sometimes uses tears to highlight a moment in which one has experienced a great truth. That's the meaning behind the phrase "being moved to tears."

I had just had my first TME. There were no words to describe it, as is often the case with mystical experiences, and all the more so for a ten-year-old. The soul wanted to make sure that I would never forget it. All of my listening ever since has been an attempt to find that experience again. Tears, otherwise an infrequent occurrence in my life, have often let me know when I've succeeded.

In retrospect, it seems that the great truth the soul wanted me to perceive in listening to *Danse Macabre* had little to do with ghosts and graveyards. The real message behind my tears was that if music moved me so much, pursuing it in some fashion was part of the soul's master plan for my growth.

The second life-determining TME occurred when I was in high school. Somewhere I'd read about the mystical music of a nineteenth-century Austrian composer by the name of Anton Bruckner (1824–1896). I became curious, and went to my dad's record collection. He had a recording of Bruckner's Ninth Symphony, his last, which was left unfinished at his death.

The first time I listened to the piece, I found the pace so slow that I nearly fell asleep. Many people disparage Bruckner's music as boring. But I was determined to find out why this music had been described as mystical. I practiced listening to Bruckner's Ninth over and over, trying to adapt my mind to its slow unfolding.

Without knowing what I was doing, I'd begun training myself in meditation. I would lie on the floor of my bedroom with my head between the speakers of the stereo. I remained motionless, hands folded on my chest, for the entire first movement, which took up one side of the record. Then I would turn the record over and do the same thing with the two movements on the other side. If my thoughts wandered, I would constantly bring them back to the music.

The piece was nearly an hour long. It wasn't easy for a fifteen-year-old to lie so still and listen so single-mindedly. Yet the practice had an unexpected payoff.

The first movement of Bruckner's Ninth ends with a gradual buildup of volume and intensity over several minutes. I discovered that if I began to breathe deeply, in long slow breaths that paralleled the pace of the music, by the time the final brass chords were resounding in my ears, I would experience powerful orgasmic waves pulsing from one end of my body to the other.

Eventually, I bought recordings of all of Bruckner's symphonies and listened to them in the same meditative way. Some were more likely than others to produce the ecstasy I experienced with the Ninth.

I was so moved by this music that I listened to it almost every night for months. Gradually, the idea dawned on me that I wanted to do for others what Bruckner's music was doing for me. I wanted to become a composer, a mystical composer like Bruckner.

So I began buying books on music theory, melody, harmony, and counterpoint. I spent hours doing the exercises. I bought scores of Bruckner's music and tried to analyze them. And I filled musical sketch books with chords and phrases discovered through improvising at the piano. Even now, thirty years later, if my determination to compose begins to falter, all I need to restore it is to listen again to Bruckner's Ninth.

These two TMEs had the force of conversion experiences. The first converted me into a lifelong classical music listener, the second into a composer.

I have little doubt that similar conversion experiences lie behind many musicians' determination to pursue music as a career. The secret influences that spark such conversions, TMEs, have their origin in the soul, and guide those of us who are musically inclined toward realizing the soul's master plan for our growth as composers and performers.

The third life-changing TME I'll describe here occurred many years later. I had just completed my course work for a master's degree in music composition at the University of Illinois (U of I) in Champaign-Urbana. I was now required to create a portfolio of original compositions, which, if approved, would allow me to earn my degree.

The prevailing style at the U of I was ultradissonant, based on the twelve-tone method of composition (also called dodecaphonicism or serialism) originated earlier in the twentieth century by Arnold Schoenberg (1874–1951). This method of composition involves the manipulation of the twelve tones of the chromatic scale according to strict mathematical principles, which determine each note in a piece of music, and sometimes other musical characteristics, such as rhythm, volume, and instrumental tone color.

I couldn't relate to this cerebral manner of composing, which resulted in pieces that were empty of enjoyment at the sensual, emotional, and spiritual levels. It wasn't surprising that I had a creative block for most of the two years I was in graduate school, and was able to complete only one of the three pieces I needed for the portfolio.

What I didn't yet know was that a number of contemporary composers both in the United States and abroad were rebelling against this academic approach to composing. They were evolving a neoromantic compositional style that would appeal once again to the senses, the heart, the mind, and in some cases the soul.

While at the U of I, I heard a piece written in this new style by the American composer Joseph Schwantner (b. 1943), *Sparrows*, for voice and chamber ensemble. I didn't know what to make of it. I wanted to love the emotionally appealing, and often mystical, beauty of its settings of haiku by the Japanese poet Issa. Yet I was afraid to consider a compositional style that my peers and teachers were likely to condemn.

After my two years at the U of I, I moved to Chicago. I wanted to get away from the composition department, whose influence I found stultifying, and see whether I could overcome my creative block and discover my own compositional style. I bought every recording and score of music by Schwantner that I could find. When I discovered that I had just missed the premiere of a new piece of his for soprano and orchestra, *Magabunda (Witchnomad)*, I wrote to the composer telling him how liberating his music had been for me. To my surprise, he not only wrote back, but also sent me a tape of the premiere.

Magabunda is in four movements. The third movement, "Black Anemones," had an effect on me unlike that of any other piece of contemporary music. Every time I listened to it, I was transfixed. Even though I must have listened to it a hundred times, I was always in tears by the end, not because it was sad, but because it was so beautiful.

"Black Anemones" seemed like the perfect crystallization of everything I'd wanted my music to be, although I hadn't known it until I heard it. The music I'd written in college had been gropingly headed in a similar direction, but I'd gotten sidetracked in graduate school by the twelve-tone method, resulting in my creative block. As I listened to "Black Anemones," I cried because I recognized the goal I was heading toward, but didn't know how to get there. Like Deb, through listening to this music, I glimpsed "a picture of who I was and didn't know it yet."

Schwantner's music gave me a new direction to work in: not to imitate his style, but to absorb what attracted me about it and forge my own. Gradually, my creative block dissolved, and I was able to finish my portfolio of compositions and get my degree.

My soul used the TMEs that I continually experienced when listening to "Black Anemones" to help me find my own personal style as a composer. These TMEs contributed directly to my process of self-actualization—first, by showing me the way I needed to follow to realize myself as a composer; then, by giving me permission to follow that path. Time and again I've been struck by these functions of listening-induced TMEs: They *show the way* and *give permission.*

The most striking example I've encountered of music showing the way and giving permission involves my friend Beth, a visual and performance artist. When she was seven years old, her father, a college professor, took her into his library, seated her on the couch, and played a recording of the entire opera *Madama Butterfly* by Giacomo Puccini (1858–1924), narrating the events of each act as they transpired.

Beth lost awareness of her body on the couch. She felt as if she had left her body and *become* Madame Butterfly. She felt "older, wounded, tragic." When Madame Butterfly knew that she had lost Pinkerton, her American husband, forever—when he returned to their home in Nagasaki with a new American wife—Beth had an almost physical sense, in her heart, of "having lost something forever," and knowing that she "would never retrieve it again."

The story her father told and the beautiful music that accompanied it gave Beth "the feeling of what it meant to be in another life and have that life experience, just from hearing the music." She says that this experience has "stayed true" for her ever since, as if she "had really lived it, almost like a past or parallel life."

Like my friend Deb, Beth had glimpsed "a picture of who I was and didn't know it yet." The music showed her how to face loss, and gave her permission to plumb the depths of those feelings, so that she "lived the life of a tragic figure at seven years old."

Beth's story demonstrates how TMEs can show the way and give permission in the emotional realm, by helping us to get more deeply in touch with our feelings, even those we may never have experienced before. Similarly, my exposure to Schwantner's "Black Anemones" demonstrates how TMEs can show the way and give permission in the creative or intellectual realm.

TMEs can also show the way and give permission for us to become more completely present in our bodies—for example, when we're listening to dance music and feel the urge to move. They can show the way and give permission for us to experience a closer relationship with our souls, as well—for example, through singing or listening to gospel music.

The power of music lies precisely in these secret influences of the soul: the TMEs that guide us toward, and give us permission to realize, the soul's plans for our growth in the physical, emotional, intellectual, and spiritual aspects of our lives.

Music, Morals, and Higher Powers

According to composer and esotericist Cyril Scott, author of *Music: Its Secret Influence throughout the Ages*, the hidden, guiding influences of music may operate not only on us as individuals, but on society at large. Scott believed that "each specific type of music has exercised a pronounced effect on history, on morals, and on culture." Music molds character more potently "than religious creeds, precepts, or moral philosophies." Furthermore, musical form "tends to reproduce itself in human conduct."[1]

For example, Scott asserted that the music of Bach acts on the mind, and thus allows the intellect to develop. I can attest to the validity of this point. When I was in college, my method of preparing for an exam was as follows. I skimmed through the textbook and the notes I'd taken in class just once, cramming my mind with information until I felt physically ill. Then I would put on a set of headphones and listen to a side or two of my two-record set of Bach's *The Art of Fugue*.

I could feel the confusion of information in my brain sort itself out in tandem with the rigorous formality of Bach's music. It often seemed as if my mind were thinking simultaneously on more than one level, just as the music was progressing, with its several superimposed melodic lines. I would no longer feel ill after this exercise. The next day, I would usually ace the exam.

For Scott, the secret influence that music exerts on us, both individually and as a society, has its origin not in the soul, as Charles would have it, but in higher spiritual powers. These powers, Scott believed, are responsible for "that elusive *something* which renders a number of works of art immortal."[2]

Inspired composers, said Scott, are used as mediums by these higher spiritual powers, creating music that influences the spiritual, psychological, and moral evolution of humankind. TMEs may occur in reaction to the spiritual truths contained in music of this type.

Scott wrote of a "Hierarchy of Great Sages, Initiates, Adepts, known as the Great White Lodge," which "exercises a mighty influence over the evolution of mankind."[3] These high spiritual beings were cited by Scott as one of several potential sources for the inspiration behind great music.

According to David Tame, this hierarchy chooses certain great men and women—among them poets and composers like Ludwig van Beethoven (1770–1827)—to be their vehicles.[4] These individuals are commissioned to bring spiritual truth into the world in artistic form.

Such a mission is chosen or assigned before the individual enters the world in a particular lifetime. Throughout that life, he'll be guided, often without being aware of it, by the hierarchy, which trains him in how to receive the spiritual truths to be brought forth in his works.[5]

This training takes place in progressive initiations, the record of which is the series of works he creates. Tame says that, "In meditating on these works, the energies and states of consciousness necessary for spiritual attainment and initiation are transferred to us."[6]

A similar notion exists in the ancient spiritual tradition of yoga. It's called *transmission*: a mystical experience in which a guru's bliss and wisdom are transferred directly from his mind to that of a properly trained disciple. When transmission occurs through music, a TME is the result, as in the case of my friend Beth, who received spiritual wisdom and states of consciousness concerning loss that had been encoded by Puccini in the music of *Madama Butterfly*.

Scott claimed that musical inspiration may also originate from higher spiritual beings called *devas*—a Sanskrit term meaning "shining ones" or "gods." For Scott, the devas represented "a graded hierarchy of incorporeal Beings ranging from the smallest nature spirit to the loftiest archangel."[7]

Scott said that the masters of the Great White Lodge work with the devas to find the best approach to raising humanity's level of spiritual evolution. Scott's book was inspired by one such master, Koot Hoomi (also known as Master K. H.), who takes a great interest in the development of Western music.

Master K. H. was available for consultation through the mediumship of Nelsa Chaplin, a friend of Scott's. Skilled in improvising at the piano, Chaplin sometimes channeled the Master through her playing, for healing purposes. She also ran a guesthouse based on alternative healing principles, including a system of color therapy that she had channeled.

Scott knew Chaplin for the last seven years of her life. He first became acquainted with Master K. H., as channeled through her, in 1921. Master K. H. was responsible for the suggestion that led to Scott's writing his book about music.

The book was produced by the following method: Scott asked questions, made notes, wrote chapters, and then read them to Chaplin, who would provide corrections in trance. After Chaplin's death, Scott found other ways to stay in touch with Master K. H. He appears to have left his wife to live with a new woman who was able to channel the Master. In this way, Scott was able to produce a revised edition of the book, published twenty-five years later.

I experienced some resistance in reading Scott's book. Despite my own training as a channel, I found some of his assertions hard to credit. For example, Scott (or Master K. H.) opposed the idea that the characteristics of *civilization* cause the kind of music it produces. In his view, the characteristics of the *music* form those of civilization.

For Scott, eras in which music of a conventional nature predominates—such as the Victorian period in England, which seems to have produced no great composers, with the exception of Sir Edward Elgar (1857–1934)—will themselves be tradition-bound in morals and manners. Eras in which a variety of musical styles prevails will adhere less to tradition, and will often throw off conventions. Revolutionary music, says Scott, may lead to political revolution as well.

The music of Handel, composer of *Messiah*, was considered by Scott to be highly conventional. Handel's music was much beloved by the British public during the nineteenth century. Scott claimed that the extreme conventionality of the Victorian era was the *result* of the Victorian's love of Handel's music.

Scott's ideas on the secret influences of music on society go back at least as far as Plato. In Republic, Plato warns that "a change to a new type of music is something to beware of" since it unsettles "the most fundamental political and social conventions."[8]

Scott's innovation lay in his claim that changes in the types of music being composed or performed can have a *positive*, as well as a negative, influence on the evolution of society. I find few of the illustrations Scott gave of such positive influences persuasive, not because I disagree with him, but because he handled these illustrations in unconvincing ways.

According to Scott, the maximum influence of music on a society's morals can take as long as a hundred years to develop. He attributed this time lag to the infrequency with which the musical works most likely to create such changes are played. In some cases, however, these changes may show up within a generation or two of the composer's death.

Scott wrote that when the Polish pianist-composer Frédéric Chopin (1810–1849) visited England, a book was written about him. A few years later the pre-Raphaelite painters came together. The group included Edmund Burne Jones, Dante Gabriel Rossetti, and others. They were famous for their colorful, sensual, romantic images of longhaired, rosy-cheeked men and women, often inspired by quasi-medieval subjects such as the King Arthur legends.

Scott saw an esoteric cause-and-effect relationship here: The pre-Raphaelite painters were inspired by Chopin's aesthetic of "refined languor" and "delicacy of outline."[9] I could concede this point if I knew that the pre-Raphaelite painters had read the book on Chopin or were devotees of his music. Otherwise, by means of a similar logic, a cause-and-effect relationship could be adduced between any two cultural events, no matter the difference in their genres or the distance in space and time, simply because one preceded the other.

A more alarming example of Scott's tendency to see esoteric cause-and-effect relationships occurs in his remarks on the music of Richard Strauss (1864–1949). Scott claimed that certain "Dark Forces," acting in opposition to the intentions of the Great White Lodge, are constantly trying to disrupt the progress of humanity's spiritual evolution. Because Strauss's music tended to glorify war and German nationalism, his symphonic poem *Ein Heldenleben* (*A Hero's Life*) supposedly created a "thought-form which was used by the Dark Forces" to precipitate the First World War.[10]

One could just as easily say that, because of their use of musical materials with a Jewish cast, the symphonies of Gustav Mahler (1860–1911) were responsible, nearly forty years after his death, for the founding of the state of Israel. Or that the "Dark Forces" used the emergence of Jewish materials in Mahler's music to bring about the Holocaust.

There may indeed be a cultural process in which Mahler's Jewish music, the Holocaust, and the founding of the state of Israel are all involved—just as there may a relationship between German nationalism, the influence of Strauss's music and personal politics, and the onset of the First World War. But linking such things in a direct chain of cause and effect oversimplifies the dynamic in which they may be related.

I believe in the influence of higher spiritual powers on contemporary culture; and I believe that they can act on us, both individually and en masse, through a variety of media, including music. But, for several reasons, I want to exercise a certain amount of caution in assessing Scott's claims about the secret influences of music. One of these reasons is that Scott derided jazz—as well as rock, which he saw as one of the later "cumulative effects" of jazz—as a product of "the Dark Forces."[11] TMEs involving jazz or rock music can be just as ecstatic and growth-producing as those involving classical music, as we shall see.

Despite my misgivings about Scott's comments on jazz and rock music and a number of other points, I was impressed with his track record in making predictions about the future of music toward the end of the century. Some of the things he wrote in his 1958 revision of *Music: Its Secret Influence* were eerily prescient.

For example, Scott predicted that the increasing noise of urban life—which, he said, has a destructive effect on the spiritual and physical organism—would be counteracted by healing music based on "etheric vision" and acting on the subtle bodies.[12] This is the aim of New-Age music, which began to develop some fifteen years later, in the 1970s.

Scott also predicted that, going hand in hand with psychology, music would be created to correspond to "specific moods and emotional states."[13] Music therapy also came into its own toward the end of the twentieth century.

According to Scott's psychic sources, concerts would take place in semidarkness, with projected lights that changed according to the musical content.[14] Here, we have a startling prevision of musically accompanied laser light shows.

Scott foresaw that melody would return. Music would no longer be as discordant as it was for much of the twentieth century. Given the hegemony, after World War II, of highly dissonant atonal, electronic, aleatoric (chance-based), and mathematically derived music, how could Scott have known that in the 1970s a wave of neoromanticism would sweep the musical world, in which tonal harmony and melodic richness would once again come to the fore?

Scott went on to predict: "Great floods of melody will be poured forth from the higher planes, to be translated into earthly sound by composers sensitive enough to apprehend them."[15] In chapter 1, I mentioned that my friend Ruth, who composes music for film and television, has often felt that her music is being channeled through her.

Some years ago, Ruth claims, she was receiving melodies from a fleet of spaceships stationed somewhere in the vicinity of our planet. She was told that these melodies contained coded messages about such things as the existence of love beyond death. Ruth wove these messages into her scores, so that the people who were exposed to them on TV could benefit from them, even if the program was on a relatively mundane subject.[16]

The most impressive of Scott's predictions was that a new species of violin would be invented, to be played by "famous executants" born in America.[17] In chapter 1, I mentioned an American composer by the name of George Crumb. In 1970, Crumb composed a string quartet called *Black Angels*, which requires electrically amplified instruments. I've seen the piece played, not just with a new species of violin, but a whole quartet of fancifully designed instruments.

The world-renowned Kronos Quartet, founded by an American violinist, often performs the piece.

Scott predicted that "more subtle" sounds would be possible on this new species of violin.[18] Crumb's *Black Angels* exploits such sounds, which include quarter tones. Much of Crumb's quartet is frighteningly dissonant, which might have shocked Scott. But, in the wonderful section called "God-music," the violin soars above icy chords played by bows drawn across water-tuned crystal goblets. The effect is strangely beautiful and moving, like a prayer of transcendental longing for union with the divine.

Could "God-music" be an example of what Scott meant by deva-inspired music? (As I pointed out previously, the word *deva* is Sanskrit for "god.") If so, then the secret influence of some higher spiritual power may lie behind it.

Unfortunately, what Scott had to say about deva-inspired music is anything but clear. Given his astonishing foresight in the predictions enumerated here, we should investigate the idea of such inspiration more deeply. It could help us determine what type of music is most likely to induce TMEs.

Another Question

Before proceeding to the next chapter, I would like you to pause for a moment and consider—either through writing, thinking, or speaking to someone else—how your TMEs or those you've collected from others may have *shown you the way* or *given you permission* in some area of life: physical, emotional, intellectual, or spiritual. You're most likely to see such effects in TMEs that have the force of a conversion experience, as opposed to those that involve chills or a heightened sense of pleasure.

Perhaps, like me, you've had a TME that showed you the way and gave you permission to become a listener, performer, or composer. Such TMEs are clearly related to the process of self-actualization, or what Charles calls realizing the soul's master plan for your growth.

Other TMEs may have shown you the way or given you permission to do or be something that you hadn't considered before. Remember what my friend Deb said about listening to the Dave Brubeck Quartet's "Take Five": that the music seemed like "a picture of who I was and didn't know it yet." TMEs that produce this effect may also be leading you to realize the soul's master plan in some way.

4

Music from the Human
to the Ethereal Realms

Scott differentiated between music of the human and that of the ethereal realms. He referred to the latter as *deva* music, which is inspired by higher spiritual beings, including nature spirits, angels, and archangels. According to Scott:

> The chief Deva characteristic is Love, but, of course, this attribute varies with the spiritual altitude of the Devas in question—in the little nature spirit it is existent, but in a correspondingly lesser degree.[1]

Deva-inspired music expresses this love. It takes people out of themselves and gives them "a glimpse" of their "Higher" selves, "in which there is neither sorrow nor disease," thereby harmonizing and aligning them, inwardly, with a "seraphic love."[2] (This idea of "harmonizing and aligning" hearkens back to the purpose of music described by Plato in Timaeus, as cited at the beginning of chapter 2.) Finally, music with ecstasy and grandeur that "doesn't touch the heart" is deva music.[3]

Scott made a further distinction between "Deva-music" and "Buddhic music." In the music of Beethoven, we have a representation of "human love." In that of Bach and Handel, we have "love for God." But in certain pieces by Richard Wagner (1813–1883), we have *buddhic* love, "that love which *is* God."[4] Such music has the power to transport listeners to a higher spiritual plane, where they may experience a state of unity, as well as "selfless, unconditional Love."[5]

It seems likely, from Scott's descriptions, that deva music and buddhic music would produce TMEs. But what, exactly, are they? How would we recognize deva music and buddhic music if we heard it? Could we compose, perform, or listen to such music in ways that would maximize its potential for inducing TMEs?

Inferring what Scott meant by these terms from verbal descriptions and the few examples of such music that he gave is not easy. I wish that Scott's sources had revealed more about the nature of "Deva-music" and "Buddhic music."

In the conclusion of his book, Scott proclaimed that

> the great Initiates have vast and important plans for the musical future and we are authorized by Them to say that it depends on the reception of the present volume how much more They will feel justified in making known.[6]

Although Scott's book remained in print for decades after the publication of its first edition and a 1958 revision, the new revelations that he promised were never published. Yet, by scouring Scott's book for clues and listening to the musical examples that he cites, I've not only discovered what he meant by deva-inspired and buddhic music, but also assembled his observations on the secret influences of music into a coherent and usable system, designed to help listeners achieve transcendent musical experiences of their own.

What Scott called music of the human realm is that with which we're most familiar, involving feeling and emotion. Music of the ethereal realms involves inspiration from higher planes of spiritual evolution that lie beyond the human realm, including deva music and buddhic music. Such music provides illumination, mystical insight, and spiritual wisdom.

Many TMEs also include aspects of illumination, mystical insight, and spiritual wisdom. In order to achieve them, as listeners, performers, and composers, we need to know the difference between music of the human and ethereal realms, that which stimulates our emotions, and that which stimulates our capacity for mystical experiences.

One of the great mysteries in *Music: Its Secret Influence* is Scott's distinction between the human and ethereal elements in music. My first step in trying to clarify this distinction was to determine what Scott meant by deva music and buddhic music. I began by listening to recordings of Scott's own music. I assumed that, because of the esteem in which he held ethereal music, he would attempt to compose it himself.

The New Grove Dictionary of Music and Musicians, second edition, supplied me with an impressive catalog of Scott's works in all genres of classical music, from short piano pieces to sonatas, songs, and chamber music; orchestral music, including overtures, symphonies, rhapsodies, and piano concertos; and works for the stage, including a ballet, and several operas. Much of this music, especially that written during the latter half of his life, was unpublished and may never have been performed.

When I began my research, two CDs were all that I could find to represent this vast body of work. The first was a selection of orchestral music so under-rehearsed and badly played that, if there were any devas behind it, they must have hidden themselves in shame. The second was a selection of piano music, including a sonata and a number of lighter piano pieces. Unfortunately, every-thing on the CD was composed before Scott's interest in the esoteric aspects of music had developed.

Scott dismissed most of his piano compositions as salon music, written to pay the bills. He constantly rued the fact that such pieces as "Lotus Land" and "Danse Nègre" ("Negro Dance") were so popular that they diverted critical and public attention away from his more serious, larger-scale compositions. This was clearly music from the human realm.

A finely performed and recorded CD of Scott's Piano Quartet and Piano Quintet was recently released.[7] Scott said in his autobiography that the Piano Quartet, written in his twenties, and therefore predating his interest in esoteri-cism, was "unrepresentative and old-fashioned." He even wished "that it had never been published."[8]

The Piano Quintet also had its origin during this early period but was revised frequently until its eventual publication in 1925. By then, Scott had already met Nelsa Chaplin and Master K. H., as channeled through her. But this music is preoccupied with intellectual rather than spiritual concerns, and so belongs to the human realm.

Browsing through bins of old phonograph records in a used record store, I found two recordings of Scott's music made in the 1970s, during a short-lived revival of interest in his work. These recordings included Scott's two piano concertos and a piece for solo piano and orchestra called *Early One Morning*.

In both recordings, the piano playing is technically accomplished and the orchestral playing merely adequate. *Early One Morning* is the most accessible work of the three. Based on a folk tune, this piece bears a resemblance to *The Lark Ascending*, by Vaughan Williams, which I mentioned in chapter 1. Scott's piece is soothing in a way that anticipates much New-Age music.

According to Scott, music inspired by nature may be deva-inspired, as well. Folk music is closer to nature, so it too may contribute to the development of deva music.[9]

In deva music, "All is enchantingly indefinite, between the notes, varied, yet in a sense charmingly monotonous."[10] Scott couldn't have written a better description of *Early One Morning*. Here was my first clue to the nature of deva-inspired music.

Scott's First Piano Concerto, written in 1913 to 1914, attempts to reproduce another characteristic of deva music: that it should sound improvised. The meter is irregular and constantly changing, which makes performers nervous about playing it accurately. Such nervousness can cause even the most spiritual music to sound like an intellectual exercise—and anything but improvised.

The performers on this recording seem to have considered Scott's music merely impressionistic and eccentric. No wonder Scott has so little presence on LPs or CDs. With new and unfamiliar music, a bad or mediocre performance is usually blamed on the composer, not on the lack of spiritual understanding of the players.

The recording of the Second Piano Concerto suffers in much the same way. This music seems to be more abstract, less appealing than the other two works for piano and orchestra described above. It reminds me of Scott's claim that deva music sounds impersonal, yet ecstatic, and that it may not touch the heart. In this performance, however, it sounds remote and cerebral.[11]

Nature Music

If Scott's verbal descriptions of deva music and the rare recordings of his compositions were the only existing examples of what he meant, it would be hard to get a clear picture of how deva music differs from the music that we're used to. Luckily, Scott gave several examples of deva music in the works of other composers.

According to Scott, Claude Debussy (1862–1918) was one of the first composers to write deva-inspired *nature* music. Nature music appears to be a subcategory of deva music, one that's inspired by the nature-spirit variety of devas.[12]

Scott claimed that nature spirits "know no passions or sorrows." Furthermore, "They sing, they dance, they bathe in the sun- or moonbeams, they love to mould the clouds into countless different shapes, they love to play pranks and transform themselves into various substances."[13] Music inspired by nature spirits partakes of these characteristics.

Scott listed the following pieces by Debussy as examples of deva-inspired nature music: the orchestral works *L'après-midi d'un faune* (*The Afternoon of a Faun*), *Nuages* (*Clouds*), and *La Mer* (*The Sea*); and piano pieces such as *Jardins sous la pluie* (*Gardens in the Rain*) and *Reflets dans l'eau* (*Reflections on the Water*).[14] *La Mer*, for example, is an attempt to capture in music the many moods of the sea, from tranquil to violent to majestic.

It seems that what music history textbooks call musical impressionism roughly corresponds to Scott's category of deva-inspired nature music—especially when it's based on folk song, attempts to capture some aspect of nature, sounds improvised, and, as noted previously, is "enchantingly indefinite" and "charmingly monotonous."[15]

Seraphic Music

Scott asserted that the Belgian organist and composer César Franck (1822–1890) was also inspired by devas—though of the seraphic (angelic) rather than the nature-spirit variety. In his discussion of Franck's music, Scott made a distinction between the human element of the second movement of Franck's popular Violin Sonata in A Major and the ethereal element of the "noted *cantilene*" of Franck's Piano Quintet in F Minor.[16]

In listening to the second movement of the Violin Sonata, I determined that what Scott called the human element in Franck's music runs the gamut from agitated to exalted emotion, including pathos and passion. I had a harder time figuring out what Scott meant by the "noted *cantilene*" of the Piano Quintet. *Cantilene* is Italian for "singing line." Sometimes the term is used in the tempo marking or name of a section or movement. No such section is mentioned in the score of the quintet.

Franck's music is often based on a single theme that reappears in different guises in each movement of the work. In the Piano Quintet, this theme is marked *cantabile*—another word for "singing." If this is what Scott meant by the "noted *cantilene*," I'm still not sure how he understood it to be ethereal.

Much of the Piano Quintet exists in the same human realm as the Violin Sonata. However, in the cyclical theme of the quintet, an odd chord progression briefly hints of something out of the ordinary. If this is what Scott meant by the ethereal element of Franck's music, it wasn't enough for me to understand the distinction he was attempting to make.

Scott also mentioned a "sublime" oratorio by Franck for vocal soloists, chorus, and orchestra called *Les Béatitudes* (*The Beatitudes*).[17] The piece, a favorite of Franck's, took him ten years to complete.

Les Béatitudes lasts for over two hours. It's comprised of a Prologue and eight movements, each based on one of Jesus' famous sayings from the Sermon on the Mount. These movements usually begin with the chorus representing some aspect of suffering humanity, petitioning God for a remedy, and end with the voice of Jesus singing a Beatitude. Sometimes the chorus plays the role of a heavenly choir. Both Satan and the "Mater Dolorosa" (the Virgin Mary) also make appearances.

Here, the distinction between the human element (the choir's depiction of emotional agitation and suffering) and the ethereal (the spiritual balm of the Beatitudes of Jesus, sung by a baritone soloist, and the choir's depiction of heavenly bliss) is absolutely clear.

Scott made extraordinary claims for Franck. As an unworldly man, Franck's disdain of fame and material things, his modest lifestyle, and his devotion to the Catholic Church, in which he served for decades as organist, made him an ideal, though unknowing, pupil of Master K. H. Scott stated that Franck would appear in his next lifetime as an advanced initiate, gifted with "the ability to see, to hear, and to heal by super-physical means."[18]

Given the spiritual content and ethereal nature of the music in *Les Béatitudes*, it's not hard to believe that Franck was a more advanced soul than the ordinary composer or that he was inspired by some higher power. This piece could easily fulfill Scott's definition of deva music by: taking people out of themselves; giving them "a glimpse" of their "Higher" selves, "in which there is neither sorrow nor disease"; and harmonizing and aligning them, inwardly, with a "seraphic love."[19]

Scott's definition of devas places the nature spirits at the bottom of this hierarchy of spiritual beings, and angels and archangels at the top. "Seraphic love" is another way of saying "angelic love." So, within the realm of ethereal music, the seraphic music of Franck seems to rank higher than the nature music of Debussy.

Buddhic Music

According to Scott, Wagner "was the first to portray that Love which *is* God, the Divine Love or what in certain schools of occultism is termed the Buddhic."[20] If this divine love lies beyond the seraphic love associated with deva music, then the buddhic music of Wagner must have a spiritual effect similar to, if not greater than, that of Franck's *Les Béatitudes*.

Although I'd been exposed to the music of Wagner in music appreciation and history classes in college, I hadn't found it compelling enough to explore on my own afterward. In the process of researching this book, I bought a couple of CDs of Wagner's orchestral music. One of them contained the Prelude to Wagner's opera *Lohengrin*.

The first time I listened to this piece, I experienced a TME. I had no idea what the opera was about. But I felt a reaction in my inmost being that went beyond any I'd experienced when listening to most sacred music: a sense of divine grace, which made me want to live a deeper, truer life. Although Scott didn't mention the Prelude to *Lohengrin* as an example of "that Love which *is* God," his description of Wagner's buddhic music perfectly corresponded with my feelings as I listened to this piece.

Later in my research, I encountered Wagner's own description of what the Prelude to *Lohengrin* portrays. I was amazed at how the spiritually uplifting and purifying experience I'd had while listening to the Prelude matched what Wagner had written about it:

> Out of the clear blue ether of the sky there seems to condense a wonderful yet at first hardly perceptible vision; and out of this there gradually emerges, ever more and more clearly, an angel host bearing in its midst the sacred Grail. As it approaches earth it pours out exquisite odours, like streams of gold, ravishing the sense of the beholder. The glory of the vision grows and grows until it seems as if the rapture must be shattered and dispersed by the very vehemence of its own expansion. The vision draws nearer, and the climax is reached when at last the Grail is revealed in all its glorious reality, radiating fiery beams and shaking the soul in emotion. The beholder sinks on his knees in adoring self-annihilation. The grail pours out its light on him like a benediction and consecrates him to its service; then the flames gradually die away, and the angel host soars up again to the ethereal heights in tender joy, having made pure once more the hearts of men by the sacred blessing of the Grail.[21]

At this point, I had samples of what could be called the lower end of the deva-music spectrum: the nature-music of Debussy (*La Mer*, for example). I also had a specimen of the seraphic upper end of that spectrum: Franck's *Les Béatitudes*. Now, I'd identified an example of buddhic music, which had, just as Scott predicted, transported me to a higher spiritual plane, in which I experienced the divine grace of a "selfless, unconditional Love."[22]

I found the effects of listening to seraphic deva music to be more intense than those of listening to nature-spirit music—and the effects of listening to buddhic music more intense than either. This observation suggested the possibility that these three types of music could be arranged in a continuum of rising intensity, with nature-spirit music on the bottom and buddhic music at the top.

What Scott called the human element in music, with all of its emotional turbulence, would presumably lie below these three levels of ethereal music. The idea that deva music may express ecstasy and grandeur but "doesn't touch the heart"[23] further suggested that these elements could be arranged on a vertical continuum: human, nature-spirit, seraphic, buddhic. If I were to place the human element on the bottom of such a continuum and the buddhic element at the top, then upward movement along this continuum would reflect an increasing degree of spiritual intensity, while downward movement would reflect an increasing degree of emotional turbulence.

Other kinds of music could perhaps be added to such a continuum, filling out the human range. Like many musicians and avid listeners to music, I've noticed that different categories of music affect me in different ways. I began quantifying these effects. Songs, for example, seemed to work directly on the emotions, dance music on *joie de vivre*, symphonies on the intellect.

In listening to certain songs, especially those by Schubert, I could feel my heart opening. The feeling was surprisingly physical. My chest seemed to expand, as if there was more room for containing my feelings.

Dance music—for example, the numerous ländler (an ancestor of the waltz) for solo piano by Schubert—would lift my spirits. Symphonies would engage my analytic side, as if they were essays on what could be done with certain musical ideas.

Other kinds of music, especially highly dramatic or discordant music, had the opposite effect of opening the heart. I could feel a contraction in my chest—an emotional tension from which my body seemed to want to turn away or protect itself.

Sacred music also created a feeling of uplift, less physically based than that of dance music. The latter produced exuberance, whereas sacred music inspired spiritual exaltation.

Finally, there was ambient music, soothing, often electronic background music played, for example, by massage therapists while they're working. The effect of such music was not emotional. It elicited relaxation or mild pleasure, without dramatic tension—a trancelike sensual bliss.

My responses to these different categories of music reminded me of things that I'd read about yoga. Scott was a student of yoga, so it seemed natural for me to use his notions of human and ethereal music as a springboard for further research into this ancient spiritual tradition. In the next chapter, I present what I discovered.

A Useful Distinction

Before we proceed, it might be helpful for you to *hear* the distinction that Scott made between human and ethereal music. To do that, you'll need examples of each.

I've already mentioned a couple of possibilities in the classical realm: Franck's Violin Sonata (which is also sometimes played on the cello), with all of its emotional turbulence, is an instance of human music. His *Les Béatitudes* is an example of the serenity of ethereal, or seraphic, music. Unfortunately, it may not be easy to locate a recording of the latter. It tends to get pushed out of the CD store bins by Franck's more popular works, such as his Symphony in D Minor.

I've also listed a number of works by Debussy, each of which, according to Scott, is an example of ethereal music. I would recommend *La Mer*, which has the sense of ecstasy and grandeur that "doesn't touch the heart." Try contrasting *La Mer* with music by Peter Ilich Tchaikovsky (1840–1893), which definitely partakes of the emotional turbulence of the human realm. The first movement from his Fourth Symphony in F Minor, Op. 36 provides an effective contrast to the ethereal music of Debussy.

The Prelude to Wagner's *Lohengrin* is yet another example of ethereal music, this time of the buddhic variety. An effective contrast, here, too, is with the emotional turbulence of the human realm, as expressed in Tchaikovsky's symphony.

Gustav Mahler composes music of both the human and the ethereal realms. The emotional turbulence of the first movement of his Sixth Symphony in A Minor is an excellent example of human-realm music. The opening of the second movement of his Eighth Symphony in E-flat Major, which is a literal evocation of nature spirits, represented by the chorus, is an excellent example of ethereal music of the nature-spirit variety.

Scott claimed that the Russian mystical composer Alexander Scriabin (1872–1915) was "the greatest exponent of Deva-music."[24] Scriabin wrote two major orchestral pieces that qualify as ethereal-realm music: *The Poem of Ecstasy*, Op. 54, and *Prometheus, the Poem of Fire*, Op. 60.

What if you're not a classical music aficionado? No problem. Scott's distinction between music of the human and ethereal realms can also be applied to other kinds of music. For example, everything I've heard by the Irish New-Age singer and songwriter Enya (b. 1961) sounds like music of the ethereal realms. Contrast a song of Enya's—such as either of the two hits from her 1988 album *Watermark*, "Exile" or "Orinoco Flow"[25]—with one by a blues singer like Billie Holiday (1915–1959)—such as her rendition of the jazz standard "Solitude"[26]—and you'll immediately get the distinction between ethereal and human music.

Another possible way to experience this contrast directly is through watching, or listening to the soundtrack of, Peter Jackson's film of J. R .R. Tolkien's *The Fellowship of the Ring*.

The music that accompanies the hobbits in the Shire, toward the beginning of the movie ("Concerning Hobbits"), may not be emotionally turbulent, but is very much of the human realm, depicting the bustle and self-satisfied hominess of village life. Later in the film, the music that portrays Rivendell, the realm of the elves, has many of the qualities that Scott attributed to ethereal music. Enya collaborated in the creation of this music, which goes under the title "The Council of Elrond."[27]

Another example of deva-inspired ethereal music, by the jazz-rock fusion guitarist John McLaughlin (b. 1942), is "A Lotus on Irish Streams," from the Mahavishnu Orchestra's 1971 album *The Inner Mounting Flame.*[28] Contrast that with a human-realm song by Madonna (b. 1958), such as "Justify My Love," and you'll have the distinction down.[29]

Being able to make a distinction between music that represents our humanness, by touching our often turbulent emotions, and that which represents our spiritual nature, by touching our souls, is a basic skill in the yoga of listening that I hinted at in chapter 2. It will help us to determine the kinds of music most likely to produce TMEs. When I lay the groundwork for the yoga of listening in part 2 of this book, however, I'll exchange the terms *human, ethereal, devic, seraphic,* and *buddhic* for others that are more systematic and useful.

5

The Serpent Power
and the Yoga of Sound

As I mentioned in the previous chapter, while considering the possibility that Scott's categories of human and ethereal music could be arranged along a vertical continuum, with the human element on the bottom and the buddhic element at the top, I became intrigued by the possibility that some relationship might exist between this continuum and certain principles of yoga.

Spiritual teacher Eknath Easwaran says that "Yoga is neither belief, nor dogma, nor metaphysics, nor philosophy. It is a method of union, a way of uniting all that is divided within us." In the ancient Hindu scriptures upon which the principles of yoga are based, the word "refers to the method, the spiritual disciplines, used to unify our consciousness."[1]

As I pointed out in chapter 2, Plato claims that music exists for the purpose of creating harmony between the various aspects of ourselves. In Timaeus, he says that music may help us bring the soul "into harmony and agreement with herself."[2]

Charles states that music is a way of bringing us closer to our souls. It would seem that yoga, with its purpose of unifying our consciousness, and music, with its purpose of harmonizing ourselves, have a natural affinity for each other. If we could combine yoga and music, we might have a powerful tool for integrating body, mind, and soul. One purpose of this book is to lay the groundwork for such a yoga, the yoga of listening.

There are many varieties of yoga, some having to do with the cultivation of the body, others with producing ecstatic and transcendent states of consciousness. One type, Tantra, develops the potentials of both body *and* consciousness.

Tantra's approach to enlightenment is body-positive. It doesn't deny the value of the senses and pleasurable physical experiences for spiritual growth, as do some world religions and a number of other brands of yoga. Hatha yoga, the type taught in most Western yoga classes, is a variety of Tantra.[3]

One of the esoteric branches of Tantra deals with a mysterious force of spiritual awakening called *kundalini*, which is said to produce ecstatic and transcendent states of consciousness. The kundalini energy has its origin at the base of the spine. When awakened, it rises to the crown of the head, activating a number of psychic energy centers located between these points. These psychic energy centers are called *chakras*, Sanskrit for "wheels," referring to their spherical appearance when seen by persons gifted with clairvoyant vision.

I was intrigued by the possibility that Charles's concept of life force and the Tantric idea of kundalini could be related to one another. I began to wonder whether the connections that I noted in the previous chapter between music and various physical, emotional, intellectual, and spiritual sensations could somehow be linked with the chakras.

I learned from my research that most Tantric traditions describe seven chakras—although some include as few as five, and others eight or more. In the seven-chakra system, the first is located at the base of the spine, and the seventh at the crown of the head. Each chakra is associated with certain aspects of human life or states of consciousness.

There is much disagreement between authorities on the chakras about what these associations are. I've investigated both ancient and modern chakra systems and have come to the conclusion that those put forward by the early twentieth-century Indian mystic Sri Aurobindo and the late twentieth-century yogi Swami Satyananda Saraswati are the most useful. The following is my own synthesis and paraphrasing of these systems.[4]

The first, or root, chakra, located at the base of the spine, is associated with the survival of the physical body; the second, genital, chakra, located in the genital area, with the sensual aspect of life.

The third, or navel, chakra, located in the area of the navel or solar plexus, is associated with self-assertion and the exercise of the will; the fourth, or heart, chakra, located in the area of the physical heart, with unconditional love.

The fifth, or throat, chakra, located in the region of throat, is associated with communication and community; the sixth, or brow, chakra, located on the forehead, at the root of the nose, between and slightly above the eyebrows (the location of the so-called third eye mentioned in some Western esoteric traditions), with intellect, intuition, and inner vision.

The seventh, or crown, chakra, located at the top of the head, is associated with states of mystical ecstasy and illumination.

As I thought about possible relationships between music and the chakras, it seemed to me that ambient music, with its sensual appeal, could be associated with the second, or genital, chakra. Dramatic music, such as opera, which often involves the contesting of wills between two or more characters, could be associated with the third. Music that opens the heart, such as songs, could affect the fourth, or heart, chakra; while music that stimulates the intellect, such as symphonies, could affect the sixth, which is often linked with the workings of the mind. Sacred music, as well as Scott's ethereal music, could express the enlightenment potential attributed to the seventh chakra.

At this stage in my thinking, I wasn't sure which chakra would best be associated with dance music. Because the first chakra is connected with our presence in the physical body, it could perhaps be related to such music. Yet the fifth chakra, which is concerned with community, could also be related to dance music, since dancing often involves a social, or communal, component.

Over many months, I attempted to refine this sketch of possible associations between the chakras and different types of music. As I mentioned previously, I was intrigued by a possible connection between the ancient yogic notion of kundalini and what Charles calls life force.

In the Tantric tradition, kundalini (Sanskrit for "coiled") lies wrapped around the root, or first, chakra like a sleeping snake. One of the synonyms for kundalini is a Sanskrit word meaning "serpent power."

Yogic practitioners attempt to arouse or awaken the kundalini by means of meditation and other spiritual practices. They draw it up or let it rise along the spine, so that it moves through each of the chakras in turn, thereby activating them. Such practitioners may experience feelings of transcendence or attain a state of ecstatic illumination at the point when the kundalini reaches the crown, or seventh, chakra.

Charles has said that TMEs are the result of an increased flow of life force generated by the soul. Could an increased flow of life force be related to the yogic notion of kundalini? If so, then the chakra system might be a useful means of organizing our perceptions of how different kinds of music—from the human to the ethereal—relate to each other. They could be connected along a vertical continuum of increasing life-force flow.

Linking the chakras with music in this way might also enable us to achieve transcendent musical experiences more easily and frequently. The idea would be to listen to music that corresponds to the upper end of this continuum— what Scott called devic, seraphic, or buddhic music—to maximize the flow of life force through us, thereby triggering TMEs.

In this chapter, I investigate the relationship of the kundalini, or serpent power, to Charles's notion of life force. In chapter 6, I demonstrate how music and the chakra system can be linked along a vertical continuum of rising life-force flow.

Kundalini Awakening

In Tantra, the awakening of the kundalini, the sleeping serpent power that activates the chakras, is responsible for states of ecstasy and feelings of transcendence. This concept may be useful in pursuing our goal of achieving TMEs. However, the literature on the subject of kundalini is rife with warnings not to tamper with it. The yogis say that doing so without the guidance of a spiritual master may lead to psychological or physical damage.

The effects of awakening the kundalini may range from slight disturbances in one's normal consciousness and sense of physical well-being—such as intense feelings of heat or itching along the spine—to potentially distressing, if not dangerous, ones that involve startling involuntary behaviors. Other, more positive, effects involve states of bliss, which can be accompanied by the development of paranormal powers. If the serpent power has a bearing on the TME, we should clearly investigate it with caution.

One yogi, Swami Vishnu Tirtha, lists the following symptoms of awakened kundalini.[5] The root chakra begins to throb, leading to a trembling in the rest of the body and forceful involuntary breathing. The hair may stand on end, accompanied by various manifestations that a modern psychologist might call hysterical: involuntary laughter, tears, animal-like vocalization, and possibly even physical orgasm. Meanwhile, the experiencer may witness terrifying visions. (Of these symptoms, only the hair rising and involuntary tears seem to apply to TMEs.)

Various yogic postures, both stationary and active, may develop spontaneously and involuntarily, and be practiced for lengthy periods with no pain or fatigue. The same may occur with certain meditation practices and *pranayama* (yogic techniques of breath control), including chanting. Both the postures and the breathing techniques are accompanied by blissful feelings, as well as the sense that someone else may be performing these activities, as if one were possessed. (In chapter 1, I described several instances in which performing musicians have experienced a similar sense of heightened awareness, in which the piece under performance seemed to play itself.)

Sensations like those described by veteran out-of-body experiencers may also develop: inner sounds, vibrations along the spine, electrical jolts in the limbs, losing awareness of one's presence in the body, and so-called sleep paralysis. Bodily fainting while maintaining consciousness, convulsions, even the feeling that one is dying may occur, along with spontaneous leaps from a cross-legged seated position. The same state of electrified, blissful lucidity may be present whether one is awake or asleep. (Of these symptoms, only that of losing awareness of one's presence in the body seems to apply to TMEs.)

Effects that would not be out of place in a Pentecostal church, including speaking and singing in tongues, may sometimes develop. One may experience an inability to concentrate on anything but God-intoxication, which causes one to remain silent and avoid other activities. Or one may find oneself endowed with an apparently inexhaustible supply of energy for physical activity or work, as well as an unflappably buoyant mood. (The latter effect correlates strongly with what Charles has said about increases of life-force flow from the soul.)

In meditation, one may have extraordinary experiences, including the stimulation of the five physical senses as if by the divine counterparts of colors, sounds, smells, tastes, and textures. Effects akin to channeling may also develop, in which one receives direct instructive communication from divine beings. (Handel seems to have experienced something like these kundalini effects when he was composing *Messiah*.)

There may be a spontaneous awakening of superior spiritual insight, including knowing the future, being able to interpret even the most abstruse scriptures with ease, and expounding on spiritual matters with surpassing inspiration and eloquence. Eventually, one may experience the more desirable of these effects at will, rather than spontaneously and involuntarily. (I comment later on the kundalini effect of spontaneous scriptural interpretation.)

Some of the symptoms of kundalini awakening described above may sound frightening. Yet, when asked in an interview whether kundalini was dangerous, a prominent teacher of kundalini yoga, Yogi Bhajan, quipped, "Is money dangerous?"[6] The implication is that both kundalini and money are merely tools. They serve certain needs under certain conditions, and create potential problems under others, especially if used ignorantly, unwisely, or with inappropriate intent.

Gopi Krishna—who became one of the foremost researchers on the serpent power as a result of the negative effects of having awakened it in himself without proper preparation—believes that the kundalini phenomenon is not limited to yogic practitioners. It may also occur in "the born mystic, the man and woman of genius, the prodigies, the mediums, and the psychotics."[7] These people, too, may experience transcendent knowledge, spiritual insight, startling creative revelations, visions of divine realms, and the sense of receiving dictation from on high.

Another yogi, Swami Narayanananda, states that any form of intense, one-pointed concentration has the capacity to activate the serpent power, even obsessive grieving over the loss of a loved one.[8] Because listening to music or composing, practicing, or performing on a musical instrument can bring about such one-pointed concentration, each could conceivably become a means of awakening the kundalini.

Yet another yogi, Swami Vivekananda, has stated that "a little current of kundalini" is responsible for "any manifestation of what is called supernatural power or wisdom."[9] Perhaps the highly concentrated trance state that the mystics and seers of old, as well as contemporary channelers, have used to receive visions and divine guidance is a Western equivalent of the yogic state of *samadhi* (bliss), an ecstasy achieved through the similarly one-pointed focus of meditation.

As I mentioned in chapter 2, Handel composed *Messiah* in a mere twenty-four days, claiming that he experienced visions of God and heaven while he worked. One biographer of the composer has stated "Considering the immensity of the work, and the short time involved, it will remain perhaps forever the greatest feat in the history of musical composition."[10]

The abilities required to achieve this feat certainly seem paranormal, and resemble those associated with kundalini awakening, including an inexhaustible supply of energy for work and a propensity for visions of the divine. Perhaps Handel's high level of concentration on composing during this period resulted in a kundalini awakening. As I've indicated, any form of one-pointed consciousness can raise the kundalini.

Another manifestation of the serpent power that may have some bearing on the art of music is the spontaneous ability to interpret even the most obscure scriptures with clarity. Such a manifestation of kundalini-inspired wisdom could be of inestimable value to a performer. Just change the word *scripture* to *musical score*.

I was in graduate school at the University of Illinois during the centenary of the birth of Hungarian composer Béla Bartók (1881–1945). One of the musicologists on the faculty held a seminar on Bartók in honor of the occasion.

Bartók had been my favorite twentieth-century composer since I was in high school. I enrolled in the seminar and relistened to Bartók's oeuvre. One piece I'd never heard previously was his Viola Concerto.

The Viola Concerto was left unfinished when Bartók died. One of his associates attempted to complete the score from the composer's sketches. These sketches had been

notated on odd bits of manuscript paper in such a way that the intended sequence was by no means apparent. Earlier sketches appeared on some of the same pages; there were no page numbers nor movement indications, and, most discouraging of all, Bartók wrote over passages instead of erasing them, with the result that parts of the score were almost illegible.[11]

The first time I listened to a recording of the Viola Concerto, I was disappointed. The piece didn't hang together well.

As I was immersing myself in Bartók's music, I was also undertaking the experiments in psychic development that led to my contact with Charles. As a result of the conjunction of these two activities, I experienced a startling effect as I listened to the Viola Concerto—a TME with a strong component of illumination.

I seemed to have a direct line to Bartók's intentions in composing the piece, as if I were in touch with the deceased composer himself or some internally perceivable version of the piece that existed on another plane of consciousness. Later, I would learn from Charles that what I'd perceived was a *process configuration*, a constellation of nonphysical energy that encapsulates both the process by which a piece of music unfolds in time and the process of composing it.

As I listened to Bartók's concerto, some passages sounded wrong. Because of my intuitive perception of the process configuration behind the piece, I was convinced that these passages didn't belong where Bartók's associate had put them. Not only was their order within a particular movement sometimes incorrect, but also certain passages in the first movement should have been placed in the third, and vice versa.

Perhaps, given access to the original sketches, I could have used sensations of this sort to reconstruct the piece, so that it would have been more in line with Bartók's intentions. The kundalini-inspired ability to see through the greatest textual obscurities would then have been quite handy.

Perhaps my experiments in channeling had temporarily sparked the serpent power within me, providing me with a glimpse of how the paranormal ability of interpreting obscure scriptures might be applied to music. At the time, however, I knew nothing about the kundalini energy and its effects.

I've often listened to unfinished compositions by other composers that were completed by a student, associate, or musicologist, sometimes many years after the composer's death. But I never again experienced such a strong conviction that the job had been botched. When listening to other sorts of music, however, I frequently have an intuitive sense of how closely the performer is realizing the composer's intentions, and of what needs to be done to improve the performance.

Perhaps this is a low-level version of the paranormal ability of spontaneous scriptural interpretation mentioned in connection with kundalini awakening. Charles has said that it's a result of "tuning in" to the process configuration behind a piece of music, an ability that anyone who learns to trust his intuition can develop. Such an ability is a key element of the yoga of listening, as we shall see.

Over and over, the yogis stress that the best way to brave and survive the awakening of the serpent power, which one writer on yoga has called an "onslaught of enlightenment,"[12] is proper preparation. According to Swami Sivananda Radha, such preparation involves "finding a teacher, studying texts, doing spiritual practice, cultivating observation, and finally having personal experience little by little."[13]

Gopi Krishna believed that without such preparation, what could have been a positively experienced release of the kundalini energy becomes a negative one. Divine light becomes "blinding glares"; divine sounds, "distracting glares and shrieks"; divine visions, "nightmares"; divine insights, mere "crazy whims"; and the sense of "spiritual exaltation" promised by the Tantric scriptures, little more than "grandiose delusions."[14] The upshot seems to be that, under certain conditions, people who have undergone a spontaneous kundalini awakening may fear for their sanity.

A psychiatrist who has studied numerous cases of spontaneous kundalini awakening makes a clear differentiation between the kundalini phenomenon and psychosis. He suggests that the primary function of the kundalini phenomenon is a process of internal purification that removes various blocks to self-realization, especially at the physical and emotional levels. This experience is positive if one goes along with it, negative if one resists it.[15]

Even though kundalini experiencers may feel that they've gone insane while undergoing such an awakening, a higher level of self-integration and spiritual health is the eventual result, not the more or less permanent dysfunctionality of true mental illness.[16]

Nada Yoga

Luckily for us, despite the claims of many yogis that awakening the serpent power is dangerous, Swami Satyananda Saraswati mentions "a most tender and absorbing way of awakening" that involves music: *nada yoga*. In Sanskrit, *nada* means "sound."

As traditionally taught, this yoga of sound involves mantras and melodies associated with each chakra.[17] A mantra is "thought or intention expressed as sound." Mantras are sometimes single syllables or vowel sounds, sometimes a phrase or sentence that "may or may not have communicable meaning."[18]

Mantras may be chanted inwardly or audibly as a means of developing concentration and achieving transcendence. They may also be used to achieve magical ends. Their power derives both from constant repetition and from their having been activated or energized by a guru.[19]

Here's what Sri Aurobindo said on the subject:

> The Mantra can not only create new subjective states in ourselves, alter our psychical being, reveal knowledge and faculties we did not before possess, can not only produce similar results in other minds than that of the user. But can produce vibrations in the mental and vital atmosphere which can result in effects, in actions and even in the production of material forms on the physical plane.[20]

While singers may spend a certain amount of practice time on repeating single-pitched vowel sounds without "communicable meaning," I doubt that these vocalizations would have any of the powers that Aurobindo mentioned. But the acts of rehearsing and performing a piece of music *could* potentially have such effects.

A piece of music being prepared for performance, whether by individual musicians in private practice or by the entire ensemble for which it was composed, is often repeated again and again. Such public or private rehearsal acts as an aid to concentration, enabling the musicians involved to achieve the best possible performance—perhaps even a transcendent one. Thus the actual sound of a piece being practiced, rehearsed, or performed is much like a mantra.

Have such sounds been energized by a guru? In the West, especially in Europe, many composers, conductors, and teachers of music are reverently referred to as Master or Maestro. They often expect or receive a level of devotion on the part of their students similar to that accorded to gurus by their disciples. A charismatic conductor can greatly enliven a performance just as a guru can energize a mantra.

Furthermore, many of Western music's greatest composers, such as Bach or Beethoven in the classical world, John Coltrane (1926–1967) and Miles Davis (1926–1991) in the jazz world, and the Beatles and Kurt Cobain (1967–1994) in the realm of rock music, are often revered by musicians and listeners alike, as if they were gurus.

Both composers and conductors seek to move an audience in various ways. That feeling of being moved by a performance, resulting in anything from toe-tapping, to tears, to spiritual transcendence, could perhaps qualify as mantra-like, in the sense described by Sri Aurobindo. New subjective states are created, the psychic being is altered. We may discover within ourselves capacities for feeling that we didn't know we had. And the world itself could be affected in visible and invisible ways by such performances, as Cyril Scott claimed in *Music: Its Secret Influence.*

Composers may find that the music they write has spiritual effects on themselves similar to those that Sri Aurobindo ascribed to mantras. For example, mystical composer Alexander Scriabin had this to say about composing:

> Music is the path of revelation. You can't imagine how potent a method of knowledge it is! If only you knew how much I have learned through music! All I now think and say, I know from my composing.[21]

According to yoga scholar Georg Feuerstein, mantras "are creative forces that act directly on consciousness."[22] Musical scores may also manipulate the consciousness of an audience in quasi-magical ways. If nada yoga—the yoga of sound—can provide a gentle means of spiritual awakening, through using mantras and the chakras, perhaps a yoga of listening that uses musical scores and the chakras can achieve a similar end. In parts 2 and 3 of this book, I develop just such a yoga of listening—one that avoids the potentially dangerous effects of arousing the kundalini.

Charles sees no essential difference between what he calls life force and what the yogis call the serpent power. For him, both terms lie along a vertical continuum. At the lower end is the least intense form of life force—what the yogis call *prana*—which keeps our bodies healthy and motivates us to satisfy our basic physical needs. At the upper end of the continuum is kundalini, the serpent power, a more intense version of the same force, whose purpose is to expand consciousness beyond its normal parameters and put it more directly in touch with the soul.

Here, then, is the basic framework of the continuum of increasing life-force flow that I mentioned at the beginning of this chapter. In chapter 6, I demonstrate how this continuum relates to music and the chakras.

We've already seen that, according to Charles, the soul guides us through fluctuations in life-force flow. But the ego, too, is often responsible for such fluctuations. Charles defines the ego as a self-regulating valve of life-force flow. It can willingly expand to increase that flow, which results in satisfaction, happiness, or ecstasy. Or it can willfully contract to reduce it, resulting in dissatisfaction, unhappiness, or depression.

In some cases, the soul provides more life force than the ego is capable of experiencing without fear for its own survival. Such fear may result from feeling out of control, overwhelmed, or consumed by the intensity of the experience.

Yogic practices designed to awaken the kundalini can maximize the ego's openness to the flow of life force, resulting in ecstasy. If the ego becomes afraid of such a state, Charles says, it will try to resist this flow of life force and shut down. The ego may then inadvertently cause the unpleasant side effects of kundalini awakening that I noted above.

According to Charles, some yogic practices attempt to achieve kundalini awakening through what he calls *ego-shattering*. Such practices involve a willful desire to destroy not only the ego's control of the body and mind, but also the ego itself as a means of apprehending and dealing with physical reality. To this end, the more extreme versions of yoga starve and mortify the body, often depriving it of sleep, while at the same time undermining the ego's sense of I-ness through self-isolation, extended periods of silence, and constant meditation.

Charles says that the frightening forms of spontaneous kundalini awakening described above cannot occur without a willful desire on the part of the ego to destroy itself. This desire may arise from the positive goal of wishing to transcend the ego and become more closely aligned with the soul; or it may arise from the negative goal of self-destruction, the so-called Freudian death wish.

In the case of the positive goal, the effort to destroy the ego is chosen consciously and pursued willfully. In the case of the negative goal, this effort is undertaken unconsciously—though it may also be pursued with a certain degree of intensity.

For Charles, the idea of destroying the ego is of questionable value. He advocates *expanding* the ego and bringing it more closely into alignment with the soul. As long as one avoids self-isolation, dietary restriction, and mortification of the body, there's little need to fear an accidental awakening of the serpent power.

Esotericist Alice Bailey claims that the best way to prevent damage from *any* sort of spiritual practice is "to lead normal busy lives" involving service, an effective antidote against isolation and unhealthy self-absorption. One should at the same time work toward realization of oneself on every level—physical, emotional, intellectual, and spiritual.[23]

Yoga teacher Stephen Cope says that he deals with unpleasant experiences caused by the kundalini energy by connecting "with the ground—gardening, getting my hands dirty, or walking in the woods." He also says that such experiences may be the result of yogic "practices that heighten purification of the body and mind." These practices include not only extended periods of isolation, fasting, and dietary restrictions, but also celibacy.

Cope states that unpleasant energy experiences can "be heightened during periods of sexual celibacy. Having sex can often lower their intensity."[24]

Much music-making requires the presence of other people in bands, chamber ensembles, and orchestras. Even the act of listening to music, especially live performances, is often a social event. By keeping in mind the guidelines mentioned here, there's little chance that the methods of spiritual development outlined in this book will result in an unintentional and potentially destructive kundalini awakening. Still, it may be important to balance extended hours of self-isolation in practicing one's instrument, or long periods of listening to recorded music by oneself, with social contact.

Charles says that making and listening to music are among the gentlest ways of expanding the ego so that it can experience a sense of union with the soul. This state of union is also the goal of yoga.

To Charles, expanding the ego means discovering and fulfilling as much as we can of the soul's master plan for our growth. Doing so should maximize the flow of life force through us, producing—and perhaps even prolonging—experiences of the transcendent bliss that the yogis call samadhi.

Charles says that such experiences are available to all human beings. Any soul-supported activity can produce them. But composing, performing, and listening to music may be among the safest and most potent means of doing so.

In my own process of spiritual development, I've learned not to hurry things along. New abilities or awarenesses have manifested themselves as I became ready for them. Because I trust my soul not to provide me with more life force than I may be able to handle in a given moment and don't demand or push for more, I've rarely felt overwhelmed by my TMEs, or any other mystical experience that has come my way. Here's an example of what I mean.

In chapter 3, I described how I taught myself to meditate by listening to the symphonies of Bruckner. In the case of the first movement of his Ninth Symphony, I was able to achieve one-pointed concentration as well as a quasi-orgasmic state of ecstasy by coordinating my breathing with the rhythm of its closing measures. Without knowing it, I'd discovered one of the fundamental tenets of yoga: breath control can lead to higher states of consciousness.

During the period in high school when I was listening so avidly to Bruckner's symphonies, I had another TME. This one involved the Finale of his Eighth Symphony in C Minor.[25] Bruckner identified the movement's opening rhythm with a horde of galloping Cossacks. Its austere and majestic harmonies, however, suggested to me some kind of solemn festival.

In my TME, I found myself in the midst of a dreamlike vision. I was aware of the music, so I was not asleep. But I was unaware of my body, which was lying on the floor of my dark bedroom, with my head positioned between the speakers of my stereo system.

The music was loud enough to drown out other sounds in my family's house, but not loud enough to become uncomfortable during the passages when the orchestra was playing at full volume. Meanwhile, the scene and actions that I perceived inwardly, with my eyes closed, had a stability and vivid reality akin to those of a lucid dream.

I seemed to be inside the central chamber of a vast temple with a vaulted ceiling. The floor, the vault, and the columns that supported it were all carved from blue-black stone. From three sides, long, high colonnades came together. They met before a raised platform backed by a wall. The platform, also carved from stone, rose a couple of steps above the floor. It was perfectly square, perhaps fifteen feet per side.

A large circular area was cut from the surface of the platform, opening downward into a deep pit. From the pit came a lurid red glow, emanating from a subterranean fissure filled with molten lava. On the wall behind the platform was a huge sheet of beaten gold, polished so that it picked up the red glow of the lava and projected it throughout the temple chamber. There was no other source of light.

I was brought forward, at the head of a line of robed priests who were approaching the platform, wall, and mirror along the central colonnade. My hands were bound. I was a prisoner. Meanwhile, two other files of priests approached from the temple wings, along the left and right colonnades.

I was led to the platform and urged up the steps. At the edge of the pit, I gazed down at the seething lava below, dimly aware of the image of myself that was reflected in the golden mirror. I was expected to jump or fall into the pit, a sacrificial victim.

I remained on the edge of the pit for what seemed like an eternity, feeling the intense heat of the lava below me. Meanwhile, the music built to its grandiose climax, and suddenly ended, along with my vision. I moved my limbs, opened my eyes, and turned on the light, wondering what had just happened.

The musical architecture of Bruckner's symphonies has often been described as cathedral-like. The temple in which I found myself may have been a visual representation of that architecture.

The Finale of Bruckner's Eighth has the tempo marking *Feierlich*, German for "solemn" and "ceremonious." So the presence of priests was not surprising as a visual expression of the music's mood.

The pit of molten lava, however, as well as my being a sacrificial victim, is not explainable in terms of the music. Such images, like those in a dream, must have had a more personal meaning.

One often-reported symptom of kundalini awakening is a sense of intense inner heat. My experiments with one-pointed concentration and rhythmic breathing while listening to music may have led me to the edge of a kundalini awakening—symbolized, in my vision, by the edge of the pit. I wasn't ready yet to take the next step, which the yogis say would require that I sacrifice my ego to the consuming fires of the serpent power.

Making a Playlist

When it comes to new technology, I've always been a slow learner. It took me years to upgrade my phonograph player to a CD player. My car stereo still plays cassettes, unless I plug in a recently bought adapter that allows me to play CDs. I've had portable cassette players with headphones for about two decades, but a portable CD player for less than five years.

So, when my housemate, Kevin, got rid of his old computer and upgraded it with one that his best friend from high school was ready to pass on, I was unprepared for the brave new world of music listening that this machine opened up for me. It contained a collection of 5,500 songs, in genres ranging from ambient music to rhythm and blues, jazz, punk, and alternative rock to country-western. In its entirety, this collection would have required just over two weeks of twenty-four-hour-a-day play time.

Kevin's new computer arrived at an auspicious time. While working on this book, I became concerned about my relative lack of exposure to music other than classical. Compared with that of my contemporaries, both older and younger, my knowledge of nonclassical music was rather spotty.

Back in high school, in addition to dozens of classical albums, I owned two 45s: "American Pie," by folksinger Don McLean (b. 1945), and "Brown Sugar," by the Rolling Stones. I also owned a handful of albums: the Who's rock opera *Tommy*, *Jesus Christ Superstar*, and Uriah Heep's 1972 release, *Magician's Birthday*, which I liked more for the cover art than the music. And that was it.

In college, a friend who was a jazz aficionado acquainted me with the group Oregon and pianist Keith Jarrett (b. 1945). In graduate school, a friend who worked at the University of Illinois radio station introduced me to the music of jazz bassist Eberhard Weber (b. 1940). I bought a couple of LPs of each.

The rest of my exposure to nonclassical music has taken place through immersion in contemporary culture: rock or jazz songs played by my brothers in their bedroom; in the college cafeteria, and down the hall from my dorm room; in movies, at the dentist's, and the houses of friends; at dance clubs and a favorite bar in Chicago in the early 1980s, where music videos were shown before the advent of MTV; at the YMCA health club to which I've belonged for twenty years; and so on.

I don't own a television and haven't watched TV, except on rare occasions, since I was fifteen years old. That cut out another possible venue for educating myself about rock and jazz. When I listen to the radio, I prefer the classical music stations.

One result of being exposed to nonclassical music in this haphazard way is that I can recognize many rock songs, and some jazz standards and instrumentals, by ear, without knowing who wrote or performed them. For example, when my friend Deb told me about her TME when listening to "Take Five," I told her I'd never heard it before. When I bought the CD to check it out, however, I recognized the piece immediately from past hearings.

In a similar way, when I began to explore the collection of songs on Kevin's new computer, I thought that the music of, say, Led Zeppelin, with the exception of "Stairway to Heaven," was completely unexplored territory. I was surprised to discover that I knew about half of the two hours of music stored there.

The software that managed the 350 hours of music on Kevin's computer was also a revelation. It could sort this vast body of musical information by genre, artist, and album title, and allow users to create their own playlists.

A playlist tells the computer what tunes to play and in what order, turning a computer equipped with loudspeakers into a digital jukebox. Such playlists can also be burned onto CDs for playback on other systems, including portable CD players.

From a newspaper article that appeared just as I was beginning to explore the music on Kevin's new computer, I learned about the digital listening file format called MP3 that allows people to download music from the Internet. I was surprised to discover that it's now possible to carry around a pocket-sized MP3 player with as much storage and software-based sorting capacity as a stationary personal computer or laptop.

Multiple-disc CD players with the capacity to move randomly from one CD or track to another have long allowed people to create a jukebox-like listening experience. MP3 players greatly enhance this capacity, adding that of *consciously* creating playlists from a wide variety of genres, moods, or musical periods.

Not only is it possible to download MP3 files from the Internet, but also to transfer the audio content of any CD to a computer's hard drive and convert it to MP3 format. Thus, at least theoretically, the entire history of Western music, in both the classical and popular modes, as well as non-Western music, could contribute to an MP3 playlist. The only requirements are that the music must be recorded in some form and available in MP3 format.

It won't be necessary for you to purchase a computer, software, or portable listening device that acts as a digital jukebox to pursue the yoga of listening described in this book. But the new ways of thinking about music upon which such digital listening systems are based will be useful to us, especially the idea of playlists.

Despite the allure of such technology, many of us who love music will no doubt continue to own and enjoy nonvirtual collections of music. I have a couple hundred classical LPs that I treasure, most of which have never been released on CD. I've also amassed extensive audiocassette (for in-car listening) and CD collections. I don't have any downloaded music. Nevertheless, I have a catalog of all the recorded music to which I have access stored in my head. Perhaps you do, too.

The human brain may not be as efficient as a computer in sorting large batches of information. But, given the right criteria, the brain is perfectly capable of generating a cross-referenced index of its own contents in many areas. Paper and pen can sometimes be a useful support in this process.

So, what I would like you to do is scan your memories of your music collection and create a playlist based on the criteria listed below. I recommend coming up with from one to three selections in each category. These selections may refer to individual pieces, movements, songs, or parts thereof.

Consulting the music itself before adding the title to your playlist is fine. It's a good idea to write down your playlist as an aid in the process of creating it and for future reference. Without such a playlist, the listening practices that I recommend in part 2 of this book may not be as useful to your spiritual development as I hope they'll be.

Don't worry if you're unable to come up with selections for one or more of the categories listed here. I offer some suggestions for you to consider in part 2.

First, I would like you to think about, and add to your playlist, from one to three items in which your main source of pleasure lies in the *rhythm*. Pieces, songs, or passages that feature or are dominated by the drummer of the band or the percussion section of the orchestra, or in which the rhythm is especially complex and fascinating, are best.

Second, I would like you to think about, and add to your playlist, from one to three items in which your main source of pleasure lies in the *melody*. Pieces, songs, or passages in which some especially beautiful or moving tune is featured are best.

Third, I would like you to think about, and add to your playlist, from one to three items in which your main source of pleasure lies in the sense of uplift they give you, their *upbeat* quality. Pieces, songs, or passages that cheer you up, sustain a buoyant mood, or make you want to dance are best.

Finally, I would like you to think about, and add to your playlist, from one to three items in which your main source of pleasure lies in how things are done—in other words, the *form*. Pieces, songs, or passages that are shaped in especially satisfying ways are best. This satisfaction could come from the formal aspects of the piece, song, or passage, or from the way that a performer plays or improvises them. You should be looking for a feeling of rightness, inevitability, or perfection—a sense that the piece could only be composed or played in just that way.

If you would like to check your playlist, once you've written it down, by listening to the music you've included on it, by all means do so. Or set your playlist aside for now. We'll add to it at the end of the next chapter, and use it as the basis for listening activities in part 2 of this book.

6

Building a Continuum
of Human Potential

In the previous chapter, I promised to demonstrate how music and the chakra system could be linked along a continuum of rising life-force flow. I pointed out that at one end of such a continuum lies prana, the life force that keeps the body healthy and motivates us to satisfy our physical needs. At the other end lies the serpent power, or kundalini energy, whose purpose is to expand consciousness and allow us to develop a closer relationship to the soul. I conceive of this continuum as a vertical hierarchy, with prana at the bottom, rising into kundalini at the top.

Sufi mystic and musician Hazrat Inayat Khan (1882–1927) said, "Man is one individual with two ends." As in the continuum of rising levels of life-force flow, "One end is man, the other end is God."[1]

As I pointed out previously, the kundalini, or serpent power, is said to run through seven psychic energy centers in the body called chakras. I identify the first, or root, chakra with the lower end of the continuum I've described, since it deals with our basic physical needs. I identify the seventh, or crown, chakra with the upper end of that continuum, since it deals with expanded consciousness and our relationship with the soul. Between these two points lie the other chakras, from the second to the sixth, each of them corresponding to a higher level of life-force flow.

Although I'm using the concept of the chakras as a framework for the continuum of rising life-force flow, my interpretation of what the chakras are—both individually and as a system—is not the same as that put forward by the ancient yogic texts I've studied or by certain modern authorities.

Attempts have been made to link the chakras with various organs and nerve plexuses of the body. In modern descriptions of the chakras, the traditional Sanskrit names have often been replaced by words that indicate their location in the body. For example, the fifth chakra, called *vishuddhi-cakra* (pure wheel) in the ancient texts, is nowadays referred to as the throat chakra.

But the association of the chakras with the physical body is contradicted by the ancient texts, which make clear that the chakras are phenomena belonging to an *energetic*, or subtle, body—one that's related to, but not identical with, the physical body. The subtle body resides on a spiritual, rather than a physical, plane.

Some contemporary yogis even claim that the chakras are imaginary. According to Sri Ramanana Maharshi, they "are merely mental pictures and are meant for beginners in yoga."[2] In alignment with this view, certain Tantric scriptures assert that the chakras are "creations of intense yogic visualization,"[3] as if they were in some way produced by the process of meditation.

Swami Satyananda, on the other hand, believes that there may be a link between the concept of the chakras and various aspects of the brain. The first and second chakras may be associated with the primitive reptilian brain and our most basic physical instincts. The mammalian brain, and the limbic system that controls it, may be associated with the emotional realms of the third and fourth chakras—the range of feelings from rage and fear (third chakra) to pleasure and love (fourth chakra). The neocortex involves the higher mental functions, and may be symbolized by the actions and attributes of the fifth and sixth chakras.[4]

The seventh chakra is not included here, since Satyananda claims that it exists in the subtle body, rather than the physical body. For him, this chakra is located *above* the crown of the head, and has no direct correspondence to any part of the brain.

Midway between the notions that the chakras are imaginary and that they have some direct bearing on the physical body is the view that they represent stages in the evolution of consciousness. Swami Radha, for example, says, "The chakras are best understood as levels of consciousness."[5]

Along similar lines, Swami Rama claims that when the kundalini manifests itself in any of the chakras, "the result is a particular frame of reference through which the individual experiences the world." For example, when the kundalini manifests itself through the second chakra, the result is a preoccupation "with sensual enjoyment"; whereas, when it manifests itself through the fourth chakra, the result is love, compassion, and "taking care of others."[6]

Despite his speculations about the relationship of the chakras to the brain, Swami Satyananda sees the chakras as a graded continuum of human potential: "The chakras span the full spectrum of man's being, from the gross to the subtle."[7] In this case, the "gross" aspect of our being is represented by the first, or root, chakra, with its firm grounding in the physical body. The "subtle" aspect is represented by the seventh chakra, which is said to open into realms beyond normal waking consciousness and the physical plane.

Whether or not the chakras are real in the usual sense of the word, the idea behind most teachings about them is that enlightenment may be achieved by activating and harmonizing them one with another. Doing so causes the chakras to "vibrate in unison," thereby producing a state of ecstasy.[8] As I noted in chapter 2, Plato says that music has "motions akin to the revolutions of our souls" and serves to bring the soul "into harmony and agreement with herself."[9]

Listening to music can allow us to harmonize not only the "revolutions of our souls," but also the chakras, which have often been described as whirling disks. A yoga of listening—something like the nada yoga of the Tantric tradition—would allow us to isolate each chakra and stimulate it through listening to a certain kind of music. Listening to types of music that stimulate *all* of the chakras would harmonize them with each other. The result, perhaps, would be the ecstasy of a TME.

Categories of Expression

In chapter 5, I made a tentative identification of certain genres of music with the chakras. Ambient music was associated with the second chakra, dramatic music with the third, songs that opened the heart with the fourth, and so on. How do these types of music relate to a continuum of increasing life-force flow?

In order to answer this question, I need to introduce a concept from the Charles material: *categories of expression*. According to Charles, what it means to be human involves having a very large, but finite, number of possible ways of expressing ourselves. These are the categories of expression.

Our personalities are formed by our preferences for these categories of expression: the ones we actualize through our behavior and those we suppress, either intentionally or because we're not aware of their existence. Cultures, too, are defined by the categories of expression that they support and those that they ignore. According to Charles, one of our challenges in life is to manifest as many of these categories of expression as possible.

The chakra system, which moves from the root chakra, associated with our grounding in physical reality, to the crown chakra, associated with the nonmaterial aspects of our consciousness, is an effective way of describing the categories of expression as a vertical continuum. Every conceivable category of expression finds a place on this continuum, depending on how related it is to the body at one end, or the soul at the other. I call this manner of describing the categories of expression the *continuum of human potential*.

One value of music is that it exposes us to categories of expression that we might not otherwise be aware of, thereby expanding our perception of human potential. The purpose of this chapter is to build a continuum of human potential, based on the categories of expression as they relate to music. To do so, I'll use the chakra system and the concept of rising levels of life force as a framework.

Such a continuum, to be explored in depth in part 2 of this book, will be useful in laying out the principles of the yoga of listening. These principles involve stimulating individual chakras and harmonizing them with one another in order to achieve TMEs.

Many people think of music as primarily expressive in nature. If asked what it expresses, they'll reply, "emotions." But music—especially classical and jazz music—can also express intellectual and spiritual aspirations, as well as act directly on the body by arousing it to movement or dance, as does rock music.

Just as different kinds of music can stimulate body, heart, mind, or soul, so the categories of expression may be grouped into four basic *ranges*: physical, emotional, intellectual, and spiritual. These ranges aren't limited to music. Any human activity can involve them. They relate to the four psychological functions identified by the Swiss psychologist Carl Jung as basic to the human personality, and existing in each of us in varying degrees of development: *sensing, feeling, thinking,* and *intuiting.*

According to Jung, these functions "correspond to the obvious means by which consciousness obtains its orientation to experience."[10] Our personalities are determined by the different ratios in which these functions are developed in each of us.

Placing these functions in a certain order (sensing, feeling, thinking, intuiting) can allow us to create another aspect of the continuum of human potential. The physical, or sensing, range is at one end of the continuum; and the spiritual, or intuiting, range is at the other. There's a continuous progression from one range to the next: Sensing shades into feeling, which shades into thinking, which shades into intuiting.

I conceive of this continuum, too, as a vertical hierarchy. Like the chakra system, it begins with the physical (sensing) range on the bottom, and extends upward to the spiritual (intuiting) range on the top. Thus it might be more apt to say that sensing *rises* into feeling, which rises into thinking, which rises into intuiting.

The word *rise*, here, can allow us to link the continuum of human potential to the continuum of increasing life-force mentioned earlier, as well as to the chakras. Of the first two chakras, the root has to do with our centering in the physical body, whereas the genital chakra has to do with sensual pleasure. These chakras correspond to the physical, or sensing, range on the continuum of human potential.

The third and fourth chakras—the navel, having to do with the will, and the heart, having to do with love—correspond to the emotional, or feeling, range, whereas the fifth and sixth chakras—the throat, having to do with communication, and the brow, having to do with mind power—correspond to the intellectual, or thinking, range.

That leaves the seventh—the crown, having to do with expanded consciousness—to represent the spiritual, or intuiting, range.

For the sake of symmetry, I would like to round off the spiritual, or intuitive, range of our continuum of human potential with an eighth psychic center, or chakra, so that each range is represented by a pair of such centers. There are two reasons for my wishing to make this change. The first is that I've encountered several sources in which eight psychic centers, instead of the usual seven, are convincingly set forth. For example, in *The Yoga Tradition*, Georg Feuerstein mentions ancient texts that describe an eighth center lying "'twelve digits' above the crown" chakra.[11]

Sri Aurobindo also said that there's a seventh center at the crown of the head and an eighth center lying beyond the seventh. The eighth center has to do with receiving what Aurobindo called the "Supramental Consciousness," or "Supramental Truth, which seems to be the source of all consciousness human and otherwise."[12] For Aurobindo, the purpose of raising the kundalini was to open oneself up to that universal consciousness—which he called the *supermind*—and bring it back to Earth, through teaching and service.[13]

Aurobindo associated this eighth center with what he called the *overmind*. The supermind lies beyond that center. The overmind acts as a receiving apparatus for the supermind. For the purposes of our continuum of human potential, I'll call this eighth center the *transpersonal center*, since it exists beyond the range of higher consciousness described in chakra systems with the usual seven centers.

The Eight Components of the Psyche

The second reason that I would like to include an eighth psychic center in the continuum of human potential involves another key concept of Charles's teaching. Early in my career as a channel, nearly twenty years ago, Charles delivered some fascinating material on what he called the *components of the psyche*, also known as the *eight dream characters.*

These eight characters constantly appear in our dreams, as symbols for the workings of the mind. We tend to project them onto the people who surround us in waking life, as well. These dream characters, or components of the psyche, are useful in demonstrating how the chakras relate to one another, in a progressive way, along the continuum of human potential.

The eight components of the psyche include one for what Charles calls the body consciousness, the sum total of the bits of consciousness present in each individual cell. He identifies this dream character as the *Soma*, the Greek word for "body."

This component of the psyche represents our relationship with the body. We project it onto the people around us who reflect our ideal image of the body, or what we'll look like if we don't take proper care of ourselves. In dreams, this component of the psyche may appear as a person or an animal, for example, a dog, pig, or horse.

On the opposite end of the scale is the dream character that represents our relationship with the soul. Charles calls this component of the psyche the *Numen*, a Latin word meaning a minor deity or nature spirit that makes any object or location *numinous*—which is to say, infused with supernatural energy.

The soul, or Numen, is the source of the life force that infuses the body. In waking life, we project the Numen onto anyone whom we consider to be a spiritual teacher, or guru. In dreams, the Numen may appear as a wise, often magical, old man or woman. If our parents or grandparents seem wise and helpful to us, they too may represent this dream character.

The remaining six components of the psyche refer to subdivisions of the ego. Charles defines the ego as the personal aspect of ourselves that results when the nonphysical soul and the physical body consciousness come together at birth.

The first component of the psyche associated with the ego is the *Participant*, whose purpose is to motivate us to take action. In dreams, the Participant appears as ourselves, or as a heroic figure who has taken our place as the dream's protagonist. In waking life, we project the Participant onto people we consider to be heroes, because they've taken action in some area of life in which our own ability to act may be limited or blocked.

The next component of the psyche is the *Witness*, which represents memory. The Witness is the portion of the ego that observes and records everything we experience, in both dreaming and waking life. When it appears in dreams, it takes the form of a passive observer, or of someone who represents memory, such as a teacher, librarian, parent, or grandparent. In waking life, we project the Witness onto anyone whose memory of a historical or personal situation is valuable to us, especially a situation that may have involved us in some way.

The component of the psyche that Charles calls the *Shadow* represents the subconscious mind, anything that we may want to avoid confronting in ourselves and that obstructs the soul's master plan for our growth. In dreams, the Shadow usually shows up as a dark or sinister figure, the sort of person or being that one would run from, as in a nightmare. In waking life, we project the Shadow onto people we don't trust or who make us angry—anyone who seems to be undermining or obstructing our growth.

The next component of the psyche, the *Anima/Animus*, represents our ability to love and be loved, especially in the context of an intimate relationship. In both dreams and waking life, this component of the psyche usually appears as someone to whom we're sexually attracted or with whom we're romantically involved. The Anima (feminine form) ordinarily appears in the waking life and dreams of a heterosexual male; the Animus (male form) in the waking life and dreams of a heterosexual female.

Homosexual individuals may see this dream character as someone of the same or the opposite sex, depending on the specifics of their gender identification and erotic attractions. Regardless of how the Anima/Animus appears to us, it represents the challenges and rewards of opening ourselves to love.

The love of parent for child or child for parent can also be represented by this component of the psyche. Thus, when the subject of a dream is filial or parental love, the Anima/Animus dream character can sometimes appear as child or parent.[14]

The component of the psyche that Charles calls the *Counterpart* represents the issues that come up in relation to our life purpose, especially as it pertains to our friends, colleagues, and social relations. In both waking life and dreams, the Counterpart appears as the people we commonly encounter in work or social settings, especially our closest friends. This dream character can also be projected upon, or appear in dreams as, our siblings.

Finally, the component of the psyche that Charles calls the *Delimiter* represents the part of us that sets goals and determines how we should achieve them. It has to do with limitations—those we may need to impose on ourselves in order to achieve a goal, or those we may need to free ourselves from to achieve that goal. In both dreams and waking life, the Delimiter typically appears as an authority figure, such as a boss, president, dictator, governmental official, or member of the police force.[15] If we perceive our parents as authority figures, then we'll represent them as the Delimiter in dreams.

Like the chakras, the eight components of the psyche can be related to one another on a vertical continuum, with the Soma (or body consciousness) at the bottom, and the Numen (or soul) at the top. When arranged in this way, the order of the eight components of the psyche is as follows: Soma, Participant, Shadow, Anima/Animus, Counterpart, Delimiter, Witness, Numen. There's a direct correlation between this order and that of the chakra system.

According to Sri Aurobindo, each chakra "is the centre and the storing-house of its own particular system of psychological powers, energies and oper-ations,—each system corresponding to a plane of our psychological existence."[16] The opening of the chakras allows us to access each of these psy-chological planes, which puts us "in communication with the worlds or cosmic states of being which correspond to them."[17]

So it is with the eight components of the psyche. They, too, represent "psy-chological planes," if not also "cosmic states of being." They can also be arranged in a spectrum "from gross to subtle," or Soma (body consciousness) to Numen (soul). And they have their own "psychological powers, energies and operations."

As do the chakras in some systems, the components of the psyche repre-sent a graded series of lessons in the evolution of human consciousness. Seeing them in this way allows us to take the next step in building a contin-uum of human potential: linking each of these components of the psyche to a particular *lesson* on the spiritual path, and a particular *element* of music.

The Continuum of Human Potential

In the following discussion, for the sake of convenience, I've standardized the names of the chakras, using English rather than Sanskrit terms, and ordered them according to their traditional positions in the body. I include them here because the continuum of human potential is based in part on the chakra system. These names provide familiar points of reference along this continuum for people who have had some exposure to the chakra system.

In the literature on the subject, the chakras are often referred to as psychic *centers*, and given names that refer to their functions. I expand on this tradi-tion by referring to the chakras as centers, numbered one through eight, while providing each with a name that describes its function. Some of these names derive from my research into various chakra systems, especially those of Sri Aurobindo and Swami Satyananda. Others are of my own invention.

At the close of this discussion, I present the continuum of human poten-tial in tabular form, listing the centers and chakras by name; pointing out the categories of expression to which they pertain, from the physical/sensing range to the spiritual/intuiting range; and identifying not only the component of the psyche and lesson that each is associated with, but also the element of music.

The first center in the continuum of human potential, also called the root chakra, is associated with the Soma, or body consciousness. The lesson of the Soma is *embodiment*, which helps us become more fully focused in the physical body. The aspect of music that helps us embody ourselves more fully is *rhythm*. Rhythm arouses our attention and holds it. Thus, when music acts on us through the first center, it does so through arousal. For this reason, I call the first chakra the *center of arousal*.

Most Western music involves the first center in some way. Little of it targets this center alone. Sound scores for film, dance, performance art, or an artist's installation may sometimes do so, by using random or ambient noise that's just rhythmic enough to arouse our attention.

The second center, also called the genital chakra, is associated with the Participant, the part of us that takes action in the world. The lesson of the Participant is *motivation*, which spurs us into action. The aspect of music that motivates us to listen more deeply is the sensual quality of sound—its beauty— which I call *sonority*. Sonority is a musical representation of desire, a primary source of motivation. Many of our actions are motivated by desire. For this reason, I call the second chakra the *center of desire*.

Second center music is often unemotional in content and soothing or pleasurable in effect. Ambient and minimal music often target the second center.

The third center, also called the navel chakra, is associated with the Shadow, the part of us that blocks action. The lesson of the Shadow is *identity*, which is often created through friction with other people, and a sense of drama. The aspect of music that best represents this process is *intensity*, a combination of dissonance and volume. For this reason, I call the third chakra the *center of intensity*. Third center music is often dramatic in nature, like opera.

The fourth center, also called the heart chakra, is associated with the Anima/Animus, or the beloved. The lesson of the Anima/Animus is *union*, which helps us to overcome the separation from others involved in developing our identities. The aspect of music that best represents this process is *melody*, which allows us to express the pain of separation, the yearning for connection, and the elation of achieving union with the beloved. For this reason, I call the fourth chakra the *center of expression*. Fourth center music often takes the form of songs, including the blues.

The fifth center, also called the throat chakra, is associated with the Counterpart, or friend. The lesson of the Counterpart has to do with discovering and fulfilling our *life purpose*, a project that often involves the support of friends, colleagues, and other social relations.

Because the soul provides us with an increase of life force when we're realizing plans for our growth, we experience a sense of happiness and satisfaction when we're fulfilling our life purpose. The aspect of music that best represents this process is *tempo*—the speed of the music, which allows it to express a range of happiness from mellowness to joy to exuberance.

The upbeat music of the fifth center is similar to that of the fourth center, but speeded up. Note that the word *upbeat* even implies the notion of increased tempo. Happy or upbeat music cheers us up by exuding a sense of satisfaction—that it's good to be alive. For this reason, I call the fifth chakra the *center of well-being*.

Fifth center music often takes the form of dance music, from classical minuets to swing and rock and roll. Many jazz instrumentals also target this center.

The sixth center, also called the brow chakra, is associated with the Delimiter, the part of us that sets the limits for our growth. The lesson of the Delimiter is *analysis*, which allows us to determine which limits are supporting us *in*, and which are blocking us *from*, achieving our goals. The aspect of music that best represents this process is *form*. Form is the means by which a composer structures or limits a piece of music, commands our attention, and directs us through it.

In traditional yoga, the sixth chakra is called the *center of command*, because gurus use it to communicate their instructions telepathically to their disciples. When we listen to a piece of music, the composer becomes the guru, attempting to pass on his or her own degree of awakening through the medium of sound, and stimulating the psychic energy centers, or chakras, of the listener. As we listen to their music, composers, like gurus, communicate through the command center what they want us to think and feel.

Sixth center music often takes the form of symphonies and other large-scale compositions, including visionary masterpieces such as Debussy's *La Mer*. The variety of deva-inspired music that Scott attributed to nature spirits is often a form of sixth center music.

The seventh center, also called the crown chakra, is associated with the Witness, which has to do with memory. The lesson of the Witness is *wisdom*, which allows us to transform our memories of what we've experienced in life into lessons on the path of spiritual growth. The aspect of music that best represents this process is something that I call *macrorhythm* (*macro-* is Greek for "large" or "long"). Macrorhythm is a way of organizing music into long swells of accumulating and dissipating energy. Music organized in this way has a transformative effect on the consciousness of a listener. For this reason, I call the seventh chakra the *center of expanded consciousness*.

Seventh center music often takes the form of sacred music, including Gregorian chant and modern gospel. Music that targets this center is more likely than any discussed so far to trigger TMEs. It corresponds to the seraphic variety of what Scott called deva music.

The eighth center, which I call the transpersonal chakra, is associated with the Numen or soul. The lesson of the Numen is *transcendence*, which allows us to experience a sense of oneness with the divine. The aspect of music that best represents this process is something that I call *metarhythm* (*meta-* is Greek for "beyond"). Metarhythm is a means of organizing music to create the impression of timelessness, or that the music is unfolding outside of, or beyond, time. Music organized in this way can open us up to a sense of oneness with God or the universe. For this reason, I call the eighth chakra the *center of cosmic consciousness*.

Music that targets this center is the most likely of all to trigger TMEs. Unfortunately, eighth center music is relatively rare. It corresponds to what Scott called buddhic music.

The table on page 76 summarizes this continuum of human potential.

In part 2, each of the centers along the continuum of human potential gets its own chapter, in which I go into more detail about its characteristics, the kinds of music associated with it (genres and specific pieces), and how to identify it when listening to music. These chapters also introduce the principles of the yoga of listening, by including exercises designed to activate the centers and begin the process of harmonizing them with each other. The goal of this yoga is to prepare us for achieving transcendent musical experiences as listeners, performers, and composers.

Completing Your Playlist

Now that you have some idea of how the chakras line up with different kinds of music, I would like you to look at the playlist that you created at the end of the previous chapter.

The first category for which I asked you to come up with selections emphasized the rhythmic aspects of music and therefore corresponds to the first chakra, or center of arousal, on the continuum of human potential.

The second category emphasized the melodic aspects of music and therefore corresponds to the fourth chakra, or center of expression.

The third category emphasized the upbeat or up-tempo aspects of music and therefore corresponds to the fifth chakra, or center of well-being.

The fourth category emphasized the formal, or intellectually satisfying, aspects of music and therefore corresponds to the sixth chakra, or center of command.

Table 1. The Continuum of Human Potential

Center	Chakra	Range	Dream Character	Lesson	Musical Element
First: Arousal	Root	Physical/Sensing	Soma (Body Consciousness)	Embodiment	Rhythm
Second: Desire	Genital	Physical/Sensing	Participant	Motivation	Sonority
Third: Intensity	Navel	Emotional/Feeling	Shadow	Identity	Dissonance and Volume
Fourth: Expression	Heart	Emotional/Feeling	Anima/Animus	Union	Melody
Fifth: Well-being	Throat	Intellectual/Thinking	Counterpart	Life Purpose	Tempo
Sixth: Command	Brow	Intellectual/Thinking	Delimiter	Analysis	Form
Seventh: Expanded Consciousness	Crown	Spiritual/Intuiting	Witness	Wisdom	Macro-rhythm
Eighth: Cosmic Consciousness	Transpersonal	Spiritual/Intuiting	Numen (Soul)	Transcendence	Meta-rhythm (Timelessness)

Please note that I asked you to come up with selections based on the *pleasure* you experienced in connection with listening to music. The first principle of the yoga of listening is: *The kind of pleasure you experience while listening to music will help you determine the chakras or centers that it affects.*

In the previous chapter, I asked you to come up with playlist selections for the first, fourth, fifth, and sixth chakras because rhythmic, melodic, upbeat, and formal pleasures are among the easiest to detect and remember. Now I would like you to come up with playlist selections for the remaining centers.

This exercise may be a bit more difficult than the previous one. Once again, don't worry if you're unable to come up with playlist selections for one or more of the following categories. I offer suggestions for you in part 2, in the chapters devoted to each center.

First, I would like you to think about, and add to your playlist, from one to three items in which your main source of pleasure lies in the sensual beauty of the *sound* (sonority). Pieces, songs, or passages that feature little in the way of dramatic tension, emotional expression, or intellectual challenge are best.

If you have any ambient or minimalist music in your collection, that would be a good place to look for selections that target the second center—for example, music by Philip Glass (b. 1937). If you're a lover of classical music, then consider slower music by any of the impressionists, such as Debussy, Maurice Ravel (1875–1937), or Frederick Delius (1862–1934).

Second, I would like you to think about, and add to your playlist, from one to three items in which your main source of pleasure lies in their dramatic tension, or *intensity.* Pieces, songs, or passages that feature some sort of conflict are best. Operas and movie soundtracks (especially those for thrillers and horror films) may give you some ideas here, as well as the harder-hitting varieties of popular music, in which volume and dissonance are prominent characteristics. If you're unable to come up with selections for this category, you might try turning on the TV and watching a few minutes of some crime-based show or horror movie that includes a soundtrack.

Moments of tension or violence target the third center. Many people shy away from such moments, and find music that targets the third center unpleasurable. Much twentieth-century classical music, such as *The Rite of Spring* by Igor Stravinsky (1882–1971), involves the third center in some way, which is why audiences often have a hard time with it. Yet such music can also be exciting or thrilling if you're in the mood for it.

Third, I would like you to think about, and add to your playlist, from one to three items in which your main source of pleasure lies in the sense of the *sacred, holy,* or *spiritual* that it invokes in you. Pieces, songs, or passages that evoke the divine in some way are best. Sacred music of any sort, such as

Gregorian chant, hymns, and gospel music, are obvious sources for such selections.

Some New-Age music might also provide you with possibilities, as well as any of the openly spiritual works of John Coltrane, such as *A Love Supreme*. Of the three categories described so far, this one, which targets the seventh center, may be the easiest for you to come up with selections for.

The only remaining center is the eighth. As I noted previously, music that targets this center is rare. Rather than ask you to come up with selections that match the criteria for this center, I'll simply remark that Wagner's Prelude to *Lohengrin* is an excellent example of the type, and leave it at that. I have more to say about the eighth center, and provide a list of music that targets it, in part 2 of this book.

Once you've added selections that target the second, third, and seventh centers to your playlist, you may wish to rewrite it, with your selections arranged in order of the centers, from one to seven. Try listening to the selections on your playlist in that order, ending with the Prelude to *Lohengrin*, if you have access to it. If you have the capability, you might wish to burn a CD in which your playlist is so arranged.

By listening to such a playlist, you're giving yourself a musical tour of the continuum of human potential, from bottom to top. Such a tour can begin the process of activating and integrating each center on that continuum. In the yoga of listening, such a process can lead to achieving TMEs.

The Yoga of Listening

7

The Yoga of Listening

The yoga of listening involves exposing ourselves to the widest range of music along the continuum of human potential in the most receptive, meditative way. The goal of such listening is to produce transcendental musical experiences.

I've mentioned that the inspiration for this spiritual practice comes in part from an already existing variety of yoga—that "most tender and absorbing way of awakening" called nada yoga, which uses mantras and melodies to open the chakras.[1] But it also has parallels in the Sufi tradition of classical Indian music.

For Sufi teacher and musician Hazrat Inayat Khan, "Music has been made a pastime, the means of forgetting God instead of realizing God."[2] Yet music is "the closest, the nearest way to God—that is, if one knows which music and how to use it."[3] The yoga of listening can teach listeners to identify the music that provides "the closest, the nearest way to God."

According to Inayat Khan, the ancient Sufis developed the art of meditating with music, "by having a certain piece played which had a certain effect upon the development of the individual."[4] In the yoga of listening, the idea is to expose oneself to music that accesses specific centers, or that activates as much of the continuum of human potential as possible. The effects of such exposure can be therapeutic, developmental, integrative, or transcendent.

The therapeutic aspect of the yoga of listening involves healing. An emotionally wounded person could benefit from learning to open the heart. Fourth center music would be useful for this purpose. According to Inayat Khan, "If one can focus one's heart on music, it is just like heating something that is frozen."[5]

In a similar way, a depressed person might be cheered up by the well-being of fifth center music. Someone who's paralyzed by fear or anger could benefit from the catharsis produced by third center music.

Inayat Khan said that what we seek in music is "the life behind it, which comes from the expanded consciousness, from the realization of the divine light, which is the secret of all true art, and which is the soul of all mysticism."[6] When he says, "It is that life which everyone desires" and "Music can heal," provided that such life "is put into it," he sounds like Charles expounding on the relationship between the soul and the life force that sustains us.[7]

For Inayat Khan, the therapeutic aspect of music is only "the beginning of development through the art of music, the end of which is attaining . . . *samadhi*."[8] Samadhi (bliss) is also the goal of yoga, the result of achieving oneness with the divine through meditation. In the yoga of listening, oneness with the divine is achieved through composing, performing, or listening to music, "the closest, the nearest way to God."[9]

The developmental aspect of the yoga of listening involves opening up portions of the continuum of human potential that a listener may never have accessed previously. According to Sri Aurobindo, in most of us, under ordinary circumstances, the chakras are undeveloped. They do little more than provide us with the minimum energy required to conduct our daily affairs.[10] We need to learn how to activate them fully. The yoga of listening can help us do so.

Swami Satyananda says that we all have different starting points for our spiritual evolution. In awakening the kundalini, a particular chakra may be more attractive to us or more developed than the others. This is the one to begin our meditation practice with.[11]

So, in the yoga of listening, we start with the music we prefer, determining the center or centers it targets. Then we expose ourselves to genres, pieces, composers, or bands that target the other centers.

Some yogic traditions insist that in order to awaken the kundalini safely, the beginner should meditate on the fourth, or heart, chakra. Significantly, a great deal of popular and New-Age music touches this center. Meditating while listening to such heart-opening music might be an excellent starting point for those who want to use the yoga of listening to open up the other centers.

Swami Satyananda believes that it's best to begin the process of awakening the kundalini through meditation on the sixth chakra. In this way, the beginner can avoid getting caught in the potential pitfalls of activating the lower chakras first. Such pitfalls can involve obsessions with desire, in the case of the second chakra, or power, in the case of the third.

Much classical music has its origin in the sixth chakra. In the yoga of listening, using classical music as a focal point for meditation is the equivalent of following Satyananda's advice.

The integrative aspect of the yoga of listening involves not merely activating the eight centers, but welding them together into a seamlessly functioning whole. As I pointed out in chapter 2, Plato believed that music exists for the purpose of creating harmony between the various aspects of ourselves. In yoga, enlightenment may be achieved by activating and harmonizing the chakras with each other. Doing so causes them to "vibrate in unison," thereby producing a state of ecstasy.[12]

The purpose of the integrative aspect of the yoga of listening is harmonizing the various aspects of the soul, as represented by the eight centers on the continuum of human potential, and getting them to "vibrate in unison," in order to produce the ecstasy of TMEs.

Some music, especially the late works of composers such as Beethoven or Schubert, spans most, if not all, of the continuum of human potential. The practice of listening to such music with an awareness of the centers it touches can have an integrative effect on the listener. The result may be not only the isolated peak experience of a TME, but Maslow's high-plateau experience, in which it becomes possible to "live casually in heaven and be on easy terms with the eternal and the infinite."[13]

Some listeners may only be capable of responding to music on the sensual level of the second center, no matter how many other centers are active within it. The same may be true of the expressive level of the fourth, the feel-good level of the fifth, or the analytic level of the sixth.

Inayat Khan stated, "There are different kinds of music, each kind appealing to certain souls according to their evolution."[14] He went on to say, "For a self-satisfied person there is no chance of progress, because he clings contentedly to his taste according to his state of evolution."[15]

Inayat Khan further explained that "The true way of progressing through music is to evolve freely, to go forward, not caring what others think."[16] Such a listener, by going beyond what normally lies within the range of his taste, "in the end attains to the highest perfection."

"No other art can inspire and sweeten the personality like music," said Inayat Khan. "The lover of music attains sooner or later to the most sublime field of thought."[17]

Using music as a means of promoting spiritual growth requires becoming attuned to all of the centers, not just those to which we normally gravitate. Exposure to music that targets as much of the continuum of human potential as possible accomplishes this end, which can be both developmental *and* integrative.

Perhaps the concept of harmonizing the centers along the continuum of human potential by means of listening to music is a metaphor for the ways in which different genres of music affect the brain. We've seen that Swami Satyananda links the chakras to various parts of the brain. I've also noted that the word *soul* may be a useful metaphor for the most comprehensive organization of the brain's components of which we're capable.

The centers on the continuum of human potential may refer to mental subsystems or hierarchies, rather than nonphysical or psychic ones, as the chakras are purported to be. The purpose of such subsystems and hierarchies is to organize various components of the brain to perform specialized tasks. By calling them centers, we may be able to isolate these subsystems and hierarchies, make more conscious use of them, and integrate them into a more highly functioning whole.

The transcendent aspect of the yoga of listening involves the production of TMEs in receptive listeners by composers and performers who have become consciously aware of the continuum of human potential. Composers with such an awareness would attempt to create music intended to activate certain centers in the listener, as well as to develop and integrate them. Performers would become aware of the centers present in the score of a piece of music and attempt to activate them in performance.

Satprem, a pupil of Sri Aurobindo, said that music "can be a powerful means of opening up the consciousness." Composers who produce "music as a result of a conscious handling of higher vibrations" may "create masterpieces endowed with initiatory power."[18]

The "conscious handling of higher vibrations" mentioned by Satprem applies to composing from the expanded consciousness of the seventh center or the cosmic consciousness of the eighth, an ability developed by some of the greatest composers of Western music, whom I call musical adepts. These composers pass on such higher states of consciousness to us through their music, by means of transmission.

I mentioned transmission in chapter 3. The term refers to a mystical experience in which a guru's bliss and wisdom are transferred directly from his mind to that of a properly trained disciple.

Transmission is one kind of initiation. When transmission occurs through music, a TME may be the result, allowing us to participate directly in the higher states of consciousness achieved by the great composers of Western music. By means of musical transmission, we can try on these higher states of consciousness, become familiar with them, then work to develop and sustain them within us.

Using the yoga of listening, we can learn to identify the types of music in which such transmissions are encoded, as well as make ourselves, as listeners, ideally receptive to such transmissions. A key concept that will allow us to achieve these ends is that of the dominant center.

The Dominant Center

The pleasure of listening to music is the basis of the yoga of listening. For those of us brought up with traditional Christian values, pleasure is often suspect. In fundamentalist Christian sects, as well as those of some other world religions, music and dancing are sometimes completely banned.

In yoga, however, especially the body-positive approach of Tantra, the concept of *ananda* (joy) is a primary goal. Sri Aurobindo said that "beauty and plenitude, a hidden sweetness and laughter in things, a sunshine and gladness of life are also powers and expressions of the Spirit."[19]

Aurobindo also spoke of a "need of bodily happiness," "joy and rapture," "mental delight," and "peace and divine ecstasy—all aspects of ananda."[20] These four types of ananda correspond with the four ranges of the continuum of human potential: physical, emotional, intellectual, and spiritual.

In any given song, dance, or piece of classical music, more than one center along the continuum of human potential may be active. Usually, one center is *dominant*. When I say that a piece of music targets a certain center, I mean that that center is dominant.

When listening to music, how do we tell which center is dominant? As I explained in the previous chapter, the first principle of the yoga of listening is: *The kind of pleasure that you experience while listening to music will help you determine the chakras or centers that it affects.*

When you ask yourself what kind of pleasure you're taking in listening to a piece of music, you're beginning to determine the dominant center. Use the ranges along the continuum of human potential to take the next step. If the pleasure is primarily physical or sensual, then you're dealing with centers one or two. If the pleasure is primarily emotional, then you're dealing with centers three or four; if intellectual, then centers five or six; if spiritual, then centers seven or eight.

After determining the range, you may be able to zero in on the dominant center by noticing other internal sensations that accompany your pleasure. In the paragraphs that follow, I provide some hints about how to determine the dominant center based on these sensations. Further information on how to do so and musical examples of each center are given in subsequent chapters.

The first center, arousal, is active in almost all Western music. If a piece of music has captured your attention and contains rhythmic activity of any sort, then this center is present. Music in which the first center is dominant is rare. I give some examples of such music in the next chapter.

The second center, desire, is also active in most Western music. When the second center is dominant, the music produces relaxation or sensual pleasure in beautiful, lush harmonies.

Fear, anger, drama, or conflict usually indicates that the third center, intensity, is dominant. If the music of the second center produces a sense of relaxation, of lolling about in sensual beauty, the music of the third center produces excitement and a sense of internal tension.

I often want to withdraw from such music, as if taking a step back from it. I may feel a tightness or contraction in the middle of my chest, a sign that my body is drawing itself in, as if to protect itself from an assault. I feel relieved when this internal tension releases itself when the music is over or begins to target another center.

Music in which the fourth center, expression, is dominant has the opposite physical effect: a sense of the chest or heart area opening up. Instead of fear and anger, we experience pity, yearning, elation, a hundred different degrees and shades of love.

Much of the world's most beloved popular and classical music touches this center. In a culture such as ours, which tends to repress its emotions, the music of the fourth center often seems refreshing and liberating. It helps people to feel more real, alive, and human.

Music in which the fifth center, well-being, is dominant is usually bouncy, lively, full of pep. This is the feel-good center. Any music that brings about or enhances a pleasant mood targets the fifth center.

Music in which the sixth center, command, is dominant sounds sophisticated and intellectual. Its hallmark is changeability of mood, tempo, tonality, character, and structure.

Usually, when I've been unable to determine which center is dominant in a piece of music, I eventually figure out that it's the sixth. I've come to think of this as a rule of thumb: *If you can't figure it out, then it's the sixth.*

Another way of determining when you're listening to sixth center music is to notice whether, in describing it to yourself or others, you're likely to call it "interesting." As a composer, I'm often fascinated when the brilliance of a piece's compositional technique has captured my attention. If I call it "interesting," then the sixth center is likely to be dominant. Other listeners may use the word "interesting" pejoratively, in which case it may indicate a lack of appreciation for the intellectual dimension of a piece.

Music in which the seventh center, expanded consciousness, is dominant often seems solemn, awe-inspiring, sublime, spiritually uplifting, or larger than life, in terms of its glory, nobility, or ecstatic joy. I often feel an eerie sense of expanding consciousness when I'm exposed to it. My psychic senses open up, with a mild frisson or tingling in the spine.

The chief characteristic of music in which the eighth center, cosmic consciousness, is dominant is that it seems to come from elsewhere, as an answer to one's prayers. Such music often elicits an overwhelming urge to change one's life. It seems to emerge from God, the source of all consciousness, demanding, in a gently insistent way, that we align ourselves more closely with the divine.

Levels within the Centers

As I evolved the yoga of listening described in this book, I came across a number of pieces that seemed to blend the characteristics of two adjacent centers. This is what happens on a continuum: One labeled point gradually shades into the next. As the transition from one center to the next occurs, the characteristics of the lower center fade out, while those of the upper one increase.

For example, there's a lower range of the fourth center that shares some characteristics of the third, a middle range of the fourth center in which the fourth center characteristics are pure, and an upper range of the fourth center that shares some characteristics of the fifth.

In the chapters that follow, I apply descriptive labels to the lower, middle, and upper ranges of each of the eight centers on the continuum of human potential. Since this continuum is arranged to reflect a rising level of life force, each of the three levels within a center corresponds to an increase in the amount of life force within that center.

In the case of the fourth center, the lower range is *pathos*. Lower 4, as I call it, shares some of the emotional intensity of the third center. Middle 4, in which the expressive nature of the fourth center is pure, is *yearning*. Upper 4 is *elation*, a love that carries with it some of the joyful well-being of the fifth center.

In the chapters that follow, I explain the lower, middle, and upper ranges of each center and provide musical examples of these ranges.

Crisis Points

In Tantra yoga, it is said that the kundalini can get stuck at any of three points called a *granthi* or "knot." These knots occur at the root (first) chakra, the heart (fourth) chakra, and the brow (sixth) chakra. Such knots are considered to be "obstacles on the path of the awakened kundalini."[21] They must be dissolved in order for the kundalini energy to continue rising into the next higher chakra.

In my work with music and the chakras, I've found that something similar to these knots may occur at the transition point between *each* of the centers in the continuum of human potential. I call this knot the *crisis point.*

Composers or performers end up in the crisis point between centers when they've overdone the characteristics of one center while on their way into another. When unintentional, such exaggeration indicates that composers or performers are stuck at the level of life-force flow represented by that center, unable to move on to the next. They don't know how to make the transition, or don't care to do so. Instead, they ramp up the characteristics of that center, trying to satisfy themselves with an increase in intensity. Sometimes the results are thrilling, risky, unheard of, even cool. But they can also make audiences feel acutely uncomfortable.

When intentional, the musical exaggeration that occurs at a crisis point means that composers or performers are trying to teach us a moral or spiritual lesson: what it feels like when the flow of life force gets stuck between centers and what to do to move beyond that stuck point into the next center.

In the following chapters, I explain what these crisis points are and how to identify the music that targets them.

Becoming a Spiritual Listener

The remaining chapters in this section deal with each of the centers on the continuum of human potential, in ascending order, from the first or arousal center, associated with the body consciousness, to the eighth or cosmic consciousness center, associated with the soul. I explain the function of each center, the musical element it works through, and the lessons it has to teach.

I also define the lower, middle, and upper levels of each center and its crisis point, giving musical examples of each. At the end of each chapter, I suggest a number of musical tours of the featured center, using jazz, rock, and classical music. Some tours are made up of several songs or pieces, others of a single work that touches all of the levels within the featured center, including the crisis point. I then sum up the material presented in the chapter in tabular form, including a playlist of all the music to which I've referred.

The examples provided in these chapters are drawn from many genres of music, from classical to jazz to rock. Some are well known and may already have a place in your collection of recordings: classical pieces such as the symphonic suite *The Planets* by Gustav Holst (1874–1934) or *Symphonie Fantastique* by Hector Berlioz (1803–1869); jazz albums such as *Sketches of Spain* by Miles Davis and *A Love Supreme* by John Coltrane; and various tunes by popular rock groups from the Beatles to Nirvana. Others are more obscure but worth seeking out for the adventuresome listener.

The purpose of the musical examples in this section is to demonstrate what the centers and levels on the continuum of human potential sound like. By listening to these examples, you're not only activating a particular center and level on the continuum, but also learning how to identify that center and level when you hear other pieces or songs that target them.

Some of these musical examples may serve other purposes in the yoga of listening than merely demonstrating the differences between the levels and centers. When this is true, I note the use to which a piece, song, or album may be put, and the conditions most advantageous for listening to it. In some cases, I recommend specific recordings, since the points I make may not be discernible in every available performance.

Finding pure examples of the lower, middle, and upper ranges of the first three centers proved to be more difficult than doing so for the fourth through eighth. Only during the twentieth century did composers begin to explore the first three centers musically, isolating them from the higher ones. Thus, in the chapters concerning the first three centers, the musical examples may be more obscure, less easy to locate, than those in the chapters for centers four through eight.

If you don't own any of the recordings I list, you may nevertheless be able to think of other musical examples in your collection of recordings that fit the criteria I describe. The reason I asked you to produce a playlist in part 1 was so that you might begin thinking about your collection in terms of the centers.

You might want to check your playlist against some of the examples I give. An easy way to do that is to go to one of the commercial sites on the Internet that sells recordings, either as CDs or downloads. In many cases, you can listen to thirty-second excerpts from these recordings and get an idea of the musical characteristics I'm talking about. This approach works better for popular music, since it doesn't change centers as often or as radically as does much classical music.

Most of the recordings I list are still in print and for sale, if you wish to purchase them from a regular or online CD store or for download from the Internet. Used CD stores and the audio holdings of libraries can also be valuable resources for those interested in pursuing the yoga of listening without spending a lot of money on new recordings.

The yoga of listening involves exposing yourself to as many of the categories of expression as possible. The result will be an advance in your understanding and practice of what it means to be human. This advance will occur whether or not you're aware of the centers active in a piece of music, or the levels or crisis points involved. However, I've noticed that the more aware I am of the centers activated by a piece of music, the more I can open myself to their beneficial effects.

The yoga of listening described in these pages takes what happens naturally in listening to music for passive enjoyment and makes it more conscious. The result may be not only an increase in the frequency and intensity of your TMEs, but also an acceleration in your overall development as a human being.

In order to take full advantage of the therapeutic, developmental, integrative, and transcendent benefits of the yoga of listening, you need to become a spiritual listener. The following "rules of conduct" for "becoming a good listener," as advocated by classical Indian musician Pandit Patekar, will allow you to do so.[22] Keep them in mind when you're listening to any of the musical examples in the following chapters, and whenever you listen to music.

The first of these rules is to let go of "the usual way of thinking" so that you can concentrate on "the higher, spiritual aspects of life."[23] In yoga, this is done through closing the eyes, turning the thoughts inward, releasing the attention from your daily concerns, and focusing on the breath. In the yoga of listening, this process involves directing your attention toward the music, to the exclusion of all other activities and thoughts.

Certain kinds of music, especially those intended to entertain, suffer little from accompanying other activities, such as work. Such music may actually improve concentration, efficiency, and productivity in some people.

Music intended to expand consciousness, such as that which targets the seventh and eight centers, is only truly effective when listeners are capable of turning their full attention toward it. Such music is best heard live, in the quiet of a concert hall; or with headphones, while seated or taking a walk in a beautiful natural setting; or at home, while sitting or lying down in a distraction-free environment.

The second rule for becoming an ideal listener is to let go of critical thinking. Such thinking involves comparison and analysis.

Much Western classical music requires a degree of analysis in order to be performed and heard properly. Composers use musical form to project their ideas, which may be emotional, intellectual, or spiritual in nature. Being able to recognize and participate in the formal unfolding of a piece of music can greatly contribute to a listener's pleasure. But it would be a shame if music were to be heard only intellectually.

Comparison, on the other hand, is an often unhelpful kind of critical thinking. It focuses on the "quality" of a performance, the style of a piece or performer, based on one's past experience as a listener. Such thinking can often get in the way of appreciating the value of what a composer or performer has to say.

Few performances are perfect, so all good listeners must be tolerant of the human element that goes into making them. Even so, there are times when a performance or a piece of music really does seem boring, disappointing, or "bad."

Bad performances can result from many factors, including inadequate preparation, nerves, fatigue, memory lapses, faulty intonation, mechanical problems with the instruments involved, acoustical issues, distractions in the audience. Even the best of listeners can do little to ameliorate the effects of such accidents. But some performances are called bad by unreceptive listeners simply because the music is not to their taste.

The yoga of listening is based on the *pleasure* of listening to music. It won't do you any good to force yourself to listen to music you don't like. Neither will you develop along the continuum of human potential if you listen to music that, like much popular music, targets only the fourth or fifth centers.

Luckily, there are composers and performers of popular music who target the higher centers for those who have no interest in classical music. I'll point out a number of these composers and performers as the book progresses.

The third of Patekar's rules of conduct for becoming a good listener is to allow a meditative state to develop. According to Hazrat Inayat Khan, listening to music can provide an excellent means of developing meditative concentration: "When you tell a person to concentrate on a certain object, the very act of trying to concentrate makes his mind more disturbed. But music, which attracts the soul, keeps the mind concentrated."[24]

The first step in allowing a meditative state to develop is to make yourself comfortable. I like to lie on the couch in my living room, wearing a set of headphones that surround my ears and block out unwanted sounds from my noisy neighborhood. I prefer darkness or semidarkness. I also turn off the phones, so I won't be interrupted.

To induce a meditative state, I turn the full focus of my attention on the music. When I find that my attention has wandered, I return it to the music.

Over time, I've developed the capacity not only to stay focused on the music, but also to observe how the music is affecting my state of consciousness. I try to be aware of the dominant center, even if it changes from moment to moment, making myself as receptive as possible to the pleasure it promotes.

The fourth rule of being a good listener, according to Patekar, is to "Establish a link with the supernatural aspects of reality."[25] By "supernatural," Patekar means aspects of reality that lie beyond the reach of our ordinary waking consciousness, such as TMEs and other mystical states.

The centers along the continuum of human potential are based on ancient yogic ideas about the chakras and the mystical kundalini energy that activates them, and therefore have a supernatural element. To connect with the supernatural through them, choose one of the centers along this continuum to concentrate on, then experience the music from that perspective as much as possible.

You could listen only to the rhythms (first center) or the sensual play of sonority (second center). You could concentrate on the rise and fall of volume, level of dissonance, and dramatic intensity (third center), if they're present in the piece; or the expressive and heart-opening nature of the melody (fourth center).

If you're listening to the music of well-being (fifth center), how does the upbeat tempo affect your mood? Let it cheer you up. If you're listening to music with a strong appeal to the intellect (sixth center), focus on how the form or the musical ideas evolve.

If the music targets the seventh center, notice how it expands your consciousness. Let it put you in touch with the soul or God. If the music targets the eighth center, allow it to penetrate you with what Scott called "that love which *is* God," the chief characteristic of buddhic music.[26]

Focusing in any of these ways on the pleasure produced by a piece of music is the point of the yoga of listening. Doing so not only allows you to become more receptive to the music, and to enjoy it and be moved by it more deeply, but also activates the continuum of human potential within you, thereby contributing to self-actualization and possibly producing a TME.

The fifth of Patekar's rules for being a good listener is to "Leave aside all inner preconceptions."[27] Maslow mentioned an innocence "of perceiving and behaving" as an aspect of the creative attitude toward life. Such innocence allows one "to receive whatever happens to be the case without surprise, shock, indignation, or denial."[28]

Sometimes, when I'm listening to a well-known composition, I strip away any preconceptions or biases I may have about it by imagining how it sounded to an audience at its premiere. Even the most beloved masterpieces of the past were once examples of modern music. To play or attempt to hear them in that way can often bring them vividly to life, no matter how often one has heard them.

The sixth of Patekar's rules for becoming a good listener is: "Try to think your way inside the artist. In other words, try to feel with him and to become one with both artist and theme."[29]

This rule sets up the receiving end of the transmission process on the listener's side. Focusing on the pleasure produced by a piece of music using the continuum of human potential can accomplish this task.

Such pleasure, and the resulting transmission of wisdom, can often be enhanced by knowing something about the composer's personal life—for example, the conditions under which the piece was composed. This is the purpose of the program notes handed out at concerts and the liner notes included with recordings.

When we feel drawn to certain composers and performers as spiritual teachers, it may help to know more about them, to read biographies, autobiographies, interviews, selections of their letters, or the reminiscences of people who knew them.

The seventh and last of Patekar's rules for becoming a good listener is a summary of all of the others: "Be still and spiritualized—both inwardly and outwardly." He ends with the Sanskrit words *Om Shantih*, which means "Peace within the Absolute."[30]

In yoga, Om is considered to be a universal sound or vibration that represents the Absolute, the source of all consciousness. One purpose of yoga is to achieve inner peace *and* union with the Absolute, however we might define it, whether as the soul, God, or in some other way.

The blessing *Om Shantih* seems especially appropriate for the yoga of listening, which is based on the vibrations present in music. So, through reading the descriptions of the centers along the continuum of human potential in the following chapters and listening to the music listed there, may you achieve peace within the Absolute.

8

The First Center: Arousal

According to Inayat Khan, "Motion is the significance of life, and the law of motion is rhythm. Rhythm is life disguised in motion."[1] He could just as well have said that music is life disguised as rhythmic motion.

Performed music seems to have a life of its own, by virtue of this rhythmic motion. As music touches the various centers on the continuum of human potential, it both illustrates and transmits to us the fluctuations in the flow of life force by which our souls guide us toward realizing the master plan for our growth.

Rhythmic motion is the most basic aspect of music. For this reason, when I asked you to add to your playlist from one to three items in which your main source of pleasure was the rhythm, you probably had little difficulty in doing so.

I recommended pieces, songs, or passages that featured or were dominated by the drummer of the band or the percussion section of the orchestra, or in which the rhythm was especially complex and fascinating. But rhythmic motion is so pervasive in all forms of music, both Western and non-Western, that the first center is almost certain to be active in it, no matter the genre. Whatever you put on your playlist is likely to be an example of first center music, whether or not that center is dominant.

The first center is the *arousal* center. It's associated with the dream character that Charles calls the Soma, or body consciousness.

Arousal works directly on the body consciousness, with or without the participation of the conscious mind. Arousal is not limited to sex. It embraces all of the ways in which we become awake to ourselves as physical beings. The arousal center is the first in the pair that corresponds to the physical, or sensing, range of the continuum of human potential.

94

Sounds capture our attention through arousal, whether they take the form of disorganized noise or highly organized music. The musical factor that most enhances arousal is rhythm, the musical element of the first center.

Among the most basic aspects of our physical existence are the cyclic rhythms of the breath and the heartbeat. Some psychological theories trace the origins of music back to these fundamental rhythms. Cyclic rhythms are so basic to music, life, and physical matter—for example, the planets spinning on their axes and revolving around the sun—that a Sanskrit proverb says "tone is the mother of nature, but rhythm is its father."[2]

Examples of music that work only on the arousal center are not common in the musical traditions of the West. I cite a few of them in this chapter. Drumming, whether the simple, uniform beat of the shamanic drummer, the more complex rhythms of a conga player, the multilayered texture of an African drumming ensemble, or a rock or jazz musician playing solo on a drum set, targets the first center.

Because rhythm underlies most music, the first center is almost always present in a subordinate function beneath a piece or song's dominant center.

I call the awakening of the Soma, or body consciousness, through arousal *embodiment*. This is the first lesson on the developmental path represented by the continuum of human potential.

The body is the basis of all our learning in physical reality. Whereas many spiritual traditions ignore or attempt to transcend the body and its needs, both Tantra and the Charles material are "body friendly." They teach that there's nothing inherently unspiritual about our presence in the body, and that experiences of higher consciousness can be more reliably produced through a thorough grounding in the body than through disdaining the physical aspect of our existence.

As jazz composer and Sufi practitioner W. A. Mathieu (b. 1937) says in *The Listening Book*, "Sound is sense, and it is more intensely pleasurable the more open your ears are. Naked hearing confirms the sensual nature of the world; it is a basic act that feels good, plain and simple."[3] What Mathieu is talking about is the embodiment aspect of the first, or arousal, center. The three levels of this center, from lowest to highest, are *immersion*, *interest*, and *entrainment*.

Immersion (Lower 1)

When the lower range of the first center has been activated, the result is a sense of being immersed in what I call a *sonic environment*. For example, at this moment, I can hear wind chimes, cars on the main road half a block from my house, a subway train rumbling toward the station that's about a ten-minute walk from my apartment, birds singing in the trees outside my window, my housemate's electric razor in the bathroom, a neighbor clapping hands to get the attention of a dog, and the click of my own word-processor keys. This is the sonic environment in which I'm presently immersed.

Take a moment to close your eyes and become aware of your own sonic environment. In doing so, you're experiencing the immersion of lower 1.

Because our ears remain physically open and able to receive sound at all times, we're perpetually immersed in sonic environments of various kinds. We can choose to pay attention to these environments, especially when we're awake, or ignore them, as we do when we're asleep.

The chief characteristic of music that acts on lower 1 is that it has no recognizable organizational pattern. Nonorganized sound is often called noise. It doesn't have to be loud to merit such a label.

From the latter half of the twentieth century to the present, some avant-garde composers have focused on presenting listeners with noise, an unorganized sonic environment. One of the first pieces of this kind was 4'33" by the American avant-gardist John Cage.

Cage's score instructs a pianist to sit at a piano keyboard in front of an audience for the specified four minutes and thirty-three seconds without playing a single note. The sonic environment created thereby consists of the audience's reactions to this spectacle: their shuffling feet, coughing, whispering, the jangling of jewelry, and so on.

When he heard about Cage's piece, Igor Stravinsky was characteristically dismissive. He called it "Mr. Cage's most successful opus" and looked forward to its influence on younger avant-garde composers, hoping to hear similarly silent works from them "of major length."[4]

Yet, in 4'33", Cage, a Zen practitioner, framed environmental noise to demonstrate that this too is music—the music of the everyday. At the same time, he forced not just a single listener but a whole audience to take a few minutes of silence for introspection.

In our busy lives, we rarely allow ourselves time for silence, turning inward, meditation. The soul is often forgotten, buried beneath the inner noise of our daily concerns. Cage's piece provides the soul with an opportunity to show itself.

I've been told that witnessing 4'33" can produce a TME. An artist friend of my mother's once reported that a performance of Cage's piece had an effect on him similar to that of Zen meditation, a quiet sense of ecstasy. He'd never been so aware of the sounds that surrounded him as when 4'33" placed them within a musical time frame and drew his attention to them. He not only had the experience that I call immersion in a sonic environment, but also a sense of connection with his soul, which is what produced his TME.

Music that involves immersion in sonic environments is not limited to the avant-gardists of classical music. It's a favorite device of composers for film and video, dance, art installations, and so on. For example, I once attended a concert by the Merce Cunningham Dance Company in which one of the pieces was accompanied by a recorded sound score by Cage that consisted of the random rhythms of dripping water. This is another instance of lower 1 music.

On another occasion, at a Boston venue for performance art, I witnessed a piece in which three performers walked through the pitch-black performance space crinkling their leather jackets. That too created a lower 1 sonic environment.

One of the most powerful TMEs I've ever had occurred as the result of exposure to a sonic environment, though not an intentionally composed one. I was camping one summer near Moab, Utah, at a place called Moonflower Canyon. This red rock box canyon was about a third of a mile long and opened out onto the Colorado River. It must have been a sacred place for the Native Americans; there were petroglyphs at the entrance to the canyon. At the upper end, rain would collect in a large freshwater pool that must have once been good for drinking.

None of the other campsites were taken. I was completely alone. After dark, I was amazed at the number of insect sounds I could hear, perhaps because the canyon's vegetation was well shaded and watered. There were a dozen different hums, as well as salsa-like rhythms that sounded as if they were played on maracas, and miscellaneous other knocking and creaking noises.

All of these sounds were amplified by the closeness of the canyon walls. I was also able to hear the distant rumbling of thunder and the occasional splattering of raindrops on my nylon tent, like light, random tapping on a drum.

Lying in my tent, surrounded by echoing nature and no human sounds but my own, I felt small. The insect noises seemed to penetrate not just my ears, but my entire body. I experienced myself as dissolving into a sea of vibrations, as if I were shedding the flesh and becoming sound.

I couldn't sleep, I could only listen. I was unable to tune out the insect sounds or think of anything else. I felt a rising sense of ecstasy that frightened me with its intensity and sense of limitlessness. How high could I go and still be me?

Just at the point when I thought I would lose my identity in ecstasy or go mad, a couple of vehicles full of young people pulled into the campground. I only knew them by their sounds: talk, laughter, a few chords played on a guitar, singing, the thump of logs to be used for firewood as they were thrown from the back of a pickup to the ground.

The familiar humanness of these sounds radically changed my experience of the sonic environment that surrounded me. I no longer felt oppressed by the insect noises or the sense of ecstasy they had produced. Both faded into the background, and I was eventually able to fall asleep.

One way to develop and enhance the sense of embodiment produced by the first or arousal center is through finding a pleasant place in nature in which you can close your eyes as if for meditation and allow yourself to become as deeply immersed as possible in the sonic environment that surrounds you. According to Mathieu, "The idea is to create a space that not only protects you from unwanted sound, but also releases you from any impulse to close your ears."[5] During the cold winter months, you can accomplish a similar end by listening to recordings of ocean surf, woodlands, or meadows provided on CDs in series such as *Soundscapes* or *Environments*, often sold along with New-Age music.

In the yoga of listening, the value of lower 1 music is that it turns on the ears, so to speak, by drawing our attention to our presence in a sonic environment. Without realizing it, we often expend a certain amount of mental energy on ignoring the sounds that surround us, protecting ourselves from what Mathieu calls "unwanted sound."[6] The result of this practice, which can be unintentional and automatic, is the production of "stuck places" in our hearing.[7]

The music of lower 1, with its focus on sonic environments, can help our hearing get unstuck, making our listening to music in which other centers are dominant more responsive and pleasurable. As Mathieu says, "the more you listen the more you hear." In *The Listening Book*, he provides a number of "exercises and games to trick people into hearing more."[8] Many of these exercises involve the immersion of lower 1.

Interest (Middle 1)

Music that targets the middle range of the first center produces *interest*. At this point, sound has become organized enough to capture the listener's attention.

Organized sound is no longer merely noise. Something about it seems special, different from the chaotic sounds of an ordinary sonic environment. One actually begins listening to organized sound. What arouses the listener's interest is an incipient sense of rhythm, created by the purposeful alternation of sound and silence.

Middle 1 interest is strengthened when the listener is able to distinguish patterns of recurrent sounds. In middle 1, such patterns are usually barely discernible, not at all like a drummer's rhythmic groove.

In music that targets middle 1, silence is placed between minimally organized musical events to separate them from each other. Such events are usually simple: an isolated unpitched sound, a couple of notes, a brief rhythmic motif.

What composers are after here is the creation of an *enhanced* sonic environment. The sounds are no longer the result of random selection or chance. Though still retaining some of the characteristics of noise, these sounds are carefully chosen, ordered, and woven together with silence between them to create an auditory tapestry. Such a tapestry captures and holds our interest in ways that a sustained immersion in random sound rarely can.

Composers in the latter half of the twentieth century have often targeted the middle range of the first center. An example occurs in the fourth movement of George Crumb's *Music for a Summer Evening* for two amplified pianos and percussion, completed in 1974. Entitled "Myth" to emphasize its primitive, premusical nature, this five-minute movement employs a variety of largely unpitched, exotic percussion instruments, usually played alone.

The sonic tapestry is woven from a single sound struck on a drum or tam-tam (large bronze gong); a single shake of a rattle; a brief rhythmic motif here and there; a couple of pitches on a slide whistle or kalimba (African thumb piano) that don't quite add up to a melody; and occasional, clipped, monosyllabic shouting by the musicians. There are no chords, no tunes.

On the rare occasions when one of the pianos is heard, the player is instructed to lean his forearms into all the black and white keys in the bass range at once, producing a rich percussive noise called a tone cluster. This description of the piece makes it sound more disjunctive than it actually is. The result does indeed hold the listener's interest.

The alternation between sound and silence is one of the most basic musical rhythms, underlying all music, not just that which targets middle 1. This alternation can set individual notes, phrases, sections, movements, and pieces off from each other, determining what could be called the musical words, sentences, paragraphs, and essays a composer uses to direct our attention.

Most people are unaware of the activity of middle 1 interest in a piece of music. But listening to music in terms of the alternation between sound and silence can produce a TME.

My friend Elizabeth, for example, attended a piano recital in college at which some solo piano music by Debussy was played. She experienced a TME when she realized that the silences between the notes were as important as, perhaps more important than, the notes themselves.

As Elizabeth sensed how the silences sculptured the sonic environment created by the music, she entered an altered state that caught her by surprise, since she wasn't looking for such an experience. Yet she knew it was important, a root understanding of silence, stillness, and emptiness such as that arrived at through meditation.

Elizabeth told me that she has no idea what in that particular performance triggered her TME. But she has remembered it for thirty-five years as "a major consciousness experience." What triggered Elizabeth's TME was her accidental discovery of how to listen to music at the level of middle 1, by paying attention to the alternation of sound and silence.

In the yoga of listening, the value of middle 1 music is that it can allow us to do what Mathieu calls unlistening: "Unlistening means clearing sounds from their associations, which are often unconscious."[9] Unlistening requires that we shoo away the associations that particular sounds may have, including whether we like or dislike them. "The more completely you do this," says Mathieu, "the more deeply sound will enter you and reveal its true nature."[10]

In the stripped-down music of middle 1, the composer has helped us to shoo away many of the things we tend to associate with music: the sensual beauty of harmony (second center), the drama of conflict (third center), the emotional expressiveness of melody (fourth center), the upbeat tempo that makes us feel good (fifth center), the formal elements that fascinate us intellectually (sixth center), even the inspirational spiritual dimension (seventh center). What we get is an enhanced sonic environment, created by the rhythmic alternation of sound and silence—a reminder of our embodiment in the sensual realm of physical reality, where life is motion is rhythm.

Entrainment (Upper 1)

In the upper range of the first center, rhythm comes to the fore. According to Inayat Khan, "Rhythm produces an ecstasy which is inexplicable, and incomparable with any other source of intoxication."[11] What produces this intoxication is entrainment.

The dictionary defines entrainment as the act of one thing pulling another after itself. This is what rhythm does—it pulls our attention after itself.

In physics, entrainment refers to what happens when two identical pendulum clocks are placed next to each other: The pendulums tend to synchronize themselves. In a similar way, the steady rhythmic pulse called meter that lies beneath most Western music organizes or entrains everything from the right and left hands of a pianist to an orchestra made up of a hundred or more players on dozens of different instruments.

The sense of oneness among audience members that's sometimes so palpable in a concert hall may be a result of rhythmic entrainment. The entrained playing of the musicians results in an entrainment of breathing, heart rate, and brain waves in the listeners, bringing the latter into synchrony.

The entrainment of upper 1 can be so compelling that it produces a mildly altered state of consciousness or light trance, a state in which the passive listener experiences the mind as awake and aware, while the body runs on automatic, requiring little or no attendance to its needs. The body may even seem to others as if asleep.

Certain people can hardly refrain from moving to rhythmic music, even when listening passively. Such movement will often be automatic, rather than intentional—swaying, head-bobbing, and so forth. It may not disturb the trance of entrainment. Even dancing to rhythmic music can have an automatic, trancelike element, as if the music and not your own volition were impelling you to move.

TMEs can result from the trance induced by entrainment. Inayat Khan reported that at certain feasts in India where drums are played, some people "instantly enter into ecstasy" and are capable of miraculous feats. They can "jump into the fire without being burned; they can cut themselves with a sword and they are instantly healed; they can eat fire and not be burned by it."[12]

The entraining music of upper 1 is highly organized, usually percussive, noise. Although recurrent patterns are clearly perceivable, there's no melody or harmony, just the sense of a constant beat as a backdrop for rhythmic phrases of varying complexity. Think of a teenager improvising a rock-based rhythmic groove or backbeat pattern on a drum set and you've got the idea of upper 1.

Upper 1 abuts the second, or desire, center and so shares some of its characteristics. The second center is responsible for a sense of beauty and pleasure in music. The music of upper 1 combines arousal with pleasure to produce entrainment. This is where the pleasurably trancelike effects of one's own drumming or of listening or dancing to the drumming of others can come to the fore.

Perhaps the most highly developed music that targets the intoxicating entrainment of upper 1 is African drumming. My multitalented cellist friend, Stephen, who has also performed as a drummer and percussionist for dance classes, is an aficionado of African drumming. One of his favorite recordings of African drumming is *Djabote*, by Senegalese master drummer and composer Doudou N'Diaye Rose (b. 1928).[13]

Djabote consists of twelve tracks, ten composed by Rose and two arranged by him from traditional sources, played by a remarkable ensemble of fifty Muslim percussionists and eighty Catholic singers. The many-layered rhythmic complexity of Rose's music is entrancing, allowing the receptive listener to go deeper and deeper into the "inexplicable" and "incomparable" intoxication that Inayat Khan attributed to rhythmic music.

When Stephen played the album for me, I was surprised by the degree to which certain tracks resembled the ecstatic soundscape I experienced at Moonflower Canyon. It made me wonder whether African drumming may have had its origin in an attempt to reproduce the nocturnal sounds of the jungle.

Some contemporary composers have attempted to bring the complexity of African drumming into concert music for percussion ensemble, for example, *Ku-Ka-Ilimoku* by American composer Christopher Rouse (b. 1949). This five-minute piece for percussion ensemble is named after the Hawaiian war god.

Listening to the Crumb example and following it with the Rouse will allow you to hear the difference between the interest-generating, barely organized sonic tapestry of middle 1 in the former and the highly organized rhythmic entrainment of upper 1 in the latter. (This exercise can be easily accomplished by checking out the brief audio clips of both pieces on an Internet-based music store such as www.towerrecords.com.)

All three ranges of the first center are active in virtually all Western music, from pop to jazz to classical. Western music creates sonic environments and arouses interest in them. It entrains the mind so that the listener's attention becomes self-sustaining. Only in special cases, like those I've noted, does first center music appear in isolation from the effects of the other centers.

Composers sometimes briefly zero in on the first center as a special effect—a sonic clearing of the air that temporarily eliminates the influence of the other centers and prepares the ear for a new beginning. An example of this technique appears in the long first movement of Gustav Mahler's Third Symphony in D Minor.

About two thirds of the way through the movement, Mahler reduces the thick orchestral texture to a single snare drum playing a long marching-band-like rhythmic flourish, which heralds the return of the music that opened the movement. This is the earliest instance I'm aware of in the history of Western classical music in which the first center was isolated in this way.

A similar effect sometimes occurs in jazz or pop music, when all the other players fall silent and allow the drummer an opportunity to play solo. Some jazz and rock music may begin with rhythmic grooves that go on for a while before the tune comes in. They establish the entrainment of upper 1 and add the other centers later.

The role of the drummer in jazz is complex. Under certain conditions, jazz drumming can target other centers on the continuum of human potential, including the second, through building up rich layers of sonority (especially through using various sizes of drums and cymbals); the third, through manifesting dramatic intensity; or the fifth, through playing recognizable dance rhythms.

African drumming, too, with its high level of rhythmic complexity, can access more than one center. The simpler the rhythm, the fewer the number and variety of instruments playing, the more likely that drumming is targeting the first center alone.

In the yoga of listening, the ecstatic and intoxicating rhythms of upper 1 have obvious value. The music of entrainment induces a trance state more or less automatically, an excellent starting point for meditation, perhaps while sitting or lying down, with the eyes closed. When combined with dancing, such music may result in a greatly enhanced sense of physical embodiment, and perhaps a TME. As I pointed out in chapter 1, Maslow said that dancing is a frequently reported trigger for peak experiences.

Boredom (Crisis Point)

The first center's crisis point is *boredom*, which develops when arousal is exaggerated to the point of failure. For example, a rhythmic pattern that goes on too long without changing becomes predictable and therefore boring. Sometimes the trance-inducing aspect of rhythm is too successful, putting the listener to sleep. These are usually unintentional failures on the part of the composer or performer.

When a rhythmic pattern is overly random or complex, the mind may hear it as an undifferentiated wash of sound and lose interest. Some avant-garde composers of the last several decades have created random or overly complex rhythms intentionally in order to subvert or overwhelm a listener's attention. Such music targets the first center crisis zone of boredom.

The monotonous beat of shamanic drumming targets this crisis point on purpose. The intention behind such drumming is to lull the listener into an altered state of consciousness between waking and sleeping. The sounds used to induce this trance state must be soporific enough not to draw attention to themselves. At the same time, they must be sufficiently entraining for the shaman to recall any interesting experiences that might develop within such a state.

TMEs induced by shamanic drumming allow practitioners of shamanism to make trance-based journeys into other, nonphysical, realities. During these journeys, shamans seek information on a variety of subjects, from the ills of patients who require healing to the wishes or instructions of godlike beings or the dead.

Some audio products created for the purpose of self-hypnosis or meditation also target the crisis point of boredom intentionally. For example, Robert Monroe, a veteran out-of-body traveler and pioneer in the use of sound to produce altered states of consciousness, invented an auditory technology called Hemi-Sync. Its purpose was to use sound to produce altered states by synchronizing brain-wave patterns in the two hemispheres of the brain.

Hemi-Sync involves feeding a simple sound into one ear through head-phones, while feeding another sound with a slightly different frequency into the other. The resulting binaural beat pattern is eventually resolved by the brain into a third sound without beats—indicating that the brain waves in each hemisphere are now synchronized.

One of the simplest altered states produced by Hemi-Sync technology is called "mind awake, body asleep." This state, like the trance induced by shamanic drumming, can become a jumping-off point for adventures in consciousness, such as out-of-body experiences.

Some Hemi-Sync tapes mask their mind-altering sound technology with relatively simple synthesized music. But the binaural beat pattern is usually enough to produce entrainment. More complex music might interest the mind too much, preventing it from achieving an altered state of consciousness.[14]

"Mind awake, body asleep" can be a useful tool in the yoga of listening, creating an ideally receptive state for listening to music in which centers other than the first are dominant. Even without Hemi-Sync technology, you may be able to create this state by lying down in a darkened room and listening to music with headphones. If the music is sufficiently absorbing, the mind will be awake and active while the body disappears from your awareness, as if it were asleep. The function of first center entrainment is to produce such a state.

If music were nothing but rhythm, we might indeed end up bored with it. Even the most complex rhythm is only one dimension of music, just as arousal is only one aspect of what it means to be human. We need something more.

While rhythm may be fascinatingly intricate, it's rarely considered beautiful in itself. The sensual beauty of sound is the realm of the second center. When we become bored with rhythmic entrainment and reach for that beauty, our level of life force rises. We overcome the crisis point of boredom and move on to the second center.

A Musical Tour of the First Center

The first Western composer to write a piece that isolates the arousal center for its entire duration was Edgard Varèse (1883–1965): *Ionisation*, composed in 1929 to 1931. The beginning of this six-minute piece for percussion ensemble provides an example of music from the middle range of the first center. It creates a sonic environment, generates interest, but doesn't use repeated rhythmic patterns to produce entrainment.

Table 2. The First Center

Center	Chakra	Range	Dream Character	Lesson	Musical Element
First: Arousal	Root	Physical/Sensing	Soma (Body Consciousness)	Embodiment	Rhythm

Table 3. A First Center Playlist

Center	Level	Characteristic	Musical Genres and Examples
First: Arousal	Lower 1	Immersion	Classical: Cage, 4'33". Other: Nonorganized sound; sonic environments; recordings of natural soundscapes for meditation.
	Middle 1	Interest	Classical: Crumb, *Music for a Summer Evening*, fourth movt.; Varèse, *Ionisation* (beginning).
	Upper 1	Entrainment	Classical: Mahler, Third Symphony, first movt., snare drum solo; Rouse, *Ku-Ka-Ilimoku*; Varèse, *Ionisation* (middle). Other: African drumming such as Rose's album *Djabote*.
(Transition)	Crisis Point	Boredom	Other: Shamanic drumming; Monroe's Hemi-Sync technology.

Eventually, some rhythmic grooves develop, bumping the music into the upper range of the first center (entrainment). Toward the end of the piece, when the piano and bells come in, *Ionisation* has achieved the lower level of the second center, sonority (explained in the next chapter). Because Varèse's *Ionisation* begins in middle 1 and ascends through upper 1 to the second center, it has successfully avoided the crisis point of boredom.

The pattern of beginning at one point along the continuum of human potential and rising to another occurs frequently in Western music. Many of the musical tours of the centers provided in subsequent chapters follow this pattern.

The continuum of human potential is based on rising levels of life-force flow. *Ionisation* reflects such a rise, from the arousal of rhythm in the first center to the sensual beauty of sound in the second.

9

The Second Center: Desire

Unless you're a fan of ambient, minimalist, or New-Age music, you may have had some difficulty coming up with examples for your playlist of music in which the second center is dominant. In such music, the main source of pleasure is the sensual beauty of the sound, which I call sonority.

Few bands, songwriters, or classical or jazz composers target the second center exclusively, except to create special effects. Yet the second center, like the first, is active within virtually every kind of Western music, from classical to jazz to pop.

Some pop songs start off with just the drummer playing the beat (first center). Then the keyboard player comes in with a progression of chords (second center). What everybody is waiting for, of course, is the tune (fourth center) that enters a minute or two later. The tune is usually what's remembered, not the buildup or what's going on behind it in the rhythm and harmony. Thus, despite the fact that the first and second centers may remain active from the beginning of the song to the end, most people may never notice them.

The Dave Brubeck Quartet's "Take Five" has this shape.[1] The drummer starts the piece, then the piano and bass player enter, and finally the saxophone comes in with the tune. During the long drum solo in the middle of the piece, the piano and bass keep playing the same simple chord progression. Only the first and second centers are involved for a period of about two and a half minutes, which is nearly half the length of the piece.

If you're familiar with "Take Five," or can acquaint yourself with it, you should have an easier time thinking of other pieces or songs in which the first and second centers start things off or are featured for an extended period.

Examples of the second center without the first are rare. My massage therapist has played a CD of bells and singing bowls (bronze or crystal bowls coaxed into vibration by gentle rubbing with a wooden stick) to relax me during bodywork sessions. The buildup of tones (sonority) is eerily beautiful and largely arrhythmic. This is the closest thing I've heard to pure second center music.

The second, or genital, chakra, which I call the center of desire, is associated not only with the pleasure of sonority, but also with the dream character Participant and the spiritual lesson of motivation. This center is the other member of the pair associated with the physical, or sensing, range of the continuum of human potential.

As I pointed out in part 1, Charles says that the soul guides us by means of increasing and decreasing the amount of life force available to us. The actual mechanism of this guidance is the perception and satisfaction of needs.

Any unsatisfied need creates disquiet, which indicates that our level of life force has dropped. As we become aware of the need, we find ourselves motivated to satisfy it and relieve this disquiet. Once we've done so, the level of life force available to us rises again and we experience satisfaction, pleasure, or happiness.

What motivates us to satisfy a need is desire. In the beginning, this motivation is little more than a niggling awareness at the back of our minds: Something may not be quite right with us. That niggling is an impulse sent by the soul, intended to direct us toward some activity that will allow us to realize its plans for our growth.

As an impulse grows in intensity, it becomes a need. A need occupies more and more of our awareness until we're motivated to satisfy it by taking action. The satisfaction of a need can be physical, when the need is for food; emotional, when the need is for connection with a loved one; intellectual, when the need is for information; or spiritual, when the need is for some activity that brings us closer to the soul, such as meditation or attending a worship service.

When a need is satisfied, the impulse behind it disappears from our awareness. It's replaced by pleasure or satisfaction. The greater the need and the better the fit between need and satisfaction, the more pleasure we'll feel.

What motivates us to satisfy our needs is the desire to minimize our disquiet and maximize our pleasure. Desire can become a powerful motivation for us to realize the soul's master plan for our growth. Desire can also become a powerful distraction from that growth when we seek to duplicate and enhance past pleasures that may have nothing to do with our current needs.

Desire is compounded not only of the impulse from the soul that sets the process of need satisfaction in motion, but also of memories of past pleasure or how past needs were satisfied. Desire is both an impetus to satisfy a need and an anticipation, based on memory, of the pleasurable results of doing so. Anticipation of pleasurable results is what motivates people to satisfy their needs.

In the previous chapter, I pointed out that the lesson of the first center is embodiment. Once our souls are focused in the body and awareness has been aroused, it becomes possible to sense our needs and we're driven to fulfill them. Hence, the lesson of the second center is motivation.

In the process of embodying awareness and motivating it to satisfy our needs, our personalities come into being. The basis of personality is a recognition not only of the cast of our needs—their particular flavor, unique in each of us—but also of the ways in which we attempt to satisfy them and how doing so gives us pleasure.

The anticipation of pleasure, the process of seeking it out, our recognition of it when we experience it, and how much of it we'll allow ourselves to feel are all highly personal matters—some having their origins in the way the human body in general, or ours in particular, is wired; and some in the soul, with its master plan for our growth. Such things make up the foundation of our personalities, which are also shaped by our accumulated experience in the world and what we decide that experience means about ourselves and the universe in which we live.

Because needs come in physical, emotional, intellectual, and spiritual forms, they're present as a shaping force along the entire continuum of human potential. But the personality has its origin in the second center, in the simple process of impulse-need-desire-satisfaction.

The dream character associated with the second center is the Participant. This component of the psyche represents our ability to act in physical reality. It's the basis of our personality, the part of us that seeks to experience pleasure and develop itself through the process of impulse-need-desire-satisfaction.

In music, as in life, impulse moves to need and need moves to desire along an increasing arc of tension. That tension is released through the satisfaction of the need and the resulting pleasure, creating a rhythmic pattern of alternating tension and release. In such a pattern, the primary field of action is not rhythm itself but the so-called vertical dimension of music, which I call sonority.

By the vertical dimension of music, I mean the *simultaneity* of sounds rather than their succession in time, which is often called the horizontal dimension. Harmony is another name for the vertical dimension of music, as melody is for the horizontal. On the staff lines of musical scores, harmony is written vertically and melody horizontally—hence the terms.

I could have chosen the word *harmony* to label the vertical dimension of music. But sonority is a more comprehensive term. It refers to *any* combination of sounds, not merely ones that we would call harmonious. It's just as possible to find pleasure in constant mild harmonic dissonance as in the relatively pure consonance of the simplest folk ballad. Impressionistic music, such as *The Afternoon of a Faun* by Debussy, is full of such dissonance.

Tension and release are usually created in music by alternating sonorities that are relatively more *dissonant* (tension) with those that are relatively more *consonant* (repose). The alternation of moments of tension (corresponding to impulse, need, and desire) and repose (corresponding to satisfaction) is a fundamental aspect of life *and* music.

Wagner was so aware of this fact that, according to music critic Ernest Newman, he identified the opening of the Prelude to his opera *Tristan und Isolde* "with the Buddhist theory of the origin of the world—the troubling of the primal cloudless heavens by a breath that swells and swells and finally condenses into our visible world." This breath is "Desire, for ever expanding and retracting, for ever seeking to realize itself and for ever being frustrated."[2]

The three levels of the second, or desire, center are *relaxation, pleasure,* and *intoxication.* The crisis point is *overload.*

Relaxation (Lower 2)

The relaxation of lower 2 emphasizes the point of repose—what happens after one cycle of impulse-need-desire-satisfaction has completed itself and before the next cycle arises. Any music whose purpose is to induce a state of relaxation in the listener acts on the lower range of the second center.

Some New-Age music is designed to create such a state of relaxation. This is why it often shows up in the offices of massage therapists. Certain kinds of music therapy also promote the calming aspects of music, and therefore act on lower 2. The CD of singing bowls that I mentioned above is an example of music that targets lower 2.

Relaxation is an enhanced version of the light trance induced by activating the highest level of the first center, entrainment. Composers create a state of relaxation with a quiet succession of chords that are primarily consonant or very mildly dissonant.

There's little in the way of rhythmic movement or tonal direction in lower 2 music, and no harmonic or dramatic tension. Melodic material generally takes the form of inexpressive fragments rather than tunes. The composer provides just enough auditory information, and allows it to change or evolve just fast enough, to keep the mind interested—to relax it without putting it to sleep.

Brian Eno (b. 1948), a pioneer of ambient music, targets lower 2 in his 1978 album *Ambient I: Music for Airports.*[3] The first of the album's four tracks (entitled "1/1") provides nearly seventeen minutes of exposure to lower 2 relaxation. The first center is also present, in a subsidiary role. From time to time, the music rises toward the pleasure of middle 2, then falls back again to lower 2.

In the second track ("2/1"), lower 2 is also targeted, but the first, or arousal, center is attenuated. The result is eight and a half minutes of relaxing music that could easily result in sleep.

The third track ("1/2") contains some of the same music as the second, but with the rhythmic entrainment of the arousal center added back in. The effect of this eleven-and-a-half-minute track is similar to that of the first.

In the final track ("2/2"), Eno once again attenuates the first center, but targets a point between lower 2 relaxation and middle 2 pleasure. The result is a nine-and-a-half-minute tug-of-war between boredom and pleasure.

In the yoga of listening, the first and third tracks could provide an excellent means of off-loading stress and calming the mind. I recommend them as preludes to silent meditation or as focal points for practicing meditation with music.

If you decide to use this music as a focal point for meditation, try listening to it with headphones while lying in a dark room. The idea is to keep bringing your attention back to the music, despite its lack of drama, emotional appeal, or intellectual engagement.

How relaxed can you become without falling asleep? The presence of first center entrainment will support you in maintaining consciousness, but the more relaxed you become, the deeper the state of meditation you will have achieved. Although this meditation practice may have no spiritual content, it can prepare you for practice with pieces that do—those that target the seventh or eighth centers.

In classical music, lower 2 relaxation is often used for special effects, such as creating a moment of repose after a climax, or the sense that a piece is beginning from or dissolving into silence, tranquility, or a sense of nothingness. Lower 2 can depict dawn, before the activity of the day begins, or nightfall, when it ceases. It can also depict the silence that exists before or after the act of creation or a human lifetime.

The first three minutes of the ballet *Appalachian Spring* by Aaron Copland (1900–1990) is an example of lower 2 relaxation. This passage represents dawn on a spring day in the Appalachian high country. Copland uses a single complex and mildly dissonant chord for the entire passage. This chord provides an excellent demonstration of the distinction between sonority and the simple chords of conventional harmony.

The beginning of *Appalachian Spring* is unusual in that it's almost entirely without rhythm in the normal sense. The staggered entrances of the instruments playing the individual notes of the basic sonority provide the barest sense of rhythmic flow.

The rhythmic entrainment of the first center is usually active beneath second center music. As we rise through the centers, the higher ones will usually subordinate the lower ones. The opening of *Appalachian Spring*, however, is a rare example of relatively pure second center music, in which the presence of the first center has been reduced to a minimum.

A more typical specimen of lower 2 music is the beginning of the second movement of Bartók's Second Piano Concerto. Here, the muted strings play a constantly shifting pattern of quiet, mildly dissonant sonorities, creating an effect of tranquil floating. There's no melody, no sense of harmonic goal, no dramatic tension, and no emotional expressiveness.

First center rhythmic entrainment, however, is clearly present, establishing the duration of each sonority: these sonorities shift from one to the next according to a slow, regular pulse. The passage lasts for just under two minutes, before the piano enters and the targeted center changes.

Pleasure (Middle 2)

The pleasure of middle 2 derives from the process of impulse-need-desire-satisfaction described previously. Music described as "beautiful," without necessarily expressing much of anything else, targets middle 2. Such music is usually based on the simple pattern of mild dissonance accumulated and sustained for a longer or shorter period of time, followed by a consonance in which the dissonance seems to be resolved.

The longer the consonance, the more tranquil the music, which tends toward lower 2 relaxation. The longer the dissonance, however, the more the music tends toward middle 2 pleasure or upper 2 intoxication. Such dissonance can even push the music toward the crisis point between the second and third centers, which I call overload—not necessarily because the dissonance is sharp, but because it has lasted for a longer period than the mind is comfortable with.

In the opening and middle sections of "Take Five," the dominant center is middle 2 pleasure.

In classical music, an example of middle 2 pleasure appears in the symphonic excerpt from Wagner's *Tannhäuser*, sometimes called Overture and Venusberg Music or Overture and Bacchanal.

Many of the higher centers are accessed during the Overture and the Venusberg Music. The latter represents the scene of the opera's opening: the lush, erotic garden of Venus, concealed within a mountain called the Venusberg. But the last six minutes or so of the Venusberg Music is pure middle 2: waves that alternate between mild dissonance, full of desire, and relaxing consonance.

Though pleasurable, middle 2 music, like that of lower 2, is often without emotive expression (a characteristic of the fourth center), and has no dramatic contrast (a characteristic of the third). There may be little in the way of harmonic motion, beyond the simple succession of tension and repose. Middle 2 music acts purely on the sensual level.

"Venus, the Bringer of Peace," from *The Planets* by Gustav Holst, is another example of middle 2 pleasure. Here, however, the alternation between dissonance and consonance is not as pronounced as in Wagner's Venusberg Music. But the harmonies are lush and impressionistic—beautiful, without expressing anything but their beauty.

"Venus" begins with what sounds like a musical question in the French horn—a mildly yearning, ascending question, expressing the desire of the second center. This question is answered by a descending succession of mildly dissonant, tranquil chords in the woodwinds, expressing the possibility of repose to follow the tension of desire. This alternation of question and answer appears several times in the course of the movement, like a masculine request for peace, followed by a feminine promise of peace.

Long passages in "Venus," especially in the opening and closing sections, are made up of lush, impressionistic chords, alternating between those that promote tension and those that promote repose. In these sections, not much happens in the way of melody—a typical characteristic of second center music.

In the middle section of the piece, however, there's more melodic activity, of a mildly yearning character. Melodies of this nature—in fact, melody itself—are characteristic of the fourth center, which corresponds to the heart chakra.

In the yoga of listening, a piece like "Venus" can remind us that we're sensual beings living in a world full of beauty. Such a realization can bring healing and peace when we need a rest from aspects of life that seem stressful, ugly, or harsh. With that healing, we may also experience a renewed motivation to satisfy our needs and fulfill the soul's master plan for our growth.

Intoxication (Upper 2)

Having once experienced pleasure, we want to experience it again, often seeking to maximize it. Typically, we'll do so by enhancing previously pleasurable experiences, using the simple formula that more is better.

The intoxication of upper 2 music is the result of enhancing the pleasurable elements of middle 2 music. Such enhancements may involve increases in volume, speed, number of instruments playing, dissonance levels, and the length of time between the buildup of harmonic tension and its resolution.

Upper 2 music is already approaching the third center, whose modus operandi is intensity. Some of that intensity spills over into it, though not enough to make upper 2 music genuinely dramatic.

An example of achieving upper 2 intoxication through enhancing the musical element of sonority is the Prelude to Wagner's opera *Das Rheingold*. This four-and-a-half-minute piece is famous for the fact that it consists of nothing but an E-flat major chord and associated scale. The music is intended to represent the flowing of the Rhine River, as well as the glinting of sun on its waves.

The Prelude to *Das Rheingold* begins in lower 2, with the gradual building of the E-flat major chord, as if from nothing, at first in the bass instruments, then with arpeggiated triads in the lower brass instruments. By the two-minute mark, the higher string instruments have joined in. With the entry of the clarinets about forty seconds later, we're on the way to middle 2.

It's hard to say exactly where we cross over into middle 2, but by the four-minute mark, we're definitely there. Wagner keeps gradually adding more instruments and increasing the volume until, at about four minutes and twenty seconds, he begins throwing in rapidly played E-flat major scales.

At this point, the tension level has also increased, since an E-flat scale contains several tones that aren't present in an E-flat chord, and are mildly dissonant with it. Now we've achieved the intoxication of upper 2. The Prelude ends and the opera begins when the first singer enters about fifteen seconds later.

In the yoga of listening, intoxication is the peak of sensual pleasure, a form of body-based ecstasy. TMEs can easily result from music or performances that target upper 2.

Almost all Western music targets the second center to some degree, even though a higher center may be dominant. When composers or performers emphasize the sensual pleasure of sonority, through attending to the richness of a piece's harmony and orchestration, the balance and intonation of each note in a chord, their music becomes irresistibly seductive, thereby increasing the chances of producing intoxication in the listener, and possibly a TME.

Wagner was well aware of the intoxication-producing power of the second center. No matter what higher center may be dominant in a given passage of his music, the second center will always be strongly active beneath it.

Overload (Crisis Point)

At the crisis point between the second and third centers, the attempt to reproduce and enhance pleasure backfires by producing a sense of overload.

Without dramatic contrast or variations in texture and tempo, music based in the second center can overload the brain with sensory stimuli, creating discomfort, annoyance, restlessness, and impatience for change or an ending.

Such discomfort is the result of the mind's fighting against the music's potentially overwhelming combination of first center entrainment and second center sensory pleasure. The mind becomes bored with the music's lack of variety or fearful of losing self-control or its sense of identity as a result of being bombarded with more auditory information than it can make sense of and enjoy. Minimalist music can cause overload in just these ways.

According to one of the pioneers of minimalism, Philip Glass, the intention behind such music is to create "a pure medium of sound freed of dramatic structure."[4] A "pure medium of sound" is exactly what we would expect of music that targets the second center, whose musical element is sonority. The "dramatic structure" that has been stripped away is a product of the third center (drama) acting in concert with the sixth center (structure).

Minimalism often targets the intoxication of upper 2. At times, however, it approaches the sense of overload associated with the crisis point, pushing the intoxicating combination of sonority, rhythm, and speed to the limit of the mind's ability to enjoy it. The result is music that behaves like an out-of-control pleasure machine, ratcheting up the lesson of the second center, motivation, to the point of frenzy.

Middle 2 pleasure, upper 2 intoxication, and the crisis point of overload may each be found in *Sextet*, by American minimalist composer Steve Reich (b. 1936). The piece is scored for three marimbas, two pianos, two synthesizers, and a variety of percussion instruments, all to be managed by six performers.

The second and fourth of the piece's five movements target the pleasure of middle 2, and the third movement the intoxication of upper 2. The first and last movements target the second center's crisis point. They produce overload by means of relentless, high-speed repetition of nonexpressive melodic fragments within a harmonic context of constant, though not jarring, dissonance that's never quite resolved.

All five movements are played without a pause, although transitional sections between them break up the otherwise unchanging texture of one movement and clear the air for the next. The transitional sections involve the analytic sixth center, since they're concerned with the musical problem of maintaining continuity while shifting from the tempo of one section to that of the next.

In *Sextet*, as with all second center music, no dramatic tension or emotional expression is involved. Often there's very little change in texture or volume. In the first and last movements, the increased dissonance, as well as the relentless, rapid flow of constantly repeated, yet gradually shifting, musical information pushes the music into overload. The mind can't take in so much information. It becomes uneasy and wants to withdraw, creating lapses in attention.

In the yoga of listening, such a piece is useful as a demonstration of what happens when desire gets out of control. Out-of-control desire is the result of the mind's continuing to reproduce and enhance pleasure, even when there's no soul-based need to satisfy or the point of satiety has been reached and surpassed.

A Musical Tour of the Second Center

Perhaps the most famous example of classical music in which the second center is dominant is *Boléro* by Maurice Ravel. In the beginning, the mesmerizing bolero rhythm that is constantly in the background produces the entrainment of upper 1. A simple harmonic accompaniment that alternates mild tension with relative relaxation adds the dimension of sonority characteristic of the second center. There's also a quietly insistent, lulling melody, which derives from the fourth center. The overall effect, however, is the pleasure of middle 2, the dominant center.

The movement from pleasure to intoxication commences when Ravel begins to harmonize the melody by doubling and tripling it on various other degrees of the scale. From this point, which occurs six or seven minutes into the piece, the harmonic texture grows thicker and the level of dissonance increases. The number of instruments playing and the relative volume of the music also grow constantly.

It's hard to say exactly when the crossover into upper 2 takes place. When the key suddenly and unexpectedly changes, about fifteen minutes into the piece, *Boléro* has clearly achieved the intoxication of upper 2, which it maintains until the end. The players even sound drunk, especially during the piece's last half-minute, after returning to the original key, with wild trombone slides and an even higher level of dissonance.

Throughout *Boléro*, the insistent rhythm produces a trance, the melody expresses nothing, and the simple, though increasingly dissonant, harmonic accompaniment adds an element of sensual pleasure, but without dramatic intensity. Constant shifts in orchestral color and a gradual increase in volume provide just enough interest to keep the listener from falling asleep.

Ravel is reputed, by fellow composer Arthur Honegger (1892–1955), to have said: "I've written only one masterpiece—*Boléro*. Unfortunately, there's no music in it."[5] Wry as this remark may seem, it contains a degree of truth.

Table 4. The Second Center

Center	Chakra	Range	Dream Character	Lesson	Musical Element
Second: Desire	Genital	Physical/Sensing	Participant	Motivation	Sonority

Table 5. A Second Center Playlist

Center	Level	Characteristic	Musical Genres and Examples
Second: Desire	Lower 2	Relaxation	Classical: Bartók, Second Piano Concerto, second movt. (beginning); Copland, *Appalachian Spring* (beginning); Wagner, Prelude to *Das Rheingold* (beginning). Other: Eno: *Music for Airports*; New-Age and ambient music.
	Middle 2	Pleasure	Classical: Holst, "Venus"; Ravel, *Boléro* (first half); Reich, *Sextet* (second and fourth movts.); Wagner, *Tannhäuser*, Overture and Bacchanal (closing section), Prelude to *Das Rheingold* (middle). Jazz: The Dave Brubeck Quartet, "Take Five" (beginning and middle section).
	Upper 2	Intoxication	Classical: Ravel, *Boléro* (second half); Reich, *Sextet* (third movt.); Wagner, Prelude to *Das Rheingold* (ending). Other: Minimalism.
(Transition)	Crisis Point	Overload	Classical: Reich, *Sextet* (first and last movts.). Other: Minimalism.

For most people, music is about dramatic intensity (third center) or emotional expression (fourth center). Ravel's experiment was to see what would happen if he stripped away the aspects of music with which most people are familiar. What he ended up with was a piece that acts almost exclusively on the second center.

Like Reich's *Sextet*, Ravel's *Boléro* also seeks to reproduce and enhance musical pleasure through constant repetition and increases in volume and dissonance. But *Boléro* achieves the intoxication of upper 2 without passing into overload.

In the yoga of listening, second center music like *Boléro* can serve a function similar to the body-positive branch of yoga called Tantra. Such music reminds us that the roots of who we are as human beings lie in physical embodiment and the enjoyment of sensory pleasure.

Our spiritual growth may be limited if we go no further than developing the physical and sensory aspects of ourselves. But without the relaxation, pleasure, and intoxication of the second center, we may not feel motivated to undertake the growth challenges posed by the higher centers on the continuum of human potential.

10

The Third Center: Intensity

Unless you're an opera or heavy metal fan, or an aficionado of twentieth-century music such as Stravinsky's *The Rite of Spring*, you may have had trouble coming up with musical instances of dramatic tension, intensity, or conflict for your playlist, as I asked you to do in chapter 6. In that case, I recommended that you try turning on the TV and watching a few minutes of some crime-based show or horror movie that includes a soundtrack.

When I visit my folks in Ohio, I'm often aware of such soundtracks. While I do yoga in the evenings on an Oriental carpet in the entryway of their house, two rooms away, my father is watching TV. I can usually tell what sort of show he's watching from the music. When it's a crime drama, thriller, or war or horror movie, I can even get some sense of where the plot is going, whether I can hear the dialogue or not.

If the music is quiet, but dissonant, tense, and brooding, then a crime is about to occur, or the haunted house has just been entered. If the music is loud and dissonant, but not fast, then someone's emotional reaction of fear or rage is building.

If the music becomes agitated, then the invasion of dangerous aliens, insects, or snakes has occurred, or someone is fleeing a pursuer or about to go insane. As the scene builds to its climax, the music becomes more passionate and overwrought, until some violent tragedy occurs—a raging battle, horrifying murder or suicide, or alien bloodbath.

Most of us aren't aware of the background music in a film or on TV. We're too absorbed in the story line. But film composers know how to make the feelings of fear, rage, or horror present in the plot vivid enough that we'll feel as if we've lived through them ourselves. To do this, they use the third center on the continuum of human potential.

The third center, intensity, is associated with the third, or navel, chakra. This center is the first of the pair associated with the emotional, or feeling, range of the continuum of human potential. It correlates with the dream character that Charles calls the Shadow.

Third center music is about our confrontation with the Shadow. It adds dissonance and volume to the rhythmic contribution of the first center and the sonority-based contribution of the second. The result is dramatic music that projects conflict and passion, fear, rage, and lust.

In the second center, the personality has been awakened. The relationship between the state of desire that accompanies needs, and the pleasure that results from their fulfillment, has been established. We've achieved both embodiment in physical reality (first center) and the motivation to acknowledge and fulfill our needs and desires (second center). This motivation not only allows us to sustain the body, but also drives our spiritual growth through the remaining chakras, or centers.

In the third center, we begin to encounter obstacles to the satisfaction of our needs. These obstacles generate feelings such as frustration and anger.

One such obstacle is the feeling of being cut off from other people. The skin that contains us seems to separate us from others, leading to a sense of loneliness and isolation. We desperately want to connect with people somehow.

Another obstacle is that we want other people to be just like us, to see things exactly as we do—especially the needs we hope they'll satisfy for us. Yet they have bodies, personalities, and needs of their own, often quite different from ours. The differences between their needs and our own often generate conflict.

A third obstacle is that we expect others to satisfy our needs. When they don't, we experience emotional pain, which further adds to our sense of loneliness and isolation. We become obsessed with the question of why they won't satisfy our needs: *Is there something wrong with me?* Meanwhile, frustrated desire can lead us through anger to conflict, as we try to persuade, manipulate, or coerce other people to do our bidding.

As our needs continue to go unsatisfied or create conflict with others, we may begin to feel sorry for ourselves, in addition to feeling alone and unloved. Our motivation to satisfy our needs diminishes. We may even begin to resist the impulses from the soul intended to direct our growth. What's the point of following them, we tell ourselves, if the outcome is emotional pain? Depression ensues.

Yet our constant rubbing up against the differences between ourselves and others can also help us become aware of who we really are. Through such friction, which can show up as anything from a fascinated exploration of otherness to a violent conflict or rejection, we begin to develop a sense of individual identity.

In the second center, as we move from impulse to need, to desire, to satisfaction, we have little awareness of ourselves as individuals. We're like infants: We *are* what makes us happy. But we each have individual destinies to fulfill as well—the soul's master plan for our growth.

Our awareness of that individual destiny often develops from experiencing the differences between ourselves and others. At first, we may be disappointed to discover that others are not like us, don't have the same needs, and aren't just as willing to satisfy our needs as we are.

The pain that accompanies these disappointed expectations often becomes evidence that something *is* wrong with us: We're unlovable. We may conclude that the more we differentiate ourselves from others, by discovering and living from our individual destinies, the more unlovable we'll become.

Herein lies the source of much of our resistance to becoming who we truly are: the fear of becoming unlovable. The Shadow dream character is the embodiment of such resistance, the source of everything that blocks our realization of the soul's master plan for our growth. The dramatic music of the third center forces us to acknowledge this resistance, to confront the Shadow, by experiencing its often tragic effects on our lives and those of others.

The lesson of the third center is to develop a soul-based sense of identity. We can do so only by accepting our differences from other people as we involve them in the process of satisfying our needs, and hoping to overcome our sense of separation from others and our feelings of unlovability.

The process of satisfying our needs can sometimes be taken over by the Shadow. Motivated by feelings of unlovability, we'll *pursue* certain people in the hope that they'll help us to satisfy our needs, all the while fearing their rejection and the resulting emotional pain. Meanwhile, we'll *flee* from others who are seeking to do the same thing with us.

When we pursue, we're acting from what Charles calls a *desire projection*. We're seeing others as potential objects of need satisfaction, without regard for what's going on inside of them—whether they're willing to satisfy our needs. When we flee, we're acting from what Charles calls a *fear projection*. We're attempting to get away from people who see us as objects of need satisfaction to protect our identities.

Desire pursues and fear flees. This is the basic plot of most drama. Drama, including dramatic music, is a product of the third center.

Most fear- and desire-based projections operate covertly within our psyches. We want to conceal them from ourselves and others, so they have a shadowy, subconscious existence. They may burst out from time to time, often violently, in socially inappropriate behaviors—what psychologists call "acting out." Conflict, war, murder, revenge, rape, incest, humiliation, and victimization are examples of such acting out.

Possessed by fear- or desire-based projections, we may even perform actions that later seem attributable to an evil alter ego. The Shadow dream character *is* that potentially evil, and usually unacknowledged, alter ego. The Shadow represents everything in us that stands in the way of our spiritual development, especially the issue of unlovability; and how our fear- and desire-based projections distort the development of our identities.

Many operas bring the Shadow into our awareness by showing us the tragic results of acting out under the influence of fear- or desire-based projections. Much operatic music targets the third center, in which the intensity that results from increased dissonance and volume enhances the emotions of fear and desire, allowing us to acknowledge, feel, and release them.

This process is called *catharsis*, the Greek word for "purging." Catharsis allows us to watch a dramatic work and witness its characters dealing with life in a variety of inappropriate ways. We get to see how fear- and desire-based projections distort their personalities and behavior. We also become aware of the results that their acting-out has on other people—their lovers, mates, family, friends, and community.

Canadian novelist and music critic Robertson Davies had this to say about opera in his novel *The Lyre of Orpheus*:

> There they sit, all those stockbrokers and rich surgeons and insurance men, and they look so quiet as if nothing would rouse them. But underneath they are raging with unhappy love, or vengeance, or some point of honor or ambition—all connected with their professional lives. They go to *La Bohème* or *La Traviata* and they remember some early affair that might have been squalid if you weren't living it yourself; or they see *Rigoletto* and think how the chairman humiliated them at the last board meeting; or they see *Macbeth* and think how they would like to murder the chairman and get his job. Only they don't think it; very deep down they feel it, and boil it, and suffer it in the primitive underworld of their souls.[1]

But opera does more than just bring up all this dark thinking, feeling, boiling, and suffering from the "primitive underworld" of the soul. It also gives such things a visible and auditory form, allowing us to witness the tragic outcomes of acting on our primitive, fear- and desire-based impulses, so that we don't have to do so in real life.

Third center music can force us to acknowledge and confront the Shadow, allowing us to feel things that we may be afraid to feel—for example, our own murderous intentions toward our bosses. The purpose of this confrontation is catharsis, to help us purge ourselves of negative emotions and put them behind us.

Opera performances can often produce TMEs as a result of third center catharsis. My friend Sue Ellen, a computer programmer, became an opera convert after having such a TME. Under the dual influence of a book about opera inherited from her grandmother and a friend who was an opera fan, Sue Ellen decided to attend her first opera, *Aida*, by Giuseppe Verdi (1813–1901).

To prepare herself for the experience, Sue Ellen read a synopsis of the plot in her grandmother's book. *Aida* takes place in ancient Egypt and deals with military triumph, political and personal betrayal, a romantic triangle, vindictive jealousy, and the undying love of a pair of star-crossed lovers. "You've got to be kidding," she thought, "this plot is absurd."

But at the performance, with Shirley Verrett singing the title role, Sue Ellen found herself "totally transported." Although she was feeling physically uncomfortable at the beginning of the opera, by the end she was no longer aware of her body. She cared about the characters and believed the story. During the final scene, in which Aida and her lover sing a duet as they're sealed in a tomb where they'll die, Sue Ellen was so moved that she wasn't conscious of the tears streaming down her cheeks until after the lights had come up at the end.

The passions and dramatic conflicts that bring the opera to this tragic and cathartic end are developed by means of the third center. But the love duet in the final scene of *Aida* targets the heart-opening fourth center, described in the next chapter.

The three levels of the third center are *tension*, *agitation*, and *eruption*. The crisis point is *violence*.

Tension (Lower 3)

In the lower range of the third center, the musical materials are little different from those developed in the second: rhythm and sonority. But the sonority is no longer pleasurable, as in the second center. The addition of volume and dissonance has increased its intensity, creating a range of musical tension from brooding disquiet to impending threat.

The gratification of some desire has been blocked. Friction is beginning to develop. Frustration builds in the pursuer and fear in the pursued. But no action has yet been taken on either side. The music illustrates only the potential for action, the tension that precedes it. The Shadow is on the scene.

Lower 3 is commonly used by composers for film and television to let the listener know that something is beginning to go wrong. Often it becomes the starting point for a dramatic buildup of emotional intensity involving lust's pursuit, fear's flight, or the rage of ungratified desire.

An example of the tension of lower 3 occurs in Stravinsky's ballet *The Rite of Spring*, which portrays pagan rites in ancient Russia, in the section called "Action rituelle des ancêtres" ("Ritual of the Ancestors").[2]

Agitation (Middle 3)

In middle 3 music, the sense of brooding menace or impending threat typical of lower 3 gives way to emotional agitation or flight and pursuit. Not only is the Shadow on the scene, it has begun to take action.

An example of middle 3 emotional agitation occurs at the opening of the second movement of the *Symphonie Fantastique* of Hector Berlioz. For about thirty seconds, the music portrays the welling up of unfulfilled desire, after which this sexual agitation crystallizes into a fifth center waltz. (I deal with this movement more extensively in chapter 12.)

An example of action-based middle 3 agitation, including fear, occurs in the Prelude to Act I of Wagner's *Die Walküre*. The music portrays a storm through which Siegmund is fleeing from pursuers who intend to kill him.

In both lower and middle 3, the intensity created through dissonance and volume is usually more important than the expression of feeling, which is a fourth center characteristic. As in both the Wagner and Berlioz examples just cited, the music of lower and middle 3 is usually unmelodic: harshly dissonant chords to increase the tension, or scurrying instrumental lines to increase the agitation. There may be melodic fragments, sometimes repeated insistently, but rarely a discernible tune.

Composers tend not to spend much time in the lower ranges of the third center. They tap into lower and middle 3 for special dramatic effects, passing through them briefly on their way to the eruption of dramatic conflict typical of upper 3. In the twentieth century, however, some composers began to base entire movements on the tension and agitation of lower and middle 3.

Threnody for the Victims of Hiroshima, by the avant-garde Polish composer Krzysztof Penderecki (b. 1933), targets lower 3 tension and middle 3 agitation exclusively, constantly shifting between them. Composed in 1959 to 1961, this ten-minute piece for string orchestra contains no melodies or harmonies, just rhythm (first center), sonority (second center), and intensity (third center).

The intensity is created by extremely high levels of dissonance, at times soft and brooding, at others loud and menacing. The passages in which there's little rhythmic activity generate tension (lower 3). They alternate, and sometimes combine, with passages in which there's a great deal of rhythmic activity, which produces agitation (middle 3).

I had one of my few unpleasant TMEs when I first heard *Threnody for the Victims of Hiroshima* in a music appreciation class. The music completely took me over. I heard the screams of the bomb victims, the panic and flight of the survivors, even the propellers of the plane that dropped the bomb. I left the classroom in horrified shock and swore that I would never listen to the piece again.

In the process of researching this book, however, I gave the piece a second hearing. It's fascinating, if unpleasant, and certainly potent in its protest against the nuclear violence perpetrated upon Japan at the end of World War II. Here, the confrontation with the Shadow forces us to acknowledge our capacity for such horrifying mass destruction.

In the yoga of listening, *Threnody for the Victims of Hiroshima* can be used not only to force such a confrontation, but also to demonstrate the distinction between the lower and middle ranges of the third center. The piece is too disturbing, however, for me to recommend it as a focus for meditation.

Eruption (Upper 3)

Some composers avoid the tension and agitation of lower and middle 3 entirely and focus exclusively on the eruption of passion and dramatic conflict typical of upper 3. Because upper 3 abuts the expressive fourth center, it carries with it some of the elements of that center, though in a primitive form.

In upper 3, the emotions of fear or desire behind the tension and agitation of lower and middle 3 fully declare themselves, usually in a dramatic and passionate way. The resulting eruption of conflict is usually expressed through the emergence of brief themes or melodies, often fragmentary, signifying the music's proximity to the expressive fourth center, whose element is melody.

These melodies or fragments are often added to the dissonant chords and scurrying instruments of lower and middle 3. Such melodies represent the extent to which the baby-like, pleasure-based personality developed in the second center has taken on a powerful sense of individual identity through the friction of the third. In the passionate eruption of upper 3, we have a fully developed, though primitive human being, an embodiment of the Shadow capable of feeling fear, lust, and the rage of ungratified desire—but not love. Love comes with the fourth center.

An example of a full-bodied eruption of upper 3 passion occurs in the third and final movement of Beethoven's *Moonlight* Sonata (Piano Sonata No. 14 in C-sharp Minor, Op. 27, No. 2). This movement, which lasts for seven or eight minutes, depending on the tempo of the performance, targets upper 3 for its entire duration.

In third center music for stage, film, or television, fear-based projections are often represented by an innocent victim, and desire-based projections by an evil victimizer. An anxious victim may turn against an angry victimizer in order to defend herself. Or the victimizer may attempt to destroy the victim. Or the victim may be driven to destroy himself. The eruption of this sort of conflict is often the core of any dramatic work, and requires upper 3.

Several sections of Stravinsky's ballet *The Rite of Spring* use upper 3 to portray such eruptions of dramatic conflict, notably those called "Jeu du rapt" ("Mock Abduction"), and "Jeux des cités rivales" ("Games of the Rival Tribes").

Violence (Crisis Point)

The crisis point between the third and fourth centers has been reached when an eruption of dramatic passion spills over into violence and some tragic act occurs. The victimizers triumph and the victims are murdered, put to death, or kill themselves. This crisis point is also useful in mob scenes when the potential for violence has become acute, whether or not a tragic act occurs. Stravinsky's *The Rite of Spring* contains such a moment in the section called "Cortège du Sage" ("Procession of the Wise Elder").

Conflicts that lead to tragedy symbolize the personal and social problems that ensue when identity is based only on the friction that develops when our needs go unsatisfied and our desire for pleasure has gotten out of control. In such a state, we perceive people not as souls but as objects to be manipulated, bullied, bent to our will, and destroyed if they do not cooperate. Or, as victims, we destroy ourselves because we no longer want to live in such a world. In either case, the Shadow has triumphed.

As long as we perceive other people as objects, convenient when they satisfy our needs, inconvenient when they don't, we're stuck in the third center. Our life force can only rise into the fourth when we're ready to learn that identity must be tempered with love, a sense of union with others in which we perceive them as people, not as objects of potential need satisfaction.

A Musical Tour of the Third Center

A good example of music that touches upon each level of the third center is "Mars, the Bringer of War" from Holst's *The Planets*. The insistent rhythm is not much different from that in Ravel's *Boléro*, just louder. But the harmony is harsher, not at all pleasurable or intoxicating.

The movement is nearly seven minutes long. The first minute and a half expresses the tension of lower 3. Thereafter the music increases in intensity, touching on middle 3 (agitation) for about forty seconds, then upper 3 (eruption of passion) for another forty seconds.

This is Holst's procedure throughout the movement: to keep the tension of lower 3 going—adding middle 3, then upper 3, and then wiping them away, bringing lower 3 back into the foreground. Fear and frustrated desire are continually building up, creating a sense of brooding menace or impending threat.

Meanwhile, a melody keeps trying to emerge from all this tension—representing the sense of personal identity that I mentioned as a characteristic of upper 3. This melody appears after slightly more than two minutes have elapsed, in the French horn, and is answered by the trumpets.

At about the three-minute mark, we're back in lower 3, for most of the next three minutes, with brief overlays of middle and upper 3. There's a good clear burst of middle 3 agitation toward the end of the movement, when Holst sends the strings scurrying.

The unresolved dissonance insistently repeated in the final moments of the piece represents the crisis point—a suggestion of the violence and horror of war, something Holst must have felt while composing the piece in the midst of the First World War.

In "Mars," we're forced to confront the Shadow's relentless tendency to escalate our frustration over unsatisfied needs to the point of violence or war. The purpose of the piece is not only to portray the buildup of martial feelings, but also to help us purge them. "Mars" evokes these feelings in our bodies through its harmonic intensity and volume, its relentless marchlike motion.

By the time the next movement begins, "Venus, the Bringer of Peace," we've experienced a catharsis of aggressive feelings. We can relax now, having lived through the horror of war in the emotions and physical tensions evoked by the music of "Mars" with its constant, unresolved dissonance.

In placing "Venus" after "Mars," the composer has made a powerful political point: Wouldn't we rather have the soft, sensual pleasure of "Venus" than the harsh violence of "Mars"?

If you'd like to check out how the third center sounds in popular music, try the fifth and seventh tracks from the 1997 album *Imaginary Day* by jazz-rock fusion guitarist Pat Metheny (b. 1954) and his keyboard collaborator Lyle Mays (b. 1953).[3] The first two minutes or so of the fifth track, "The Heat of the Day," which is strongly influenced by Indian music, employs middle 3 agitation, with occasional eruptions into the passion of upper 3.

In the seventh track, "The Roots of Coincidence," lower 3 tension is present for about two thirds of the seven-and-a-half-minute piece. Middle 3 agitation is strong at the beginning. There are two outbursts of heavy-metal-like violence (the crisis point between centers 3 and 4), both followed by an ambient-music-like drop to lower 2 relaxation. The expressive fourth center is also touched upon at various points.

In popular music, various kinds of rock, punk, heavy metal, and rap can also target the third center, especially the passionate eruption of upper 3 and the crisis point of violence. This is a favorite center for the disenfranchised, who may use it to express and purge themselves of fear- and desire-based projections, whether they suffer from racial injustice or adolescent angst.

In the yoga of listening, the purpose of third center music is emotional purification, or catharsis. In musical works for film, TV, and stage, including opera, we confront the Shadow by seeing characters in an unfolding drama behaving fearfully and aggressively. The music enhances this confrontation with the Shadow, evoking similar fearful and aggressive feelings in us. Purification takes place as the music guides us to feel our way to the bottom of these negative emotions.

Third center music can also appear in purely instrumental music, as in the case of Holst's "Mars." No discernible characters may be involved, yet the music leads us from the buildup of tension over unsatisfied needs, through the agitation of desire-motivated pursuit and fear-motivated flight, to the eruption of passion or a dramatic conflict and possibly the violence of some tragic act.

The spiritual purpose of experiencing such confrontations with the Shadow is to encourage us to learn from and avoid them. Some spiritual teachers advocate the avoidance of violence in all forms, which might include composing, performing, or listening to third center music. While I don't recommend immersing oneself exclusively in third center music as composer, performer, or listener, if one is drawn to it, then one needs the lessons it has to teach, including catharsis through confrontation with the Shadow.

Most composers use third center intensity to make a special point. They usually don't dwell on the third center for the entire duration of a piece, but pass through it briefly in order to create a moment of drama. Or, as is often the case with the first and second centers, they'll subordinate the third center to some higher center. The use of third center intensity in a supportive role is like adding shadow effects to a drawing to make the subject more three-dimensional and lifelike.

When we've achieved the emotional purification or catharsis effected by third center intensity and our confrontation with the Shadow, we're ready to experience the love expressed in the fourth center.

Table 6. The Third Center

Center	Chakra	Range	Dream Character	Lesson	Musical Element
Third: Intensity	Navel	Emotional/Feeling	Shadow	Identity	Dissonance and Volume

Table 7. A Third Center Playlist

Center	Level	Characteristic	Musical Genres and Examples
Third: Intensity	Lower 3	Tension	Classical: Penderecki, *Threnody for the Victims of Hiroshima*; Stravinsky, *The Rite of Spring*, "Action rituelle des ancêtres." Jazz: Metheny, "The Roots of Coincidence."
	Middle 3	Agitation	Classical: Berlioz, *Symphonie Fantastique*, second movt., opening (beginning); Penderecki, *Threnody for the Victims of Hiroshima*; Wagner, Prelude to Act I of *Die Walküre*. Jazz: Metheny, "The Heat of the Day" and "The Roots of Coincidence."
	Upper 3	Eruption	Classical: Beethoven, *Moonlight Sonata*, third movt.; Stravinsky, *The Rite of Spring*, "Jeu du rapt," "Jeux des cités rivales." Pop/Rock: Some rock, punk, heavy metal, and rap.
(Transition)	Crisis Point	Violence	Classical: Stravinsky, *The Rite of Spring*, "Cortège du Sage." Jazz: Metheny, "The Roots of Coincidence."

11

The Fourth Center: Expression

Creating a playlist including from one to three items in which your main source of pleasure was the melody should have been easy. Any trouble you may have had probably arose from too many possibilities to choose from rather than too few, as with the second and third centers.

I've already pointed out that the rhythm of the first, or arousal, center, and the sonority of the second, or desire, center underlie almost all Western music, whether classical, jazz, or popular. It was difficult for me to identify pure examples of music that touches these centers. The lessons that these centers entail—embodiment and motivation—are so basic to our growth that we may not be aware of them as such, in music as in life.

It was somewhat easier for me to identify pure musical examples of third center intensity. The increases in volume and dissonance, as well as the presence of passionate, often self-destructive, emotions typical of this center are commonly found in works for the stage: opera, ballet, and background music for plays, films, or television shows with dramatic or tragic themes.

The painful, shadowy side of the lesson of the third center—identity—was also a challenge for me to describe, perhaps because so much of this lesson resides in, or has been relegated to, our subconscious. We're less familiar with the shadowy side of ourselves, just as we're often unaware of the background music in a stage work, film, or television show. We're too caught up in the unfolding drama to notice the music, just as in life we may be too caught up in conflict to notice how it helps us build our identity.

Third center music not only is *about* the subconscious parts of ourselves, but also *acts* on us subconsciously, creating feelings of anxiety, agitation, or terror to accompany or illustrate dramatic action. For this reason, third center music is often easy to detect by our tendency to shrink from it inwardly or physically.

With the fourth center, we emerge from the relatively unconscious lessons of embodiment and motivation, and the subconscious lessons of identity building, with their accompanying sense of unlovability, pain, and resistance to growth. We've had enough of separation, fear-inspired flight, and desire-inspired pursuit. We're ready to reach out to others, share our feelings with them, and invite them to join us on the basis of what's similar between us, rather than what's different. We're ready to add the lesson of union to the lesson of identity.

The fourth center represents the level of growth at which many people will find themselves on the continuum of human potential. For this reason, the music that targets this center is quite familiar to us. We're exposed to it all the time, on the radio, at work, while shopping, even in the dentist's chair.

The fourth chakra is located in the area of the physical heart. In the ancient Sanskrit scriptures, "the heart rather than the head has been considered the true bridge between consciousness [represented by the upper chakras] and the body [represented by the lower chakras]."[1] The heart chakra is less likely to cause the yogic practitioner to fall into self-limiting obsessions, as the lower chakras sometimes do, or ungrounded experience of mystical states, as the upper ones sometimes do.

Some yoga masters consider this center to be the safest with which to begin meditation practice. They advise cultivating virtues such as "kindness, compassion, dispassion, calmness" to open the heart center and counterbalance or eliminate the ego-based drives of the lower chakras.[2] Listening or meditating to music that targets the fourth, or heart, center can have the same effect. This is one purpose of New-Age music.

Swami Satyananda says that the heart chakra "is responsible for all the creative sciences and fine arts."[3] For this reason, I call the fourth chakra the center of *expression*. It's the second of the pair of centers associated with the emotional, or feeling, range of the continuum of human potential. I correlate this chakra with what Charles calls the Anima/Animus dream character, which represents the beloved as partner, father, mother, or child. Much of the music that targets this center, however, refers to romantic love.

One of the key tasks of our spiritual growth, according to Charles, is to balance identity and union within us. Identity refers to the part of us that seeks to differentiate ourselves from others. Developing identity can lead to greater separation from others. Under the auspices of the third center, such separation often creates emotional pain, fear of unlovability, and resistance to growth.

Union represents our attraction to others, the experience of loving and being loved that helps us to overcome our sense of separation from them, heal the pain of disappointed expectations, and let go of the resulting feelings of unlovability and resistance to growth.

The function of the expressive fourth center is to enable us to communicate our need for connection to others, whether through the arts or a personal sharing of feelings. Developing the heart center allows us to open ourselves up to union, which is the lesson of the expressive center.

The interaction between the third center's Shadow-based issues of separation and identity and the fourth center's Animus/Anima-based issues of attraction and union generates much of the drama of growth on the physical plane. A great deal of Western music, from classical to jazz to pop, derives from this interaction.

Swami Satyananda claimed that when the fourth center is awakened, one acquires "the freedom to escape from a preordained fate and to determine one's own destiny."[4] This freedom is possible only when the powerful forces of physicality, sensuality, and the lower emotions (anger and so on) represented by the first three centers have been overcome.

The obstacles that we encounter on the journey of self-realization—those that block the satisfaction of our needs, while at the same time building character in the form of identity—can seem like fate. Music that portrays a battle with fate, especially the apparently losing battle that generates tragedy, has its origin in the third center.

Examples of such encounters with fate abound in opera—for example, *Carmen* by Georges Bizet (1838–1875). In *Carmen*, the desire of a Spanish officer for a Gypsy woman who betrays him for another man destroys the lives of all three characters. The notion of fate also crops up in certain symphonic works, such as Tchaikovsky's Fourth Symphony.

The lesson of the fourth center is that love can be a powerful redemptive force, more powerful than fate. Many romantic movies and musicals have this theme, as well as certain operas—for example, Wagner's *The Flying Dutchman*, in which the redemptive love of a woman saves the captain of a ghost ship who is condemned to sail the world forever for having committed blasphemy.

If the third center represents the intensity of raw emotions such as anger, the fourth begins a process in which such emotions are acted upon, through expression rather than violence. At the level of the third center, where inappropriate action leads to tragedy, as in opera, acting out emotions can have a cathartic effect.

With the fourth center, a process of analyzing and abstracting such emotions begins—one that continues through the remaining centers beyond it. Feeling becomes something to be observed and acted upon, communicated and transcended, through the fourth center's power of expression.

The element of music that corresponds to this power of expression is *melody*. Melody is a prime carrier of emotion in music. Though the music of the centers below the fourth may have melodic qualities, in the fourth center, the emphasis is on emotional expression through songlike melodies, which are often called tunes.

Tunes form the basis of most songs, from the lieder of Franz Schubert or Robert Schumann (1810–1856) to the hits of Billy Joel (b. 1949). In tunes such as those in "Im wundershönen Monat Mai" ("In the Wonderful Month of May") from Schumann's song cycle *Dichterliebe* (*Poet's Love*), Op. 48, or Billy Joel's "The Longest Time," from his 1983 album *An Innocent Man*,[5] to name two of my favorites, the expressive fourth center is dominant.

In the yoga of music, songs like these, as well as tuneful instrumental music that targets the fourth center, has the purpose of opening the heart. Hazrat Inayat Khan spoke of the "heart—which is often cold and frozen" and how listening to music can heat it up and bring it to life again.[6]

I've often experienced this heating and opening up of the heart. It's one of the ways to differentiate fourth center music from that in which another center is dominant. Think of the moment when the musical theme of a romantic movie swells as the credits roll at the end and you're weeping in sadness or joy. That's what I mean by the heating and opening of the heart.

This effect of fourth center music is especially noticeable in several famous pieces by the early-twentieth-century Russian composer Sergei Rachmaninoff (1873–1943): the second movement of his Piano Concerto No. 2 in C Minor, Op. 18; the eighteenth of the twenty-four variations that make up his Rhapsody on a Theme by Paganini, Op. 43; and the third movement, or Adagio, of his Symphony No. 2, Op. 27.

Once when I was going through a difficult period, I listened to the Adagio of Rachmaninoff's Second Symphony. My oboist friend George had recommended it to me when I asked him about whether he had ever had a TME. George told me that this adagio was a "musical journey," like "riding down an energy stream and looking at the sparkling lights along the way."

I had never been a fan of Rachmaninoff's music. I'd avoided it for years as sentimental. But I decided to listen to the Adagio of the Second Symphony to see what George was talking about.

Lying down to hear to the music, I became aware that my lower jaw was extremely tight. This tension had been present for weeks. In my determination to get through my difficulties, I'd somehow forgotten how to smile, as if my brain didn't have access to those muscles of my face any longer. But I didn't know this until after I'd finished listening to Rachmaninoff's music. At that point, not only was the tension gone from my jaw, but I also found myself able to smile again. How strange, new, and wonderful it felt to be able to do so!

My heart had apparently been frozen, and Rachmaninoff's music melted it. This was not the most dramatic of my TMEs, but it made me a fan of Rachmaninoff.

My performance artist friend Beth, who had the Puccini-induced TME that I described in chapter 3, once told me about what she called a "transmission of healing" through listening to music that touched her heart. She had been listening to a song called "Father, Father," by our mutual friend Stephen Katz (b. 1956), from his 1991 self-produced album *First Person Singular.* The song expresses the love that Stephen feels for each member of his family.

Beth said that after her father died, she was so stricken with grief that she felt cut off from the love of her family. Old wounds resurfaced. But Stephen's song allowed her to open her heart "in a particular way" that allowed her to "repattern" her feelings, making it possible for her to mourn her father's death. Through listening to "Father, Father" multiple times while crying and dancing to it, she was "doing the work" of healing herself, moving from feeling wounded by her family to forgiving and loving them.

Beth's heart, too, was unfrozen by music that targeted the fourth center. In the yoga of listening, such music teaches us how to love. The three levels of this center are *pathos, yearning,* and *elation.* Its crisis point is *delirium.*

Pathos (Lower 4)

The word *pathos* means "suffering" in Greek. After the tension, agitation, passionate eruptions, and violence of the third center comes an emotional reaction to the resulting tragedy.

Pathos in art tends to arouse feelings of sympathy, pity, or tenderness in an audience. Music that expresses a sense of deep sadness, melancholy, depression, or despair is lower 4 music. Such music arises when the fatelike obstacles to becoming ourselves presented by the third center cannot be entirely overcome by the desire for union that corresponds to the fourth. Instead, these obstacles overcome the possibility of love itself—just as, in Shakespeare's *Romeo and Juliet,* the love of the title characters is overcome by the feud between their families.

Shakespeare's play has been a favorite of classical and modern composers because it offers such rich opportunities for the musical expression of third center tragedy and fourth center pathos. Berlioz, Tchaikovsky, Prokofiev, and Leonard Bernstein (1918–1990), in *West Side Story,* have all been inspired by it.

Lower 4 music may not only lament the loss of love, but also complain bitterly over the inability to attain love at all. The feelings of unlovability that developed, along with our sense of identity, in the third center, come to the surface and find expression. Instead of covertly acting them out in the dramas of flight and pursuit typical of the third center, we acknowledge them as our own and share them with others. Through the sympathetic response of other people, we're able to begin the process of healing our sense of separation from others. Torch songs, which lament the loss of love, can often serve this purpose.

The pathos expressed by lower 4 music need not be only for lost love. The complaining, melancholy, or depression associated with many blues songs indicates that they, too, are examples of lower 4 music. In the Madonna song "Papa Don't Preach," from her 1990 anthology of greatest hits *The Immaculate Collection*, the singer takes on the character of a teenage girl who has just discovered that she's pregnant, thereby eliciting the pathos of lower 4.[7]

Many jazz standards target lower 4—for example, "Solitude," as sung by Billie Holiday.[8] Two jazz instrumentals that target lower 4 are Miles Davis's "Générique," from his 1958 *Ascenseur pour l'echafaud* (*Lift to the Scaffold*, a.k.a., *Elevator to the Gallows* and *Frantic*);[9] and "Naima" by John Coltrane, from his 1960 album *Giant Steps*.[10] "Naima" is an example of melancholy, which falls between the pathos of lower 4 and the yearning of middle 4.

The Beatles classic "Yesterday," from their 1966 album *Yesterday and Today*, full of nostalgia for lost love, is also an example of lower 4 pathos.[11]

A good example of lower 4 music from the classical repertoire is the melancholy first movement of Beethoven's *Moonlight* Sonata (Piano Sonata No. 14 in C-sharp Minor, Op. 27, No. 2).

In the yoga of listening, the pathos of lower 4 teaches us how to grieve for lost love or a lost loved one.

Yearning (Middle 4)

Unhappy love songs are typical of lower 4, but bittersweet love songs are typical of middle 4. Bittersweet love songs express a yearning for love that has elements of both pathos *and* elation.

The music of middle 4 wants to open the heart up to love and communicate its joy more fully, but also expresses anxieties and doubts about doing so. These doubts arise from fear either of losing oneself in one's beloved (identity overcome by union) or of losing or being ignored or rejected by one's beloved.

Some middle 4 songs alternate between joy and doubt one phrase at a time. Others convey both feelings simultaneously. Middle 4 music can communicate both the poignant blessing of new love and the impassioned wistfulness of a doubting lover. These feelings are expressed in the Schumann lied mentioned previously, "Im wundershönen Monat Mai."

The majority of jazz standards that deal with love target the yearning of middle 4: "The Man I Love," "Night and Day," "The Very Thought of You," and "You Go to My Head," to name a few. I especially like Billie Holiday's soulful renditions of these tunes.

In instrumental jazz, Coltrane's "Central Park West" is a good example of middle 4 yearning.

The Beatles songs "Michelle" and "Something" also target middle 4.[12] Just as with jazz standards, the repertoire of pop songs that deal with yearning for love is huge. Such yearning, for example, appears in "Time after Time," by Cyndi Lauper (b. 1953), from her 1983 album *She's So Unusual*.[13] I also know this song in a moving instrumental rendition by Miles Davis.

Madonna's song "Rescue Me" captures the yearning of middle 4. "Cherish" still contains yearning, but is more on the elation side of middle 4.

In classical music, an example of middle 4 yearning is the second movement of Beethoven's *Pathétique* Sonata (Piano Sonata No. 8 in C Minor, Op. 13).

The middle section of "Jupiter, the Bringer of Jollity," from Holst's *The Planets*, also targets the yearning of middle 4. Its expansive, folk-song-like melody has a slightly melancholy cast that makes it bittersweet, the hallmark of middle 4. (The more boisterous beginning of the movement, as we shall see in the next chapter, is an example of fifth center music, which does indeed involve jollity.)

In the yoga of listening, the music of middle 4 teaches us how to achieve the difficult, bittersweet balance between pathos and elation. On one side are past experiences of hurt and disappointment, our present melancholy, fear of rejection, doubts about our lovability. On the other are the possibilities of healing and satisfaction, our future happiness, hopes for acceptance, belief in our ability to love and be loved. We have to learn to live with both the bitter and the sweet, so that the heart neither breaks from past pain nor bursts from encountering a potential joy.

Elation (Upper 4)

At the upper end of the fourth center, love undergoes a transformation. Less conditioned by feelings of unlovability, it becomes more joyous, free of inner and outer obstacles to expression. It *celebrates* the experience of union, instead of simply yearning for it. According to Swami Satyananda, when the heart chakra is awakened, "we have a sublime relationship with God, with our family members and with every being."[14]

The feeling that goes along with this "sublime relationship" is elation. Any happy love song expresses it, as contentment or gratitude for the love of another or ecstatic ardor.

Because upper 4 music is already beginning to shade into the sense of well-being associated with the fifth center, it can sometimes be difficult to tell the difference between the elation of upper 4 and the contentment of lower 5. Many popular rock songs fall into this anomalous category. The lyrics often profess love, but the rhythm is bouncy and danceable, a characteristic of fifth center music.

Along the whole of the continuum of human potential, the more abstract the feeling, the higher the center. The movement from the lowest to the highest center is from subjective and personal to objective and universal. Thus, if the lyrics are about the love of a specific individual, the song is rooted in upper 4. If the lyrics are about the feeling of love in general, the song may be emanating from a higher center. Brotherly love, for example, may express itself through the fifth center. Even more abstract and universal is the love of humanity, which expresses itself through the seventh center.

The Billy Joel song that I mentioned previously, "The Longest Time," is a good example of the elation of upper 4 music, even though it contains two moments of doubtful yearning, when it goes from major to minor.[15] Early in their career, the Beatles produced many tunes that targeted upper 4, among them: "And I Love Her," "Eight Days a Week," and "She Loves You."

The Madonna song "Like a Prayer" also targets the elation of upper 4, as does the Billie Holiday standard "I've Got My Love to Keep Me Warm."

In classical music, a good example of this upper 4 elation occurs in the eighteenth variation of Rachmaninoff's Rhapsody on a Theme by Paganini. This variation comes about fifteen minutes into the piece and provides a two-and-a-half-minute dose of radiant human love. (The other two examples of fourth center music by Rachmaninoff mentioned previously, the second movement of the Second Piano Concerto and the third movement of the Second Symphony, move freely between each of the levels of the fourth center.)

In the yoga of listening, the lesson of upper 4 elation is that of opening our hearts to experience more love than we've ever felt before. Allowing our frozen hearts to be heated and opened up by music can seem safer than doing so with another human being. But once our hearts are open again, we may feel more able to make the experiment of keeping them open with those we love. Then we can pass on to others the healing we've received from listening to the heart-opening music of the fourth center.

Delirium (Crisis Point)

When the elation of upper 4 gets out of control, it turns into erotic or lovesick delirium. Here the desire for union threatens to destroy one or the other, or both, of a pair of lovers, and may even threaten the stability of the community that surrounds them. Erotic delirium needs to be brought under control by the next higher center, the fifth, which has to do with our social selves.

I've used the phrase "eruption of passion" to describe upper 3 music. I was referring to anger rather than erotic passion. An eruption of erotic passion is more characteristic of the crisis point between the fourth and fifth centers.

Some popular music is saturated with sexuality in the lyrics and an elation bordering on delirium in the instrumental background, which makes full use of the entrainment of the first center, the sensuality of the second, the passionate intensity of the third, and the emotional expressiveness of the fourth. When such music attempts to portray erotic passion, it targets the crisis point between the fourth and fifth centers. Examples are the Madonna song "Justify My Love" and two songs by the Irish rock band U2: "Two Hearts Beat as One," from their 1983 album *War*, and "Desire" from their 1988 album *Rattle and Hum*.[16] The former deals with an obsessive and socially condemned love, the latter with an intensifying erotic obsession.

Flamenco and tango can often express erotic delirium. But the act of channeling such passion into dancing brings it under control, as the life force behind it breaks through the crisis point and achieves the fifth center, which is targeted by most dance music.

In opera, the foremost example of music that targets the crisis point of erotic delirium is the second scene of Act II of Wagner's *Tristan und Isolde*, in which the forbidden love of the title characters goes beyond social and personal propriety as they seek self-annihilation through physical, emotional, and spiritual union.

In the yoga of listening, the lesson of erotic delirium teaches us what happens when elation gets out of control, when we attempt to pursue and maintain it at all costs, including those that might accrue to ourselves, our beloved, and those around us. *Tristan und Isolde* is a complete expression of this lesson, in a way that few pop songs, no matter how deliriously passionate, could ever be.

A Musical Tour of the Fourth Center

At this point, if you would like to take a pop-song-based tour of the fourth center, you could create a playlist of your own from the examples already given. An all-Beatles tour might look something like this: "Yesterday," "Something," and "Eight Days a Week" will give you a sense of how the life force rises from lower to middle to upper 4. An all–Billie Holiday tour that achieves the same end might include: "Solitude," "The Very Thought of You," and "I've Got My Love to Keep Me Warm."

A Madonna-based tour of the fourth center that includes the crisis point would run like this: "Papa Don't Preach" (lower 4 pathos), "Rescue Me" (middle 4 yearning), "Like a Prayer" (upper 4 elation), and "Justify My Love" (crisis point, erotic delirium).

If you want to create a mixed-artist playlist that includes the crisis point, it might go something like this: the Beatles, "Yesterday" (lower 4 pathos); Cyndi Lauper, "Time After Time" (middle 4 yearning); Billy Joel, "The Longest Time" (upper 4 elation); U2, "Desire" (crisis point, delirium).

You could also mix genres: Miles Davis, "Générique" (lower 4 pathos); Beethoven, second movement of the *Pathétique* Sonata (middle 4 yearning); Billie Holiday, "I've Got My Love to Keep Me Warm" (upper 4 elation); and U2, "Two Hearts Beat as One" (crisis point, delirium).

Any of these playlists will effectively illustrate not only the qualities of the lower, middle, and upper ranges of the fourth center, as well as the crisis point, but also how the mood of the music changes as the level of life force rises. If you don't have access to the selections listed, but would like to get some sense of how music targets the different ranges of the fourth center, you may be able to use the Internet to listen to thirty-second clips of these selections wherever CDs or downloadable music is sold.

You can take a classical music tour of the fourth center, including the crisis point, by listening to the first movement of Berlioz's *Symphonie Fantastique*. The work as a whole is subtitled "Episode in the Life of an Artist" and consists of musical realizations of opium-inspired dreams about the composer's beloved. The second movement is called "Reveries—Passions."

The first ninety seconds or so of "Reveries—Passions" expresses the melancholy of lower 4. At the point when the violins begin scurrying along in a more lively fashion, the music moves briefly into the elation of upper 4.

Throughout the symphony, a recurrent theme that Berlioz calls an *idée fixe*, an obsessional melodic idea, which in this case represents his beloved, is woven into the texture of each movement. Its first appearance comes immediately after the moment of elation described previously. This tune is an example of the bittersweet yearning of music that targets middle 4. It soon gives way to the lower 4 melancholy with which the movement began.

After the fast section of the movement has started, about six minutes from the beginning, there's a brief moment of erotic delirium (crisis point), which is repeated just over a minute later.

An odd passage that occurs about two thirds of the way through the movement also touches this crisis point of delirium, illustrating lovesickness, one way in which delirium may be expressed. The passage has a queasy effect, as if the piece's otherwise strong sense of tonality is becoming unstable. You'll recognize it by the prominence of the oboe.

Shortly after this passage, you'll hear two outbursts of elation that last longer than the one in the movement's slow introduction. These outbursts represent the musical climax of the movement. They should give you a clear idea of what upper 4 music sounds like, in this case pushing toward, but never quite crossing over into, erotic delirium.

A Musical Tour of the Third and Fourth Centers

In classical music, Tchaikovsky's *Francesca da Rimini, Symphonic Fantasia after Dante*, Op. 32, allows you to tour both the third and fourth centers in a single work. All three ranges of the third center, plus the crisis point between the third and fourth centers, and all three ranges of the fourth center (but not the crisis point) can be heard in this symphonic poem.

Tchaikovsky borrowed the tale of Francesca da Rimini from Dante's *Inferno*. She and her brother-in-law, Paolo, carried on an adulterous affair. They were caught in flagrante delicto and murdered by Francesca's husband, Giovanni the Lame. After death, they were doomed to swirl around forever in the second circle of Dante's Hell, carried by the wind of their illicit passion.[17]

The first third of this approximately twenty-four-minute work unfolds entirely within the third center.[18] It begins with a passage of brooding chords (lower 3) that lasts for just over a minute, then gradually picks up energy, becoming increasingly agitated (middle 3). This agitation symbolizes the eternal swirling of the doomed lovers through Hell.

The music returns to lower 3 at about the three-minute mark. By the end of four minutes, it has risen again to middle 3.

There's an eruption of passion at the five-minute mark with the entry of the trumpets, which signal the music's arrival at upper 3.

Until this point, we've had only melodic and thematic fragments. Now the tragic emotions of the piece declare themselves by coalescing for several minutes into clearer melodic and thematic shape. The intensity begins to build and, at about seven and a half minutes, becomes almost excruciating, having approached the third center crisis point of violence.

The music falls back from the crisis point, however, returning briefly, at the eight-minute mark, to the brooding chords of lower 3. By the nine-minute mark, it's clear that we've broken through the crisis point into the next higher center, the fourth.

The lamenting cello melody that follows the brooding chords is an example of lower 4 pathos. It introduces the eleven-minute central section of the tone poem, intended to portray fond memories of the illicit love that the doomed couple Francesca and Paolo shared while they were still alive.

Table 8. The Fourth Center

Center	Chakra	Range	Dream Character	Lesson	Musical Element
Fourth: Expression	Heart	Emotional/Feeling	Anima/Animus	Union	Melody

Table 9. A Fourth Center Playlist

Center	Level	Characteristic	Musical Genres and Examples
Fourth: Expression	Lower 4	Pathos	Classical: Beethoven, *Moonlight* Sonata, first movt.; Berlioz, *Symphonie Fantastique*, first movt., opening; Tchaikovsky, *Francesca da Rimini* (beginning of middle section). Jazz: Coltrane, "Naima"; Davis, "Générique"; Holiday, "Solitude." Pop/Rock: Beatles, "Yesterday"; Madonna, "Papa Don't Preach."
	Middle 4	Yearning	Classical: Beethoven, *Pathétique* Sonata, second movt.; Berlioz, *Symphonie Fantastique*, first movt., *idée fixe* theme; Holst, "Jupiter" (middle section); Tchaikovsky, *Francesca da Rimini* (middle section). Jazz: Coltrane, "Central Park West"; Davis/Lauper, "Time After Time"; Holiday, "The Man I Love," "Night and Day," "The Very Thought of You," "You Go to My Head." Pop/Rock: Beatles, "Michelle," "Something"; Lauper, "Time After Time"; Madonna, "Cherish," "Rescue Me."
	Upper 4	Elation	Classical: Berlioz, *Symphonie Fantastique*, first movt., climax; Rachmaninoff, Rhapsody on a Theme by Paganini (18th variation); Tchaikovsky, *Francesca da Rimini* (middle section, climax). Jazz: Holiday, "I've Got My Love to Keep Me Warm." Pop/Rock: Beatles, "And I Love Her," "Eight Days a Week," "She Loves You"; Billy Joel, "The Longest Time"; Madonna, "Like a Prayer."
(Transition)	Crisis Point	Delirium	Classical: Berlioz, *Symphonie Fantastique*, first movt., various points (as noted in text); Wagner, *Tristan und Isolde*, Act II, Scene 2. Pop/Rock: Madonna, "Justify My Love"; U2, "Desire," "Two Hearts Beat as One."

The section begins with a bittersweet oboe melody, which sets the tone for much of the music that follows: middle 4 yearning. The climax comes at about eighteen and a half minutes, when the music finally settles on the elation of upper 4, for about a minute.

At the twenty-minute mark, the music falls back into the third center, touching briefly on lower 3, then moves into the agitation of middle 3 for the next two minutes. Just before the twenty-two-minute mark, we've arrived once more at upper 3. From the twenty-three-minute mark to the end, the music again achieves the almost unbearable intensity of the third center crisis point of violence.

Composers sometimes target the third center's crisis point to illustrate an act of violence, such as murder or vengeance. Such acts seem to be a natural outcome of the thwarted desire or constantly building anxiety associated with the third center.

Murder or vengeance results from a failure to see another individual as a person or soul. The murderer sees him or her only as an object standing in the way of releasing anxiety or gratifying desire. Only the ability to love that comes with the fourth center is able to prevent such violence.

The third major section of *Francesca da Rimini*, where it drops from the fourth center to the third, could be seen as simply a repeat of the lovers' doomed whirling in Hell. But just before the transition occurs, Tchaikovsky brings in the French horns. They play a brief strain of hunting or chase music (a long-standing musical and theatrical cliché), which lets us know that Francesca's husband has arrived on the scene. Thus the final section of the piece represents the husband's chasing down and murdering the lovers, an act that occurs when the music reaches the crisis point of violence during its last minute.

The place of Tchaikovsky's *Francesca da Rimini* and Berlioz's *Symphonie Fantastique* in the yoga of listening is a moral and cautionary one. In the case of *Francesca da Rimini*, the moral has to do with the danger and potential tragedy of pursuing an illicit love. In the case of the *Symphonie Fantastique*, the whole work, not just the first movement, deals with the possibility of purging obsessive love by means of musical creativity.

12

The Fifth Center: Well-Being

As with the fourth center, when I asked you to add to your playlist from one to three items in which your main source of pleasure was their upbeat quality, you may have had too many possibilities to choose from. Just turn on the radio, and whether you're listening to a classical music station that plays the music of Wolfgang Amadeus Mozart (1756–1791) or a rock station that plays the songs of Madonna, chances are that you're hearing the fifth center music of well-being.

Fifth center music like that of Mozart and Madonna is so popular because it inspires a sense of happiness. Such music has the capacity to lighten a heavy or depressed mood, which is its primary function in the yoga of listening.

When played in the background at work, health clubs, shopping malls, and dental offices, fifth center music creates a relaxed and festive mood. It can also aid in concentration, as long as its volume isn't loud enough to command our full attention.

The fifth center, or throat chakra, is the first of the pair of chakras associated with the intellectual, or thinking, range of the continuum of human potential.

It may seem odd that I've linked the pleasure of listening to feel-good music to the thinking/intellectual range of the continuum of human potential. Connoisseurs of classical music often consider feel-good music to be virtually brainless. The intellectual content of fifth center music, however, is covert. In a subtle way, such music educates people about social mores.

In Tantric scriptures, the throat chakra is sometimes referred to as the abode of the goddess of speech. For this reason, in both ancient and modern chakra systems, the throat chakra is often linked with communication. Throat chakra communication is involved less with expressing emotions (a fourth center attribute) than with conveying information about how we feel.

An example of this distinction is an emotion-based conversation with a partner about how one has been hurt by his behavior, versus an information-based conversation with a friend about the same incident. A higher level of abstraction is present in the latter conversation. As we ascend through the centers on the continuum of human potential, from first to last, the level of abstraction constantly increases.

The fifth center is associated with the dream character that Charles calls the Counterpart, represented by the best friend. By extension, this dream character represents all friendships and social relationships, from one's siblings to one's social set. Such relationships are based on a more abstract sense of love than that expressed in the fourth center. Fifth center love expresses itself in the feeling of brotherhood.

The function of the Counterpart is to resolve the conflict between separation and identity (third center), on the one hand, and attraction and union (fourth center), on the other. This resolution occurs in the notion of *life purpose*.

Each life purpose is unique, so it seems to separate us from the rest of humanity, representing the utmost in our differentiation from others and the development of our identity. Yet every life purpose is also an offering of service to humanity. It has the potential to lead us to a deeper sense of union (brotherhood) with others.

According to Charles, the ability to blend identity and union is one of the key lessons of our spiritual development. The trick is to do so without fearing that our individuality will dissolve while we're experiencing union—whether with a single person, humanity, or the divine; or that we'll lose our sense of union by focusing too exclusively on our differentness from others. Our life purpose is what allows us to blend identity and union in just this way, under the image of the Counterpart.

This component of the psyche reflects both our social and our work relationships—the friends, colleagues, and co-workers who support us in discovering and fulfilling our life purpose. Charles claims that our life purpose includes not only what we do to serve humanity, but also the ways that we develop ourselves as human beings, including recreational activities, such as dancing.

According to Charles, our life purpose is more than our career. It consists of the *lifestyle* we create through integrating the following modes of service: (1) service to the body (diet and exercise); (2) service to the soul (self-awareness activities, such as therapy, journal writing, or interpreting dreams); (3) service to the Creator (activities that develop our creative abilities); (4) service to the personality (activities that develop the full range of what it means to be human); (5) service to family (not just blood relatives, but the spiritual family of our closest friends as well); (6) service to humanity (this is what most people think of as life purpose, connecting it to the idea of career); and (7) service to all life (living in a way that has minimal impact on the environment and other forms of life on the planet).

Each of us has a unique configuration of activities related to these seven modes of service that will comprise our life purpose. The Counterpart dream character, or best friend, can reflect and support us in developing any of these activities.[1]

The product of combining first center embodiment, second center motivation, third center identity, fourth center union, and fifth center life purpose is a sense of well-being. When we've been able to achieve this combination of centers, by learning their respective lessons, we've greatly increased the amount of life force available to us from the soul. The result is a higher level of what Charles calls *willingness to be here*, by which he means willingness to be present in the body and on the planet.

Willingness to be here is both the result of, and the counterbalance to, fulfilling our life purpose. As I know from my own experience as a composer, the more willing I am to compose, the more life force is available to me from the soul for fulfilling this aspect of my life purpose. The result is a greater sense of satisfaction and joy, or willingness to be here.

When I channel that joy into activities that further increase my pleasure in being in the body and on the planet—hiking, camping, bicycle riding, attending a concert, or visiting a museum—I become even more willing to fulfill my life purpose. Whereas, if I do nothing but compose, day in and day out, my joy gradually diminishes. Pleasurable activities that further increase my willingness to be here must counterbalance fulfilling my life purpose, or I'll experience burnout.

Music of the fifth center enables the fulfillment of our life purpose by constantly reinforcing our well-being, or willingness to be here. At the same time, such music keeps us open to the friendships and social ties we need to support us in fulfilling our life purpose. When fifth center music has lyrics, it also often affirms the values that support our lifestyles.

Any music that makes people feel good is fifth center music. But the type of music most characteristic of this center is dance music, from courantes and gigues by Bach, to the hits on the radio that make people want to boogie.

The musical element associated with the fifth center is *tempo*, the speed of the music, which often has a strong effect on a listener's sense of well-being.

Tempo variations exist in music associated with the other centers as well. But with fifth center music, especially dance music, the *degree* of well-being expressed is a result of the tempo.

Classical Indian musician Ravi Shankar (b. 1920) had this to say about the relation of tempo to mood, not only in his own musical tradition, which makes use of scalelike modes called *ragas*, but also in Western music: "Each *raga* has to have its own psychological temperament in relation to its tempo, or speed." Thus, "the heavy, serious *ragas*" are usually "sung or played in a slow tempo." Those that are lighter in mood "are best rendered in a medium or medium-fast tempo."

Shankar continued:

> This relationship of speed to the predominant expression of the music also exists in the West and is quite obvious, even to a nonmusician. A joyful *raga*, full of laughter, could not be executed in a very slow tempo any more than could a playful scherzo.[2]

Some dance music, such as the so-called slow dance, is more expressive in nature. That kind of music belongs to the lower end of the fifth center. It's colored by its proximity to the expressive fourth center.

At the upper end of the tempo scale, the mood of many faster dances is more ebullient. Salsa and the music used in aerobics classes, for example, access the upper range of the fifth center.

As I pointed out in chapter 3, Cyril Scott emphasized the moral influences of music. Such influences are strongly at work in music that targets the fifth center. For example, in the previous chapter, I mentioned that the delirium of the crisis point between the fourth and fifth centers can be transcended through dance. I used the examples of flamenco and tango.

Many social dances, from tango to waltz to square, contra, and folk dancing, involve elaborate steps and gestures, as well as clearly defined roles for each gender. Such movements serve to tame, condition, or socialize physical and sexual attraction, as well as public displays of affection, from flirting to the deeper intimacy of long-time married couples. They *contain* the possibilities of passion or delirium, making them socially acceptable, while at the same time teaching and reinforcing codes of appropriate behavior between the sexes.

Social dancing and the music associated with it is a fifth chakra form of communication, transmitting personal and social values in connection with love and sexuality. Such values tend to be union-based.

The more anarchic, free-form dancing associated with rock music also communicates social values. These values have to do with throwing off social conventions and expressing oneself as an individual. They're more identity-based.

Like Cyril Scott, David Tame believes that a society's morals are determined by its music and expresses alarm over what he feels to be the deleterious effects of jazz and rock. Overemphasis on the individual's right of expression can indeed threaten the stability of society and lead to anarchy. On the other hand, Scott also decried the conventionality of English musical taste, which rejected his own music as ultradiscordant. Overemphasis on social values may support social stability but can also prevent progress.

Charles sees individual expression versus social acceptance as a matter of identity-based values versus union-based values. Both sets of values are equally valid, but they should be integrated with, rather than oppose, each other.

As I've pointed out, our life purpose allows us to develop a personal identity and, through service, a social one as well. Creating a lifestyle that supports us in fulfilling our life purpose allows for self-expression *and* social stability.

Fifth center music can also be a strong influence on social relations in ways other than dancing. The lyrics of much popular music tell the listener what feels good and why—including sex, drugs, love, rebellion, and dancing—while underlining these messages with the sense of well-being associated with fifth center music.

The close relationship between well-being and brotherhood or belonging means that the implicit message of such music is often: *You will belong and be loved if you do what we do.* Cultural groups, even whole societies, can be formed on the basis of what people agree upon as feeling good, as well as the methods they sanction for achieving that feeling.

When it's not about disappointed love (fourth center), country-western music is about family and other wholesome small-town, often Christian, values. The videos that accompany such music on the Country Music Television (CMT) network often dramatize or illustrate the values expressed in the music, creating a powerful social statement about what's wrong in the world and what to do about it.

Both the music and the videos act upon the fifth center. Their covert message is: You will feel good if you live this way.

Social mores represent a feeling-based intellectuality, as we might expect in association with the fifth center, which stands between the emotional expressiveness of the fourth and the intellectual rigors of the sixth.

Rock music, too, has a set of values and a lifestyle to promote, one that often rebels against parental and social authority. The values and lifestyle presented in MTV and CMT music videos couldn't be more different, and are almost diametrically opposed to each other.

The music of the fifth center may *seem* to be about feeling good, apparently a personal matter. But it's really about lifestyle: the choices we allow ourselves to make in order to produce the experience of feeling good. Such choices also involve the social group to which we belong or wish to belong—a group that shares similar motivations.

Charles says that values are beliefs that motivate to action. When a belief is about the actions we'll take to feel good, it creates a lifestyle. The music we listen to is often a reflection of that lifestyle, as well as a subtle proselytizer for it. That proselytization takes place through the communication aspect of the fifth center.

I once saw a subway performer who was using a programmable portable keyboard. The keyboard was producing a typical bouncy rock beat, over which the performer was playing happy-sounding chord progressions while he sang about joining up with Jesus and the Lord. The message was clear: You will feel good if you get religion.

That's what I mean by proselytizing. If you've got a product to sell or a lifestyle you want people to join, your power of persuasion increases when you back up your sales pitch with the fifth center. Advertisers who use music in the background of radio and television ads often choose fifth center music to emphasize the connection between feeling good and the product they're pushing.

The connection between music, feeling good, and belonging is the basis of the alarm often expressed by adults over the possible negative effects of popular music on their children. Yet, when I'm at the YMCA working out and listening to the lyrics of the songs played through the loudspeaker system, I often find that they affirm such basic values as the wonder of love and being in the body and the world.

Is popular music morally suspect or dangerous? Charles says that valuing social acceptance at the expense of fulfilling our life purpose can lead to what he calls the *cool disease*, which develops when we choose belonging to some in-group over developing our own identities and abilities. Under the influence of the cool disease, which many aspects of our consumer culture condone, we act, dress, and speak in ways that our peers—or advertisers—define as cool, instead of focusing on the more important issue of discovering and fulfilling our life purpose.

The cool disease is the downside of the tendency of TMEs to result in conversion experiences. If we and our friends accept as gurus a composer or band whose music we love, adopting their values and lifestyle, we need to make sure that doing so supports us in fulfilling our life purpose and realizing the soul's plans for our growth.

If the values or lifestyle we adopt contribute to our willingness to be here, they're probably fine from the soul's perspective. But if they distract us from, or block our ability to realize, the soul's plans for our growth, the soul will reduce the amount of life force available to us, resulting in dissatisfaction, unhappiness, or depression.

Drug and alcohol abuse are often associated with the feel-good music of the fifth center. Substance abuse has nothing to do with well-being or willingness to be here, which are based on rising levels of life-force flow.

In fact, substance abuse is the opposite of well-being and willingness to be here. Although drugs and alcohol seem to provide a temporary escape from mental, emotional, or spiritual pain, addiction to the feel-good states they promote may actually cause a gradual withdrawal from the world and even destroy the body. Luckily, we don't need drugs or alcohol to feel good. The right kind of music often is enough, especially when it induces TMEs.

TMEs associated with fifth center music are most likely to develop when dancing is involved. As I pointed out in chapter 1, psychologist Abraham Maslow said that dancing was often cited as a trigger for peak experiences by the self-actualizing individuals he interviewed.

Dancing to fifth center music combines feeling good with the first center's intoxicating rhythm and sense of embodiment, producing not just well-being, but willingness to be present in the body and on the planet. An ecstatic sense of willingness to be here is the chief characteristic of fifth center TMEs.

From lowest to highest, the levels of the fifth center are *contentment*, *joy*, and *exuberance*. The crisis point is *mania*.

Contentment (Lower 5)

There are so many varieties of fifth center music that it would take a whole book to do them justice. The examples that I provide here are for the most part from well-known songs, composers, singers, or groups, in the genres of pop, rock, jazz, and classical music, with a few others such as reggae and bluegrass thrown in for good measure.

In doing the research for this chapter, my appreciation for the depth and quality of popular music grew tremendously. But finding the right examples was tricky, especially in the case of songs with lyrics.

I'm amazed at how often the music in some pop songs targets the fifth center, but the lyrics are about something else. Sometimes the music says "I feel good" while the lyrics are full of complaining. Some songs set tender lyrics to bouncy rhythms, resulting in a joyful expression of well-being in which the poor love object doesn't seem to matter much.

I've learned that fifth center music can appropriate the expressiveness of the fourth center and still remain dominant. In a similar way, the analytic sixth center can dominate over the fifth center, resulting in bouncy upbeat music in which the lyrics complain about something. Such music is still about lifestyle, a fifth center characteristic. But the analytic sixth center is trying to determine what's wrong, what the singer isn't getting in order to be happy.

My research reminded me of an important lesson in the yoga of listening: The higher centers often subordinate the lower ones. As you'll learn in the next chapter, this is especially true of the sixth center. If you're wondering whether a song targets the fourth, fifth, or sixth centers, just remember this rule of thumb: If you can't figure it out, it's the sixth.

Even though the discovery and fulfillment of life purpose is the lesson of the fifth center, most fifth center song lyrics are about willingness to be here. Writing lyrics and composing and performing songs can all be aspects of life purpose, involving creativity, self-expression, and service to humanity. Why sing about your life purpose when you're already fulfilling it?

Fifth center music in which the lyrics support the fulfillment of one's life purpose sometimes occurs in musicals with themes such as overcoming all odds to achieve a goal, discovering oneself, or developing a career. All three of these themes, for example, appear in *Fame* and *Rent*.

As much as possible, the examples in this chapter come from a single artist in each genre who is able to target all three levels of the fifth center. The best way to tell the difference between these levels is through comparing how the energy rises as the tempo increases. Such comparison is more difficult with single tunes from a variety of artists.

When listening to these examples, keep in mind that I'm not endorsing the morals or lifestyle they represent, or that of the artists who produced them. My only concern is to demonstrate the levels of energy that come through in each level of the fifth center.

Again, tempo is the major factor determining which level of the fifth center is being accessed. Slower feel-good music, targeting lower 5, expresses contentment, a relaxed and mellow sense of well-being. The tempo of such music usually ranges from eighty-four to ninety-six beats per minute.

Slow dances, such as the ländler of Schubert (a slower ancestor of the waltz), mentioned in chapter 4, often express lower 5 contentment. So does reggae, for example, the song "Roots, Rock, Reggae" by Bob Marley (1945–1981), from his 1976 album *Rastaman Vibration.*[3] As we might expect, the lyrics are about dancing and feeling good.

The Beatles didn't produce much fifth center music. Their songs usually concern love (fourth center), as we saw in the previous chapter, or social satire (lower 6) as we shall see in the next chapter. "A Little Help from My Friends," from *Sgt. Pepper's Lonely Hearts Club Band*, however, targets lower 5 contentment.[4] The lyrics are about how the lead singer feels or wants to feel. The languorous "Sun King" from *Abbey Road* also targets lower 5.[5]

The Madonna song "La Isla Bonita" is another example of lower 5 contentment, in which the lyrics express how good it feels to be in the exotic location of the title.[6]

"Villanova Junction" by Jimi Hendrix (1942–1970) is a hard-rock version of lower 5 contentment, without lyrics.[7]

Much jazz activates the fifth center. The mellow or cool variety expresses the relaxed well-being of lower 5. A good example is Miles Davis playing "Now's the Time," from *The Essential Miles Davis*.[8]

In classical music, a special genre of "pastoral" music often illustrates a relaxing day in the country or the well-being of shepherds or peasants. Such music usually targets lower 5. The second movement of Beethoven's *Pastoral* Symphony (Symphony No. Six in F Major, Op. 68), which portrays a brookside scene, complete with birdcalls, provides a good example of such music.

The third movement of Mozart's famous *Eine kleine Nachtmusik* (Serenade in G Major, K. 525), called Menuett, targets lower 5. Its mellow, relaxed sense of well-being takes the form of a slow dance.[9] The songful middle section of this movement reminds us that the lower 5 carries with it some of the expressiveness of the fourth center.

A similar pattern is noticeable in a song by the young bluegrass band Nickel Creek: "Out of the Woods," from their popular 2000 album *Nickel Creek*.[10] This song alternates between the mellow feel-good music of lower 5, especially in the solo instrumental sections that feature plucked strings, such as mandolin, bazouki (a Greek relative of the mandolin), and guitar. A violin solo in the middle brings in the expressive warmth of the fourth center. The lyrics are about imagining how good it would feel (fifth center well-being) to be in a relationship with a person one has a crush on (fourth center love).

As noted in the previous chapter, I've found that it's sometimes difficult to tell the difference between upper 4 and lower 5. The contrast between the mellow plucked string music and the expressive warmth of the violin solo in "Out of the Woods" makes this distinction clearer.[11]

In a similar way, the second movement of Mozart's *Eine kleine Nachtmusik*, called Romanze, helps to clarify the difference between lower 5 and upper 4 (along with a surprise appearance of middle 3 agitation).

The form of the movement is A-B-A-C-A, which means that the music that begins the movement (A) returns three times. These repetitions are separated from each other by the B and C sections, in which Mozart presents contrasting musical materials. These contrasts are created along the lines of the third, fourth, and fifth centers.

The A section of the movement is expressive, affectionate, and tender, without yearning (upper 4). The B section is less feelingful, more abstract and spirited, though relaxed. This is the mellow sense of well-being of lower 5. The C section provides a brief, unexpected, descent into middle 3 agitation.

Joy (Middle 5)

Most dance music, whether rock, big band, jazz, country-western, or folk, expresses the joy of middle 5. Such music, with or without lyrics, is often intended to encourage our willingness to be present in the body and on the planet. The tempo of such music is faster than that of lower 5, ranging from 108 to 132 beats per minute, and often centering on 120. The joyous energy level of middle 5 music comes through clearly, whether you're aware of its exact speed or not.

The Beatles hit "Here Comes the Sun" from *Abbey Road* targets the joy of middle 5. "The End," from the same album, begins in middle 5, but takes off in other directions as it progresses.

Much pop music expresses the joy of middle 5—for example, the following songs from Madonna's *The Immaculate Collection*: "Express Yourself," "Holiday," "Into the Groove," "Lucky Star," "Open Your Heart," and "Vogue." Of these, "Express Yourself" merits singling out, since the lyrics offer lifestyle advice about a girl's valuing herself enough to expect and request the best treatment possible from her beloved.

Note that I've listed six Madonna songs here, but only one each in connection with lower 5 and upper 5. I suspect that a survey of the levels targeted by pop music will tend to reproduce the ratio implied here. When pop music targets the fifth center, it rarely ventures above or below middle 5.

The music of Jimi Hendrix's song "Spanish Castle Magic" targets middle 5 joy, even though the lyrics, which speak of flying to a place far away, have a visionary aspect that links them to upper 6 (fantasy). Music that targets upper 6 is often lighter and airier, sometimes making use of special effects that sound otherworldly. "Spanish Castle Magic" is more down-to-earth than that.

In folk music, "Smoothie Song," from Nickel Creek's 2002 album *This Side*, expresses the unbridled joy of middle 5.[12] This album won a 2003 Grammy for Best Contemporary Folk Album, and "Smoothie Song" got a lot of play time on the radio.

In jazz, Miles Davis's rendition of "Jeru" from *The Essential Miles Davis*, targets middle 5.

In classical music, the familiar first movement of Mozart's *Eine kleine Nachtmusik*, called Allegro, also targets the joyous middle range of the fifth center. Note that the title of the movement (also its tempo marking) means "happy" in Italian. Music with such a tempo marking often targets some level of the fifth center.

Exuberance (Upper 5)

Upper 5 music is characterized by its brisk tempo, which results in a mood of exuberance. Once again, the tempo is faster than that of the previous level, ranging from 144 to 168 beats per minute.

Salsa and aerobics music usually target upper 5. Swing-style, big-band jazz runs the gamut from middle to upper 5. Dixieland is usually an upper 5 phenomenon.

March music, such as that by John Philip Sousa (1854–1932)—"The Stars and Stripes Forever," for example—also targets middle to upper 5. The same thing is true of the ending of Tchaikovsky's 1812 Overture, with its bells, cannons, and air of martial celebration.

"Polythene Pam" from the Beatles' *Abbey Road* is certainly lively enough to qualify as an example of upper 5 exuberance. The lyrics, however, are humorous, which is a characteristic of lower 6 (wit). I could argue that the fifth center is dominant, and the humor comes in because upper 5 is approaching lower 6; or that lower 6 is dominant, and appropriating or subordinating upper 5.

There's no need to split hairs. Lining this song up with the other Beatles songs mentioned in this chapter will give you a sense of how upping the tempo increases the sense of well-being from contentment to (in this case) exuberant laughter. But remember the rule: If you can't figure it out, it's the sixth.

The Madonna song "Material Girl" not only exemplifies the exuberance of upper 5 music, but also clearly demonstrates the connection between fifth center music and lifestyle. The lyrics unabashedly describe, even gloat over, the material things that this girl demands in order to be happy.

The Jimi Hendrix instrumental "Jam Back at the House" (no lyrics) adds third center intensity to the exuberance of upper 5. This is a typical hard-rock pairing.

Folk music, especially bluegrass, often targets upper 5. The instrumentals "In the House of Tom Bombadil" and "Ode to a Butterfly," from Nickel Creek's album *Nickel Creek*, express the exuberance of this level. The title of the first of these tunes refers to chapter 7 of J. R. R. Tolkien's *The Fellowship of the Ring*.

In jazz, Miles Davis's "Compulsion," from *The Essential Miles Davis*, exemplifies the exuberance of upper 5.

In classical music, the fourth, and final, movement of Mozart's *Eine kleine Nachtmusik*, called Rondo, is more high-spirited than the first. Its faster tempo targets the exuberant upper range of the well-being center.

Mania (Crisis Point)

The crisis point between the fifth and sixth centers is *mania*. Exuberance has risen to the point of getting dangerously out of control. It needs to be brought under control by the intellectual and analytic abilities of the sixth chakra.

Some kinds of hyperfast dance music target this crisis point—for example, "No Time This Time" by the Police, from their 1979 album *Regatta de Blanc*.[13] The tempo here is close to 200 beats per minute.

In this song, the music illustrates the lyrics, which concern a manic or out-of-control lifestyle, one in which there's no time to do what one wants to do. Even though "No Time This Time" targets the crisis point of mania, it does so for moral teaching purposes, by warning us against such a lifestyle.

Manic music often requires extremes of instrumental and vocal virtuosity. In some cases, such virtuosity, rather than portraying mania as something to be avoided, demonstrates the inability of a composer or performer to move through the fifth center's crisis point into the next center.

Manic virtuosity can occur in any type of music, but is especially notice-able in improvised music in which performers pass beyond exuberance into sheer technical display. In some cases, the intention of the performers may be to work themselves into a state of ecstasy, a TME that will transport both them and their audience. In others, the intention is to impress or wow the audience.

Either way, performers run the risk of slipping into musical exhibitionism. For an audience, such exhibitionism may be neither sensually (second center), dramatically (third center), nor expressively (fourth center) enjoyable. It may seem more egotistical than exuberant (fifth center).

According to Charles, just about any expression of what it means to be human is valid, as long as it does nothing to prevent the growth of others through such means as torture, imprisonment, neglect, rape, or murder. From the soul's perspective, however, certain kinds of behavior tend to build up the ego at the expense of the soul.

Musical exhibitionism does exactly that. While it may be a valid human behavior, and even please some crowds, it does nothing to further the spiritual growth of the performer. It may even be misleading, in that it can tempt other musicians to abandon their growth in favor of building up their egos through the desire to impress audiences in the same way.

Musical exhibitionism is an abuse of the fifth center's joy at being in the world. Performers may delight in it, but possibly at the expense of the audience's enjoyment.

My image of musical exhibitionism comes from the first *Back to the Future* movie, in which the character played by Michael J. Fox grabs a guitar in a dance band during a high-school dance in the 1950s. He gets carried away with improvising in the atonal, heavy-metal style of his own time period, twenty-some years in the future, with a sexually suggestive physical stance and gestures that shock the happily dancing crowd into motionless silence.

In some kinds of avant-garde jazz and rock, there's no conventional musical structure or unity among the players. The manic improvisation of the entire ensemble often targets the fifth center's crisis point. Parts of John Coltrane's 1965 free jazz piece *Ascension* exemplify such music.[14]

Jazz record producer and spiritual seeker Joachim-Ernst Berendt has said that *Ascension* "is what the title implies: an ascension into heaven, from humanity to God, taking in both—the divine and the human, the whole cosmos."[15] He hears *Ascension* as "hymnlike, ecstatic music of the intensity of a forty-minute orgasm."[16] But he also admits the piece's "mad intensity" strains "the limits of the appreciable and physically tolerable"[17]—a characteristic of music that targets the fifth center crisis point of mania.

I hear the spiritual intentions behind *Ascension* during the first few minutes, which are sublime. But I'm unable to appreciate the "mad intensity" of the rest, which seems more like musical exhibitionism than a spiritual orgasm.

The two alto and three tenor sax soloists, two trumpeters, two bassists, drummer, and pianist on the album play as loudly and as quickly as possible for nearly forty minutes. Perhaps doing so resulted in ecstatic TMEs for them as performers. Berendt reports that Marion Brown, one of the alto sax players, said, "You could use this record to heat up the apartment on those cold winter days."[18]

Toward the end, the pianist, McCoy Tyner, comes to the fore with a solo that temporarily raises the music from fifth center manic chaos into sixth center order. The analytic abilities of the sixth center can often bring manic virtuosity under control.

The jazz-rock fusion guitarist and spiritual seeker John McLaughlin calls the exhibitionism frequently encountered in freely improvised music "indulgent." He says that to play such music:

> First of all, harmonically and melodically you have to know everything, and then you have to be a real big person, a developed human being. Only a developed human being would not indulge himself. But as an ordinary human being—and that's what we mostly are—you indulge yourself. It's not making music; it's self-indulgence; it's not real.[19]

Free or manic jazz can be exciting, even liberating, for some listeners, especially when a jazz ensemble temporarily allows the structure of a piece to break down into free improvisation and then return to structure. "E.S.P.," from the 1965 Miles Davis album of the same title, does this. The improvisational sections push the envelope of mania without going overboard. The analytic sixth center is also present, setting tasteful limits on the technical display.

Compare *Ascension* and "E.S.P." and you'll see that the problem of musical exhibitionism has nothing to do with free improvisation as a musical texture, only with the intentions of the musicians. The desire to impress or show off, as McLaughlin points out, is self-indulgent. That's what leads to musical exhibitionism.

The problem of musical exhibitionism is less apparent in classical music. Some of the great nineteenth-century and early twentieth-century piano and violin virtuosi were guilty of excessive and lengthy displays of technique when playing improvised cadenzas in concertos. Fortunately, this kind of improvisation has largely fallen out of favor.

These same virtuosi sometimes composed bravura pieces designed to show off their technique. Such music can also be self-indulgently manic, targeting the fifth center's crisis point—for example, the fifth, tenth, and sixteenth of the Twenty-Four Caprices for solo violin by Italian violin virtuoso Niccolò Paganini (1782–1840).

Bravura pieces such as concert études can also have the pedagogical intent of developing the technique of performers. The test is whether they're more fun to play than to listen to. When under the control of the sixth center, virtuosic music can be not only impressive, but also clever and entertaining—for example, Chopin's "Minute Waltz" (Waltz in D-flat Major, Op. 64, No. 1).

Because tempo is the determining factor of level in the fifth center, a performer intent on showing off can push an exuberant upper 5 piece into the crisis point of mania by playing it too fast. This, too, is a form of self-indulgent musical exhibitionism.

The remedy for musical exhibitionism is inner listening, which can put performers in touch with their souls and the audience. Inner listening as a basis for improvisation can result in moving and impressive performances regardless of speed and volume.

My cellist friend Stephen once experienced a performance-based TME induced through inner listening. He was playing his first gig with the Paul Winter Consort. The piece was called "Ballad in 7/8," a transcription by Paul Winter (b. 1939) of a piece by twentieth-century Hungarian composer Béla Bartók.

After the opening sections of the piece, several of the performers had a chance to improvise a solo—piano, percussion, and cello. There had been no time to prepare a solo. Stephen had to improvise it, with no instrumental backup from the other players.

He was nervous. The spotlight was on him. The other members of the ensemble had temporarily cleared the stage.

The spotlight made a dark space before him that seemed like a black pool of cool water. Stephen played a few notes quietly with silences between them. They seemed like drops of water in the pool, spreading ripples out into the audience. He got a feeling of perfection from this image of moving water.

As his TME developed, Stephen sat in silence feeling this perfection and that the audience had joined him in that feeling. Then he would play a few more notes. He felt that his playing was more visual than musical, as if he were making a painting. Every note seemed to come at the right moment in time.

When he returned to the opening rhythm of the piece, the rest of the ensemble came back on stage and brought it to a close. Afterward, during a break in the performance, someone who knew his playing well and had never heard him play that way before came up to Stephen and asked if his solo had been composed beforehand.

In the yoga of listening, when you're an improvising performer, the best way to create TMEs in yourself and an audience is through inner listening.

A Musical Tour of the Fifth Center

In order to learn about and activate the various levels of the fifth center, you could put together a jazz-based tour from Miles Davis's renditions of "Now's the Time" (lower 5 contentment), "Jeru" (middle 5 joy), "Compulsion" (upper 5 exuberance), and "E.S.P." (crisis point, mania). The value of this tour is that no lyrics are involved. You can experience the moods and energy levels represented by the music of each level without the lifestyle issues that so often come in with the words.

A hard-rock-based tour of the fifth center might include the following Jimi Hendrix tunes: "Villanova Junction" (lower 5 contentment), "Spanish Castle Magic" (middle 5 joy), and "Jam Back at the House" (upper 5 exuberance).

A tour based on the Beatles could include "A Little Help from My Friends" (lower 5), "Here Comes the Sun" (middle 5), and "Polythene Pam" (upper 5).

Madonna's *The Immaculate Collection* allows you to put together a pop-based tour of both the fourth and the fifth centers, minus the crisis point of the latter: "Papa Don't Preach" (lower 4 pathos), "Rescue Me" (middle 4 yearning), "Like a Prayer" (upper 4 elation), "Justify My Love" (fourth center crisis point, erotic delirium); "La Isla Bonita" (lower 5 contentment), "Into the Groove" (middle 5 joy), and "Material Girl" (upper 5 exuberance).

A folk-based tour of the fifth center might include Nickel Creek's "Out of the Woods" (lower 5 contentment), "Smoothie Song" (middle 5 joy), and either "In the House of Tom Bombadil" or "Ode to a Butterfly" (upper 5 exuberance).

For the sake of completeness, the Police tune "No Time This Time" could be added to any of the above tours to represent the crisis point of mania. Any number of cross-artist and cross-genre tours are also possible.

During classical music's Baroque period (ca. 1600–1750), composers often compiled suites of dances in various tempos. Bach's French and English Suites for keyboard, and his six Suites for cello solo are well-known examples of the type. Within these suites, some dances access lower 5 (Allemande), some middle 5 (Menuet, Gavotte), and some upper 5 (Courante, Bourée, Gigue). The slow Sarabande is often more songlike than dancelike and usually targets the fourth center.

Like the second movement of Mozart's *Eine kleine Nachtmusik*, the "Jupiter" movement from Holst's *The Planets* accesses several levels in the fifth center and one in the fourth. The exhilarating opening fanfares touch upon upper 5 (exuberance). They give way to a rambunctious tune that those who like to tap their toes or nod their heads in time to the music may find irresistible—still in upper 5.

A slower, dancelike section expresses the more restrained, mellower sense of well-being of lower 5 (contentment). Slower still, a folk-like tune in the middle of the piece, solemn and wistful, targets the bittersweet expressiveness of middle 4 (yearning).

These centers and their associated music return as the piece progresses. Note that the difference in tempo between them is largely what determines their place on the continuum of human potential.

The second movement of Berlioz's *Symphonie Fantastique*, entitled "A Ball," runs the gamut of the fifth center. It begins, however, with middle 3 agitation. Strong feeling is present but hasn't yet declared itself as passion.

The main waltz tune that develops from the introduction targets lower 5 (contentment). Note the slightly melancholy cast of the tune, an indication that lower 5 shares some of the expressiveness of the fourth center. The same is true of the next major section, in which the *idée fixe* that I mentioned in the previous chapter is absorbed into the waltz.

When the waltz theme that began the movement returns, however, it's played at a somewhat faster tempo. Note how this change of speed reduces the melancholy elements in the tune and increases the joyous ones. Now we're in middle 5 (joy).

There are two further increases in tempo as the piece progresses. The first ratchets up the music into the exuberance of upper 5, and the second carries

Table 10. The Fifth Center

Center	Chakra	Range	Dream Character	Lesson	Musical Element
Fifth: Well-being	Throat	Intellectual/Thinking	Counterpart	Life Purpose	Tempo

Table 11. A Fifth Center Playlist

Center	Level	Characteristic	Musical Genres and Examples
Fifth: Well-being	Lower 5	Contentment	Classical: Beethoven, Sixth Symphony, second movt.; Berlioz, *Symphonie Fantastique*, second movt., waltz theme and *idée fixe*; Holst, "Jupiter," second theme; Mozart, *Eine kleine Nachtmusik*; third movt. Folk: Nickel Creek, "Out of the Woods." Jazz: Davis, "Now's the Time"; mellow or cool jazz. Pop/Rock: Beatles, "A Little Help from My Friends," "Sun King"; Hendrix, "Villanova Junction"; Madonna, "Isla Bonita"; Marley, "Roots, Rock, Reggae."
	Middle 5	Joy	Classical: Berlioz, *Symphonie Fantastique*, second movt., return of waltz theme (first tempo change); Mozart, *Eine kleine Nachtmusik*, first movt. Folk: Nickel Creek, "Smoothie Song." Jazz: Davis, "Jeru"; Swing. Pop/Rock: Beatles, "The End" (beginning), "Here Comes the Sun"; Hendrix, "Spanish Castle Magic"; Madonna, "Express Yourself," "Holiday," "Into the Groove," "Lucky Star," "Open Your Heart," and "Vogue."
	Upper 5	Exuberance	Classical: Berlioz, *Symphonie Fantastique*, second movt., second tempo change; Holst, "Jupiter," opening and first theme; Mozart, *Eine kleine Nachtmusik*, fourth movt.; Sousa, "The Stars and Stripes Forever"; Tchaikovsky, 1812 Overture (ending). Folk: Nickel Creek, "In the House of Tom Bombadil," "Ode to a Butterfly." Jazz: Davis, "Compulsion"; Dixieland. Pop/Rock: Beatles, "Polythene Pam"; Hendrix, "Jam Back at the House"; Madonna, "Material Girl"; aerobics music; salsa.
(Transition)	Crisis Point	Mania	Classical: Berlioz, *Symphonie Fantastique*, second movt., third tempo change, and ending; Paganini, Caprices 5, 10, and 16. Jazz: Coltrane, *Ascension* (parts); Davis, "E.S.P"; free jazz; exhibitionistic improvisation. Pop/Rock: The Police: "No Time This Time"; exhibitionistic improvisation.

it into the manic range of the crisis point. A poignant moment of yearning, more expressive, quieter, in a much slower tempo, brings back the *idée fixe*, shifting the music into middle 4 (yearning). The end of the movement once again returns to the crisis point.

Note how the virtuosity of the violins, which seem to be playing as fast as possible, helps to create the effect of mania. Berlioz's intention is to represent the feverish opium dreams of an artist obsessed with his beloved. Thus the manic virtuosity of the end of this movement of the *Symphonie Fantastique* is justified by the dramatic program of the piece rather than being merely exhibitionistic.

13

The Sixth Center: Command

In music, the intellectual pleasure in how things are done arises when the sixth, or command, center is dominant. Pieces, songs, or passages shaped in especially satisfying ways contribute to this pleasure, which can arise from their formal aspects or from the way that a performer plays or improvises them.

A key element in this satisfaction is a feeling of rightness, inevitability, or perfection, a sense that the piece could only be composed or played in just that way. Formal pleasures are a characteristic of much classical music, jazz, and progressive and alternative rock.

In Sanskrit, the sixth chakra is called *ajna* or "command." It's associated with the brow, or middle of the forehead. This chakra allows for the transmission and receiving of telepathic messages, "especially those between the *guru* and the disciple"—hence the name. Known as the third eye in the Western occult tradition, this chakra is responsible for paranormal abilities such as remote viewing.[1]

Sri Aurobindo stated that the sixth center involves "inner vision." Opening it results in seeing "the inner forms and images of things and people" and allows for an understanding "of things and people from within." Such understanding can lead to clairvoyant vision.[2] This center is the second of the intellectual/thinking pair.

The process of abstracting feeling that began in the fifth center continues in the more involved intellectual work of the sixth. The lesson of the sixth center is *analysis.* Composers working from this center charge their musical materials with feeling, then manipulate them like variables in a mathematical equation, producing certain moods, thoughts, or inner visions in an audience.

The sixth center not only manipulates musical ideas, but also commands the effects of each of the centers below it. In any piece of music in which the mood constantly changes, often with uncanny rapidity, the sixth center is dominant.

Composers use the command center to impose their will on performers or listeners, supplying them with what to feel, think, and see. In this way, composers become gurus for their performers and listeners—in some cases for the duration of a concert, piece, or song, in others for a lifetime of enthusiastic performing and listening.

The sixth center is associated with the dream character that Charles calls the Delimiter. The Delimiter is the component of the psyche that establishes and dissolves the parameters (or limitations) that affect our growth in the world. For example, when we've set goals for ourselves and decided on the steps necessary to achieve them, we've established the parameters of our growth and imposed limits on ourselves. We're acting under the influence of the Delimiter.

As I've pointed out, the first center involves our physical embodiment. The second triggers our motivation to grow through desires, needs, and the pleasure of their satisfaction. The third develops our identity as we come up against obstructions to the satisfaction of our needs. The fourth resolves the pain of separation that develops along with our identity in a sense of union with others. The fifth blends identity and union in the discovery of our life purpose. The sixth helps us to fulfill that life purpose through the establishment of goals and limitations.

The Delimiter also enables the dissolving of limitations that may prevent us from achieving our goals. Such limitations can spring up as a result of the improper functioning of the lower centers.

For example, the intellectual sixth center can help us dissolve the rage that sometimes develops from within the third center when we encounter obstacles to the satisfaction of our needs. Dissolving that rage requires that we analyze the conditions under which it developed, then come up with a solution that allows us to break it down and get past the obstacles that caused it.

The Delimiter is often represented in dreams by an authority figure. In Hindu spiritual traditions, the primary authority figure is the guru.

Swami Satyananda points out that the sixth chakra acts as a mental and psychic "bridge" between guru and disciple, allowing for the transfer of thoughts from one to the other—especially spiritual directives, or commands.[3] The development of the sixth center also helps us hear the voice of the soul, the inner guru that guides our spiritual growth.

In music, the commands of the sixth center are given first as instructions in the score for the performers to realize. In performance, the realized sounds carry commands for the listeners to feel, think, or perceive in ways intended by the composer.

The sixth, or command, center is essential for the composition of music. Like the first center, with its musical element of rhythm, and the second center, with its musical element of sonority, the analytic sixth center is active in virtually every genre of Western music.

As noted, the Delimiter component of the psyche is involved in the creation and dissolving of boundaries and limits. Any creative work requires the establishment of limits in order to come into being. For example, the composer of a piece of classical music must choose the instruments for which she'll write. Such a choice imposes certain limits on the range of the piece and the technical difficulties she may challenge the player with. But this is only one of many choices that will limit and eventually determine the final form of the piece.

The sixth center is always active in Western music, sometimes more prominently than others. It coordinates the other centers, creating numerous subtleties of shading.

The sixth center can make itself dominant, subordinating the others, as it does in music with intellectual appeal. Or it can subordinate itself, making another center dominant, as in the musical examples in the previous chapters, each of which targets a level or crisis point of centers one through five.

The sixth center can share dominance with another center or attenuate itself, making its contribution to the music barely noticeable, as it does when the music targets the fourth center to express feelings and open the heart. Finally, the sixth center can attenuate or eliminate any other center, as it often does with the seventh and eighth centers, producing secular music that acts on the body, heart, or mind, but not the soul.

In the playlists in the previous chapters, in order to facilitate your understanding of how music targets each center of the continuum of human potential, I tried to use selections in which the dominant center was clear from beginning to end. If a selection targeted a point between the lower and middle range of the fourth center, for example, I usually avoided it. Unless otherwise noted, I also avoided selections in which the dominant center changes, or in which the sixth center's presence is strong enough to compete with your perception of the dominant center.

Nor did I list selections in which more than one center was equally strong, or in which the dominant center shifted from one moment to the next. In either of these cases, the dominant center was usually the sixth. But it would have taken several paragraphs to explain why.

For example, the presence of lower 5 in the Beatles song "A Little Help from My Friends," mentioned in the previous chapter, is strong enough to impress a sensitive listener as the dominant center. But the song takes the form of a witty exchange of questions and answers, not unlike a press interview set to music. Thus lower 6 (wit) is also strongly present.

Which center is dominant? In the yoga of listening, it doesn't matter. It's enough to note that both are equally strong. Knowing this may deepen your appreciation of the song, as well as your receptivity to the two centers in question.

If for some reason you have to decide on the dominant center, call it the sixth. As I've pointed out before, not being sure of the dominant center is usually a sign that it's the sixth.

The musical element associated with the sixth center is *form*. The creation of form may be rigorous and abstract, playful and imaginative, or merely clever. It often involves the exposition and development, through variation and transformation, of musical ideas or themes.

In *The Lyre of Orpheus*, novelist Robertson Davies playfully compares musical form to a business meeting: "The theme is announced, developed in major and minor, pulled about, teased, chased up and down dark alleys, and then, when we are getting tired of it," the composer, like the director of the business meeting, "whips us up into a lively finale and with a few crashing chords brings us to a vote."[4]

Our life purpose is like a musical theme. Just as we can learn to analyze a piece of music by following its theme through all of its variations and transmutations, so can we analyze each moment of our lives to see how the themes that make up our life purpose have impacted it.

The lesson of life purpose has two parts. The first is undertaken in connection with the fifth center. It involves laying the groundwork for fulfilling our life purpose. Fifth center music reminds us of the joy of being present in the body and on the planet and of the importance of connecting with others socially in order to support the fulfillment of our life purpose.

The second part of the lesson involves the sixth center, which enables us to establish the parameters or limitations necessary to achieve goals that pertain to the fulfillment of our life purpose. This center also enables us to analyze the ways in which the components of our life purpose weave together to form the fabric of our experience, like musical themes.

My life purpose, for example, involves not only composing music, but also writing poetry, channeling Charles for my own and others' guidance, and authoring books such as this one. Each of these activities, or themes, weaves through my life on a daily basis, sometimes at the forefront of my attention, sometimes in the background.

For example, this book brings together several aspects of my life purpose like themes in a fugue. In particular, it draws upon my experience as a composer, performer, and listener, my interest in yoga, and my channeling abilities.

The ability to keep track of these themes in my life as they weave in and out of my daily experience developed through listening to music, especially through listening to the ways in which composers manipulate their thematic material. This ability is developed by listening to music that targets the sixth center, with its lesson of analysis.

The levels of the sixth center, from lowest to highest, are *wit*, *invention*, and *fantasy*. The crisis point between the sixth and seventh centers is *irrationality*.

Because the sixth center is active in all Western music and composers use it to transmit their feelings, thoughts, and inner visions to listeners, it's possible to speak of three categories of composers: *entertainers*, who compose from lower 6 wit; *formalists*, who compose from middle 6 invention; and *visionaries*, who compose from upper 6 fantasy. The catchphrase of the entertainers is *Feel as I do!* that of the formalists, *Think as I do!* and that of the visionaries, *See as I do!* Each type uses the sixth center to express these commands in music.

Wit (Lower 6)

I mentioned Chopin's "Minute Waltz" in my discussion of virtuosity in the previous chapter. It's an example of the wit of lower 6 music, in which the potentially manic virtuosity of the crisis point between the fifth and sixth centers has been brought under control by the sixth, turning what could have been a brief but impressive display of technique into an entertaining commentary on both waltzes and showing off.

Any form of playfulness, cleverness, or humor in music targets lower 6, as in Chopin's "Minute Waltz." Another example of the wit of lower 6 is the pointed second movement of Beethoven's Eighth Symphony in F Major, Op. 93, which parodies the recently invented metronome by means of an exaggerated emphasis on the quarter-note pulse.

Much rock music takes the form of clever social satire and therefore targets lower 6. Many Beatles songs are of this variety. The lyrics mock social mores while the form of the song parodies musical conventions. For example, "Back in the USSR" is a parody of the Beach Boys, with words that can be read equally as an indictment of Socialist or American values. Other Beatles songs that target lower 6 are "Drive My Car," "Paperback Writer," "Lady Madonna," and "Penny Lane."[5]

Another example of middle 6 wit with an edge of protest is the famous solo electric guitar rendition of "The Star-Spangled Banner" by Jimi Hendrix.[6] The music of protest, when not merely a third center outpouring of frustration and anger, requires a degree of social analysis, and so is often a sixth center phenomenon.

Symphonies frequently include a movement called *scherzo*, Italian for "joke," which targets lower 6, for example, the lighthearted third movement of Beethoven's Second Symphony in D Major, Op. 36. "Mercury, the Winged Messenger," from Holst's *The Planets*, though not identified by the composer as a scherzo, is nevertheless an excellent example of the type: light, fleeting, constantly darting about from one musical idea to another. The chief characteristic of all sixth center music is its restlessness, how it tends to mimic the erratic movement of thought.

When composers first begin creating their own music, their motivation is usually a desire to express what they feel, influence our moods, or entertain us. They compose from lower 6 (wit), even if their intention is to target some other center. The creators of such music are entertainers.

I mean nothing disparaging by this term. Many well-known songwriters are lower 6 entertainers—for example, Madonna and Elvis Presley (1935–1977). The songs on Madonna's *The Immaculate Collection*, consisting of her greatest hits, target a variety of levels in the fourth and fifth centers, but have all been composed from lower 6.[7]

Typical reactions to lower 6 music and the entertainers who produce it range from knowing smiles to delight, amazement, and laughing out loud. Such music is often created by brilliant composer/performers, from the nineteenth-century violin virtuoso Paganini, the best of whose Twenty-Four Caprices for solo violin entertain as they cleverly extend the techniques of fingering, bowing, and plucking the instrument to the limits of playability; to the jazz-influenced Bobby McFerrin (b. 1950), who brilliantly combines so many unheard-of ways of using his body and voice to produce music, especially in his earlier albums, such as *The Voice* (1984).[8]

When showing off not only impresses but also entertains, it's more of an offering to the audience than an indulgence of the ego, and has therefore transcended the empty virtuosity of the crisis point between the fifth and sixth centers.

In the yoga of listening, the cleverness and wit of music that targets lower 6 help us make light of our personal problems and social ills, remind us of the importance of laughter and delight in overcoming heavy moods, such as depression, and, in the case of entertaining virtuosos, demonstrate the amazing things we human beings can do once we've discovered and mastered our life purpose.

Invention (Middle 6)

The middle range of the sixth center moves beyond cleverness to the extension and development of musical ideas into large-scale musical forms. I call this range "invention" to emphasize the high level of creativity, logical thinking, and serious intellectual play that goes into the making of middle 6 music.

The major forms of Western classical music target middle 6, from fugues like those of Bach to sets of variations on a theme, such as his Goldberg Variations, and the sonata form that composers often use in the first movements of symphonies, sonatas, concertos, and chamber music. Robertson Davies was referring to sonata form in his musical description of a business meeting, cited above.

Jazz composers or performers also target middle 6 when they base a song on variations or improvisations on a well-known tune. For example, John Coltrane's "Summertime" is based on a famous tune from the opera *Porgy and Bess* by George Gershwin (1898–1937).[9]

All musical forms that target middle 6 have in common the attempt to manipulate one or more musical ideas in as many ways as a composer can conceive or invent. TMEs induced by sixth center music often trigger or are triggered by an awareness of its form. Such TMEs may have a strong noetic element, involving what William James calls "states of knowledge,"[10] because of the analytic bent of the sixth center.

The following TME, which occurred when I was in college, was induced by listening to a recording of Bach's only six-voice fugue, entitled Ricercare, from *The Musical Offering*, a collection of pieces in various forms based on a single theme written by King Frederick the Great. Most fugues are made up of only three or four voices ("voice" here is the technical term for the number of musical lines to be played together simultaneously), so the work is a tour de force. Fugues usually target the sixth center.

Bach didn't specify the instrumentation for his six-voice fugue, which lasts about six and a half minutes. It's performed in a multitude of arrangements, ranging from a solo harpsichord to a string sextet or full orchestra. The version of the piece that I was listening to was for solo harpsichord.

The challenge in listening to this fugue is to follow the theme, announced by itself at the beginning, as it crops up in a variety of guises in each of the six voices. It's easier to do this when listening to multiple-instrument arrangements of the piece than to a single harpsichord.

Closing my eyes to listen to the music, I was surprised to see the score of the piece, divided into six lines called staves, one for each voice. Each of these staves had the usual five lines, closely spaced, upon which the notes appeared, as in a printed version of the score. But the score that I was seeing inwardly seemed to be more three-dimensional than two. I was not just looking at it, I was *in* it. The five-line staves were like bars on a jungle gym. I seemed to be physically climbing from one to another as I tried to follow the fugue theme.

At one point, I ended up on a staff in which nothing was happening for what seemed like a long time. That voice had temporarily dropped out of the fugue. For some reason, I was unable to free myself from this staff, to climb above or below it to another one where there was musical activity. I became frustrated, and even felt panicky, as if experiencing claustrophobia in a small, tightly closed room. Eventually, that line picked up again and carried me to the end of the piece, whereupon I felt greatly relieved.

Like Bach's six-voice Ricercare, "Uranus, the Magician," from Holst's *The Planets*, is an example of the invention of middle 6 music. "Uranus" not only demonstrates what I mean by musical development, but also teaches us how to listen to a piece thematically, thereby developing our own sixth center analytic abilities.

"Uranus" begins with the brass instruments. They state a musical idea that consists of four loud sustained notes—not enough to make a melody, and without harmonic background. To emphasize that the piece will be "about" these four notes, Holst immediately repeats them in the lower brasses, but in shorter note values. They go past twice as fast as they did in the first statement. This is one of the techniques of invention, or development, called *diminution.*

These four notes return in a number of guises throughout the movement. The fun of listening to this piece—an intellectual pleasure, rather than a sensual or emotional one—derives from spotting restatements and transformations of the original idea. For Holst, such imaginative play, or invention, constitutes the magic that he's trying to illustrate in "Uranus." The composer, as the master of such play, is the magician of the movement's title.

Most string quartets, concertos, and symphonies, when considered as wholes, target middle 6 invention—for example, Beethoven's First through Fifth symphonies, and Seventh and Eighth symphonies. The Sixth targets upper 6, as we shall see. The Ninth Symphony primarily targets the seventh center, as explained in the next chapter.

When entertainers have mastered self-expression and the attempt to amuse or move an audience, they begin exploring the formal aspects of music. Their focus is on the exercise of the intellect, perfection of form, and sometimes formal innovation. They compose from middle 6 (invention), becoming formalists. Again, I don't mean anything disparaging by this word. It simply refers to composers for whom the formal aspects of music are paramount, including the invention of new forms, sounds, and chord progressions.

Conservative classical composers are usually middle 6 formalists—for example, Dimitri Shostakovich (1906–1975), primarily known for his symphonies. The symphony, as a musical form, is highly appealing to formalist composers. The twelve-tone style of composition developed by Schoenberg, a highly inventive formalist, has appealed to many twentieth-century formalist composers, especially in academia.

Solo jazz musicians who improvise on standard melodies often are also highly inventive formalists—for example, Oscar Peterson (b. 1925). Many jazz composers and arrangers are formalists, or have gone through a formalist phase, such as Duke Ellington (1899–1974) and Keith Jarrett (b. 1945).

Much of the music of John Coltrane and Miles Davis is composed from middle 6. I've already mentioned Coltrane's "Summertime" as an example of middle 6 invention. Another is Miles Davis's performance of "Petit Machins (Little Stuff)."[11] The 1974 album *Winter Light* by the jazz ensemble Oregon is one of my favorite examples of middle 6 invention.[12]

The Beatles began their career as lower 6 entertainers. By the time they created *Abbey Road* (1969), they were middle 6 formalists, experimenting with different styles of songwriting and techniques of recording and performing.[13]

One sign that a composer or group has moved from lower to middle 6 is the tendency to link songs into suites, or to produce entire albums that are organized musically and thematically, as the Beatles were doing at this time.

Middle 6 invention is especially apparent in *Abbey Road*. The second side of the original LP was composed as a suite of interconnected numbers, rather than individual songs. On the CD, this suite begins with the seventh track, "Here Comes the Sun," and ends with the sixteenth, "The End."

As is typical of music that targets the sixth center, the moods and tempos shift restlessly, often drastically, from song to song, sometimes even within the song itself. The sixth center is commanding the other centers below it. "Here Comes the Sun," for example, targets middle 5 (joy), whereas the next song in the suite, "Because," targets lower 4 (pathos).

The invention of middle 6 also appears in the opening of "Sun King," which is a slowed-down and reharmonized version of part of the tune of "Here Comes the Sun." In another case of such invention, the tempo of "Polythene Pam" is the same as that of "She Came in through the Bathroom Window," but sounds twice as slow because of a metric shift in which the quarter-note pulse in the first song becomes a half-note pulse in the second.

In the yoga of listening, music that targets the invention of middle 6 pleasures the intellect while it develops our analytic, inventive, and creative capacities.

Fantasy (Upper 6)

Having mastered the formal dimension of music, composers often challenge themselves to represent other realities in sound. By "other realities," I don't necessarily mean other planes or planets—although a composer *could* seek to represent such realities in music. Rather, I mean realities that are not as intrinsic to music as the formal dimension is.

Thus the upper range of the sixth center, fantasy, embraces a larger chunk of the world than that of musical ideas and the feelings they inspire. Here, a composer attempts to create new worlds and present them to the listener.

The traditional musical forms, stretched to their limits by extremes of invention, begin to dissolve. The composer tries to do the impossible: to make the audience see or experience something that has nothing to do with music, for example, an aspect of the real world, such as the ocean, or a magical fairyland.

Anyone who has thrilled to the beginning of Wagner's Overture to *The Flying Dutchman* will know what I mean. Wagner portrays the surging ocean, on which the ship of the damned must sail eternally, by means of rolling chromatic scales in the lower strings. Such musical realism attempts to put us directly on the scene.

Beethoven's Sixth Symphony in F Major, Op. 68 (*Pastoral*), does something similar with its musical depiction of a day in the country, complete with bird calls and a thunderstorm. Although I've cited the second movement as an example of lower 5 music, the symphony as a whole targets upper 6.

At the other end of the scale from such musical realism are Stravinsky's *The Firebird* and Ravel's *Ma Mère l'Oye* (*Mother Goose*). These ballets are musical depictions of fairyland.

The element of the fantastic in such pieces is an indication of the proximity of the soul and its nonphysical reality. They remind us that in the music of upper 6, we're already beginning to feel the influence of the seventh center's expanded consciousness. We're standing on the threshold of what Scott called the ethereal realms, about to leave the human behind.

Stravinsky's 1913 ballet *The Rite of Spring* is another example of upper 6 music. Here the "fantastic land" that Stravinsky attempts to create is that of prehistoric, pagan Russia.

In note 2 to chapter 10, I remarked on the difficulty of coming up with pure examples of middle 3 agitation in *The Rite of Spring*, even though Stravinsky makes frequent use of it. As noted in this chapter, extreme changeability is a characteristic of sixth center music. With the exception of the sections cited in chapter 10, *The Rite of Spring* is so restless in its movement between levels and centers that as a whole it could only be attributed to the sixth center.

Stravinsky's 1911 ballet *Pétrouchka* involves a fantastic *situation*, rather than a fantastic land, in which the characters in a puppet show magically come to life. Musical evocations of magic and its results are also often upper 6 phenomena.

Between the musical depiction of the real world and that of fairyland lies the portrayal of nonmusical ideas or energies in musical terms. Although I've been using movements from Holst's *The Planets* to illustrate types of music associated with centers below the sixth, the intention of the piece as a whole is that of upper 6.

Various aspects of what it means to be human can also be portrayed by upper 6 music. For example, the early twentieth-century Danish composer Carl Nielsen (1865–1931) wrote a symphony intended to bring the four temperaments of the medieval medical treatises to auditory life. The four movements of his Second Symphony, Op. 16, reflect the choleric, phlegmatic, melancholic, and sanguine temperaments in turn.

Prokofiev's *Lieutenant Kijé* is a series of movements intended to portray the life and death of an imaginary soldier. Its primary focus is upper 6. The final movement, however, contains a tour de force of musical invention (middle 6), in which a lovely, slow, middle 4 theme, expressing melancholy yearning, is combined simultaneously with a jaunty, quick, middle 5 march.

Each theme maintains its sad or happy character, as if Prokofiev were commenting on the bittersweet nature of life, in which tragedy and comedy are sometimes inextricably entwined. As pointed out, the command center is capable of enhancing or suppressing any of the centers and levels below it, as well as mixing and matching them. Here, the command center has granted two other centers, middle 4 and middle 5, equal dominance.

Wagner's famous operatic technique of the leitmotif—the recurrent use of brief musical themes to indicate characters, things, and relationships, whether portrayed on stage, or referenced in the thoughts or sung conversations of his characters—is an upper 6 approach to composing. Any form of music intended to enact a drama or tell a story targets the upper range of the sixth center, including much film music.[14]

Modest Mussorgsky's (1839–1881) famous piano piece *Pictures at an Exhibition* (best known in its orchestration by Ravel) is another specimen of visionary upper 6 music. This music not only depicts a number of drawings by a deceased artist friend of Mussorgsky, touching on many other centers in the process, but also portrays the composer's thoughtful wandering from one drawing to the next in the exhibition itself.

I used the first two movements of Berlioz's *Symphonie Fantastique* to illustrate levels in the fourth and fifth centers. Yet the "fantastic" conception of the piece as a whole—an "Episode in the Life of an Artist," as Berlioz called it, comprised of opium dreams about his beloved—links it to upper 6.

The third movement, "Scene in the Country" is another example of the upper 6 attempt to turn a visual scene into an auditory one, including shepherds calling to each other across a distance on musical pipes, and the sound of far-off thunder. The nearer of the two shepherds is represented by the English horn, the farther by the oboe.

As with much other sixth center music, the lower centers are constantly being targeted, though often fleetingly, to create an auditory scene like this one. Such changeability can make it difficult, if not impossible, to point out to a listener what center the music is accessing from one moment to the next. That's a sign that the sixth center is dominant. Once again, if you're puzzled by the question of the dominant center in a piece of music, it's probably the sixth.

As noted above, a third type of composer works primarily from upper 6: the musical visionary. Such composers extend the expressive and intellectual possibilities of music beyond the development of purely musical ideas into other areas of life, including musical depictions of the real world or fantasy lands, as well as stories, ideas, or characters, as described above.

In classical music, Holst and Berlioz are upper 6 visionary composers, as is Debussy. Many composers of stage works, such as operas (Verdi and Puccini) and ballets (Stravinsky), fall into this category, as well as composers of symphonic poems, such as those by Richard Strauss (*Don Quixote*, Op. 35, for cello and orchestra, for example).

Much of the music composed and arranged by Gil Evans (1912–1988) for Miles Davis's 1960 album-length masterpiece *Sketches of Spain* is also visionary, a dreamy evocation of Spain through flamenco rhythms and folk melodies, inspired, like Debussy's visionary tone poem *Iberia*, by the sounds of Spanish festivals.[15] An especially clear example of upper 6 fantasy from this album is "The Pan Piper."

A jazz-rock fusion example of visionary upper 6 music is "A Lotus on Irish Streams," from the Mahavishnu Orchestra's 1971 album *The Inner Mounting Flame*.[16] I cited this song in chapter 4, as an example of what Cyril Scott meant by ethereal music. Its heart-opening aspects indicate that the fourth center is strong. But, as in Scott's definition of deva music, "All is enchantingly indefinite, between the notes, varied, yet in a sense charmingly monotonous."[17]

In popular music, the visionary phase often attempts to illustrate images and story lines from the Middle Ages, as in King Crimson's 1969 album *In the Court of the Crimson King* (excluding the first track, to be discussed later)[18] and the progressive rock band Genesis's 1976 release *Wind and Wuthering*;[19] or mysticism, as in the 1975 album *Initiation* by Todd Rundgren (b. 1948), based on the teachings of the early-twentieth-century esotericist Alice Bailey,[20] and Yes's 1974 release *Tales from Topographic Oceans*, based on Paramahansa Yogananda's *Autobiography of a Yogi*.[21]

Some Beatles songs express the visionary qualities of upper 6, such as "Magical Mystery Tour," "Across the Universe," and "Lucy in the Sky with

Diamonds." The latter is said to be a portrayal in music of hallucinogenic drug experiences. According to John Lennon (1940–1980), the song refers to a drawing by his then four-year-old son Julian, along with images from Lewis Carroll's *Alice in Wonderland.*

Visionary music began to appear in the Beatles' songs around the time of *Magical Mystery Tour* (1967), and was combined into a suite with formalist elements in *Sgt. Pepper's Lonely Hearts Club Band* (1967). Two years later, in *Abbey Road*, the Beatles were working more as middle 6 formalists than upper 6 visionaries. Had they not broken up, perhaps they would have mastered form at this level, then moved on to further exploration of the visionary qualities of upper 6. The progression from entertainer to formalist to visionary is noticeable in the careers of many classical and nonclassical musicians, including leaps from entertainer to visionary, and backsliding from a higher level to a lower one.

Does composing from a higher level of the sixth center produce better music than composing from a lower one? A long critical battle has waged over whether *absolute* music is aesthetically superior to *program* music. Absolute music has reference to nothing outside itself, and deals only in musical ideas, such as a string quartet by Beethoven. Such music targets middle 6. Many critics consider such music to be aesthetically superior to program music, which relies on extramusical elements to tell a story, such as a symphonic poem like Strauss's *Don Quixote.* Program music targets upper 6.

Saying that the visionary music of upper 6 is superior to the formal perfection of middle 6 music would force me into making specious comparisons, in which I'd have to rate a Wagner overture over a fugue by Bach. Yet many technical innovations that have expanded the expressive possibilities of music have been the result of visionary composers trying to do something impossible, such as portraying the waves of the Rhine in music, as Wagner does in the Prelude to *Das Rheingold*, an example of composing from upper 6 (even though the music targets the second center, as pointed out in chapter 9).

In the yoga of listening, music that targets upper 6 helps us to develop our imagination, visualization, and dreaming abilities, as well as clairvoyance, when it opens the third eye. Thus, in terms of consciousness development, upper 6 music may be superior to middle 6 music. Listening to upper 6 music prepares us for the expanded consciousness of the seventh center, explained in the next chapter.

Irrationality (Crisis Point)

The crisis point between the sixth and seventh centers, irrationality, involves the ego's fear of the soul. According to Charles, our egos have their origins in the soul. Yet, like rebellious teenagers, we want to have an independent existence, in which we're free to ignore the soul's plans for our growth.

At the transition between the sixth and seventh centers, the ego begins to feel the presence of the soul, whose guiding influence is distorted by what I call *transcendental fear*. Transcendental fear is compounded of two things: a sense of the soul's alienness and the ego's fear of losing its autonomy.

The ego's existence is strongly conditioned by the physical world of space and time. The soul, however, has its being in a nonphysical realm, in which space and time are experienced differently or are nonexistent. For this reason, we may fear the soul as alien, perceiving it as an evil supernatural power intent on destroying us.

The soul wants us to expand ourselves until we can see our lives from the soul's perspective, including the necessity of realizing its plans for our growth. We resist because we fear losing our autonomy and grounding in space and time.

Having gone through the development of embodiment, motivation, identity, union, life purpose, and analysis, however, we must be willing to expand ourselves beyond our groundedness in physical reality to continue our spiritual growth. We do this by willingly opening ourselves up to spiritual growth, making the transition to the expanded consciousness of the seventh center as we welcome the soul as our guide.

If we're unable to make this transition, we end up feeling threatened by death. We can have no sense of our immortality without accepting our relationship with the soul. Without this sense of immortality, we become anxious, tortured, and cynical.

The irrational music of the crisis point between the sixth and seventh centers can portray the soul as an alien and overwhelming presence, as well as express the agony we feel when the soul has withdrawn life force and guidance from us, because of our resistance to fulfilling its plans for our growth. Signs that the soul has withdrawn from us include feeling cynical about life, anxious about death, and fearful of damnation. We may also be filled with self-loathing and paranoia, which can lead to drug use, depression, and insanity.

The Beatles song "I Am the Walrus," from *Magical Mystery Tour*, is a relatively benign example of music that targets the crisis point of irrationality, one in which the lyrics seem drug-addled and make no sense, but the music is relatively normal, until the last minute or so. "Purple Haze," by Jimi Hendrix, goes a step further—both the lyrics and the music seem irrational and drug-addled.

Music that targets the crisis point of irrationality is often loud and dissonant, drawing heavily on third center intensity. It may also involve sonic distortion, achieved either through using one's voice or instrument in unusual ways, including singing or playing out of tune, or through producing bizarre microphone, loudspeaker, and electronic effects.

Such effects are prominent not only in Hendrix's "Purple Haze," but also in "Voodoo Child," another example of music that targets the crisis point of irrationality. "Voodoo Child" brings in the threatening aspects of the supernatural that Charles associates with fear of the soul.

In classical music, the fourth movement of Berlioz's *Symphonie Fantastique*, entitled "March to the Scaffold," targets the crisis point of irrationality by depicting the consciousness of a man doomed to die for having murdered his beloved. Saint-Saëns's *Danse Macabre*, which portrays a dance of the dead with death as the fiddle player, and the final movement of *Symphonie Fantastique*, entitled "Dream of a Witches' Sabbath," are also examples of the music of irrationality. Each deals with the supernatural and our transcendental fears of death and the soul in relatively benign ways.

Totentanz (Dance of the Dead) for piano and orchestra by Franz Liszt (1811–1886) and Mussorgsky's *Night on Bald Mountain*, another depiction of a witches' sabbath, are more threatening examples of music that targets the sixth center's crisis point.

Another type of music that targets the crisis point of irrationality, but without telling a story, as do the pieces just mentioned, is something that I call a *demonic scherzo*. Demonic scherzos are relentlessly whirling, pounding, often ominous and mocking dances. They sometimes show up as one of the inner movements of late-nineteenth-century symphonies, such as those by Bruckner (the second movement of his Ninth Symphony) or Mahler (the third movements of his Seventh and Ninth symphonies).

Demonic scherzos are usually loud and dissonant, indicating the presence of third center intensity. They can also be perversely exuberant, indicating that the fifth center (well-being) is contributing to the mix, though not in the healthy way implied by its name.

Demonic scherzos can be devilishly clever in how they distort the conventions of fifth center dance music, indicating that lower 6 is active, not as wit but as mockery. While listening to a demonic scherzo, it's easy to imagine devils, demons, the dead, or the damned dancing, indicating that the visionary aspect of upper 6 is also active.

There is no love, human (fourth center) or divine (seventh and eighth centers), in demonic scherzos, which depict the doubts, torments, and cynicism of the ego that refuses to accept the spiritual guidance of the soul.

The second movement of Beethoven's Ninth Symphony is an early example of the demonic scherzo, although it tends to fall away from the crisis point of irrationality into several lower centers—the wit of lower 6, the joy of middle 5 (in the Trio section that's flanked on either side by the scherzo proper). The demonic scherzo of Bruckner's Ninth, however, just keeps on pounding away.

Demonic scherzos also exist in rock music—for example, the King Crimson song "21st Century Schizoid Man" from *In the Court of the Crimson King.* After starting off in a middle 1 soundscape, the song targets the crisis point of irrationality. The sung portions are full of sarcasm and sonic distortion. The dancelike instrumental sections are demonic scherzos.

In extreme cases, demonic scherzos can target several crisis points at once. For example, the Nirvana song "Territorial Pissings," from the 1991 album *Nevermind*, targets overload (the second center's crisis point), violence (that of the third), and mania (that of the fifth), in addition to the sixth center's crisis point of irrationality.[22]

In the yoga of listening, demonic scherzos and other irrational music of the crisis point between the sixth and seventh centers help us to face and overcome our transcendental fears of death and the soul.

A Musical Tour of the Sixth Center

Given the examples already cited, several pop/rock musical tours of the sixth center focused on the Beatles are possible—for example: "Back in the USSR" (lower 6 wit), *Abbey Road*, tracks 7–16 (middle 6 invention), "Lucy in the Sky with Diamonds" (upper 6 fantasy), and "I Am the Walrus" (crisis point, irrationality).

A pop/rock tour of this center that emphasizes the difference between entertainers, formalists, and visionaries, including the crisis point, might comprise Madonna, *The Immaculate Collection* (lower 6); the Beatles, *Abbey Road*, tracks 7–16 (middle 6); and King Crimson, *In the Court of the Crimson King*, tracks 2–5 (upper 6), and "21st Century Schizoid Man," the first track on the *In the Court of the Crimson King* (crisis point, demonic scherzo).

A jazz-based tour of the sixth center that emphasizes the difference between entertainers, formalists, and visionaries, but does not include the crisis point, might comprise Bobby McFerrin, *The Voice* (lower 6); Oregon, *Winter Light* (middle 6); and Miles Davis, *Sketches of Spain* (upper 6).

A classical tour might include Holst, "Mercury," from *The Planets* (lower 6 wit in the form of a scherzo); Holst, "Uranus," from *The Planets* (middle 6 invention); Berlioz, *Symphonie Fantastique*, movements 1–3 (upper 6 fantasy), and *Symphonie Fantastique*, movements 4–5 (crisis point).

I've given sufficient examples of sixth center music in this chapter that other tours are possible, including some that cross genres. Stravinsky's 1910 ballet *The Firebird*, however, provides a tour of all levels of the sixth center, including the crisis point, in a single work.

When I was in college, my composition professor told me about a group of music majors at his alma mater that would periodically hold parties to get high on marijuana and listen, in darkness, to a recording of Stravinsky's ballet *The Firebird*. Why *The Firebird*?

As a whole, Stravinsky's ballet targets upper 6 (fantasy). The students at those parties must have responded intuitively to the visionary aspects of the music. I know of no other piece of classical music that works so strongly on the third eye. But drugs are not required to open the third eye. The music is enough.

The Firebird exists in multiple versions, including the complete ballet, which lasts about forty-five minutes, and a Suite that includes only the high points and lasts about half as long. I recommend listening to the complete ballet, which will prolong your exposure to the third-eye opening characteristics of *The Firebird*. These characteristics are especially strong in the transitional music between scenes, which has been eliminated from the Suite.

The wit of lower 6 is represented in the complete ballet by a section called "Jeu des princesses avec les pommes d'or" ("The Princesses' Game with the Golden Apples"), which is subtitled "Scherzo" by Stravinsky. This music is not present in the Suite.

While there are no fugues or theme and variations in *The Firebird*, the invention of middle 6 is present throughout. The ominous melody in the lower strings at the beginning of the piece returns in many guises, just like the theme of Holst's "Uranus, the Magician." These thematic transformations are more noticeable in the complete ballet than in the Suite.

The fantasy of upper 6 is also present throughout because the ballet is a musical depiction of fairyland. The music seems to wander through this imaginary land, as if taking it in visually. From time to time this wandering inner eye comes upon a scene or vision—such as the first dance of the enchanted Firebird—that seems to emerge from nowhere, as if crystallizing equally from the music and the magical elements of fairyland.

Such moments of magic, which resemble the lucid dream experience of seeing and shaping our dream reality as we wish, are easier to hear in the complete ballet than in the Suite. In the yoga of listening, the complete ballet music of *The Firebird* could be useful not only for opening the inner eye, but also for encouraging the development of lucidity in the dream state.

As with most music that targets the sixth center, the lower centers may become briefly dominant, sometimes in the evanescent turn of a phrase, at others for passages of some duration. For example, the lovely "Ronde des

Table 12. The Sixth Center

Center	Chakra	Range	Dream Character	Lesson	Musical Element
		Intellectual/Thinking	Delimiter	Analysis	Form
Sixth: Command	Brow				

Table 13. A Sixth Center Playlist

Center	Level	Characteristic	Musical Genres and Examples
Sixth: Command	Lower 6	Wit	Classical: Scherzos, e.g., Beethoven, Second Symphony (third movt.); Beethoven, Eighth Symphony (second movt.); Chopin, "Minute Waltz"; Holst, "Mercury"; Paganini, Caprices; Stravinsky, "Jeu des princesses avec les pommes d'or" from *The Firebird* (complete ballet). Jazz: McFerrin, *The Voice.* Pop/Rock: Beatles, "Back in the USSR," "Drive My Car," "Paperback Writer," "Lady Madonna," "Penny Lane"; Hendrix, "The Star Spangled Banner"; Madonna, *The Immaculate Collection.*
	Middle 6	Invention	Classical: Sonata form, fugue, theme and variations; Bach, six-voice Ricercare, the Goldberg Variations; Beethoven, symphonies 1–5, 7, 8 (as wholes); Holst, "Uranus"; Prokofiev, *Lieutenant Kijé* (fifth movt.). Jazz: Coltrane, "Summertime"; Davis, "Petits Machins (Little Stuff)"; Oregon, *Winter Light.* Pop/Rock: Beatles, *Abbey Road,* tracks 7–16.
	Upper 6	Fantasy	Classical: Beethoven, Sixth Symphony; Debussy, "Iberia"; Holst, *The Planets* (as a whole); Berlioz, *Symphonie Fantastique* (as a whole); Mussorgsky, *Pictures at an Exhibition*; Nielsen, Second Symphony; Prokofiev, *Lieutenant Kijé* (as a whole); Ravel, *Ma Mère l'Oye*; Strauss, *Don Quixote*; Stravinsky, *The Firebird* (complete ballet), *The Rite of Spring* (as a whole); Wagner Overture to *The Flying Dutchman*; Prelude to *Das Rheingold.* Jazz: Davis, "The Pan Piper," *Sketches of Spain*; McLaughlin, "A Lotus on Irish Streams." Pop/Rock: Beatles: "Across the Universe," "Lucy in the Sky with Diamonds," "Magical Mystery Tour"; Genesis, *Wind and Wuthering*; King Crimson, *In the Hall of the Crimson King* (tracks 2–5); Rundgren, *Initiation*; Yes, *Tales from Topographic Oceans.*
(Transition)	Crisis Point	Irrationality	Classical: Berlioz, *Symphonie Fantastique,* movts. 4 and 5; Liszt, *Totenanz*; Mussorgsky, *Night on Bald Mountain*; Saint-Saëns, *Danse Macabre*; Stravinsky, "Danse infernale du roi Kastcheï" from *The Firebird*; Demonic scherzos, e.g., Beethoven's Ninth (second movt.), Bruckner's Ninth (second movt.), Mahler's Seventh (third movt.) and Ninth (third movt.). Pop/Rock: Beatles, "I Am the Walrus"; Hendrix, "Purple Haze," "Voodoo Child"; King Crimson, "21st Century Schizoid Man"; Nirvana, "Territorial Pissings."

princesses" ("Princesses' Round Dance"), which is present in both the Suite and the complete ballet, settles for several minutes into the heart-opening, bittersweet yearning of middle 4.

Toward the end of *The Firebird*, the "Danse infernale du roi Kastcheï" ("Infernal Dance of King Kastcheï"), present in both the Suite and the complete ballet, targets the sixth center's crisis point of irrationality. Here an evil King, representing our fear of the soul, performs a threatening dance—a demonic scherzo.

After this dance, the King's palace crashes to the ground, signifying that the crisis point has been transcended. From this point forward, the music dwells in the seventh center, to be discussed in the next chapter. The "Berceuse" ("Lullaby") of *The Firebird* is an example of the sublimity of lower 7 music. The "Finale" of *The Firebird* brings the ballet to a conclusion in middle 7 nobility. These selections are present in both the Suite and the complete ballet.

14

The Seventh Center: Expanded Consciousness

Music in which the main source of pleasure lies in the sense of the sacred, holy, or spiritual that it evokes is seventh center music. When I asked you to construct your playlist, I suggested that you consider sacred music, such as Gregorian chant, hymns, and gospel music; New-Age music; or spiritually oriented jazz, such as John Coltrane's *A Love Supreme*, as possible sources of seventh center music.

But there are also many spiritually uplifting secular works that have to do less with God than the divine potential in humankind. These works, too, may be examples of seventh center music.

In the continuum of human potential, the seventh is the first of the pair of centers belonging to the spiritual and intuiting range. I call it the *expanded consciousness* center.

The seventh center has a Janus-like aspect. It faces two ways: toward the soul or God; and toward the human, seeing life on Earth from a perspective higher than that of ordinary consciousness.

Religious music, such as that intended for the church and to glorify God—Mozart's Requiem, for example—belongs to the seventh center. So does Beethoven's Ninth Symphony, which is a secular, though deeply spiritual, work, extolling the divine nature of humanity and the brotherhood of humankind.

Many masterpieces of Western music are so-called late works. Like Mozart's Requiem or Beethoven's Ninth, they were written toward the end of a composer's life, with full awareness of the body's mortality and a strong intuition of the soul's immortality.

Such music is often composed from the seventh center. It tends to encourage TMEs in listeners more frequently than works created earlier in a composer's career, which are usually composed from the sixth.

Similar experiences of transcendence can be gleaned from music of an expressly spiritual or religious intent, written at *any* point in a composer's life, often for the church. Hence music that targets the seventh center is divided into secular and sacred varieties, depending on the "direction" in which it faces.

The music of secular seven faces toward the human aspects of life, seeing it from the soul's perspective. The music of sacred seven faces toward the soul or God.

The seventh center is associated with the crown of the head, the traditional location of the seventh chakra. This center corresponds to the Witness component of the psyche, or memory. The Witness is in direct contact with the larger nonphysical consciousness of the soul. It has a soul-enhanced viewpoint on life in the world. The Witness allows us to experience and comprehend the nonphysical reality in which the soul resides to a greater extent than we ordinarily do. That's why I call the seventh center the expanded consciousness center.

Because the Witness is responsible for memory, the lesson it involves is *wisdom*. Wisdom is memory enhanced by both the soul's perspective on life in the world and the lesson of analysis contributed by the sixth center. Such wisdom, when accumulated during a long lifetime on Earth, is often expressed in the late masterpieces of the great composers. Yet wisdom can also refer to our receptivity to guidance from the soul or God.

Swami Satyananda indicated that the psychological classification of people as extroverts or introverts is also valid in yoga. The extroverts are those whose consciousness is primarily directed outward, toward the material world. The introverts are those whose consciousness is primarily directed inward, toward the source of being.[1]

As noted above, music of the seventh center may express itself in either a secular or a religious manner. The former, like Satyananda's extroverts, looks toward the physical world. The latter, like Satyananda's introverts, looks toward the nonphysical reality of the soul or God.

Using the expanded consciousness of the seventh center, composers can turn toward the world and view it as if from above, thereby producing the transcendent, secular, late masterpieces of Western music. Or they can look beyond the world toward the soul or the source of their being in God, thereby creating transcendent sacred music.

The function of the Witness dream character associated with the seventh center is to sum up our experience in the world. That experience has been analyzed in the sixth center. Now we begin making sense of it, in spiritual terms, in the seventh.

Intuiting the spiritual meaning or significance of our experience, especially as it pertains to our life purpose, allows for the development of wisdom. Such wisdom, though often nonverbal, is transmitted to us by listening to seventh center music, especially a composer's late works. When we're able to receive it, this wisdom produces a feeling of transcendence.

The Witness also looks beyond the world toward the divine, attempting to come into a deeper relationship with it, and imploring it for guidance. This is the purpose not only of our private prayers and meditations, but also of sacred music.

TMEs that develop in connection with seventh center music contain either an element of intuitive knowing, illumination, or spiritual insight, or a sense of opening up to the soul or God. When listening to seventh center music, I often have the experience of an inner opening and expansion, as if senses beyond the ordinary physical ones were becoming active.

Recently, I had such an experience while running errands in my car. I turned on the radio to listen to a local classical music station and heard a piece of organ music unlike any I'd heard before. Within seconds, the piece produced a TME in which I felt as if the top of my head were being lifted off, a sign of the crown chakra opening. The sense of expanded consciousness was so powerful that I wondered if it was safe for me to continue driving.

The piece ended within a couple of minutes, so I kept on going. I learned that it was written by a French composer I'd never heard of, Charles Tournemire (1870–1939): his Symphonie-Choral, Op. 69. Based on the few minutes of the piece that I heard, I have no doubt that, in the yoga of listening, it could be useful, like much seventh center music, for developing intuition and psychic abilities.

What caused my TME was the strong presence in Tournemire's Symphonie-Choral of macrorhythm, the musical element that I associate with the seventh center. This element is not likely to be familiar to most readers, even those who are knowledgeable about music.

In *Music, the Brain, and Ecstasy*, composer Robert Jourdain states that "variations in information flow create their own tensions and releases—a different sort of rhythmic accentuation from the mere variations in loudness that typically define meter."[2] By meter, Jourdain means the regular, slightly accented pulse that determines, for example, whether a piece is in march or waltz time. The former has a two-pulse (duple), the latter a three-pulse (triple) meter.

Ordinary music develops variations in information flow that correspond to individual musical phrases, sections, and movements. Thus the tension of a more active section might be followed by the release of a slower, more tranquil one.

In macrorhythmically composed music, variations in information flow take the form of a long gradual accumulation of musical energy (tension) followed by a slow or sudden dissipation of that energy (release). The effect is like riding rising and falling ocean waves. The alternation of peaks and troughs in these waves creates a much larger (macro-) rhythm than that of individual beats and phrases. Macrorhythm corresponds to the larger rhythms of both consciousness and the universe.

According to Sri Aurobindo, what moves people in a work of art is "the little vibration" of truth contained within it "that goes straight to the heart." Furthermore, "the higher we rise" in our spiritual growth, "the purer, the more luminous, vast, and powerful is the vibration."[3]

At a certain point, this vibration takes the form of a *"luminous sweep*, a sudden flood of light." This sweep "may not long remain pure in a work. It "often drops to an ordinary mental . . . level, for the movement of the work follows that of consciousness, with constant ups and downs."[4] These ups and downs correspond to the rising and falling levels of energy in macrorhythmically composed music.

Whereas music emanating from the sixth center enacts the restless whirl of thought, that from the seventh enacts the calmer ebb and flow of consciousness. Listening to macrorhythmically composed music is like riding waves of rising and falling intensity. But this intensity is without the turbulent emotional ups and downs associated with music that targets the third and fourth centers. In the seventh center, we've moved from what Cyril Scott called the human realm, whose music is full of emotional turbulence, to the ethereal realm, that of deva music, which is full of love for nature and God.

Music composed macrorhythmically tends to have organically developing, unconventional forms, rather than conventional ones, such as the sonata form that opens many of Mozart's symphonies, or the rondo form that closes them. Unconventional forms are characteristic of many late works, such as Beethoven's last five string quartets.

An example of seventh center music that both is macrorhythmically composed and has an organically developing form is the stand-alone orchestral piece called Prelude and Liebestod (Love-Death) from Wagner's opera *Tristan und Isolde*. I mentioned in chapter 9 that Wagner identified the opening of the Prelude to *Tristan* "with the Buddhist theory of the origin of the world—the troubling of the primal cloudless heavens by a breath that swells and swells and finally condenses into our visible world."[5] This breath is "Desire, for ever expanding and retracting, for ever seeking to realize itself and for ever being frustrated."[6]

Wagner was attempting to portray his intuitive understanding of how the soul perceives our world in terms of *energy transformations.* According to Charles, in the nonphysical reality in which the soul resides, everything is consciousness, which Charles defines as a living, nonphysical, information-carrying energy.

Our experience on Earth looks like a sequence of events to us. To the soul, however, it looks like transformations of energy from one form to another. Whenever we go through a process that allows us to move, say, from rage to inner peace, we've participated in an energy transformation. The purpose of these energy transformations is learning and growth.

There are many kinds of energy transformations, some of them incapable of expression in words. The whole of our experience in the world will eventually be processed by the soul as energy transformations. Dreams often show us that process in action. So does music.

Music is so important to us because it provides us with the closest thing we have to the soul's manner of experiencing the world: an intuitive perception of how we're learning and growing by means of energy transformations. Whether or not they're aware of it, composers encode their music—especially that of the seventh and eighth centers—with energy transformations.

When we respond to the music of the great composers by feeling moved or having a TME, the energy transformations encoded within it have transmitted to us some truth or spiritual wisdom about how the soul experiences the world. In this book, whenever I mention the use that a piece of music has in the yoga of listening, I'm referring to the energy transformations encoded within it.

In the Prelude and Liebestod from *Tristan,* Wagner portrayed his intuitive understanding of energy transformations having to do with desire. He wasn't dealing with desire as a single human being might experience it, but with the *archetype* of desire as the whole race experiences it: a transcendental longing for union with another individual, the soul, or God.

In the Prelude and Liebestod, desire has been abstracted from the planes of sensation (second center) and emotional expression (fourth center) to that of wisdom, or energy transformations (seventh center). Stripped of the purely personal, the desire expressed in this music accumulates and dissipates as waves of energetic intensity, rather than emotional turbulence, until it's finally purged in the ecstatic spiritual union of Tristan and Isolde in the love-death of the title (Liebestod).

No preexisting musical form could have contained such an energy transformation. The music can only proceed organically, developing from the yearning expressed in the unresolved dissonance of the first chord of the Prelude. This combination of yearning and unresolved dissonance builds constantly until the final resolution of both at the conclusion of the Love-Death, nearly twenty minutes later.

The musical waves, in which an archetypal energy transformation like that expressed in the Prelude and Liebestod from *Tristan und Isolde* is encoded, can be overwhelming in their power to move a listener or an audience. Coming from the level of the soul, such waves carry the force of truth about who and what we are. Their potential for creating TMEs is immense—provided that the performers don't emphasize the purely formal or expressive aspects of the piece from ignorance of, or fear of being subsumed by, these musical waves of truth.

An example of macrorhythmically composed popular music is the jazz-rock fusion instrumental "Dawn" by John McLaughlin from the Mahavishnu Orchestra's 1971 album *The Inner Mounting Flame.*[7] This piece contains one large wave of musical energy rising, cresting, then falling back to its original level. The energy transformation behind this wave has something to do with the rising and falling flame of spiritual devotion.

Because the seventh center has both a sacred and a secular aspect, I've come up with two sets of words to describe its lower, middle, and upper ranges. In sacred seven, these ranges are *fear of God, love of God,* and *praise of God.* In secular seven, they are *sublimity, nobility,* and *divine ecstasy.*

The sacred aspect of the seventh center is targeted by religious and devotional music, from Gregorian chant to Renaissance choral masses, or from the mystical monodies of Hildegard von Bingen (1098–1179) to contemporary gospel music.

Gregorian chant is one of the purest forms of seventh center music. It contains no harmony, intensity, tempo variations, or form, thus eliminating the second, third, fifth, and sixth centers. It's rhythm is free and floating, so the first center is barely active.

Gregorian chant is pure melody, in which the love of the fourth center is directed toward God instead of another human being. Some chants, such as the Dies Irae (Day of Wrath, a reference to the Last Judgment), target lower 7, the fear of God. Most target the devotional aspects of middle 7, or love of God. Alleluias, in particular, access upper 7, in which the praise of God can sometimes heat up to the point of mystical ecstasy.

The medieval Christian mystic Hildegard von Bingen composed many chantlike monodies on Latin texts, some of which target the ecstatic range of upper 7. Among them is a spine-tingling, crown-chakra-opening antiphon (devotional composition alternating a solo voice with that of a choir) called Nunc Gaudeant Materna Viscera (Now Let the Maternal Heart), which was written for the dedication of a church.[8]

In the secular version of the seventh center, the waning fear and waxing love apply to humanity, nature, or the soul, rather than to God—to the spiritual or divine potential of humankind and its awe at, love of, and ecstatic praise of being in the world. As mentioned above, the levels of secular seven are sublimity, nobility, and divine ecstasy. Two important stations between these ranges are *transcendental longing*, at the point between sublimity and nobility and *transcendental mirth*, at the point between nobility and ecstasy.

By "transcendental longing," I mean an intense yearning for a world beyond the physical or union with the divine. Much New-Age music expresses this longing—for example, "Exile," by the Irish singer and composer Enya, from her 1988 album *Watermark*.[9] Cyril Scott would probably have classified Enya's music, like much music of the seventh center, as ethereal, or deva-inspired.

By "transcendental mirth," I mean the ability to look back on the physical world and find its failures and foibles more worthy of laughter than a painful reaction such as depression. Much of Mozart's late music is full of such transcendental mirth—for example, his last opera *Die Zauberflöte* (*The Magic Flute*), K. 620.

Fear of God/the Sublime (Lower 7)

The lower range of sacred seven, fear of God, is targeted by religious music of a solemn, ceremonial, and often supplicatory nature. It represents the approach to God, and may be characterized by a sense of awe and mystery, even terror.

Substitute the word *God* for *angel* in the following excerpt from the first of Rainer Maria Rilke's *Duino Elegies*, and you'll have a perfect illustration of the mood of such music:

> Who then, if I cried out, would hear me among the angelic
> orders? And tranquil himself, should one suddenly take
> me into his heart, I'd die of that greater
> existence. For beauty is nothing
> but *that* terror's beginning, as much as we can stand,
> and it amazes us so, because it coolly disdains
> to destroy us. Every angel is terrifying.[10]

Large portions of Mozart's Requiem in D Minor, K. 626, target lower 7—for example, the Dies Irae, a terrifying sonic depiction of the Day of Judgment.

The lower range of secular seven, the sublime, is targeted by music "which arouses sentiments of awe and reverence and a sense of vastness and power outreaching human comprehension."[11] A good performance of the first movement of Beethoven's Ninth Symphony arouses such sentiments. It's an example of secular lower 7 sublimity.

Some music critics claim that the key of D minor, that of Mozart's Requiem and the first movement of Beethoven's Ninth, is tragic in nature. Yet to hear either of these pieces as tragic is to miss the point. They're both sublime, in the truest sense of the word—full of mystery, awe, and a tragic sense of grandeur that says much about how these two great composers perceived both their own lives and human life in general.

In Mozart's case, the sense of the sublime was derived from his conception of God, in Beethoven's from his conception of the divine nature or spiritual potential of humanity. These two senses of the sublime may not be as different from one another as they seem.

Charles says that the fear and awe associated with lower 7 are derived from the ego's approach to the soul. The soul is a more comprehensive consciousness than that of the individual ego. As I pointed out in the previous chapter, the soul exists outside of time and space, as experienced by the ego, and may feel foreign, even threatening to the ego. Yet the soul also represents the highest realization of the divine potential that exists within each of us.

The soul is like a way station on the journey back to God—greater than the ego, not as great as God, though nevertheless divine. For each of us the soul is like a private God, or a highly personal version of God, more accessible than the infinitely great and distant, perhaps incomprehensible Creator.

The Rilke poem that I quoted above describes the sensations that may accompany an encounter with the soul, which the poet metaphorically likens to an angel: the sense of being embraced by a serene power that is greater than oneself, that feels as if it could destroy one, and yet is thrilling in its beauty, its power to move one spiritually, despite the awe, and even terror, it may inspire. Some TMEs, especially those induced by seventh center music, can produce such feelings.

If we see the soul not only as representing the highest realization of our potential as human beings, but also as expressing the God within us, then it becomes clear that the sacred and the secular versions of the seventh center are attempting the same thing: to help us overcome our fear of the soul and approach it, to learn to embrace and love it, and to move toward a sense of ecstatic union with it, in which we're able to retain our identities while experiencing an immeasurable enhancement of what it means to be human.

In jazz, a religious example of the lower 7 awe of God is Part 4 of John Coltrane's *A Love Supreme*, entitled "Psalm."[12]

In rock, an example of the lower 7 sublime is "Kashmir," from Led Zeppelin's 1975 album *Physical Graffiti*.[13]

My friend Marjie, an energy healer, speaks of "Kashmir" as a "consciousness building song." When she played "Kashmir" for me I could hear the expanded consciousness aspects of the seventh center active within it. The lyrics speak of being a "traveler in space and time," which Marjie interprets as a reference to astral travel.

Another example of the lower 7 sublime in rock occurs in "Emmeleia" from Dead Can Dance's 1993 album *Into the Labyrinth*.[14]

In the genre of New-Age music, Enya targets the sublime aspect of lower 7 in "Cursum Perficio," the second track of *Watermark*.

Love of God/Nobility (Middle 7)

The middle range of sacred seven, the love of God, expresses such things as reverence, contemplation, devotion, faith, and piety, as well as the deeply spiritual and often unconditional love that results when the heart opens itself up to the divine. An example of middle 7 devotion is the Sanctus from Mozart's Requiem.

Secular middle 7 expresses the divine nature of humanity, its nobility, as well as a love of life and the world comparable to the sacred middle 7 love of God. Many late works achieve the nobility of secular middle 7 through their composers' having come to terms with life, having seen and accepted what it has to offer.

Just as sacred middle 7 reflects an embracing of God, so does secular middle 7 represent an embracing of life. In Maslow's terminology, such music expresses the "high-plateau experience" in which one can "live casually in heaven and be on easy terms with the eternal and the infinite."[15]

The third movement of Beethoven's Ninth conveys a warmth and depth of spiritual love that subsumes the several loves of being in the world, of God, of humanity and its potential, and of being oneself. There's no distinction here between sacred and secular. This is middle 7 music at its best, the high-plateau experience. Such music could be called devotional or divinely noble with equal justice.

The slow second movement of Beethoven's *Appassionata* Sonata (Piano Sonata No. 23 in F minor, Op. 57) is a fine specimen of middle 7 nobility, without the religious implications of the slow movement of the Ninth.

Many hymns target the middle 7 love of God. National anthems also target middle 7, although the question of what is sacred and what secular here is somewhat blurred. The texts of such anthems may or may not mention God, but the notion of being reverent or devoted to one's nationality and the nobility of doing so is clearly expressed in them.

At the transition point between lower 7 and middle 7, what overcomes our fear of God or the soul and turns it into love is transcendental longing. In the realm of human relationships, a similar, though more physical, longing helps us overcome fear of losing our identity in our partner and moves us toward union with him or her through love.

Wagner's Prelude to *Tristan und Isolde* begins at the point where transcendental longing for the experience of soul-to-soul union becomes strong enough to overcome the ego's fear of losing its identity, both to its own and another's soul (lower 7). The music gradually mounts into the higher love of middle 7, and ends at the point where middle 7 shades into upper 7. Here, love is experienced as rapturous—the first step on the way to ecstasy.

Wagner doesn't go all the way to ecstasy in the Liebestod. For him, spiritual union in love can only take place at the moment of, or after, death, when the separation and identity imposed by our physical bodies have been transcended.

A jazz example of transcendental longing appears in the Miles Davis instrumental "Portia" from his 1986 album *Tutu*.[16]

Perhaps the most famous example of transcendental longing in rock is the Led Zeppelin song "Stairway to Heaven" from their 1971 album *Led Zeppelin IV*.[17]

I've already mentioned that Enya's song "Exile" from *Watermark* is also an example of transcendental longing, from the New-Age genre.

Holst's *The Planets* contains two movements that target secular middle 7, each showing a different side of the Witness dream character associated with the seventh center. "Saturn, the Bringer of Old Age" reflects the aspect of the Witness that involves memory and looking back on life.

Most of "Saturn" targets secular middle 7, especially the noble, yet slightly melancholy march that develops shortly after the beginning. There are also moments of awe that reflect lower 7. An odd passage involving bells that intrudes briefly a couple of times toward the end of the movement hints at the divine ecstasy of upper 7.

"Neptune, the Mystic," which rounds out *The Planets*, reflects the aspect that looks toward the nonphysical reality of the soul, or Numen. "Neptune" begins with muted mystical awe (secular lower 7), and rises to a love-filled inner peace (secular middle 7), with the entry of the wordless female chorus.

In jazz, an example of sacred middle 7 music is "Acknowledgment," Part 1 of *A Love Suprème,* by John Coltrane. Another instance of middle 7 love of God is Miles Davis's rendition of "Little Church" from his 1971 album *Live-Evil.*[18]

The Beatles classic "Let It Be" from their 1971 album of the same title is an example of middle 7 prayerful devotion.[19] Paul McCartney (b. 1942) claims that ten years after she died, his mother, Mary, appeared to him in a dream speaking the words "Let it be," which became the basis for the song.

The Christian overtones of the phrase "Mother Mary comes to me" are supposedly unintentional. Nonetheless, the keyboard introduction and the harmonies throughout the song resemble those of hymnlike gospel music, which is why I attribute "Let It Be" to middle 7. A song based on a comforting dream vision of a mother who has passed on is as much an expression of devotion and spiritual longing as a vision of the Virgin would be.

A New-Age example of middle 7 spiritual devotion is Enya's song "On Your Shore" from *Watermark.*

Praise of God/Ecstasy (Upper 7)

The upper range of sacred seven, praise of God, combines both love and awe, and converts them into action—a rapturous dance of praise that often rises to the level of mystical ecstasy. Upper 7 is a specialty of gospel music.

My composer friend Ruth tells me that good gospel singers are so well respected in their communities as religious leaders that they're often called "ordained." When churchgoers or concert attendees speak of a gospel choir or singer "raising the roof," they mean that the energy in the sanctuary or performance hall is moving into the ecstatic range that I call upper 7.

An example of sacred classical music that spans the range of upper 7, from quiet praise to mystical ecstasy, is Steve Reich's *Tehillim,* a setting of four psalms in Hebrew for female voices and an ensemble of miscellaneous woodwind, string, and percussion instruments, plus synthesizer.

The upper range of secular seven is also ecstatic, the difference being that in secular upper 7, this ecstasy celebrates the divine potential in humankind. Beethoven's choral setting of Schiller's "Ode to Joy," in the Finale of his Ninth Symphony, exemplifies this level of the seventh center.

I've mentioned that transcendental mirth occurs at the point where middle 7 shades into upper 7. The Overture to Mozart's *The Magic Flute* begins with a slow introduction that targets the nobility of middle 7. The faster section that follows is full of the laughter and high spirits of transcendental mirth. As we shall see, Wagner's opera *Die Meistersinger* (*The Mastersingers*) also contains much transcendental mirth.

In jazz, a secular example of upper 7 ecstasy occurs in the Miles Davis number "Black Satin" from his 1972 album *On the Corner.*[20]

In rock, a more joyful than ecstatic example of secular upper 7 is Led Zeppelin's acoustic instrumental song "Bron-Yr-Aur" from *Physical Graffiti.* This short piece, named after a location in Wales, expresses a spiritual sense of praise of the beauty of the world, which places it at the lower end of upper 7. A more ecstatic rock version of secular upper 7 may be found in "Saldek" from Dead Can Dance's *Into the Labyrinth.*

In New-Age music, the ecstasy of secular upper 7 appears in the Enya song "Storms in Africa," from *Watermark.*

Disillusionment (Crisis Point)

The seventh center's crisis point is disillusionment. The desire for union with God or the soul has propelled us from fear, through love, to an ecstatic recognition of the God within, and of our own divinity. Yet the actual experience of union has continued to evade us.

At this point, we may start to lose our belief in the possibility of such a union. We begin to find evidence in the suffering of humanity that there is no God. Our own suffering increases as we see the inhumanity of one person toward another. We become resigned, philosophical, and eventually deeply depressed.

The last movement of Tchaikovsky's Symphony No. 6 in B Minor, Op. 74, the *Pathétique* (meaning "tragic") is perhaps the most famous example of the music of this crisis point. Here, disillusionment takes the form of continually reaching out for God and salvation, from the depths of depression, but without receiving an answer. Within weeks of the work's premiere, Tchaikovsky died under mysterious circumstances. No one knows whether his death was by accident or suicide.

Once we've completed the process of self-actualization and achieved the high plateau of middle 7, we can continue our development only by means of a godlike compassion for others. We must learn how to embrace and understand the suffering of others, one person at a time, to see ourselves reflected in others, as if each suffering being were a stage of our own development that we might have left behind. The more people we embrace and understand in this way, the closer we come to union with the soul. This is how we move beyond the crisis point of disillusionment.

Wagner's last opera, *Parsifal*, begins at this crisis point and eventually transcends it, moving fully into the realm of the eighth center, in which union with God or the soul becomes possible.

Listening to the Prelude to Act I of *Parsifal* will give you a good idea of how the spiritual weariness that accompanies disillusionment sounds. As Wagner targets the crisis point between the seventh and eighth centers, he keeps reaching for, and falling just short of, the godlike compassion of lower 8.

Billie Holiday's rendition of "Gloomy Sunday" is a jazz-based example of the spiritual disillusionment of the crisis point between the seventh and eight centers.[21] Disillusionment can develop from weariness of the world, as in the case of "Gloomy Sunday," or weariness of the rigors of spiritual seeking, as when a spiritual seeker, approaching an important breakthrough from the divine ecstasy of the seventh center to the compassion of the eighth, despairs of ever achieving union with the divine.

The weariness of the spiritual seeker is clearer in Wagner's life and music than Tchaikovsky's. Tchaikovsky seems to have shot up to the crisis point because of the extreme nature of his spiritual conflict, which concerned his homosexuality; whereas Wagner, as we shall see in later chapters, progressed to this point in a more gradual fashion.

A Musical Tour of the Seventh Center

Mozart's Requiem in D Minor, K. 626, which he was working on when he died at the age of thirty-six, is full of sacred seven music, containing examples of the lower, middle, and upper ranges of this center. Most of the Requiem targets lower 7, or fear of God. I wonder whether Mozart wrote the Requiem in mortal terror, not only of his impending death, but also of the possible fate of his soul in the Afterlife, given his somewhat dissipated life.

The Introitus, Kyrie, Rex Tremendae, Confutatis, Amen, and Cum Sanctis movements are good examples of awe before the mystery of God. The Dies Irae, a sonic depiction of the Day of Judgment, exemplifies the fear of God as terror. The Lacrimosa, Domine Jesu, Agnus Dei, and Lux Aeterna movements bring in the element of supplication.

The middle range of sacred seven, love of God, expresses piety and devotion. Such music has greater emotional warmth than that of lower 7. In Mozart's Requiem, the following movements target middle 7: Tuba Mirum (all but the tenor solo section, beginning at Mors stupebit, which is another example of lower 7 fear of God), Recordare, Sanctus, and Benedictus.

The two Hosanna movements exemplify the rapturous praise of God that is typical of upper 7.

The Hostias movement stands at the transition between love of God and praise of God. While the text actively praises God, the music is devotional in nature.

Just as the eight centers on the continuum of human potential shade into each other, so do the three levels that I've identified within them. A rising level of abstraction usually accompanies the transition from one center or level to the next.

While I've outlined three levels in each center, more are theoretically possible, depending on the sensitivity of the listener. The number of segments into which a continuum is divided is arbitrary. More or fewer segments are equally justifiable.

For example, in Mozart's Requiem, it might be possible to divide lower 7 into the following substages, based on a rising level of abstraction: terror of God (Dies Irae), awe at the mystery and majesty of God (Rex Tremendae), a solemn and supplicatory approach to God (Lacrimosa). The latter stage then shades into the love of God (Recordare). Rising through middle 7, the fear of God wanes as the love grows, until the praise of God (Hostias) and mystical ecstasy (Hosanna) have been achieved.

Beethoven's Ninth Symphony provides a musical tour of the secular aspect of the seventh center. The first movement corresponds to lower 7 (the sublime), the third movement to middle 7 (nobility), and the final movement to upper 7 (rising from the joyful praise of the "Ode to Joy" theme to the ecstasy of its final moments).

The second movement, as I pointed out in the previous chapter, is in part a demonic scherzo, associated with the crisis point between the sixth and seventh centers. That crisis point reappears in the stormy opening moments of the Finale.

In the pop/rock genre, you could create a Led Zeppelin-based tour: "Kashmir" (lower 7 sublimity), "Stairway to Heaven" (middle 7 transcendental longing), and "Bron-Yr-Aur" (upper 7 praise of nature).

In jazz-rock fusion, the instrumental "Meeting of the Spirits" by John McLaughlin from *The Inner Mounting Flame* touches upon all ranges of the seventh center. The first and third parts move from the lower 7 sublime to upper 7 ecstasy. The slower middle section expresses the devotion of middle 7 love of God.

Other musical tours of the seventh center could be arranged by creating playlists of the jazz, rock, and New-Age numbers listed in this chapter in order of range. For example, a New-Age tour of the seventh center could be created by playing the four songs by Enya in the following order: "Cursum Perficio" (lower 7 sublimity), "Exile" and "On Your Shore" (middle 7 transcendental longing), and "Storms in Africa" (upper 7 ecstasy).

The music of the seventh center is what the yoga of listening is all about: expanded consciousness. Music that targets lower 7 helps us to overcome our

Table 14. The Seventh Center

Center	Chakra	Range	Dream Character	Lesson	Musical Element
Seventh: Expanded Consciousness	Crown	Spiritual/Intuiting	Witness	Wisdom	Macrorhythm

Table 15. A Seventh Center Playlist

Center	Level	Characteristic	Musical Genres and Examples
Seventh: Expanded Consciousness	Lower 7	Sacred: Fear of God	Classical: Mozart, Requiem: Introitus, Kyrie, Rex Tremendae, Confutatis, Amen, Cum Sanctis, Dies Irae, Lacrimosa, Domine Jesu, Agnus Dei, and Lux Aeterna. Jazz: Coltrane, "Psalm" from A Love Supreme; McLaughlin, "Meeting of the Spirits" (first and last parts).
		Secular: Sublimity	Classical: Beethoven, Ninth Symphony, first movt.; Holst, "Neptune" (first half). Pop/Rock: Dead Can Dance, "Emmaleia"; Led Zeppelin, "Kashmir." New Age: Enya, "Cursum Perficio."
	Middle 7 (Transcendental Longing)		Classical: Wagner, Prelude and Liebestod from Tristan und Isolde. Jazz: Davis, "Portia." Pop/Rock: "Stairway to Heaven." New Age: Enya, "Exile" and "On Your Shore."
		Sacred: Love of God	Classical: Mozart, Requiem: Tuba mirum, Recordare, Sanctus, Benedictus. Jazz: Coltrane, "Acknowledgment"; Davis, "Little Church"; McLaughlin, "Meeting of the Spirits" (middle part). Pop/Rock: Beatles, "Let It Be."
		Secular: Nobility	Classical: Beethoven, Appassionata Sonata, second movt.; Ninth Symphony, third movt.; Holst, "Saturn" and last half of "Neptune."
	Upper 7 (Transcendental Mirth)		Classical: Mozart, Overture to The Magic Flute.
		Sacred: Praise of God	Classical: Mozart, Requiem: Hosanna; Reich, Tehillim. Jazz: McLaughlin, "Meeting of the Spirits" (first and last parts).
		Secular: Divine Ecstasy	Classical: Beethoven, Ninth Symphony, Finale. Jazz: Davis, "Black Satin." Pop/Rock: Dead Can Dance, "Sladek"; Led Zeppelin, "Bron-Yr-Aur." New Age: Enya, "Storms in Africa."
	(Transition) Crisis Point	Disillusionment	Classical: Tchaikovsky, Pathétique, last movt.; Wagner, Prelude to Act I of Parsifal. Jazz: Holiday, "Gloomy Sunday."

fear of the soul or God and open ourselves to the sometimes terrifying beauty of the world. That which targets middle 7 opens us up to love of the soul or God, as well as love of humanity and the world. Music that targets upper 7 allows us to experience a taste of the ecstasy that comes from opening ourselves completely to the divine and fully accepting ourselves as spiritual beings, as well as our relationship with the soul and its master plan for our growth and our lives in the world.

We can use music that expresses the transcendental longing that emerges between lower and middle 7 to propel us on this journey toward oneness with the divine. And we can use music that expresses the transcendental mirth that emerges between middle and upper 7 to help us rise above and forgive the often stupid and hurtful behavior of our fellow human beings, so that we may see them, as well as ourselves, as divine.

Frequent exposure to seventh center music is the best way to prepare ourselves for achieving the transcendent musical experiences that further our spiritual growth. Such music leads us beyond our ordinary state of consciousness to the threshold of oneness with the divine. Crossing that threshold leads us into the eighth center: cosmic consciousness.

15

The Eighth Center: Cosmic Consciousness

A more spiritually refined category of music lies beyond that of the seventh center. While the purpose of seventh center sacred music is to direct our attention and prayers toward the divine, this other, less common, type of music expresses the response of the divine to such prayers. Such music, which emanates from the eighth, or cosmic consciousness, center, seems to come directly from the other side of life. It makes us want to live a deeper, truer life.

Music associated with the eighth center is so uncommon that rather than ask you to come up with examples for your playlist, I simply recommended Wagner's Prelude to *Lohengrin* as an excellent example of the type. I've encountered only a handful of other examples of eighth center music from the classical repertoire, and just three from nonclassical music. I doubt that this fact means that composers of jazz and rock are less capable of experiencing cosmic consciousness or conveying it through their music. I just don't know the many genres of such music well enough to have located other examples of eighth center popular music.

Like music of the seventh center, that of the eighth has both sacred and secular varieties. However, the impression that such music makes is so overwhelmingly spiritual that it hardly matters whether it was composed within a specific religious tradition.

The eighth center is associated with a point about twelve finger breadths above the crown, and corresponds with the component of the psyche that Charles calls the Numen, or soul. I call it the *cosmic consciousness* center.

Because the chakra associated with this center lies not only beyond the physical body, but also beyond the chakras having to do with us as individuals,

I refer to it as the *transpersonal* chakra. It's the second of the pair associated with the spiritual and intuiting range of the continuum of human potential.

At this point in the continuum, we've achieved the following: in the first center, embodiment; in the second, the motivation of desire; in the third, the formation of identity; in the fourth, the establishment of union with the beloved; in the fifth, the integration of identity and union, through discovering our life purpose; in the sixth, the analysis and setting of goals to achieve this life purpose; in the seventh, the turning of our earthly experience, as well as what we've learned through fulfilling our life purpose, into wisdom. All of this learning and growth may now be dissolved into the lesson of transcendence, a transpersonal sense of peace and union with the divine.

The goal of yoga is the bliss and inner peace of samadhi, which comes from union with the divine. In the yoga of listening, eighth center music gives us a taste of such peace and union so that we'll strive for it in every aspect of our lives.

As stated in the previous chapter, the soul is like a way station on the journey back to God—greater than the ego, not as great as God, though nevertheless divine. Beyond the soul is God, the source of all consciousness, a transcendent reality or consciousness comprised of absolute truth and wisdom.

In *The Unanswered Question*, I coined the term *cosmic normative balance* to describe this transcendent reality or consciousness. It's cosmic in the sense that it's an all-embracing, though nonphysical, reality. It's normative in the sense that all of our notions of spiritual and moral truth derive from it. And it's a balance in that exposure to it that causes our actions in life to be weighed against the spiritual and moral truths it represents.

I've experienced the cosmic normative balance in altered states that I call *adventures in consciousness*. These adventures often take the form of out-of-body or lucid dream-based forays into nonphysical reality, including the Afterlife.

During such adventures, I've discovered that what I call the Afterlife Zone, where we go when we die, is permeated with a glorious light that is also a glorious love. This light or love diminishes in intensity the farther one is from its source. I call this source the cosmic normative balance.

I've learned that in the Afterlife, we can only take in as much of the light and love of the cosmic normative balance as our level of spiritual development and the actions based on it allow us to. We shrink from this light and love, or find ourselves pushed away by it, in all the areas in which our lives are out of alignment with the cosmic normative balance. But we also change dramatically with each exposure to the cosmic normative balance, trying to align our thoughts and actions with it more completely, so that we can take in more of its light and love.

Exposure to the cosmic normative balance can take place in near-death, out-of-body, or mystical experiences. By "mystical experiences," I mean not only peak or high-plateau experiences, but also TMEs. Eighth center music may be the closest thing on Earth to exposure to the cosmic normative balance. No other type of music is as likely to produce TMEs.

As I pointed out in chapter 2, those who have had peak experiences are often driven to become self-actualizing individuals by their desire to have more experiences of this nature. Maslow called them meta-motivated, but in Charles's terms, they're fulfilling the soul's master plan for their growth. The reward for doing so is a surge of life force, with results that range from an intense feeling of happiness to a peak experience.

The people that Maslow called self-actualizing are always trying to align themselves more deeply with the soul in order to increase the number, frequency, and intensity of such experiences. In the process of doing so, they may encounter God, the cosmic normative balance.

By calling this transcendental reality the cosmic normative balance, I don't intend to make it sound impersonal. My own exposure to it has taught me that the cosmic normative balance is as much a *Being* as a balance—a Being that weighs our every action and attempts to adjust our course when we're out of alignment with it.

This Being is what some religious refer to as God. Sri Aurobindo called it the supermind. The soul, or Numen, is our personal representative of this all-embracing, cosmic consciousness, just as in Aurobindo's yoga, the overmind is a receiving station for the supermind.

Eighth center music is composed directly from the soul or overmind. Such music can open us up to, give us a taste of, or immerse us in the cosmic normative balance. The result is often a TME with the force of a conversion experience, a desire to change our lives.

The eighteenth-century Swedish mystic Emanuel Swedenborg refers to what I call the cosmic normative balance as "the light of heaven." I believe that this glorious light is the same as that encountered by many near-death experiencers on their brief, unintentional journeys into the Afterlife.

People who have had near-death experiences (NDErs) describe this light as seeming to be imbued not only with consciousness, but also with a sense of reality far greater than anything they've experienced on Earth. It contains all truth and wisdom. Merely being exposed to it answers all their questions, and fills them with an indescribable sensation of divine love.[1]

Some NDErs have reported hearing heavenly music during their NDEs. For example, the once nationally syndicated cartoonist Arthur E. Yensen had an NDE in 1932, the result of a car accident. He wrote about it in a booklet first published in 1955—twenty years before the term "near-death experience" was invented.

Yensen describes the heavenly music he heard during his brief visit to the Other Side as follows:

> [It] seemed to be coming from everywhere. I estimated it to be 100 times more beautiful than anything I had ever heard. The whole country resounded with it, and everything seemed to be in tune. It had a different swing than earth-music, which by comparison is very coarse and crass—mostly noise. Sometimes now when I listen to the best of earth-music I notice a slight resemblance to heaven-music as if the composer were consciously, or unconsciously, trying to imitate it.[2]

"Earth-music" that resembles "heaven-music" is an apt description of eighth center music. Few composers seem capable of producing music of this kind. Holst's *The Planets*, which touches each of the second through the seventh centers at least once in its seven movements, contains nothing that expresses the cosmic normative balance.

One of the most powerful examples of eighth center music that I've encountered thus far is Wagner's Prelude to *Lohengrin*. As I mentioned in chapter 4, the first time I heard a recording of the piece, I had no idea what the opera was about. I was deeply moved by the sense of a transcendent spiritual revelation that seemed to emanate from the music. Only later did I discover that Wagner's intention was to portray a vision of the Holy Grail, high in the heavens, emerging from the clouds, and then disappearing into them again.

In Arthurian legend, a vision of the Holy Grail imparts a sense of spiritual mission to the perceiver. It's an apt image for the cosmic normative balance. Once exposed to this balance, you feel an inner compulsion to change your life. Music of the eighth center, when well performed, can have a similar effect.

The musical element that applies to the eighth center is *metarhythm*. By this term, I mean a process of musical unfolding that goes beyond the use of rhythm as an organizing principle. The tempos of metarhythmic music are extremely slow, and there's little rhythmic motion. The macrorhythmic waves of accumulating and dissipating energy that characterize music of the seventh center have calmed down, creating not only a sense of tranquility, but also of immersion in the divine.

Metarhythmically composed music is timeless. It seems either to take place outside of time, or to describe a state of being, or a place, like heaven, that exists beyond our time- and space-bound physical universe.

Another characteristic of eighth center music is that it seems to radiate toward, wash over, and bathe the listener in what could be described as waves of light or goodness. It provides the closest thing we have in the physical world to exposure to the cosmic normative balance, short of having an out-of-body or near-death experience. I call this characteristic *radiance.* I discuss musical radiance in depth in chapter 19.

There are a number of ways in which a feeling of timelessness can be produced in music: extremely slow tempos; static harmonies (i.e., little sense of progression from one harmony to the next); modality (no strong sense of key center); and odd instrumental colorings. But each of these techniques may also be used to create seventh center music.

I've encountered a number of composers who have attempted to portray nonphysical reality through a sense of timelessness or spiritual peace. Yet their music may not evoke a feeling of exposure to the cosmic normative balance. It *yearns* for such exposure, and therefore expresses transcendental longing. As I pointed out in the previous chapter, transcendental longing is a characteristic of seventh center music.

The hallmark of music that *does* evoke exposure to the cosmic normative balance is a sense that transcendental longing has been fulfilled. The result is often a conversion experience. Such music makes us want to change our lives, become more closely aligned with the cosmic normative balance, and find ways to experience it more directly ourselves, whether through further TMEs or other types of mystical experiences.

Here is God's *response* to the supplication and transcendental longing of seventh center music. Eighth center music carries a sense of being utterly beyond the human—although it's not inhuman, being full of compassionate and loving understanding for human suffering. Such music can have the strongest moral effect on humanity, in the sense that Cyril Scott described in *Music: Its Secret Influence.* Eighth center music corresponds to what Scott called buddhic music.

To the composer, such music may feel like a gift from beyond, a higher inspiration that comes without effort—the result of what Scott would call "musical mediumship." Such inspiration can produce a single phrase, a whole movement, or, in rare cases, a large-scale piece.

The levels of the eighth center from lowest to highest are *compassion, grace,* and *union.* The examples described here are either secular or sacred in character. Because of the nature of eighth center music, the secular examples are, like Wagner's Prelude to *Lohengrin,* spiritual without being religious.

Compassion (Lower 8)

A secular example of lower 8 compassion is the Adagio for Strings by Samuel Barber (1910–1981). Composed when Barber was only twenty-six, the work exists in two versions: a more intimate and less well-known one for string

quartet, part of a multimovement work, his Op. 11; and the usual, often emotionally shattering, stand-alone movement for string orchestra. The latter truly
brings out the transcendent character of this music.

In the hands of a conductor who's not sensitive to the spiritual magnificence of this work, the Adagio for Strings can sound as if its purpose were
merely to express a profound sense of grief—in other words, as if it were lower
4 music (pathos).

A great performance of the Adagio for Strings is completely unsentimen-
tal. It seems to call down to Earth a Christ- or bodhisattva-like compassion and
understanding for human suffering, and to permeate the listener with it. Tears
will be a more or less inevitable response—and afterwards there's a sense of
spiritual peace.

I know of only one recording of the Adagio for Strings that expresses its full
power as lower 8 music: that of Thomas Schippers and the New York
Philharmonic.[3] In the yoga of listening, you may want to use this recording
when grieving, especially when you need to remind yourself of the compassionate embrace of the soul or God.

A religious example of lower 8 compassion is *Ein Deutsches Requiem* (*A
German Requiem*), Op. 45, by Johannes Brahms (1833–1897). Brahms wrote *A
German Requiem* after his mother died. He wanted to create a piece of music
that would provide spiritual consolation for the loss of a loved one. He chose
to set a number of texts from Luther's translation of the Bible that offered such
comfort, rather than the usual Latin text of the Catholic mass for the dead.

Under the dual influence of his personal need and his desire to serve
humanity, Brahms was able to bring through his music the bodhisattva-like
compassion of lower 8. The piece lasts nearly an hour and a quarter. While
there are moments when *A German Requiem* descends into the seventh center,
it nevertheless represents one of the most prolonged periods of exposure to the
eighth of which I'm aware. The recording by Claudio Abbado and the Berlin
Philharmonic does justice to this magnificent though mournful work.[4]

In the yoga of listening, Brahms's *A German Requiem* can also be used to
create a compassionate and spiritually protected space for grieving the loss of
a loved one. The sense of spiritual protection comes, as in Barber's Adagio for
Strings, from the embrace of the soul or God made palpable in the music.

The song "Only Time" from Enya's 2000 album *A Day Without Rain* is a
nonclassical example of secular lower 8 compassion, without the sadness of
Barber's Adagio.[5] It was used to accompany newscasts of the September 11,
2001, terrorist attacks on the World Trade Center in New York.

Enya's song is full of eighth center radiance. The lyrics communicate a forgiving acceptance of all that seems to go wrong in life, or at least not according

to our expectations. Only time knows what we've suffered, lost, or given up. Between the third verse and the fourth (a reprise of the first verse with the order of the lines changed), the music drops briefly into the ecstasy of upper 7 before returning to lower 8.

In the yoga of listening, "Only Time" is a radiant reminder of the fact that we need to have compassion for and forgive *ourselves* as much as we do others.

Grace (Middle 8)

Wagner's Prelude to *Lohengrin* is a secular example of middle 8 grace. It's spiritual without being religious. By "grace," I mean a sense of coming back into alignment with the soul and its plans for one's growth, the cosmic norma-tive balance, or whatever one names and reveres as God.

In Christianity, grace represents God's forgiveness of our sins. Charles defines *sin* as emphasizing our identity over our sense of oneness or union with God. Thus sin is advancing the satisfaction of our own needs over that of others or resisting the soul's plans for our growth.

As noted above, Wagner's Prelude is intended to portray a vision of the Holy Grail. Those who witness such a vision feel compelled to dedicate their lives to its service. The Holy Grail represents grace—and therefore the cosmic normative balance.

Charles says that we base much of our personality on resistance to the soul's master plan for our growth. Middle 8 music is like a call from beyond to give up that resistance, to realign ourselves with our life purpose. Such music encourages us to resume the quest for the Holy Grail that lies in each of us, as a symbol for the perfect blend of identity (knowing ourselves) and union (lov-ing and serving others). This blend of union and identity is one of the main goals of our spiritual life.

Many recordings of Wagner's Prelude are currently available. The middle 8 quality comes through especially strongly in those by James Levine and the MET Opera Orchestra, and Claudio Abbado and the Vienna Philharmonic.[6]

In the yoga of listening, the Prelude to *Lohengrin* is useful when you feel spiritually lost, unsure of your life purpose, and needful of realignment with the soul or God.

An example of middle 8 grace of the religious variety may be found in the Missa Papae Marcelli (Pope Marcellus Mass) by the Italian Renaissance com-poser Giovanni Pierluigi da Palestrina (ca. 1525–1594). This famous mass for unaccompanied choir resonates at the middle 8 level of grace for its entire thirty-minute duration. The recording by the Tallis Scholars is magnificent— the middle 8 effect is fully present throughout.[7]

If, in the yoga of listening, Wagner's Prelude to *Lohengrin* is useful for those of us who need to realign ourselves with the soul or God, then Palestrina's Pope Marcellus Mass is useful for those of us who have achieved that realignment and want to sustain it.

I've encountered a progressive rock example of secular middle 8 grace in a song called "The Gates of Delirium" from Yes's 1974 album *Relayer*.[8] This is one of the few instances of cosmic consciousness I've encountered in nonclassical music. I discuss this remarkable song in chapter 18.

Union (Upper 8)

Upper 8 music reflects the peace of union with God. Composers are sometimes able to access this highest level of the eighth center when they're attempting to portray paradise in music. The final movement of the Requiem, Op. 48, by Gabriel Fauré (1845–1924), In Paradisum (In Paradise), is a perfect example of such music, arresting in its sense of timelessness and simplicity.

A bad performance of this movement could easily sound sentimental, even saccharine. Once again, the quality of the conducting can make a huge difference in whether or not the eighth center qualities of a piece of music come through.

There are two versions of the Fauré Requiem, one for small, the other for large orchestra, plus organ and chorus. My recording is of the latter version, conducted by Philippe Herreweghe, who has a reputation in Europe for his sensitive renditions of music of a sacred or spiritual character. Here the eighth center qualities of the final movement are strongly contrasted with the usually middle 7 devotional cast of the earlier ones.[9]

In the yoga of listening, In Paradisum can serve as a charming reminder of what for most of us is the far-off goal of union with God. In one of my adventures in consciousness, I once heard the almost inaudible tinkle of distant chimes. These chimes were so beautiful that I felt an irresistible urge to get closer to their source so that I could hear them better. I was told by a helpful spiritual Guide that these chimes represent the nearly inaudible call of the Source to align ourselves and journey toward oneness with it.[10] In Fauré's In Paradisum, I hear something like these distant chimes, calling us back to oneness with God.

The twentieth-century mystical Catholic composer Olivier Messiaen (1908–1992) made a number of musical attempts to express a sense of union with God. The one that stands out for me as a fine example of upper 8 religious music is the fourth, and final, movement of the orchestral suite *L'Ascension* (*The Ascension*). This movement is entitled "Prière du Christ montant vers son Père" ("Prayer of Christ Ascending unto His Father").

Messiaen's "Prayer," written for strings alone, unfolds in an extremely slow tempo that illustrates what I mean by metarhythm: a music that seems to have transcended the element of time. In it, I recognize the feeling I've had in the several adventures in consciousness in which I've been exposed to the cosmic normative balance.

In one of those experiences, recounted in the first chapter of *Otherwhere*, I seemed to be in a nonphysical place made entirely of light. Tiers or terraces of light ascended across what seemed like a great distance toward the source of that light, a great sun that pulsed like a heart. Each of these pulses sent a wave of love from one end of the plane of light to the other.[11]

Messiaen's music seems to represent this experience in sound. However, I have yet to encounter an ideal performance of it. The one I own, on the Naxos label, is merely adequate. The upper 8 quality of the music comes through, but not the sense of having to change one's life to accommodate it.[12]

In the yoga of listening, the fourth movement of Messiaen's *L'Ascension* provides an ideal opportunity for meditation—a nine-minute opportunity to float in the timeless tranquillity of samadhi (bliss), basking in a sense of union with God.

"Wind on Water," the first track from *Evening Star*, a 1975 collaboration between Brian Eno and Robert Fripp (b. 1946), is another example of nonclassical secular eighth center music.[13] It has the qualities of radiance and timelessness that I attribute to eighth center music and demonstrates what I mean by metarhythm. In many respects, "Wind on Water" might make a better soundtrack for my out-of-body visits to the Afterlife than the fourth movement of Messiaen's *L'Ascension*.

I would be curious to know what spiritual beliefs or intentions on the part of Eno and Fripp went into creating this amazing five-and-a-half-minute work. It seems to be a musical portrait of the pulsing sun/heart I described, radiating waves of divine love.

"Wind on Water" offers another ideal opportunity for meditating on the upper 8 quality of union with the divine. The piece is linked directly with the next track on the album, "Evening Star," which can be a little jarring, since that track descends to the devotion of middle 7. Perhaps one could create a meditation tape in which the music of "Wind on Water" gently fades out just before that transition point.

Translation (Crisis Point)

According to Swami Satyananda, the first, or root, chakra is the first that pertains to human spiritual development and the last that pertains to evolution at the animal level. Using a seven chakra system, he claims that there are also chakras or spiritual planes above the seventh, or crown, chakra. For him, the seventh chakra represents the last in the line of human evolution and the first in the evolution of humanity into divine beings.[14]

In the continuum of human potential, the eighth center, or transpersonal chakra, serves a similar function. Whereas the seventh center, associated with the Witness, is the last in the line of human evolution, the eighth center, associated with the Numen, or soul, is the first in the evolution of humanity into what Satyananda calls divine beings. Beyond this point, our evolution takes place in nonphysical reality, where there's no music as we experience it here, because there's no physical source of sound.

The crisis point associated with the eighth center is *translation*, the transition from physicality to nonphysicality. The music of this crisis point would be inaudible on Earth: a nonphysical equivalent of music perceivable only by equally nonphysical senses.

Such senses are probably too little developed for most of us to "hear" or recognize such music. As I've pointed out, some NDErs, like Arthur E. Yensen, have reported hearing an indescribable music during their visits to the Afterlife. Perhaps they've been exposed to the nonphysical music that I'm talking about here.

The only composer I know of who has made an attempt to target the crisis point of translation, is the Russian mystic Alexander Scriabin. He wanted to compose a *Mysterium* that would end the world, transfigure humankind, and lead people into the paradise of a new age.

Scriabin died prematurely, at the age of forty-three, having done little more than sketch out a text and a few musical passages for a work that would precede the *Mysterium* and prepare people for it. Yet the motivation to write the *Mysterium* had been with him for at least a decade.

I come back to Scriabin and the *Mysterium* in chapter 24. For now, suffice it to say that I'm not surprised that Scriabin had trouble realizing his idea. He kept coming up against the crisis point of translation, beyond which there is no sound. He was unable to resolve the problem of how to write or perform a nonphysical music that could somehow be perceived by an audience based in physical reality.

Launching the Soul toward Union with God

The only music that I know of that contains the lower, middle, and upper ranges of the eighth center is César Franck's *Les Béatitudes*. Multiple hearings of the work have convinced me that it goes beyond what Scott would call the seraphic variety of deva music, typical of the seventh center, to the buddhic, which is typical of the eighth.

Les Béatitudes lasts longer than two hours and contains long stretches of music targeting other centers. Rather than provide a center-by-center analysis of it here, where my intention is to isolate the characteristics of the eighth center, I do so in chapter 19.

I'd like to conclude the present chapter with a discussion of the Adagio of Schubert's String Quintet in C, D. 956, a rare secular (spiritual but not religious) example of upper 8 union, instead of a musical tour of the eighth center. Such a tour, of course, could include Enya's "Only Time" (lower 8 compassion), Yes's "The Gates of Delirium" (middle 8 grace), and Eno and Fripp's "Wind on Water" (upper 8 union). But the Yes example is imbedded in a twenty-two-minute progressive rock suite that touches on a number of other centers. I provide a center-by-center analysis of "The Gates of Delirium" at the end of chapter 18.

The Adagio of Schubert's String Quintet is the most radiant music that the composer ever wrote. It begins with a long passage of upper 8 union, like basking in the sunlight of God's love, well above the clouds that hover over the emotional turbulence of the human world. Here is an example of what Scott would call ethereal music, buddhic in its serenity.

This opening section is an excellent example of metarhythmically composed music. The slow chord changes and attenuated rhythmic activity create a sense of timelessness, or of beingness as experienced beyond Time.

In the center section of the movement, the serene mood is broken by an outburst of what Scott would call "the human element." The music becomes tense, agitated, and passionate (third center), expressing anger and a sense of tragedy.

Schubert composed the work during the last months of his life. He must have known that he was doomed to die young as a result of the syphilis he had contracted several years earlier. The center section of the Quintet seems like a protest against his fate, directed to God, who is floating somewhere above the clouds of human suffering.

When the tranquil music of the opening section returns, a disturbing new element has been added: a cello line that keeps climbing from the depths to the heights, full of passionate yearning—as if Schubert were desperately trying to achieve the state of union with the divine expressed in the music before his angry outburst. The result is jarring. The eighth center music of divine union, which is without human emotion, continues its serene progress, while the cello, full of the seventh center's transcendental longing, keeps marring its beauty.

Eventually, the cello's yearning fades out. The music of divine union goes on for a few minutes longer, then gradually dies away, leaving open the

Table 16. The Eighth Center

Center	Chakra	Range	Dream Character	Lesson	Musical Element
Eighth: Cosmic Consciousness	Transpersonal	Spiritual/Intuiting	Numen (Soul)	Transcendence	Metarhythm (Timelessness)

Table 17. An Eighth Center Playlist

Center	Level	Characteristic	Musical Genres and Examples
Eighth: Cosmic Consciousness	Lower 8	Compassion	Classical: Barber, Adagio for Strings (secular); Brahms, *German Requiem* (sacred). New Age: Enya, "Only Time" (secular).
	Middle 8	Grace	Classical: Wagner, Prelude to *Lohengrin* (secular); Palestrina, Missa Papae Marcelli (sacred). Pop/Rock: Yes, "The Gates of Delirium" (secular).
	Upper 8	Union	Classical: Fauré, In Paradisum, from his Requiem (sacred); Messiaen, *L'Ascension*, fourth movt. (sacred); Schubert, Adagio from his String Quintet in C (secular). Pop/Rock: Eno and Fripp, "Wind on Water" (secular).
(Transition)	Crisis Point	Translation	Classical: Scriabin, *Mysterium*.

question of whether Schubert's soul, represented by the cello, was absorbed back into the divine, or gave up trying to achieve oneness with it.

In the yoga of listening, the Adagio of Schubert's String Quintet can remind us of the goal of spiritual practice, union with the divine; the emotional turbulence that prevents us from achieving this goal; the transcendental longing that causes us to rise above this turbulence; and the challenge of launching our souls from the turbulence of the human realm into the serenity of the ethereal or divine.[15]

Here ends my presentation of the eight centers of the continuum of human potential. In the next chapter, I demonstrate how listeners, performers, and composers can use their knowledge of these centers to prepare themselves for achieving transcendent musical experiences.

16

Preparing for Transcendent Musical Experiences

Before I explain how to use the yoga of listening to prepare yourself for transcendent musical experiences, here are two useful charts that present the continuum of human potential in its entirety. Table 18 is identical to Table 1 from chapter 6. Now that you've read the in-depth descriptions of the eight centers in the intervening chapters and begun to identify music that targets each center and level by means of the playlists and musical tours, this table should have new meaning.

How have the playlists that I asked you to create in part 1 changed as a result of what you've read? You may wish to revise and expand them on the basis of new knowledge.

Table 19 provides a comprehensive list of the levels and crisis points, without musical examples, allowing you to see how they flow seamlessly from one to the next.

"Through music, one can reach God," states north Indian classical musician Ravi Shankar. He explains as follows:

> Our tradition teaches us that sound is God—Nada Brahma [Sanskrit for "sound is God"]. That is, musical sound and the musical experience are steps to the realization of the self. We view music as a kind of spiritual discipline that raises one's inner being to divine peacefulness and bliss.[1]

Table 18. The Continuum of Human Potential

Center	Chakra	Range	Dream Character	Lesson	Musical Element
First: Arousal	Root	Physical/Sensing	Soma (Body Consciousness)	Embodiment	Rhythm
Second: Desire	Genital	Physical/Sensing	Participant	Motivation	Sonority
Third: Intensity	Navel	Emotional/Feeling	Shadow	Identity	Dissonance and Volume
Fourth: Expression	Heart	Emotional/Feeling	Anima/Animus	Union	Melody
Fifth: Well-being	Throat	Intellectual/Thinking	Counterpart	Life Purpose	Tempo
Sixth: Command	Brow	Intellectual/Thinking	Delimiter	Analysis	Form
Seventh: Expanded Consciousness	Crown	Spiritual/Intuiting	Witness	Wisdom	Macrorhythm
Eighth: Cosmic Consciousness	Transpersonal	Spiritual/Intuiting	Numen (Soul)	Transcendence	Metarhythm (Timelessness)

Table 19. Levels and Crisis Points

Center	Level	Characteristic
First: Arousal	Lower 1	Immersion
	Middle 1	Interest
	Upper 1	Entrainment
(Transition)	Crisis Point	Boredom
Second: Desire	Lower 2	Relaxation
	Middle 2	Pleasure
	Upper 2	Intoxication
(Transition)	Crisis Point	Overload
Third: Intensity	Lower 3	Tension
	Middle 3	Agitation
	Upper 3	Eruption
(Transition)	Crisis Point	Violence
Fourth: Expression	Lower 4	Pathos
	Middle 4	Yearning
	Upper 4	Elation
(Transition)	Crisis Point	Delirium
Fifth: Well-being	Lower 5	Contentment
	Middle 5	Joy
	Upper 5	Exuberance
(Transition)	Crisis Point	Mania
Sixth: Command	Lower 6	Wit
	Middle 6	Invention
	Upper 6	Fantasy
(Transition)	Crisis Point	Irrationality
Seventh: Expanded Consciousness	Lower 7	Sacred: Fear of God; Secular: Sublimity
	Middle 7	Sacred: Love of God; Secular: Nobility
	Upper 7	Sacred: Praise of God; Secular: Divine Ecstasy
(Transition)	Crisis Point	Disillusionment
Eighth: Cosmic Consciousness	Lower 8	Compassion
	Middle 8	Grace
	Upper 8	Union
(Transition)	Crisis Point	Translation

Shankar's tradition, although unrelated to Tantra yoga, kundalini, and the chakras, uses a continuum somewhat like that described in this book: a musical system called the nine *rasas* (affections of the mind). Shankar describes the *rasas* as follows:

1. *Shringara*, a "romantic and erotic sentiment filled with longing for an absent lover" (corresponding to what I call the bittersweet yearning of middle 4)

2. *Hasya*, which is "comic, humorous, and laughter-provoking" (the wit of lower 6)

3. *Karuna*, which is "pathetic, tearful, sad, expressing extreme loneliness and longing for either god or lover" (the former [God] is lower to middle 7, the latter [lover], lower 4; I've also seen *karuna* translated as "compassion," in which case it would correspond to lower 8)

4. *Raudra*, which portrays "fury or excited anger" (the passion of upper 3)

5. *Veera*, which "expresses the sentiment of heroism, bravery, majesty, grandeur, and a dignified kind of excitement" (triumph is upper 5; nobility, middle 7)

6. *Bhayanaka*, which is "frightening or fearful" (the tension or agitation of lower or middle 3)

7. *Vibhatsa*, which expresses "disgust" (a likely reaction to any of the crisis points between the centers: boredom, overload, tragedy, delirium, mania, irrationality, or disillusionment)

8. *Adbhuta*, which "shows wonderment and amazement, exhilaration and even a little fear, as one undergoes a strange experience" (lower 7, the sublime)

9. *Shantah*, which expresses "peace, tranquility, and relaxation" (lower 2, if this peace is merely physical; upper 8 if spiritual)[2]

Shankar also describes a tenth *rasa*: "*bhakti*, which is devotional, spiritual, almost religious in feeling; but actually this *rasa* is a combination of *shanta*, *karuna*, and *adbhuta*."[3] This tenth *rasa* aptly describes middle 7, the love of God.

While the *rasa* system of north Indian classical music has many of the same categories as the continuum of human potential that I've described, they're arranged in a different order. The first of the *rasas* listed above, *shringara*, is considered to be "the *lowest* and the *first* passion of all sentient beings"; whereas the ninth, *shantah*, is "the highest development of human feeling, leading man to the contemplation of, or pleasurable communion with, the deity."[4]

I've already mentioned Charles's notion of categories of expression, which comprise all of the possible ways of being human. Whatever they're called, however they're arranged, these categories of expression can be accessed by Western and non-Western music alike, including north Indian classical music. I've arranged these categories of expression into a continuum of human potential that reflects rising levels of life force. Other criteria might easily result in a different order, as in the case of the Indian *rasas*. The important thing in the case of the yoga of listening and north Indian classical music is that they both attempt to reach God through music by creating transcendent musical experiences in the listener.

For most of us, TMEs seem to occur at random. Is there a way to prepare ourselves so that we can achieve them more regularly?

In the previous chapters, I've hinted that listening to music that targets the visionary aspects of the sixth center (upper 6), as well as the expanded consciousness of the seventh and the cosmic consciousness of the eighth, can help us do so.

What Cyril Scott called deva music, which extends from music inspired by nature spirits to that inspired by more formidable spiritual powers, such as the archangelic, roughly corresponds to this range of the continuum of human potential, with Debussy representing upper 6 (nature-spirit music), Scriabin, the seventh (deva music), and Franck and Wagner the eighth center (seraphic deva music and buddhic music).

Applying the principles of the yoga of listening outlined in chapter 7 to such music may be enough to guarantee an increase of frequency and depth in our TMEs. But there may be other ways to do this as well.

My housemate, Kevin, had an ecstatic TME that suggests another way to prepare ourselves for such experiences. One Friday night at a weekly free-form dance, Kevin was dancing by himself when the DJ played a new song that he had never heard before. It was a slower tune, using electronics. There were no lyrics. Kevin isn't sure who wrote or performed it.

Kevin wanted to be true to himself and the music, to move authentically, with no desire to impress others. As consciously as possible, he began moving to the trancelike music, its slowly changing rhythms, and engaging, hypnotic melodies.

With his eyes closed, Kevin saw what he describes as "color and energy shapes" that were "morphing." He tried to express with his body what was happening in that "inner energy constellation."

After a while, Kevin began to feel that that energy constellation was "galactic, huge, set within deep reaches of space." As his TME developed, he "felt that there was less of a boundary" between himself and the galaxy. It seemed as if he *became* the galaxy and his body "was mirroring its movement, rhythms, and activity."

The music built up with a "crescendo of tension" to a "climactic release." Kevin reports, "At that moment, I felt that the galaxy I had become was exploding into glory."

After the song was over, he had no difficulty making the transition back to ordinary consciousness and interacting with people in typical ways. He says he felt normal, even though he had never before experienced such a sense of glory.

Process Configurations

In the yoga of listening, the idea is to align ourselves with the music as deeply as possible, so that we can achieve a TME like Kevin's. The question is how to attain an alignment deep enough to act as a springboard to inner glory.

Kevin used movement to attain that inner alignment. I've used meditative practices such as heightened concentration and synchronization of my breathing with the flow of the music. But there may be another important factor in achieving the deepest possible alignment with the music we meditate on in the yoga of listening: the process configuration that has produced the music.

I introduced this term in chapter 5. A process configuration is a nonphysical energy form that encapsulates both the process by which a piece of music unfolds in time and the process of composing it.

In chapter 2, I mentioned that nameless, imageless waves of emotional intensity or feeling-toned energy are the basis of my compositions until I find the notes that would express and embody them. I wrote: "Perhaps all art is an attempt to translate these waves into words, images, or music, so that the artist can share them with others—or, especially in the case of music, *invoke* them in others."

In chapter 14, I introduced the notion of energy transformations, which I defined as the way that the nonphysical soul experiences our lives in physical reality. Energy transformations carry us from one emotional state to another, allowing us to learn important lessons along the way. The result is spiritual wisdom.

Such wisdom is encoded in music, which is the closest thing we have in the physical world to the energy transformations experienced by the nonphysical soul. As in the yogic notion of transmission, music not only encodes such wisdom, but passes it along to receptive listeners.

The process configuration behind a piece of music is what allows this transmission to take place. A process configuration contains not only the processes by which the music was composed and by which it unfolds in time, but also the energy transformations and spiritual wisdom encoded within it.

According to Charles, process configurations reside in a nonphysical reality that he calls the *transceptual field*. The word *transceptual* has been coined from *trans-* (across) and the last two syllables of the word *conceptual*.

Charles explains that the transceptual field is a zone of nonphysical reality in which all of the ideas or concepts ever invented by humankind exist like suspended particles, capable of coming together in ever-new conglomerates. When creative artists or thinkers are trying to solve a problem, they may enter this field, usually in a meditative state. Their need for a solution to that problem carries a charge that causes the contents of the transceptual field to reposition themselves and recombine. At some point, these contents may crystallize into a form that an artist or thinker recognizes as a solution to the problem: a process configuration.

Process configurations contain not only the resolution of the artist's or thinker's problem, but also the steps necessary to realize this resolution in physical reality. When artists or thinkers seek to unravel the process configuration in time and express the solution it contains in words, pictorial images, music, mathematical equations, and so on, a translation process begins. They must find a way to realize the nonphysical energy of the process configuration in their chosen medium.

The Russian musical mystic Alexander Scriabin seems to have been familiar with process configurations. In conversation with his brother-in-law, Boris de Schloezer, a philosopher and musicologist, Scriabin described his compositional process as follows:

> [T]he music existed outside him in images that he could not express verbally. He was not creating this music out of nothing, he declared, but rather he had removed a veil that obscured it, and thus made it visible. His task was to render this inner image into sounds, without distortion; he liked to call this image a "sounding body" possessing a color of its own. He observed it in his inner self and at the same time separate from him or, rather, above him. He sensed it with his entire self, not only through the medium of sense organs.[5]

When Scriabin speaks of a "sounding body," he's describing a process configuration. Charles's notion of the transceptual field explains why Scriabin felt that such sounding bodies existed both within and outside him.

Schloezer records that Scriabin claimed he was "but the translator'" of his Fifth Piano Sonata. While composing it, Scriabin felt as though he were projecting a three-dimensional body on a flat surface, stretching and flattening in time and space a prophetic vision that he experienced as an instant revelation, simplifying and at the same time impoverishing it.[6]

When Scriabin lost his awareness of this inner image, he would "seek to regain" it by engaging in a practice he called placing himself "upon the plane of oneness."[7]

In Scriabin's description of his compositional process, I recognize my own. I'm constantly sensing and attempting to translate into sound the inner experience of a piece's process configuration, which I sense as waves of energetic intensity. Through inner listening, I try to match the sounds I produce at the piano or computer keyboard with the feel of these waves and the process configuration behind them. A deep sense of happiness and inner peace develops when I've gotten the right notes.

My friend Ruth also uses process configurations to compose. A TME lets her know when she has realized the process configuration behind a piece correctly. For example, she once transcribed a six-minute piece for string orchestra that she heard in a dream. While working with an actual orchestra on this transcription, she felt that the notes were right but the bowing techniques were not. She had the players try out a number of possibilities.

Ruth thought she was "listening for a certain sound and feeling" but was surprised when she suddenly felt that her "joints disappeared, turning into pure shafts of light." That's when she knew she had the bowing right.

This experience was accompanied by an overwhelming sense of love; otherwise she would have been terrified. Knowing when the piece was right was a result not of what she heard with her physical ears, but something deeper. Now she has a motto for when she's working with musicians on playing her music: "When my joints turn to light, that's when I know it's right."

Scriabin's, Ruth's, and my own compositional processes are also remarkably like my experience of channeling for Charles. While in trance, I feel the information that's about to come through me first as patterns of energy, a kind of inner image. The task is to sense the information content of this energy and translate it into words. If I lose my connection with the energy or information, I must deepen the trance, bringing myself closer to Charles, in order to continue—a process that corresponds to Scriabin's placing himself "on the plane of oneness."

The process of translating my adventures in consciousness, especially those that have taken me into the Afterlife, from images to energies to words, also resembles Scriabin's compositional process. Such accounts always seem to me both "simplified" and "impoverished" by this translation process, as if they were stretched and flattened, losing their multidimensionality as I try to communicate them in words.

A number of TMEs described earlier in this book have involved process configurations. In chapter 5, when I introduced the term, I described a TME in which I sensed the process configuration behind Bartók's posthumous Viola Concerto. This process configuration manifested itself as a conviction that the associate who had completed Bartók's unfinished score had put certain passages that should have been in one movement in another.

In chapter 1, I described a TME induced while performing Karel Husa's *Music for Prague 1968*. I wrote that I felt "as if I'd entered an emotional reality in which the military invasion was still going on: People were panicking, fleeing from the tanks rolling into Prague, while trying to gather up their loved ones; distress signals were being sent around the world, full of fear and outrage." The Soviet invasion of Prague in 1968 and the composer's reaction to it had both inspired the piece and were therefore part of its process configuration.

I mentioned a similar experience in chapter 10, in connection with Krzysztof Penderecki's *Threnody for the Victims of Hiroshima*. I wrote that "I heard the screams of the bomb victims, the panic and flight of the survivors, even the propellers of the plane that dropped the bomb." In this case, the composer's horror at the nuclear violence perpetrated upon Japan at the end of World War II was part of the piece's process configuration.

I described another TME that involved a process configuration in chapter 13, in my account of listening to a Bach fugue. There, I felt that I was climbing around in the score as if it were a jungle gym. The process configuration in this case had more to do with the intellectual than the emotional content of the piece.

My friend Beth tapped into a process configuration when she listened to Puccini's *Madama Butterfly* with her father when she was a child. Beth's TME, which I described in chapter 3, taught her what it felt like to lose something forever, knowing that she "would never retrieve it again," as if she had experienced "a past or parallel life" in which she "had really lived" this experience "just from hearing the music." This sense of loss, an aspect of Puccini's life experience, is a part of the process configuration behind the music.

Kevin's TME also involved a process configuration. When he began to dance to the music, his intention to move authentically attuned him to the process configuration behind the music, which he experienced as morphing colors and shapes. In chapter 1, I mentioned a type of TME in which listeners inwardly experience odd colors and geometric forms that seem to have no equivalents in physical reality. These colors and forms often indicate that a listener's intuitive senses are active and becoming aware of a process configuration.

When Kevin tried to express with his body what was happening in that process configuration, which he called an "inner energy constellation," he tapped into the soul-based energy transformations contained within it. His awareness of these energy transformations led him to an experience of his own soul in nonphysical reality, which he described as a galaxy.

By aligning himself with the energy transformations going on in his soul— a process that he experienced as *becoming* the galaxy, so that his body "was mirroring its movement, rhythms, and activity"—Kevin went beyond an awareness of his soul to encounter what Swedenborg calls the light of heaven, and I call the cosmic normative balance. He was directly connected with the source of all consciousness.

How was this possible? Perhaps the unknown music that Kevin was dancing to targeted the eighth center, which can put us in touch with the cosmic normative balance. Or, more likely, because we all come from the same source, under the right conditions, we can reach through *any* music to that source. Perhaps all music has its source in the cosmic normative balance, no matter what centers along the continuum of human potential it targets. As one of my e-mail correspondents, a jazz drummer named Roland, once put it: "Norm's the ultimate musician! (Maybe the *only* one!)"

One goal of the yoga of listening is to use the continuum of human potential to reach through the music we compose, perform, or listen to, not merely to achieve TMEs, but to have direct contact with the soul or cosmic normative balance, as Kevin did. Sensing the process configuration behind a piece of music is a way of preparing ourselves for such contact.

Thought Forms and Music Forms

As I've noted, TMEs may include inner visions such as odd colors and geometric shapes as visual representations of process configurations. A number of esotericists who have written about music mention such shapes, which they call thought forms.

For example, in a precursor to *Music: Its Secret Influence*, Cyril Scott wrote: "Every musical composition produces a thought-and-colour form in the astral space, and according to that form and colour is to be gauged the spiritual value of the composition under review." Perception of this form is accomplishable only by "someone who has developed psychic abilities."

Scott listed "lilac, violet, blue, pink, yellow, apple-green" as spiritual colors, especially when linked with "a form of lofty structure and vastness." Works whose thought forms include these colors have "intrinsic spiritual value." Works "of a lower order," however, are colored with "muddy browns, greys, cloudy reds."[8]

Scott's notion of "astral space" is roughly equivalent, if not identical, to what Charles calls nonphysical reality. The "thought-and-colour" forms he speaks of are probably identical to what Charles calls process configurations.

Scriabin perceived colors inwardly in response to hearing external sounds. He once told an interviewer that he usually had "only the 'feeling' of the colour."[9] When that feeling became especially intense, it would show up as an inner image of the color. For example, Scriabin often saw the key of C major as red, D as yellow, and F-sharp as blue.

The mystical composer Olivier Messiaen was also able to perceive sound as color. He said:

> When I hear a score or read it, hearing it in my mind, I also see in my mind's eye corresponding colours which turn, mix and blend with each other just like the sounds which turn, mix and intermingle, and at the same time as them.[10]

For example, Messiaen described the following colors in association with certain passages in his music: "an orange with red and green pigments, patches of gold and also a milky white with iridescent opal-like reflections."[11] He insisted that this experience was neither imaginative nor psychic but "an inward reality."[12]

In *Music Forms: Superphysical Effects of Music Clairvoyantly Observed*, esotericist Geoffrey Hodson hinted at the importance of process configurations, which he called "music forms," in the composition and performance of music. A music form originates in the "play" of a composer's "consciousness during composition." It's "an expression of superphysical matter, partly a creation of the composer's idea and inspiration and partly the superphysical effects of the physical sound" when the piece is performed.[13]

What Hodson called superphysical matter appears to be astral or nonphysical in nature, implying that music forms, like process configurations, develop in a nonphysical medium like Charles's transceptual field.

Hodson went on to say that in any music form "a measure" of the composer's "egoic life and consciousness is incarnated as an ensouling principle, creating a relatively permanent entity."[14] This "entity" resides in the nonphysical reality that some esotericists call the astral plane. When "a composition is performed," said Hodson, "an instant rapport with the original composer's form—and therefore with his life and consciousness—is established."[15]

Hodson believed that this rapport extends even to the music forms of deceased composers. "Apparently, success in the art of interpretation depends on the performer's ability to contact and express the composer's life and consciousness, and through that, his intention."[16] Such contact depends on the performer's conscious or unconscious rapport with the music form and its composer.

Beth's Puccini-induced TME, in which she tapped into the sense of loss in *Madama Butterfly*, allowed her to respond to emotional aspects of the "egoic life and consciousness" encoded in the music and the process configuration behind it. Something similar occurred for me, with the emotions of outrage and horror, in the TMEs induced by listening to music by Husa and Penderecki.

Value Fields

Esotericists Annie Besant and C. W. Leadbeater also wrote on the subject of music forms in their book *Thought-Forms*, which contains illustrations of inwardly perceived images and colors associated with listening to music. The authors claimed that

> sound produces form as well as color, and that every piece of music leaves behind it an impression of this nature, which persists for some considerable time, and is clearly visible to those who have eyes to see.[17]

Besant and Leadbeater selected three pieces of music as illustrations of such thought forms: Mendelssohn's *Lieder ohne Wörte* (*Songs without Words*) No. 9, in E Major, for piano; the "Soldier's Chorus" from the opera *Faust* by Charles Gounod (1818–1893); and the Prelude to Wagner's opera *Die Meistersinger*. All three examples were played on a church organ. The clairvoyantly perceived forms thus produced were described to, then rendered by, an artist in color and reproduced as plates in the book.

These plates depict a church tower in an English landscape, with the astral forms produced by the music billowing above it like atomic mushroom clouds. The Mendelssohn cloud is filled with simple lines and colors and rises 150 feet above ground level. The Gounod cloud contains a psychedelic swirl and rises 600 feet. The Wagner cloud produces a "mountain-range" that rises 900 feet into the air.[18]

Such clouds may last "an hour or two at least," during which they're "radiating forth their characteristic vibrations in every direction." The spiritual vibrations present in these clouds of astral matter have an "uplifting effect on anyone in their vicinity."[19]

The illustrations in Besant and Leadbeater's book may document something more than the process configurations behind their musical examples. The enormous size of these thought forms suggests that they may be what Charles calls *value fields*. According to Charles, a value field is established whenever a group of people who share similar values come together, as in a concert hall.

Being in the presence of others who share our values creates a sense of safety. The energy field that surrounds our bodies—what psychics call the aura, an expression of our soul's presence in the physical body and the life force that animates us—begins to expand and merge with that of others. This merging creates a value field.

The shared experience of listening to music often mediates, enhances, and accelerates the creation of a value field. The music itself may express certain values, so the process configuration behind it is the actual source of the value field.

In chapter 1, I described looking around me at the rapt audience listening to the Borromeo Quartet, which was playing Schubert's Rosamunde Quartet. That shared experience of raptness was a value field.

In chapter 2, I recounted esotericist David Tame's Bach-induced TME, in which he perceived waves of goodness emanating from the music, filling the concert hall, and radiating through the walls. He seemed to rise above his body and perceive the concert hall from outside, amidst the sprawling city that surrounded it. The concert hall appeared to him as a "glowing light amid a great, chaotic sea of darkness."[20]

Tame, too, was perceiving a value field, which had its source in the music. He described the music he was hearing as "a tangible, living filigree lattice-work of mathematical precision which I could almost reach out and touch,"[21] which means that he was in touch with the process configuration behind it.

Value fields can also develop in connection with rock concerts, sporting events, cults, and political uprisings. Sometimes a value field becomes so strong that people in its vicinity are taken over by it. They end up acting in accordance with the value field, even when the values it expresses contradict their own.

I can often sense the presence of a value field, but have never perceived one in visual terms. It's conceivable that a psychically gifted individual could perceive a value field in connection with a concert hall, during or after a performance, and perhaps from outside. If this perception were translated into color and shape, the psychic might be able to tell what sorts of people were gathered there, what kind of music was being played, and what values were contributing to the value field. The result, if recorded in visual images, would probably look something like the clouds of astral matter in Besant and Leadbeater's book.

Becoming aware of the presence of a value field in a live concert can be valuable in two ways. First, the value field is based on values present in the music being performed. Aligning yourself more deeply with these values can result in a TME, connecting you with the process configuration behind the piece, or providing you with an ecstatic sense of union with other audience members. In either case, you may find it easier to sense a connection with your soul or God.

Second, if you find yourself uncomfortable with the value field created by a piece of music, then your soul may be warning you away from it. The values expressed in that field may be too different from your own, making it difficult for you to open up to them. Or the audience doesn't feel safe to you, especially in cases in which the value field created by the music gives audience members permission to act in ways that may be dangerous to themselves and you.

Remember, TMEs give permission and show the way. When you're listening to music with others, the values expressed in that music and the value field it creates can lead to TMEs. The ecstatic feelings that result when your energy field opens and merges with the energy fields of others often carries the force of a conversion experience.

It's a good idea to make sure that the permission and sense of guidance resulting from such TMEs is in alignment with the soul's intentions for your growth before you act in accordance with a value field. Otherwise you may end up doing things that you'll regret later.

Psychic Signatures

Process configurations can be perceived in a variety of ways, from shapes to colors to something felt internally that has no visual equivalent. As I noted in *Otherwhere* and *The Unanswered Question*, everything experienced in nonphysical reality is energy. That energy needs to be translated—represented to us in quasi-physical form—in order to be understood by the mind and communicated via words to others.

Several people may inwardly perceive the process configuration of a certain piece of music. Each may describe it differently. Yet the function of what's perceived remains the same in each description: a sense of the music's having had its origin in what Scriabin called an "inner image" or "sounding body," which represents not only what the composer wished to express, but also the process of the work's creation and the process of its unfolding in performance.

Process configurations also include the ways in which the composer has targeted the centers along the continuum of human potential in any given moment. We can use our awareness of these centers as a way of putting us in touch with a process configuration.

In most music, more than one center is active simultaneously. The lower centers usually support the higher ones. Centers one (rhythm), two (sonority), and six (form) are almost always present. One or more of the other centers may be added to these, creating the specific energetic profile of a piece.

I call this energetic profile the piece's *psychic signature.* If a finished piece or a song is like a fleshed-out human body, the process configuration is like the bones that support the body. The psychic signature is like an X-ray that reveals the location of the bones. Such signatures may be dramatic, if the third center is dominant; expressive, if the fourth center is dominant; infused with well-being, if the fifth center is dominant; intellectual, if the sixth center is dominant; or spiritual, if the seventh or eighth center is dominant.

Large-scale pieces of music, such as Beethoven's symphonies or Wagner's operas, have psychic signatures. So do the subdivisions—acts, movements, or sections—of such pieces. Even a single phrase can have its characteristic energetic profile.

Hodson's book *Music Forms* contains artistic renderings of the thought forms perceived while he listened to eight pieces of classical music. In these renderings, he sought to capture the thought form as it emerged through the performance of the work, an arduous process that required many hearings, since each note, phrase, section, and movement added its own "superphysical effect" to the two-dimensional diagram he was attempting to create. Some of the features he perceived were "relatively permanent," others "evanescent."[22]

Hodson reported that during this rendering process, "changes in form" would "follow each other so swiftly" that "before the observer has correctly visualised one, another is superimposed upon it, while at the same time new ones may be appearing at other parts of the overall structure." Meanwhile, the actual "sound of the music is distracting to the observer, especially if he is a music lover, often rendering concentration at the superphysical level extremely difficult."[23]

In these ever-changing music forms, Hodson was attempting to capture what I call psychic signatures. Using a meditative state to follow how the psychic signature of a piece of music evolves over time may be a less arduous way of getting in touch with the process configuration or music form behind it than trying to illustrate it in color in a two-dimensional drawing, as Hodson tried to do.

Most songs in popular music, and many jazz instrumentals, rarely change centers. Just as the tempo, texture, tonality, volume level, and overall mood remain the same, so does the energetic signature. In longer works, especially in classical music, the targeted centers change constantly.

In the yoga of listening, determining the psychic signature of a piece or song requires the ability to differentiate between the eight centers along the continuum of human potential. Each of these centers may be in one of four states: dominant, subordinate, attenuated, or absent.

For example, in a simple love ballad, such as "A Whole New World" (also called "Aladdin's Theme") from Disney's 1992 animated film *Aladdin*, the fourth center (expression) is dominant.[24] The first (rhythm) and second (sonority) centers, which are usually active in Western music, are subordinate. The third (intensity), fifth (well-being), seventh (expanded consciousness), and eighth (cosmic consciousness) are absent. The sixth center is attenuated. It guides the composer's musical choices without obtruding itself, which might make the song seem more cerebral than expressive.

A further refinement of the song's signature becomes available if I tune into the levels of the centers involved. "A Whole New World" targets a point between middle and upper 4, in which the love expressed is more hopeful than elated, but free of yearning. The composer is an entertainer, working from lower 6, since the intent of the song is to get me to feel what the composer wants to express, rather than thinking what he thinks (middle 6) or seeing what he sees (upper 6).

The purpose of music composed with such a signature is to open the heart. This signature is fairly common in New-Age music, especially the variety that involves acoustic instruments such as solo piano or guitar.

If a composer were to add the tension, agitation, or eruptive passion of the third center into the mix, the result would be more like a rock love song. By adding lower to middle 7 instead of 3, the result would be the transcendental longing expressed in much New-Age music.

If the composer were a middle 6 formalist instead of a lower 6 entertainer, the result would be an intellectually stimulating piece about transcendental longing, richly textured and fully developed. Miles Davis's performance of "Portia," which I cited in chapter 14, would be an example of music of this type.

If a composer were an upper 6 visionary, the transcendental longing expressed by this signature would result in a musical depiction of another, perhaps utopian, world. "God-music" from George Crumb's *Black Angels*, for electric string quartet, portrays just such a world of angelic peace and our intense human longing for it.

When I began experimenting with using the continuum of human potential to place myself en rapport with a piece's process configuration, I was only able to sense the psychic signature of a piece, movement, or section in the broadest of terms. I might be able to pick out which center was dominant and nothing more. Eventually, I was able to detect whether the other centers were subordinate, attenuated, or absent. Much later came the ability to detect which level of the dominant center was targeted, and whether the composer was an entertainer, formalist, or visionary.

In chapter 7, I described the seven rules for becoming a good listener, as presented by Indian classical musician Pandit Patekar. His sixth rule is: "Try to think your way inside the artist. In other words, try to feel with him and to become one with both artist and theme."[25] Using the continuum of human potential to become aware of the psychic signature of a piece of music, and perhaps the process configuration that lies behind it, is a means of realizing this rule.

Learning to follow the ways in which composers add and subtract the eight centers from phrase to phrase, movement to movement, and piece to piece has provided me with an endless source of fascination. This is the most subtle application of the yoga of listening, preparing the listener to reach beyond the music to the process configuration behind it, and perhaps from that to the soul or cosmic normative balance.

A Musical Tour of the Continuum of Human Potential

Eberhard Weber's jazz composition "Silent Feet," from the album of the same title, touches on centers one through seven, making it a musical tour of most of the continuum of human potential.[26] The second-by-second analysis of "Silent Feet" given here can also demonstrate how to register the psychic signature of a piece, providing an X-ray of the process configuration that lies behind it. I recommend listening to "Silent Feet" a minimum of three times, perhaps on successive days.

The first listening should be without reference to the synopsis of the piece included here. The second should be conducted with reference both to this synopsis and a timer, such as that contained in many stationary and portable CD players. The third listening should occur with eyes closed, remembering what I've said about how the centers change as the piece progresses.

Subsequent listenings to "Silent Feet" might be conducted by first reviewing what I've written, then listening with eyes closed. Notice whether any inner visual effects develop as you listen, letting you know that you're in touch with the process configuration behind the piece. Because "Silent Feet" involves several passages of upper 7 music, it could perhaps launch you beyond perceiving the process configuration into a transcendent experience of your own soul or the cosmic normative balance, as Kevin achieved in the TME described.

During each hearing, try to feel how the interplay of centers affects you, rather than listening by the center numbers. Perceiving the psychic signature of a piece or the process configuration behind it requires the use of intuitive senses that are often not available when the mind is operating in its usual analytic mode.

The center numbers exist merely to draw your attention to subtle changes in energetic states that might pass by too quickly for you to notice otherwise. Over time, I've learned to detect the changes in centers in a piece without losing my openness to the energies they represent and how they might affect me. This is a skill in the yoga of listening little different from learning to balance on one leg in certain hatha yoga postures. It takes some getting used to, a little practice. The results, in terms of deeper appreciation of the music, as well as deeper receptivity to energies and states of consciousness it targets, may be well worth the effort.

Listeners can use this exercise to familiarize themselves with how the centers are added and subtracted as a composition develops. Following the piece's psychic signature in this way can not only put them in touch with the process configuration underlying a piece, but also help them develop the ability to move from psychic signature to process configuration when listening to other music.

Through using this exercise, performers may become more able to place themselves en rapport with the process configuration of a piece of music they're playing, allowing them, in Hodson's words, to "contact and express the composer's life and consciousness, and through that, his intention."[27] The result will be a more satisfying performance of the piece, perhaps a transcendent one.

This exercise is useful for composers, too, since it demonstrates how they can create various effects through adding and subtracting the centers on the continuum of human potential when composing a piece. It can also help them develop the ability to perceive the process configurations behind their own music, which can speed up the compositional process and perhaps make the piece a gateway to the soul or cosmic normative balance for future listeners, as in Kevin's TME.

In part 3 of this book, I provide other exercises to suggest how to attune yourself to the psychic signature of rock songs, jazz instrumentals, and pieces of classical music, especially those whose process configurations involve access to the soul or cosmic normative balance. All of these exercises, including the present one, are ways of using the yoga of listening to prepare yourself for achieving TMEs.

"Silent Feet" is just over twelve minutes long. Composed macrorhythmically, the piece has three parts. The first part is a gradually accumulating wave of energy. The second part rides the crest of that wave. The third part begins with a sudden dissipation of this accumulated energy, which then builds up again to its former peak and gradually dissolves.

When the acoustic bass begins the piece, its spare rhythmic motif captures and entrains our interest (middle and upper 1). Seconds later, when the piano enters, the first center is fully active and the dominant center rises to lower 2 (relaxation), using the wind-chime-like sounds typical of some New-Age music: beautiful, but not emotionally expressive.

At 0:40, the music hints at the heart-opening expressiveness of the fourth center, as the piano rises to middle 2 (pleasure).

At 1:00, the energy level of the music starts to rise. The piano vacillates between the beautiful sounds of middle 2 (pleasure) and the heart-opening expressiveness of upper 4 (elation).

At 1:30, the passion of the third center makes its first appearance. By now, the full ranges of both the first and second centers are active. The drummer joins the ensemble.

At 2:00, centers 1, 2, and upper 4 are active, but 3 has temporarily dropped out. The drums hint at the joyful range of middle 5.

At 2:30, centers 1, 2, and upper 4 continue to be active, with middle 5 (joy) dominant. The passion of center 3 drifts in and out of the piano from time to time.

By 3:10, several centers are active at once, each in a different instrument. The joy of middle 5 is present in the drums; the piano is expressing the elation of upper 4; the bass is expressing the yearning of middle 4.[28] Centers 1, 2 , and 3 are active below these.

At 3:50, middle 5 (joy) is fully established in all three instruments and the music has become more dancelike.

At 4:30, the energy has risen to the exuberance of upper 5. When the saxophone enters, joining with the piano in a contrasting rhythm, at 5:20, the music vaults over the sixth center and lands in the ecstasy of upper 7.

Ten seconds later, when the saxophone drops out, the music once again expresses the exuberance of upper 5. This pattern of alternating upper 7 with upper 5 then repeats itself. I usually feel a slight expansion of consciousness when the saxophone is playing in this section.

At 5:50, the second section begins, with a radical change in texture. The targeted center is middle 6 (invention). All instruments are improvising as inventively as possible, each going its own way, creating a typical jazz experience—one in which the pleasure is primarily intellectual.

The saxophone, however, vacillates between the heart-opening expressiveness of middle to upper 4 and the exuberance of upper 5, creating another typical jazz experience, a quasi-ecstatic sense of liberation from boundedness and structure. There's even a point (at about 7:00) when the sax player gets carried away, and briefly pushes his playing into the crisis zone between centers 5 and 6 (mania).

At 7:50, the third section begins. Weber wipes the slate clean, eliminating all but centers 1 and 2. The result is the relaxation of lower 2, a simple ostinato (repeated pattern) that has the minimal amount of rhythmic arousal and sonorous pleasure to be classified at this level. Meanwhile, middle 1 (interest) is active in the drums—a series of sounds presented in short, barely rhythmic phrases, with just enough intentionality to hold the listener's attention.

At 9:15, the music rises to middle 2 (pleasure) in the piano and bass, while the drums carry the music up to upper 2 (intoxication). Upper 2 is fully established when the saxophone enters, at about 9:30. The music is still without passionate intensity (center 3) or emotional expressiveness (center 4).

At 10:25, in a passage that recalls the music of 4:30, upper 5 (exuberance) returns (along with the passion of the third center and the emotional expressiveness of the fourth). This passage is immediately followed by another instance of vaulting to upper 7 (ecstasy), with the entry of the saxophone, seven seconds later.

At 10:50, the drums are carrying on at upper 5 (exuberance), while the piano vacillates between middle 2 (pleasure) and middle 4 (yearning), as at the beginning of the piece.

At 11:20, the piano has settled down to middle 2 (pleasure). The drums gradually relax from upper to middle to lower 5, then drop out altogether.

From 11:55 to the end, fifteen seconds later, everyone has settled into lower 2 (relaxation).

PART III

Music of the Soul

17

Listening as a Spiritual Practice

As the epigraph of this book, I chose a statement by the Irish-born British playwright George Bernard Shaw: "You use a glass mirror to see your face: you use works of art to see your soul." The composers, performers, and pieces that most deeply move us are showing us our souls. Or perhaps we see our souls in them, recognizing who we are and who we most want to be.

The music to which we're drawn reflects our inner state, level of spiritual development, and growth needs at the time. Musical taste indicates where we find ourselves on the continuum of human potential. How our taste evolves may provide a record of our spiritual development.

We may progress from the rebellious music of the third center that we worshiped in our teens, to the soft-rock love songs of the fourth center, the feel-good dance music of the fifth, the intellectual appeal of alternative rock or jazz of the six, until we've acquired a taste for the music of the soul, that of the seventh and eighth centers.

The soul may lead us from one lesson and level of the continuum of human potential to the next by means of TMEs. When we get bored with music that targets a certain center, we're ripe for a revelatory experience that shows us the pleasures of music from some higher center. If we would like to accelerate our spiritual growth, then we need to challenge ourselves to listen to music from the higher ranges of the continuum, especially those associated with the seventh and eighth centers.

The way in which my collection of recordings has grown over time, first as LPs, then as cassettes, currently as CDs, perhaps at some future point as MP3s or some other format—what I keep, what I get rid of, what I listen to again and again, my ever changing playlists—is a record of my journey through the centers in the continuum of human potential, my path of spiritual development. The growing catalog of music that I've composed provides a similar record of my development. The clarinet or piano music I practice as a performer does the same thing. As my collection of recordings, compositions, sheet music, and scores evolves, the outlines of my soul become ever clearer.

Charles and my own experience have taught me that music is not only a way of attaining higher states of consciousness and TMEs; it's also a *practice*, something that combines physical, emotional, intellectual, and spiritual training, in much the same way that Tantra or hatha yoga does. The goal of this practice is to see my soul ever more clearly and learn to realize its plans for my growth. I call this practice the yoga of listening.

I've found that in the yoga of listening, the key is learning to reach through the music that I compose, perform, or listen to and find the process configuration that lies behind it. In this way, I'm directly in touch with the energy transformations and spiritual wisdom encoded in the music.

When I'm composing, the process configuration behind the piece teaches me how to find the notes that will realize it in sound. When I perform a piece, getting in touch with the process configuration behind it enables me to transmit its encoded wisdom more directly to an audience. When I listen to a piece, I'm more receptive to the encoded wisdom transmitted from composer to performer to audience.

I mentioned the soul's plans for my growth. Those plans are also a process configuration, containing information about the composition of my own life as I realize it in the physical world. Tuning into the process configurations behind music by others allows me to sense something of the soul's plan behind their lives.

As esotericist Geoffrey Hodson says, "a measure" of the composer's "egoic life and consciousness is incarnated as an ensouling principle,"[1] in any music form or process configuration. This ensouling principle allows performers and listeners to develop "an instant rapport with the original composer's form—and therefore with his life and consciousness."[2]

In Kevin's TME, described in the previous chapter, he aligned himself with the unknown music he was dancing to, then reached through that to the process configuration behind it. Because the intuitive senses that allowed him to perceive this process configuration were open, he was able to leap from it to a direct connection with his soul and the energy transformations or process configuration behind his own life, which he saw as a galaxy. The crescendo and climax in the music then expanded his awareness still further, beyond the soul and its plans for his growth, opening him up to the glorious light of the cosmic normative balance.

As I pointed out in the previous chapter, becoming aware of the centers that are active in a song or piece of music—its psychic signature—can put us in touch with the process configuration behind it. In using the yoga of listening for this purpose, we're not only developing our ability to sense such process configurations, but also our ability to sense the process configurations behind our own lives, the soul's master plan for our growth.

In part 2, I associated certain lessons with each center in order to emphasize the connection between music, the centers, and the process configurations of our lives. The yoga of listening involves first listening to the music that gives us pleasure, moves us, or induces TMEs. Next, we become aware of the centers operating within this music, each piece's psychic signature, which, as I pointed out in the previous chapter, is like an X-ray of the process configuration behind it. In so doing, we develop the inner senses required to perceive such process configurations, which often manifest themselves as visual images such as thought forms, music forms, morphing colors or shapes.

Over time, we may be able to sense the process configuration of the composer's own life operating behind that of the music we're listening to. I've found that knowing something about that life is often helpful in achieving this stage in the yoga of listening. It's natural that we become fascinated with the lives of those whose music has the greatest effect on us. They become our spiritual teachers. The more we know about what was going on in their lives when they were composing a piece we love, the more likely we are to sense the *composer's* process configuration behind the process configuration of the piece.

Having reached through the wisdom encoded in a piece of music to a sense of the composer's soul, we've developed the ability to sense the process configuration behind our own lives, the soul's master plan for our growth. Music can lead us not only to see our souls, as Shaw says, but also to have a direct experience of the soul's presence within us. We may even be able to reach beyond that sense of the soul's presence, as Kevin did, to have an ecstatic experience of the cosmic normative balance: God, the source of all consciousness.

In the ancient texts on yoga, such an experience of God is called samadhi (bliss). Samadhi is the goal of the yoga of listening, as it is of most other forms of yoga.

The yoga of listening, like other yogas, is a spiritual practice. It can be undertaken by any listener, performer, or composer. As jazz-rock fusion guitarist John McLaughlin learned from his spiritual teacher, Sri Chinmoy, in the 1970s: "The important thing, always, is the state of consciousness because it determines (1) how you do it, and (2) the quality of what you do, and (3) the quality of what you are. So if you are a musician and you work towards enlightenment, your music will automatically be a part of it."[3]

The same thing will be true even if you're not a musician but wish to use listening to music as a means of working toward enlightenment. I explained "how you do it" in chapter 7, where I laid out the principles of the yoga of listening. In the subsequent chapters, I deepened your understanding of the eight centers and created playlists of music from various genres to improve "the quality of what you do" in the yoga of listening. Now I have some recommendations for how to develop "the quality of what you are" as you pursue the yoga of listening as a spiritual practice.

Yoga scholar Georg Feuerstein outlines eight components of the Tantric spiritual path, each of which has relevance for listeners, performers, and composers in the yoga of listening: moral restraint, self-restraint, posture, breath control, sensory inhibition, concentration, meditation, and ecstasy.[4]

In Tantra, moral restraint involves "nonharming, truthfulness, nonstealing, chastity, and greedlessness." The usefulness of these virtues for listeners, performers, and composers may not be immediately apparent, despite their undeniable social benefits. Yet practicing them would keep the mind quiet, allowing it to become more focused on the yoga of listening.

Think about the opposites of these virtues—violence, lying, dishonesty, promiscuity, and covetousness—and it's easy to understand how distracting a lifestyle dominated by such behaviors would be. This is why Feuerstein states that the virtues of moral restraint described above "are said to be valid on all levels, at all times, and everywhere."[5]

Self-restraint involves "purity, contentment, austerity, study, and devotion to the Lord."[6] The purity here is not the moral type, which is covered by moral restraint. Rather, it refers to purity of purpose: Are you serving the ego by composing or performing to impress others, or the art itself by becoming the best composer or performer you can be, through realizing the soul's plans in your work?

As a listener, are you pursuing the yoga of listening merely in the hope of increasing your pleasure through enhanced TMEs? Or are you doing so in order to bring yourself closer to the soul and realizing its plans for your growth?

In Tantric practice, the idea of devotion to the Lord refers to a Hindu god such as Shiva. In the yoga of listening, such devotion may refer to the art of music, your own soul as listener, performer, or composer, or the author of a work you're preparing to listen to or perform.

Many listeners, performers, and composers revere Bach, Beethoven,

Coltrane, the progressive rock band Yes, and other favorites as if they were gods. Their devotion yields a different listening experience from one based on mere pleasure, a different performance from one based on competitiveness or the desire to impress. Such devotion can sometimes be a factor in producing TMEs.

The virtues of contentment, austerity, and study are related to one another. In the yoga of listening, satisfaction (contentment) derives from the study and practice of composing, performing, and listening to music. Austerity means creating an outer environment as free from distractions as possible. Successful practice of moral restraint will have already created a distraction-free inner environment.

In Tantra, the cultivation of posture involves yogic asanas (poses) such as the "plow," "lotus," or "corpse," which are familiar to anyone who has taken a hatha yoga class. Composing and listening to music are usually passive activities that require a strong inward focus. In the yoga of listening, in order not to develop your capacities for expanded or cosmic consciousness at the expense of your focus in the physical body, you should make sure that you get physical exercise on a regular basis.

Charles says that there is a direct relationship between mental and physical flexibility. Pursuing one allows greater flexibility to develop in the other. So, both consciousness *and* body will become more flexible if you pursue the yoga of listening, which is a type of meditation practice, in combination with hatha yoga or some other form of developing physical flexibility.

As a performer, your playing posture may be sufficiently artificial, as in the case of tucking a violin or viola under the chin, that muscular tension may result from prolonged practice. You'll need to discover not only the most balanced and relaxed way of holding your instrument, but also how to release the physical tension that builds up through playing. Hatha yoga and other stretching exercises may help you avoid debilitating nerve and muscle damage, such as repetitive-stress syndrome.

In Tantra, breath control involves the techniques of pranayama. Such techniques may require the practitioner to take in the breath in a sustained manner, hold it for a time, and exhale it with even greater restraint; or use one nostril for inhalation and the other for exhalation.

In music, breath control may seem to apply mostly to performers, especially singers and wind players, who need to take in sufficient air to get through a phrase and modulate its dynamics. Pianists and string players also need breath control, which can involve not forgetting to breathe during difficult passages, or learning how to bring subtle emphasis to the musical phrasing of a passage with the timing of the breath.

During my first semester of study in college, my clarinet teacher had me practice "long tones"—taking in a breath and sustaining a single note on the exhalation as long as possible. This exercise not only resembles some that I've experienced in yoga classes, but also improves on them. I was required to vary the intensity of the breath exhaled through my instrument to produce fluctuations in volume from as loud to as soft as possible, a practice that helped me develop both breath control and concentration. I've also heard of wind players who have mastered the art of "rotary breathing," which allows them to take in breath through the nose while at the same time exhaling through the mouth into their instrument—another highly developed form of breath control.

In Tantra, breath control is practiced for the effect it has on consciousness—relaxing and expanding it, preparing the way for ecstasy. Breath control also has an effect on consciousness in the performance of music, as anyone who has experienced stage fright can attest. A case of nerves can have a devastating effect on a performance, making it impossible to focus on anything but the physical aspect of music-making, of simply getting through a phrase. Stage fright can also cause lapses in concentration, faulty sound production, fingering errors, memory problems, and a host of other embarrassing affronts to the art. Deep breathing between movements and during rests can often remedy or prevent such effects.

The benefits of breath control may not be as obvious for listeners or composers. In the yoga of listening, I've discovered that timing my breaths with the long phrases of a Bruckner symphony can deepen my concentration on the music and lead to the ecstasy of a TME, as I related in chapter 3.

As a composer, I've benefited from the higher levels of concentration that listening and breathing in this way make possible. I've found that any form of breath work, especially when combined with meditation, increases my clarity of mind, which can make the compositional process more efficient.

Sensory inhibition, concentration, and meditation, each mentioned by Feuerstein as an essential aspect of Tantra, are related to each other. In Tantra and the yoga of listening, as well as composing and performing music, the idea is to create a one-pointed consciousness, a trance state in which ecstasy is achieved. Feuerstein defines ecstasy as "one's complete merging with the object of meditation."[7]

In the yoga of listening, the object of meditation is the music you're listening to. In performing, it's the score of the piece you're playing. In composing, it's the new music you're in the process of realizing through improvisation or on paper, using acoustic instruments, electronics, or a computer notation program.

The idea is to get behind the notes, to perceive the psychic signature of the piece and the process configuration behind it, to jump from the piece's process configuration to that of the composer's soul or your own, and perhaps from there to an experience of the cosmic normative balance. Alignment with your soul, the master plan for your growth, or the cosmic normative balance will improve the quality of who you are whether you're a listener, performer, or composer.

Performers who are able to line themselves up with a piece's process configuration and that of the composer's soul are better able to project the wisdom encoded in the music, transmitting it to the audience, and perhaps inducing TMEs in themselves and their listeners.

Composers who are able to line themselves up with the process configurations behind a piece they're writing will find it easier to realize that piece in sonic or score form. The depth and range of what their music expresses will also be affected. They'll be composing music of the soul, full of TME-inducing wisdom to be transmitted from performer to listener.

Sensory inhibition involves learning how not to be distracted while composing, performing, or listening to music. Such distractions can originate in the body, mind, or external environment. In the yoga of listening, you develop sensory inhibition by focusing exclusively on what you're listening to, rather than having music on in the background while doing something else. When your mind wanders, you bring it back to the music.

Similar principles apply to composing and performing. You must learn to banish all thoughts other than those connected with music-making. Performers must also learn how not to become uncentered by the presence of an audience, its movements and noises.

Concentration is the key to sensory inhibition, and such concentration is mastered through meditation. Since the yoga of listening is a form of meditation, the concentration you develop as a listener can help you achieve a similar level of concentration as a composer or performer. Composition itself, which often requires deep inner listening, can be practiced as a form of meditation.

For performers, practicing your instrument with concentration can become a form of meditation. In classical Indian music, it's said, "A musical mistake is also a spiritual mistake."[8]

My guide, Charles, has often reminded me that when I'm practicing clarinet or piano, every mistake I make is merely a lapse in concentration. My not being able to play a passage may be less the result of insufficient technique or rehearsal than of doubts about whether I can play it, or internal distractions, such as personal problems. Such things can interfere with my ability to concentrate on how to produce a passage at every level, from the physical and emotional to the intellectual and spiritual.

In Tantra, one form of meditation involves intense concentration on a visual image called a *yantra*. A yantra is a drawing done on paper, wood, or cloth, intended to be "a geometric representation of the levels and energies of the cosmos and the human body." In some Tantric practices, the yantra must be "completely internalized, i.e., perfectly visualized."[9]

In the yoga of listening, the music being listened to functions like a non-visual yantra. Deep and frequent listening can allow you to hear parts or the whole of a piece or song internally, without reference to a recording.

In performing, a similar purpose is served by the score of a piece. Like a yantra, this score is a focus of concentration. Playing from it, studying it in silence, listening to others' renditions of it, and hearing it in your mind are all aids to meditation on this yantra. Some musicians perform or conduct from memory, having "completely internalized" the musical score as if it were a yantra. Many music teachers claim that a transcendent performance is only possible when one has completely freed oneself from dependence on the score.

In composing, the yantra is the process configuration behind the piece. It exists as an inner shape in the process of being realized in external form, as a written-out score or recorded sound score.

Tantric meditation may also involve the use of a mantra, a "thought or intention expressed as sound," often without "communicable meaning."[10] As I pointed out in chapter 5, repetition of a piece of music in rehearsal is similar to the repetition of a mantra, acting as an aid to concentration. Such repetition can allow musicians to achieve the best possible performance, possibly even a transcendent one.

Because mantras "are creative forces that act directly on consciousness,"[11] constant rehearsal can have a consciousness-transforming effect on performers, and through them, the audience as well. This transformative effect may be especially noticeable in sacred music with sung texts.

German record producer and spiritual seeker Joachim-Ernst Berendt points out that "mantras also exist in the realm of Christianity," for example, Amen, Alleluia, Hosanna, and so on.[12] Music such as the Hosanna in Bach's B Minor Mass "can be heard in a completely new way if in all its notes we listen to the mantric content of the word." We should try to feel "its primal sound" and "mantric power."[13] The same thing can be true of the Hallelujahs and Amens of gospel music.

In Tantra, the goal, like that of many spiritual practices, "is to transcend the experienced world, which is both external and internal."[14] In the yoga of listening, whether you're a music-lover, composer, or performer, the idea is to see music not merely in terms of "knowledge, pleasure, personal growth, or moral goodness"—although it can be used to achieve such things. Rather, the idea is to see music in terms of the "transcendence of the self and the complete transformation of human nature."[15]

Listening to music that targets each center on the continuum of human potential and integrates them all into a harmoniously functioning whole can allow us to attain transcendence and transformation. The continuum of human potential is itself a process configuration, a basic template for connecting what we feel when we listen to music with the lessons that we need to learn to fulfill the soul's master plan for our growth. As we integrate and harmonize the centers on the continuum of human potential through listening to music, we're also acquiring the wisdom we need to learn those lessons. This is how we can use the yoga of listening to achieve transformation.

In the yoga of listening, transcendence at first occurs unexpectedly, in the form of TMEs that guide and coax us onward as we attempt to duplicate them. As we listen again and again to the pieces that most pleasure or move us, we see our souls ever more clearly. We develop the skills necessary to connect with the soul directly, via process configurations, and realize its plans for our growth with greater clarity and precision.

Eventually, we achieve what psychologist Abraham H. Maslow called the high-plateau experience, a more or less constant peak experience in which we "live casually in heaven" and are "on easy terms with the eternal and the infinite."[16] Then we've achieved the goal of both Tantra and the yoga of listening, samadhi (bliss), the serene sense of union with, or being *yoked* (one meaning of *yoga*) to, the divine.

In Tantra, the relationship between disciple and spiritual master, or guru, is considered to be of primary importance. Devotion to one's guru is supposed to last not only for the duration of that revered teacher's lifetime, but also beyond it. After death, one's guru continues to be available for spiritual guidance.

In the yoga of listening, the greatest masters of Western music continue to guide us long after their deaths, by means of the scores of their music, in the case of Bach and Beethoven, and recordings of their playing, in the case of classical cellist Pablo Casals (1876–1973) or jazz saxophonist John Coltrane. Such scores or recordings and their attendant process configurations contain the "ensouling principle" of their "egoic life and consciousness"[17] for us to tune into and learn from.

As I've noted before, the sixth, or command, center is active in all Western music. This center allows composers and performers, living or dead, to transmit to us, as from guru to disciple, what they think, feel, and understand about life, the experiential, intellectual, and spiritual wisdom they've encoded in their music. The command center is powerful. As with the selection of a Tantric guru, we should choose our spiritual teachers in music wisely.

In the yoga of listening, the two main criteria for choosing spiritual teachers are easy access to the seventh center or above—a capacity of musical mystics; and access to the widest range of the continuum of human potential. The greatest spiritual teachers in music are those who, like Bach or Beethoven, have both qualities.

In *Music: Its Secret Influence*, Cyril Scott implied that a third criterion for selecting a spiritual teacher in music is a virtuous life. The mini-biographies of the composers that Cyril Scott included in his book were written to emphasize the saintliness of each, especially that of César Franck.

A criterion such as saintliness, however, would greatly narrow the field of potential spiritual teachers in music. It would eliminate not only most jazz and rock artists, but also Richard Wagner, who may be one of the greatest spiritual teachers in music, on account of his ease of access to the seventh and eighth centers, and his use of the entire range of the continuum of human potential.

Many musicians aspire to be better people in their music than they are in their lives. Character defects may get in the way of their living saintly lives. Or circumstances such as poverty may make it difficult for them to be virtuous. Or they may be overwhelmed by the desire for fame. Or sudden, unexpected financial success may allow them to gratify any conceivable desire, including physically self-destructive or spiritually inappropriate ones. Or the adulation of their fans may lead to ego inflation, isolation, or boredom.

In many of the world's religions, these are the temptations that each of us may encounter on the path to self-transcendence or enlightenment. The value of public failures to avoid these temptations by those we admire can be an object lesson for us not to fail in the same way.

Saintliness of character *may* be a useful guide for choosing spiritual teachers in music. But equally valid is the wisdom that comes from having lived deeply. The devout celibate Bruckner avoided temptations on the path of soul-realization and composed a transcendent music of the soul. But a composer such as Wagner, who succumbed to and survived indulging in such temptations, is able to access each level of the continuum of human potential, having lived it in some way—including the darker desires and passions of the lower centers. Wagner's operas are often about facing and transcending such desires and passions. We may need those lessons as much as we need the pure soul-connecting music of Bruckner.

Rock and jazz composers and groups that have led less than saintly lives can also become spiritual teachers for us. The important thing is how much of the continuum of human potential their music is able to access, and whether they're able to bring through the music of the soul—that of the seventh and eighth centers.

My friend Deanna, for example, reveres the rock band Led Zeppelin, some of whose songs express a love of nature. They've become spiritual teachers for her.

A few years ago, before she would get up in the morning to go to work, Deanna often found herself in a state half in and half out of sleep, inwardly hearing a song without words for acoustic guitar. The music "had an energetic quality" that made it seem "spiritual" to her. As she awoke, it would gradually fade away. "What is that? Where is it coming from?" she would think. The song felt "otherworldly" and made her "feel peaceful." This went on for months.

Some time later, Deanna accidentally came upon a recording of this song on the Internet. It was "Bron-Yr-Aur," a two-minute solo instrumental by Led Zeppelin, from their 1975 album *Physical Graffiti*.[18] She downloaded it and listened to it again and again.

Deanna, who is in her early thirties, has been into Led Zeppelin since she was fourteen years old. She had probably heard the song before, but it was not a popular one. It was named after a beautiful location in Wales where Led Zeppelin used to rehearse. Deanna tells me that "Bron-Yr-Aur" means "Golden Breast" and refers to sunlight on a hillside that flanks a valley.

Deanna says that listening to the music of Led Zeppelin "puts me in touch with my soul," that it's "an energetic reminder of who I am at a core level." She has created a tape of Led Zeppelin songs that she listens to on workdays while walking outdoors along the Charles River for exercise at lunchtime.

Deanna refers to this combination of walking and listening as a "walking meditation." It helps her "clear out the morning's issues," which "melt away" as the music gets her "in touch with what's really important." Afterward, she feels that she is "back in touch" with her "essence."

For Deanna, listening to Led Zeppelin is a "healing and energizing experience." No matter how often she does this walking meditation, she finds the music "always fresh" and that a certain "vibrance comes through." The songs that she especially likes are those in which the lyrics are about nature. These lyrics, she believes, "contain a hidden spirituality."

Deanna is in a class about channeling that I've been teaching for the last several years. She says that when she prepares to channel by going from a light trance into a deeper one, she often hears a couple of Led Zeppelin songs. She considers these songs to be "consciousness tools" that allow "energetic shifts to happen." Led Zeppelin's music helps her make such shifts, both in life, when she's exercising at lunchtime during the workday, and when she's "focusing on a specific task such as going into trance."

One Led Zeppelin song that Deanna frequently hears when she's going into trance is "Going to California" from *Led Zeppelin IV* (1971), the lyrics of which mention a girl with a flower in her hair.[19] On her way into trance, the song accompanies Deanna's meeting with "a spirit guide on horseback" that she describes as "a woman with long blond curly hair, radiant," who leads Deanna down a path to a waterfall.

Before I interviewed Deanna, I had discovered two hours of Led Zeppelin songs on Kevin's computer, which, as I've mentioned, he had inherited from one of his friends. When I listened to these songs, I was surprised at the number that targeted upper 6, the visionary aspect of the command center. Often, while listening to this music, I would experience a tingling in the area of the sixth chakra, just above and between the eyebrows, which esotericists say is the location of the third eye. Such tingling indicates that my third eye is opening, that my psychic senses are becoming active.

When I showed Deanna a list of songs that targeted upper 6, she said, "Oh my God, those are all my favorite songs!" They made up the majority of the tunes she listens to when she does her walking meditation.

In the yoga of listening, a cumulative effect may develop from repeated listening to one's favorite music. Thus frequent exposure to music that targets upper 6 can open the way (or in Deanna's words, become "a consciousness tool") for experiences of expanded consciousness such as channeling.

Besides "Bron-Yr-Aur," which I identified in chapter 14 as an example of upper 7 music, Deanna's Led Zeppelin playlist includes "Stairway to Heaven" (middle 7 transcendental longing) from *Led Zeppelin IV*, and the following upper 6 visionary tunes: "Thank You" from *Led Zeppelin II* (1969);[20] "The Battle of Evermore" and "Going to California" from *Led Zeppelin IV*; and "The Rain Song" from *Houses of the Holy* (1973).[21]

Several tunes on my list of upper 6 visionary music were not on Deanna's: "Ramble On" from *Led Zeppelin II*, and "No Quarter," and "Over the Hills and Far Away," from *Houses of the Holy*. In the yoga of listening, these too could be used to open the third eye.

Pursuing Union with God

At the end of each chapter in this part of the book, I include a brief sketch of the psychic signature of a piece of music that I consider to be *music of the soul*—that most likely to put us in touch with our souls because it has been composed or performed by musicians who were in touch with theirs. I consider these musicians to be among the best spiritual teachers in the yoga of listening.

The piece I choose to analyze in this way is directly related to the subject of the chapter. In addition to noting the psychic signature, I also offer some remarks about how this piece may be used in the yoga of listening. If you choose to listen to this music, keep in mind the rules for becoming a good listener that I covered in chapter 7, as well as the guidelines I gave in chapter 16 for using the centers on the continuum of human potential to attune yourself to the process configuration behind a piece of music.

The playlists given in part 2 were intended to help you develop the ability to recognize each center and level along the continuum when you hear it. The musical examples in part 3 provide you with opportunities to apply what you've learned. The purpose of these exercises is to help you develop the yoga of listening as a spiritual practice, enabling you to become more receptive to the wisdom encoded in the works I've selected.

In the present chapter, I provide a sketch of the psychic signature of a jazz piece, John Coltrane's 1964 spiritual masterpiece *A Love Supreme*. In the next chapter, I do the same for a rock song by the progressive rock band Yes. Musical examples in later chapters are from the classical repertoire, which I know best. Some are famous and may be familiar to you. They may even appear in your collection of recordings. Others are likely to be unknown.

Even before I understood what I was doing in terms of the yoga of listening, I was constantly searching for music of the soul, especially that which targeted the expanded consciousness of the seventh center and the cosmic consciousness of the eighth. Here are the results of my search. I can't guarantee that in listening to these examples you'll have TMEs. But I believe that, of all the music that I know, the selections included here are the most likely to induce them.

One of the greatest spiritual teachers in jazz is John Coltrane. In the liner notes to *A Love Supreme*, he claims to have experienced what he calls a "spiritual awakening" in 1957. Many of Coltrane's subsequent recordings exemplified spiritual aspirations dating back to that awakening. His playing and compositional styles have influenced the lives of several generations of listeners, as well as the music of many composers and performers in the fields of both jazz and classical music.

As a spiritual teacher in music, Coltrane is driven by the desire for self-transcendence, pursuing union with God through his music. According to Berendt, *A Love Supreme* "combines spiritual fervor with formal completeness in a way not heretofore achieved in jazz."[22] It embodies these words from the poem/prayer Coltrane included in the liner notes: "ELATION—ELEGANCE—EXALTATION— / All from God."[23]

The dominant center in part 1 of *A Love Supreme*, "Acknowledgment," is middle 7 (love of God, in the form of devotion). Centers 1, 2, and 4 through 6 are also present. The third center is attenuated.

In part 2, "Resolution," the dominant center is middle 6 (invention, formal play). Centers 1 through 5 are active beneath it, with the third center coming through strongly. A tinge of lower 7 (awe, fear of God) comes in at the beginning and end, in the sax melody.

In part 3, "Pursuance," the dominant center is once again middle 6. A ninety-second drum solo targets middle 1 (interest). The piano solo is middle 6. When the sax comes in again, the music gradually works its way up to upper 7 (ecstasy). The title of this section, "Pursuance," refers not only to Coltrane's intent to act in accordance (or pursuance) with his spiritual awakening, but also his pursuit of union with the divine.

Part 4, "Psalm," begins at about 10:50 in the third track, after an extended bass solo, which brings back the mood and theme of part 1 (middle 7). For nearly seven minutes, the music targets the upper range of lower 7, expressing an awe-inspired love of God that is solemn, serious, and mystical.

18

Good Music versus Bad Music

In the foreword and chapter 3 of this book, I mentioned Cyril Scott's claim that jazz "was 'put through' by the Dark Forces."[1] These dark forces, or "occult forces of opposition," as esotericist David Tame calls them, attempt to disrupt, prevent, and pervert our spiritual strivings.

Scott saw rock as one of the later "cumulative effects" of jazz.[2] Tame is unequivocal in his dismissal of rock and jazz as spiritually dangerous. According to Tame, good music, such as that of Bach and Beethoven, "gives life." Bad music, such as jazz and rock, "gives death."[3]

To Scott and Tame, my classifying the rock band Led Zeppelin and the jazz composer and saxophonist John Coltrane as spiritual teachers, as I did in the last chapter, would be heretical.

Can music be good or bad for our spiritual growth? Tame believes, as I do, that music encodes various emotions, helping us to perceive and experience them more deeply. Music may even allow us to experience emotions that we've never encountered in ourselves or those around us. Tame also believes that music acts as a means of amplifying and communicating states of consciousness from composer to musician to listener. When listening to music, we're taken over by the state of consciousness of the composer or performer. Our own consciousness takes a similar shape.[4]

Tame's ideas correspond to the yogic notion of transmission of knowledge and states of consciousness from guru to disciple. As we've seen, in music, this transmission is accomplished through the sixth, or command, center.

Tame further believes that music comes in three types, which he describes as *upward* (tending toward God and spiritual or altruistic feelings), *horizontal* (tending toward sonic representations of the material world), and *downward* (tending toward "anguish, desolation, and psychological pain").[5]

Because music amplifies and communicates states of consciousness, Tame insists that we should only listen to morally and spiritually uplifting music, that of the upward direction. Music rooted in the body, emotions, or impressions of nature and the physical world may pull us down and destroy us.

When writing about similar beliefs in ancient yogic traditions, yoga scholar Georg Feuerstein calls this the "verticalist approach" of "'in, up, and out.'"[6] By "in," Feuerstein means turning inward, as in meditation. By "up," he means attempting to achieve higher states of consciousness. By "out," he means transcending the body and the physical world. Tame's preference for music of the upward direction indicates that he's interested only in music that supports us in turning inward, achieving higher states of consciousness, and transcending the body and the world.

Feuerstein sees the body- and world-positive approach of Tantra as more balanced than the verticalist approach. I've adopted a Tantric stance in this book. Like Tame, I have a preference for classical music that tends in the "upward" direction of promoting spiritual growth—or that touches the seventh and eighth centers on the continuum of human potential. But I can't deny the value, for myself or others, of music that targets the other six.

As said in Ecclesiastes (3:1), there's an appropriate season for everything, including the passion and catharsis of music that targets the third center, the pathos, bittersweet yearning, or elation of the fourth, the various ranges of joy in the fifth, and the intellectual pleasures of the sixth.

Nor can I deny the value of nonclassical music. From the examples given in part 2 of this book, it should be clear that the continuum of human potential is fully available to musicians working in any style. Composing, performing, and listening to jazz and rock music can be used to promote spiritual evolution just as well as classical music can.

The argument that some music is good for the soul's development and other music is bad has been put forward for centuries. In the old days, sacred music was considered good and secular music bad. More recently, classical music has been cited as good and popular music as bad. Depending on who you ask, jazz is good and disco bad, country-western is good and hard rock bad, gospel is good and heavy metal bad, and so on. The grounds for these judgments run the gamut from Christian fundamentalist beliefs that the devil can possess members of a rock band to the aesthetic and philosophical arguments of critics and professors.

Rather than addressing the issue of good and bad music on spiritual, religious, or philosophical grounds, which would require a book of its own, I suggest that *all* music, no matter the genre, can be seen as music of the soul.

By acknowledging that any song, dance tune, improvisation, or symphony expresses something about what it means to be human and has a place on the continuum of human potential, we can transcend the question of good and bad music. Our only criterion for judgment should be whether composing, performing, or listening to a particular piece contributes to our growth. The music we dislike may have little use for us, but it could nevertheless spark someone else's growth.

In quoting a Sufi teacher named Sa'adi, musician and mystic Hazrat Inayat Khan said: "Every leaf of the tree becomes a page of sacred scripture once the soul has learned to read."[7] So music is for me. Through creating the yoga of listening, I've learned how to "read" music in terms of the continuum of human potential. No matter the genre—classical, jazz, rock, non-Western—if I treat whatever I hear as scripture, reading it by means of the centers it targets, then all music has something to teach me.

For example, in 1926, Inayat Khan, a contemporary of Scott, wrote that jazz

does not give the brain much to think about in the technicality of music, it does not trouble the soul to think of spiritual things, it does not trouble the heart to feel deeply. Without troubling the heart or the soul it touches the physical body. It gives a renewed strength . . . a greater strength and vigour and interest than music that strains the mind making it to think.[8]

Nothing that Inayat Khan says about jazz is pejorative. Translated in terms of the continuum of human potential, his statement indicates that early jazz didn't target the heart (fourth center), brain (sixth center), or soul (seventh or eighth center). Instead, it acted on the body (first center) and renewed strength and vigor (the fifth, or well-being, center).

Asked during a lecture about the spiritual differences between so-called higher and lower grades of music, Inayat Khan replied that "the spiritual person does not care about its grade." All that's required is "to tune oneself to the music." He adds that "better" music might be "more helpful."[9] Yet no matter where the music comes from, Inayat Khan claimed, "if the music has a soul" and we seek "for the soul in music," we "will appreciate and admire all music."[10]

Thus, despite Scott's and Tame's claims to the contrary, I believe that jazz and rock, as well as what Tame calls the bad music of the downward and horizontal directions, can be read as sacred scripture, or music of the soul.

Music of the Downward Direction

For Tame, music that expresses suffering, such as the blues, is music of the downward direction, and therefore bad. But such music is often moving. It "has a soul." If read properly, music that expresses even the deepest suffering can become sacred scripture, worthy of our appreciation.

For example, Tame sees Tchaikovsky's music as unwholesome because it deals in pessimistic emotions of the downward direction. Tame vilifies the composer for his depression over his homosexuality, this "obsessive defect," and his failure "to overcome his sexual inclinations."[11]

Tame cites the last three of Tchaikovsky's six symphonies, those considered the greatest by most concertgoers, as spiritually problematic. Tchaikovsky's Sixth Symphony, the *Pathétique*, is famous for its tragic final movement, completed shortly before the composer died, apparently in the throes of a deep depression, and possibly of suicide. For Tame, this tragic movement is pessimistic; therefore the music is downward-tending and bad.

In chapter 15, I pointed out that the final movement of the *Pathétique* is an example of the crisis point between the seventh and eighth centers: spiritual disillusionment. This tragic music portrays a desperate prayer for deliverance from suffering that goes unanswered. By identifying Tchaikovsky's music as downward-tending, Tame implies that such a portrayal of spiritual disillusionment and unanswered prayers "gives death."

Most of us have experienced depression, mild or deep, at some point in our lives. One of the hallmarks of a deep depression is the sense of no way out, no choice that will return us to a sense of happiness or emotional equanimity, and no help available, spiritual or otherwise. When depressed, we may experience such deep emotional pain that we'll contemplate taking our own lives.

The idea of listening to music that reflects our mood at such times, such as the final movement of the *Pathétique*, can indeed seem spiritually dangerous. Yet we may be attracted to it. We may even need it.

In some ways, Tchaikovsky's music is like the blues, which Tame also decries for its subject matter: "infidelity, perversion, drink, and crime," "bewilderment and depression," and "crying, desolation, betrayal and loneliness."[12] Such music, far from encouraging us to abandon ourselves to feelings like these, forces us to confront them. Depressive music shows us where our darker feelings might take us, as they ended up taking Tchaikovsky, if we don't keep them in check and turn ourselves around.

The same spiritual disillusionment portrayed in the *Pathétique* can be heard in the song "Gloomy Sunday," as sung by Billie Holiday—another example of music from the crisis zone between centers seven and eight. The song was originally written in the 1930s by a pair of Hungarians and was rumored to be the cause of many suicides. Holiday's is the most famous English version of what was popularly known as "The Hungarian Suicide Song." While Holiday did not commit suicide, she was often deeply depressed, became a heavy drinker and heroin user, and died prematurely from heart and liver trouble related to her addictions.

I find "Gloomy Sunday" and the final movement of the *Pathétique* to be deeply moving, in part because I know how the lives of Holiday and Tchaikovsky ended. Their depressions—that sense of no way out, of unanswered prayers—destroyed them. As I listen to the music of Holiday and Tchaikovsky, pitying them for their intense suffering, I experience a catharsis, purging myself of my own suffering, while feeling the truth of the phrase, "There but for the grace of God go I."

That phrase, according to Charles, comes to mind when we encounter what he calls a *wayward reflection*. Charles says that everyone around us is in some way a reflection of our growth. Wayward reflections show us a direction that our souls don't want us to go in. If we heed such reflections, they serve the important spiritual purpose of keeping our development on track. Thus both Holiday and Tchaikovsky are wayward reflections of what would happen to us if we were to give way to depression and abandon all hope, if we were unable to move beyond spiritual disillusionment.

While I mourn the loss of these talented artists and would never wish their fate on anyone, I nevertheless accept the spiritual gifts that Holiday and Tchaikovsky have given me. As spiritual teachers, they show me a way I may not want to go. If they'd been able to turn self-pity into compassion for others, perhaps they would have lived longer, gotten through the crisis zone between centers seven and eight, and taught their listeners in other ways.

Within the self-isolation that depression creates, we may find comfort in the notion that some other person has been there, understanding and expressing what we're going through. That, too, is a spiritual message encoded in "Gloomy Sunday" and the last movement of the *Pathétique*. Such music can bring on healing tears, whether for our own pain or that of others.

For me, "Gloomy Sunday" and Tchaikovsky's *Pathétique* are gifts of compassion to those of us who may be suffering in similar ways. Each is "a page of sacred scripture" in the yoga of listening.

Music of the Horizontal Direction

Tame accuses Debussy, another beloved composer, of writing music of the "horizontal" direction. He claims that Debussy's music never rises above portraying "the physical, emotional, and mental conditions of the world around him."[13] For example, Tame faults Debussy's masterpiece *La Mer* (*The Sea*) for being nothing more than a description of "the impressions conveyed by the sea to man—on the physical, emotional, and mental, but *not* the spiritual, levels."[14]

There may be truth in this statement. It's a negative way of saying that Debussy's interest lies in finding musical equivalents for experiences that take place outside the realm of music, such as those connected with the sea—a characteristic of upper 6 music. When Debussy targets the seventh (expanded consciousness) center, he does so on the secular instead of the religious side. Rather than expressing the fear of God (lower 7), Debussy portrays the terrifyingly beautiful sublimity of nature. For the love or praise of God (middle or upper 7), he substitutes the love or praise of nature.

Because of the twentieth century's long record of scientific advances, as well as reactions against the increasingly conservative and even fundamentalist attitudes of some churches, many people today have trouble accepting the idea of a personalized God. Yet their feelings of reverence for the forces of nature may be no less spiritual than prayers to God as a loving Father.

In one way or another, we all try to place ourselves in relation to the source of all life. Such attempts seem to me deeply spiritual, whether we call that source God, nature, or something more scientific, like DNA. For this reason, I hesitate to declare Debussy's *La Mer* unspiritual. For me, it's another page of sacred scripture.

What Tame calls horizontal music, which attempts to portray nature, also exists in jazz or rock. For example, the last recording project of jazz drummer Tony Williams (1945–1997), *Wilderness*, presents Williams's and several other jazz-rock fusion composers' musical impressions of wilderness.[15] His intention is to praise wilderness through music, to raise people's awareness of the value of wilderness. The result is another page of sacred scripture.

Music of the Upward Direction

For Tame, the music of Beethoven exemplifies that of the upward direction. Beethoven's music influences "man's spiritual nature, inspiring his soul with feelings of love, beauty, resolution, altruism and all good emotions."[16]

There are many instances of the seventh center's expanded consciousness, and a few of the eighth's cosmic consciousness, in Beethoven's work. The slow movement of the Violin Concerto in D Major, Op. 61, exemplifies the love of God (middle 7).[17] The Finale of the Sixth Symphony in F Major, Op. 68 (*Pastoral*), in keeping with its subtitle, "Shepherd's Song: Happy and Thankful Feelings to the Deity after the Storm," is full of praise of God (upper 7).[18] The magnificent slow movement of Beethoven's *Hammerklavier* Sonata (Piano Sonata No. 29 in B-flat Major, Op. 106) is an example of compassion (lower 8). Love of God, praise of God, and compassion are all characteristics of what Tame calls music of the upward direction.

Music of the upward direction is not confined to classical music, although Tame believes otherwise. I've also heard love of God, praise of God, and compassion in recordings of rock music played for me by my friend Marjie, who calls herself "an energy worker, soul therapist, and spiritual tour guide."

Marjie, like Deanna, is a member of my channeling class. She shares Deanna's love of the music of Led Zeppelin. I've already mentioned Marjie in connection with Led Zeppelin's song "Kashmir," from *Physical Graffiti*, which she considers to be a "consciousness building song" about an astral journey.

Marjie is also a fan of the progressive rock band Yes, a group that one of my brothers introduced me to when we were in high school in the 1970s. I liked Yes better than other rock bands of the time because their songs most resembled classical music's constant changes of mood, tone color, and texture.

For Marjie, some of Yes's music is about "moving energy around and raising consciousness." She says that every time she moves into a new apartment or house, she uses the Yes song "Close to the Edge," from the 1972 album of that name, to clear out the energy of the previous occupants and put her own "energetic stamp" on the place.[19]

When she played this song for me during our interview, I was struck by an intense, highly dissonant passage toward the beginning. It reminded me of something that Cyril Scott said in *Music: Its Secret Influence.* Scott referred to "ultra-discordant music," by which he meant the works of early-twentieth-century classical composers such as *The Rite of Spring* by Stravinsky.

According to Scott, such music has the spiritual purpose of destroying "undesirable obsessing thought forms," which are created in certain locations by the presence of "intense and continued passional emotions." These thought forms can influence people in negative ways. They "endure for a number of years, until destroyed by some specific agency."[20]

Marjie's use of the Yes song "Close to the Edge" serves a similar purpose. She claims that playing this music clears out stagnant energy—which is to say that it breaks down and destroys the thought forms left behind by the previous occupants of a place she has just moved into.

Marjie also claims that the phrase "I get up, I get down" in the lyrics of "Close to the Edge" refers to moving into heightened states of consciousness and returning to an ordinary state. She tells me that some Yes fans use drugs while listening to their music, but she has never done so. She emphasizes that the consciousness-altering aspects of Yes's songs are *in* the music. Drugs are not required to become aware of or be affected by them.

I agree with Marjie. When listening to "Close to the Edge," I observed that the music began in the everyday world of lower 1, with bird songs; moved into the section that she uses to clear energy, which occurs at the fifty-five-second mark and targets the crisis zone between centers six and seven (irrationality); catapulted itself into middle 7 (love of God or the world) at the three-minute mark; then moved back and forth between the visionary aspect of upper 6, the transcendental longing that develops between lower 7 and middle 7, and the majesty of middle 7; until it returned, at 17:40, to the world of the everyday in which it began.

During the four connected movements of this song, which lasts nearly nineteen minutes, I experienced a movement from the ordinary consciousness of the first center to the expanded consciousness of the seventh center and back—a movement that illustrates the phrase "I get up, I get down." The song keeps moving back and forth between the realm of intellect, dominated by the ego (upper 6), and that of intuition, which is closer to the soul (lower and middle 7), as if crossing a boundary. This boundary between ego and soul is reflected in the song's title, "Close to the Edge."

Marjie has given me a list of her favorite songs, along with indications of what they do for her, energetically. For example, "Starship Trooper," from *The Yes Album*, is for "moving energy up and down within oneself."[21] I hear the three parts of this song as moving through three levels of intensity within upper 6, the visionary center.

Marjie tells me that "Wonderous Stories" from Yes's 1977 album *Going for the One*, is "a storytelling song about meeting a spiritual guide."[22] It targets upper 6, which is often used in musical storytelling.

Marjie divides Yes's songs into those that are about experiences in altered states of consciousness, such as "Wonderous Stories," and those that dramatize such experiences by carrying the listener along in their wake. In the latter, the music allows us to experience the states of consciousness that it portrays. The song "Awaken," also from *Going for the One*, is of this type. Marjie says that she listens to this song for "uplift, the feeling of transcending or being transported." It reminds her "that we're not alone" in this world, that we have access to help and guidance from beyond.

"Awaken" begins in the visionary realm of upper 6 and soon crosses over into the sublime realm of lower 7. Most of the fifteen-and-a-half-minute song is a luminous macrorhythmic wave that gently undulates through each of the levels of the seventh center, providing one of the longest periods of exposure to the expanded consciousness of this center that I've heard in rock music. In the yoga of listening, "Awaken" provides an excellent object of meditation to open the seventh center for those who are more attracted to the sounds of rock than classical music.

Marjie also recommends Yes's 1973 album *Tales from Topographic Oceans* because it was inspired by Paramahansa Yogananda's *Autobiography of a Yogi*.

When I listened to this eighty-minute, four-movement suite, I was struck by its energetic similarity to Todd Rundgren's *Initiation*, which was inspired by esotericist Alice Bailey's *Treatise on the Cosmic Fire*.[23]

Both albums are so concerned with musical portrayals of their respective sources that they rarely rise above upper 6. In the yoga of listening, either could be used as preparation for higher consciousness work. Each offers prolonged exposure to the visionary aspects of the sixth center, those that awaken the third eye. For listeners who are more interested in the expanded consciousness of the seventh center, I recommend Yes's "Awaken."

Dangerous Music

So, does "good" music really produce life and "bad" music death, as David Tame believes? Charles says that the soul uses increases in life force to guide us toward what contributes to our growth. Listening to music that the soul perceives as helpful in this process can lead to an increase in life force. "Good" music of this sort would indeed give life. Such music may produce TMEs as a sign that the soul approves it.

Charles also says that the soul decreases our life force when we're doing things that don't contribute to our growth. Listening to music that doesn't contribute to our growth could theoretically lead to ever more drastic reductions in life force, even to the point of death. But we've seen that *any* music can contribute to our growth, if we know how to read it. No matter what center it targets along the continuum of human potential, music can help us to realize that potential, and is therefore inherently growth-oriented. Composed, performed, and heard rightly, any piece, song, or genre of music can give life.

That said, we should exercise caution when exposing ourselves to music that targets the crisis points between the centers. Music transmits states of consciousness from composer to performer to listener. The states of consciousness that are active at the crisis points are less desirable than those of the lower, middle, and upper ranges of each center: boredom, overload, violence, erotic delirium, mania, irrationality, spiritual disillusionment, and translation from this world into the next.

Musicians who target these crisis points may be stuck between centers, in which case we should be careful not to emulate them. Like Tchaikovsky or Holiday, they're wayward reflections. On the other hand, when musicians show us how to move through these crisis points, they're providing us with sacred scripture, as long as we know how to read it.

Under certain circumstances, noted below, music that targets the crisis points may lead to spiritually inappropriate or physically dangerous behaviors.

The crisis point between the first and second centers, boredom, is relatively harmless. It becomes a problem only if the rhythmic music that targets this crisis point makes us sleepy in a situation in which we might be brainwashed, as in a cult.

The crisis point between the second and third centers, overload, is a bit more dangerous. Music that produces overload is trying to push sensory experience to its limits. With minimalist or ambient music, the result is likely to be no more harmful than mental fatigue. The high volume level of many rock concerts, however, could create not only sensory overload, but also hearing impairment.

For example, musician and Sufi W. A. Mathieu reports that while attending a Janis Joplin concert in the 1960s, he made the experiment of placing himself directly in front of the speakers, which were double his height and "cranked to the max." "Two things happened," he reports: "I experienced a blend of ecstasy and pain so intense that I will remember it forever. And I went a little deaf."[24]

I once heard a rap song that targeted the crisis point of overload by means of a rapid tempo, an elaborate rhythmic groove, no emotional content (which is typical of second center music), and lyrics that went by so quickly it was impossible to hear what they were saying. The effect was acute discomfort. Musical information was coming too rapidly for me to assimilate. When I tried to understand the words, I felt as if my mind was being taken over (an indication that the sixth, or command, center was active).

The inner battle between maintaining my autonomy and giving it up to the music made me feel crazy. I was relieved when the song ended. Because it was part of a tape played at the Y, I never found out who produced it.

Not all rap music targets the crisis point of overload. Like other musical styles or genres, rap can access any of the centers along the continuum of human potential. I've heard rap songs that target the third center to express rage or the fourth center to express love.

Just as with boredom, overload can be used to program the mind when words accompany the music, either as lyrics or as speech in the foreground or background. In some social settings, such as bars or rock concerts, music that targets the crisis point of overload can break down our self-command, resulting in dangerous actions that seem to be sanctioned by the lyrics, such as violence, substance abuse, or sexual misconduct. This loss of self-command can be amplified when loud music is combined with alcohol or drug use.

The crisis point between the third and fourth centers, violence, may be targeted by musicians wishing to break down parental authority, social conventions, and political regimes. When reined in by the intellectual sixth center, the result is the music of protest, which can often be a powerful unifying force and rallying cry for creating necessary change.

Music that targets this crisis point can seem frighteningly out of control, especially to adults who have left the mood of teenage rebellion behind them. In social settings, the danger of such music is that it could incite a riot. Otherwise, it has a cathartic effect on listeners, allowing them to release repressed anger or fear. Heavy metal, punk, and some rap music may target this crisis point.

Music of the crisis point between the fourth and fifth centers expresses erotic delirium. It may also encourage us to act out such delirium, something like the illegal drug ecstasy, which increases one's libido while lowering social inhibitions.

The transmission of feelings, thoughts, and visions from composers and performers is especially powerful when listeners are under the influence of alcohol or drugs. They can easily be taken over by the erotic delirium expressed when a piece of music targets this crisis point and may feel compelled to act it out. The music may even seem to give them permission to do so.

Yet, like any other earthly experience, sex has lessons to teach. Music that targets the crisis point of erotic delirium could be useful in helping people overcome sexual inhibitions *without* drugs like ecstasy.

A musician friend of mine used to make love with his girlfriend in college while listening to the Prelude and Liebestod from Wagner's *Tristan und Isolde*, music which at times touches the crisis point of erotic delirium. He told me that he would set his CD player on auto-repeat so that their lovemaking would not be limited to the twenty-minute length of the piece. He was amazed at how the music inspired not only erotic passion but also tenderness.

Music that targets the crisis point between the fifth and sixth centers, mania, generates physically based ecstasy (as opposed to spiritually based ecstasy) by upping the tempo of dance music beyond the level of exuberance expressed in, say, the most active salsa music. As with the other crisis points, the danger is loss of self-control. For the dancer, physical fatigue and injury due to carelessness are the only hazards.

In jazz and rock, the crisis point of mania may be targeted through improvisation. The solo player or the whole band attempts to achieve the trancelike ecstasy of upper 7. But the ego gets in the way, aggressively asserting itself in the desire to impress, resulting in musical exhibitionism.

This crisis point poses three threats to the performer. The first is going beyond the bounds of taste, and offending, rather than impressing, the audience with competitive virtuosic display.

The second threat is to the unity of the ensemble. Some manic improvisations cause a breakdown in the structural elements of the piece, making it difficult to keep the ensemble together. In many cases, however, such breakdowns are treated as an exciting change of texture. Eventually, the musical order and unity of the ensemble are reestablished.

The third threat is that performers addicted to impressing audiences with displays of technique may strengthen their egos in ways that prevent their spiritual growth. The desire to impress others can deafen performers to the guiding inner voice of the soul.

The crisis point between the sixth and seventh centers, irrationality, serves for musical depictions of death, madness, cynicism, and evil. In such depictions, the third center is often strongly active, adding a frightening level of intensity to the visionary aspect of upper 6.

The nightmarish creatures summoned up when musicians target this crisis point are sometimes depictions of the soul. In chapter 14, I pointed out that the ego is often afraid of the soul, which, because of its origin in nonphysical reality, feels to the ego like an alien being.

The ego's fear of the soul is a transcendental fear. It can block our growth in much the same way that ordinary fear often does. In order for us to grow beyond transcendental fear, we need to learn how to confront and release it. Nightmares of evil supernatural beings can serve such a purpose. So can the irrational music of the crisis point between centers six and seven.

For example, Mussorgsky's *Night on Bald Mountain* is a musical depiction of a nightmare. We eventually wake up from a nightmare and feel a sense of relief at being in the real world, instead of the dream world created by transcendental fear. So it is with *Night on Bald Mountain*. Dawn comes at the end with the ringing of church bells—and a hint that spiritual devotion, or prayer, may be one of the ways of overcoming transcendental fear.

Yet, when not used for teaching purposes, as in *Night on Bald Mountain*, the crisis point of irrationality may be the most dangerous of all. This danger arises because irrationality is connected with the command center, by which musicians seek to transfer their feelings, experience of the world, or inner visions into the minds of an audience.

Any manifestation of the command center can so impress us with the power of the feelings, thoughts, and visions it transmits that we intentionally or unintentionally adopt a composer or band as gurus. The result is a personality cult.

Young people, whose sense of identity is still forming, are especially susceptible to such personality cults—all the more so when these cults come with a whiff of rebellion against parental authority. Many young people have a potent fascination with ESP, ghosts, witches, and other supernatural figures. Some may even consider black magic and the darker side of the occult as cool, because such things are so different from their everyday experience or religious upbringing. A performer or musical group could exploit them by projecting an image based on transcendental fear, fascination with the supernatural, and the coolness of the occult.

In many cases, such exploitation of the young does little more than extract money for concert tickets and albums from their pockets. Everyone I knew as a teenager who was thrilled by the diabolical face-paint of Kiss or the circus-geek-like stunts of Alice Cooper (b. 1948) eventually grew out of their fascination with such grotesqueries.

But what about the kid who is emotionally traumatized by the graphic nature of some musical acts that target the crisis zone of irrationality? Or the one who endangers himself or others by attempting to emulate such acts? Just as with graphic movies, parental caution may be advised.

The command center is powerful. We need to be mindful of this power, and to teach our kids self-reliance, which can prevent them from succumbing to mind control through music in advertising, politics, religious cults, and the cult of personality inspired by some musicians and musical groups.

I've already mentioned the crisis point between the seventh and eighth centers, disillusionment, in connection with "Gloomy Sunday" and the last movement of Tchaikovsky's *Pathétique*. Portraying spiritual disillusionment in music seems dangerous in that it could encourage suicide. But such portrayals can also be cathartic, allowing self-pity to become compassion for the suffering of others.

As I pointed out in chapter 15, the eighth center's crisis point, translation, seems to pose the danger of destroying the world, but is actually beyond realization in sound.

In the yoga of listening, you might wish to observe the following guidelines in order to prevent any of the possible negative effects of music that targets the crisis points. Avoid substances that reduce self-command, such as alcohol or drugs. Avoid situations such as bars or concerts in which the volume of music may lead to sensory overload and a possible loss of self-command.

Keep in mind that any musical situation that involves other people creates a value field, bringing those who share values with the musicians and each other together. In some cases, the lyrics of songs may be an expression of these shared values.

Presence in a value field creates a sense of safety and belonging. The more aligned you are with that value field, the safer and more comfortable you'll feel. Your own energy field will expand and join with the energy fields of the people who surround you. The safer and more expansive you feel, the more likely you are to give yourself permission to act on the values expressed in that value field. Even when you're not listening consciously to the lyrics of songs, they're defining the value field that surrounds you and telling you what you need to do to align yourself with it.

If the value field is spiritual in nature, as in a gospel choir concert, you may have a conversion experience, dedicating yourself more deeply to the realization of your spiritual values. If the value field has to do with sexual promiscuity, as in a singles bar, you may give yourself permission to do something you'll regret later.

Alcohol, drugs, and overly loud music are artificial ways to open your personal energy field to the surrounding value field. Because they reduce your self-command, such things can allow you, along with others in a similar state, to be taken over by the value field, resulting in mob behavior that often has unfortunate consequences: a brawl, an orgy, a rape, and so on.

If you avoid social situations in which drugs, alcohol, and overly loud music prevail, and maintain your self-command, you should be immune to being taken over by a value field and succumbing to mob behavior. Awareness of how music targets each center and crisis point on the continuum of human potential can help you identify the value field present in any social situation that involves music, even when there are no lyrics to tip you off. If you're drawn to certain music, even that of the crisis zones, it may have something to teach you. If it makes you uncomfortable, you should probably avoid it.

Beyond Good and Evil

I don't believe that dark or evil forces act through music to disrupt our spiritual lives, as Cyril Scott and David Tame have stated. In my many out-of-body and lucid-dream-based adventures in nonphysical reality, I've never encountered such things, unless they were the products of my own fears. As I've said in my previous books, thought creates experience in nonphysical reality. In that reality, fearful thoughts can create what seems to be an evil, nightmarish creature, but such creatures have no existence without my fear.

Yet, given the power of music to transmit states of consciousness from composers to performers to listeners, it would be irresponsible of me to dismiss the notion of evil beings or dark forces working through music to obstruct our growth. I may never have encountered such beings, but they could still exist. Suffice it to say, then, that I *suspect* that music that targets the crisis zone between centers six and seven, irrationality, does not portray *real* demons or satanic beings, but the transcendental fear we feel when we confront the alien reality of our own souls.

As I pointed out previously, we need to be cautious when approaching music that targets the crisis zones, unless it does so for teaching purposes. In the case of musical depictions of evil, we learn how to transcend our fear of demonic beings, real or imagined, when a composer or group forces us to confront them in the crisis zone, then shows us how to move beyond them into the expanded consciousness of the seventh center. Such music often shows the way from damnation to redemption—which even David Tame would have to qualify as upward-tending.

My friend Marjie describes "The Gates of Delirium" from Yes's 1974 album *Relayer* as "a battle between good and evil."[25] The remarkable thing about this song is that it not only moves through the crisis zone of irrationality, but eventually achieves the grace of middle 8—one of the few examples of cosmic consciousness that I've so far encountered in nonclassical music.

"The Gates of Delirium" begins in the visionary realm of upper 6, with magical sound effects that are typical of music that attempts to open the third eye.

At 6:45, the music begins to move into the crisis zone between centers six and seven (irrationality). A progressive rock version of a demonic scherzo, as defined in chapter 14, develops—a relentlessly pounding, intensely dissonant dance. By 7:30, we're fully in the crisis zone, one sign of which is the sonic distortion in the singing.

At 10:25, we're still in the crisis zone, but the texture changes. The intensity of the demonic scherzo keeps building. The lyrics even refer to demons.

At 12:50, the music transcends the crisis point and its demons and shoots up to upper 7, expressing a relaxed sense of spiritual ecstasy.

At 15:10, the music rises into middle 8 (grace), expressing timelessness and inner peace, as well as depicting the heavenly light that I call the cosmic normative balance. The lead guitar then begins to play a radiant melody full of divine love and compassion, embodying the grace of middle 8. This melody sounds like it's calling us home to the Source.

The lead singer joins in at 17:10, adding in the human yearning for transcendence associated with the seventh center. From here until the end, just less than five minutes later, the music combines our homesickness for the Source (middle 7) and the Source's beckoning us to return (middle 8).

I was moved to tears when listening to the last part of "The Gates of Delirium" and wanted to hear it again and again—a sign of the conversion experience that often occurs when we encounter music from the eighth center. In the yoga of listening, this song is another page of sacred scripture—one that can lift us beyond our fear of the soul, beyond the question of whether dark forces or evil beings are real or imaginary, into redemption. Such music aligns us with the cosmic normative balance, bringing us home to the Source.

19

Musicians as Spiritual Teachers

Certain composers, performers, groups, or pieces of music remain with us through long periods of life, like faithful companions or teachers. We go back to them again and again, always delighted, always learning something new.

For example, I've owned the Odeon Trio's recording of the Schubert Trios for piano, violin, and cello, D. 898 and 929, for over twenty years, at first on cassette and now on CD.[1] It must be the most frequently played recording in my collection. I've listened to it hundreds of times—and I mean *listened*, rather than simply turned it on in the background while doing other things. I never tire of it.

Every time I put on this recording, I have a transcendent experience. It has not only contributed to my enjoyment and understanding of life, but also has deeply influenced my thinking about the purpose of music and how to achieve TMEs as a composer, performer, and listener. The question of what made this recording so special was the driving force behind much of what I've written in this book.

Schubert's Trios seem to express the whole of what it means to be human, to live in a world where great happiness and great sadness are equally possible, and constantly giving way to one another; where mortality confronts us in every moment, challenging us to clarify what's of value (peace, truth, beauty, and many similar ideals) in our own brief experience here.

Such music, when properly played, conveys a wisdom no words can put across. It shows us how to live, think, and feel. When composed macrorhythmically, and performed with attention to the resulting swells of accumulating and dissipating musical energy, it can lead us into states of consciousness that transcend our usual understanding of what it means to be human. Composers or performers who are able to lift us into higher states of consciousness are musical adepts.

According to Sri Aurobindo, there are four levels of consciousness beyond the one we're most familiar with, which he called *thinking mind*. These higher levels of consciousness are *higher mind*, *illumined mind*, *intuitive mind*, and *overmind*.

Beyond the overmind lies the *supermind*, which for Aurobindo is the source of all consciousness. According to Aurobindo, the overmind acts as a receiving station for the supermind. Thus the overmind is roughly equivalent to what Charles calls the soul, or Numen. The supermind corresponds to God, or what I've called the cosmic normative balance.

In chapter 2, I suggested that the word *soul* may be a metaphor for the most comprehensive hierarchy of information processing that the body/mind is capable of. It may be that Aurobindo's terms reflect not only levels of consciousness, but also levels of information processing that lie beyond the ordinary workings of the mind. Thus these terms could be used equally to describe the states of consciousness achieved by spiritual masters in meditation and the psychological functioning of genius.

Composers and performers who have gone beyond the thinking mind have developed a working relationship with the supermind. According to Aurobindo, connection to the supermind allows us to experience a sense of oneness and bliss beyond the range of ideation or communication in words. When composers and performers are able to transmit something of this experience to us, they're musical adepts.

According to Aurobindo, a relationship with the supermind must be initiated from *that* level of consciousness, rather than our usual level, which corresponds to the thinking mind. Connection with the supermind manifests itself as "a presence," "power," or "stream of knowledge" that "pours in waves or currents" over our consciousness, resulting in "a flood of bliss or a sudden ecstasy."[2]

For composers and performers with a direct connection to the supermind, or for us listeners, when we're exposed to this connection through their music, the result is a TME. Such TMEs may be "occasional," "frequent," or "constant." Any connection with the supermind leaves in its wake "a longing and aspiration" for further, similar, experiences.[3]

If we try to better ourselves in order to increase the chances of reconnecting with the supermind, the result may be a gradual reorganization of the self, under the direction of this higher level of consciousness. A process of purging everything that contradicts the truth of who we are will then take place. One purpose of the yoga of listening is to facilitate this reorganization of the self.

According to Aurobindo, we tend to resist both the descent of the "supramental force" and the ascent of our own consciousness toward a higher plane of being. We fear and resent such a "direct and unveiled intervention from above" because it requires "a total submission and surrender of the lower consciousness."[4]

Charles has often said that the ego is afraid of the soul, which, like the overmind, stands between us and God. There are three reasons for such fear. The first is that the soul feels alien to the ego because it exists outside of space and time. This fear can only be overcome by a gradual process of familiarization in which the ego gets used to the soul by being frequently exposed to it, for example, through dreams.

The second reason that the ego is afraid of the soul is that the soul is the source of the life force that sustains the ego. The ego wants to be the boss. It resists the soul's attempts to assert its needs for our growth. The soul then diminishes the amount of life force available to the ego, and the latter suffers from dissatisfaction, unhappiness, or depression. This fear can only be overcome by learning how to surrender to the growth needs of the soul.

The third reason that the ego is afraid of the soul has to do with how the soul rewards the ego with higher levels of life-force flow when the latter cooperates. In chapter 5, I mentioned that the ego acts as a self-regulating valve of life-force flow. It often fears that it will be overwhelmed by the amount of life force provided by the soul. Too much satisfaction, happiness, or ecstasy can cause the ego to feel out of control and shut down—even though it may originally have been seeking to maximize the frequency and intensity of such experiences.

Ecstasy also opens us up to the soul, which, as I've pointed out, often feels alien to us. The fear of ecstasy can be overcome by allowing ourselves gradually to get used to it, which means learning not to hurry the growth processes guided by the soul or supermind.

Music is one of the best ways to overcome these three fears at once. Pieces or performances created by someone who exists in a closer than usual relationship to the soul or God can familiarize us with what such a state of being feels like: Here is someone who has gotten beyond the fear of the soul as an alien consciousness and survived.

Surrendering to such music in order to maximize its effects on us helps us to overcome the fear of surrendering to our own souls. We're allowing ourselves to be guided by the composer as if by the soul or God.

The ecstasy that we feel when listening to such music may last only as long as the performance or recording itself. The fact that there's a limit to the duration of this experience of increased life-force flow can prevent us from fearing that we'll be overwhelmed by it.

Therefore, one of the best ways to open ourselves up to the soul or God is through listening to the music of composers or performers who have done so themselves: the musical adepts. Their work encodes the characteristics of the higher states of consciousness from which it has developed, and transmits them to us. Such transmission either *prepares* us for that state of consciousness, should our spiritual development be headed in that direction, or *initiates* it directly. In the latter case, we experience a TME.

The works of musical adepts have a special quality that I call *radiance*, a term that I introduced in chapter 15, in connection with music of the eighth center (cosmic consciousness). Such works radiate a wavelike spiritual force that moves us beyond physical, emotional, or intellectual pleasure into spiritual ecstasy. At the same time, these works lift us up to a sense of oneness within ourselves, or with other players or members of the audience, and initiate a process of inner change. When exposed to radiant music, we want not only to hear it again and again, but also to transform our lives, to become better people so that we may be worthy of the spiritual exaltation it produces in us.

As related in chapter 1, David Tame experienced a Bach-induced TME in which he felt waves of goodness spreading out from the music, filling the performance hall, and passing beyond its walls. The phrase "waves of goodness" is an apt description of what I mean by radiance.

In Tibetan Buddhism, "divine grace may be received by human beings on earth in the form of waves radiated by spiritual beings."[5] Such "grace-waves" are "emanated" by gurus, living or dead, or buddhas and bodhisattvas. Their purpose is to lift the recipient from spiritual ignorance into self-transcendence.[6]

Grace waves are also encoded in the scores of musical adepts, having originated in the supermind. They produce the quality that I call radiance, which some listeners may experience, as I often have, as inner luminosity.

Radiance is an expression of the divine love that musical adepts are able to bring to us through their music. The degree of radiance increases with the composer's proximity to the supermind. Pieces or performances produced by musicians who operate at the level of the thinking mind have the least degree of radiance. Those produced by musicians who operate at the level of the overmind have the highest degree of radiance.

Perception of the degree of radiance present in a piece of music depends on the receptivity of the listener and the quality of the performance. Sometimes the radiance of a musical adept is immediately perceptible, especially when it triggers a TME. At other times, the sense of radiance dawns slowly, the cumulative effect of multiple hearings of a piece or performer.

Radiance is what I most respond to in a composer or performer. I've heard it, for example, in the lyrical saxophone playing of John Coltrane, as well as the Boston-based Borromeo Quartet.

Here is a TME in which a sensitive listener, a German psychologist and musician named Silvia Ostertag, heard and responded to the radiance of a musical adept, the cellist Pablo Casals. Ostertag was attending a cello master class taught by Casals in Switzerland. The latter played a single note, with the following effect, as reported by Ostertag: "[I]n the moment in which this tone was sounded, I felt as if I were waking up, violently and yet tenderly."

Ostertag continued: "It was as if this tone had reached an inner ear that hadn't existed before." It "struck me in my innermost self, a part of myself which I had been unaware of."

To Ostertag, this tone was one "in which all tones were sounded and in which at the same time was all silence." The result of having heard it was a process of internal reorganization like that referred to by Aurobindo. "Ever since that experience I have been trying to become the kind of person who, through my hearing and my deeds, would open my entire life for the sake of this 'tone,'" wrote Ostertag.[7]

Many jazz and rock musicians have felt something similar in response to Coltrane's playing.

As noted, the degree of radiance in composers or performers depends on their proximity to the soul or supermind. In the case of composers, it's often possible to determine from their works whether they're operating from the thinking mind, higher mind, illumined mind, intuitive mind, or overmind, and the point in their lives when they moved from one state of consciousness to the next.

The Thinking Mind Composer

According to Aurobindo, the thinking mind is made up "of mingled light and obscurity or half light."[8] It functions on the basis of "inquiring reason or reflective thought" and requires a great deal of intellectual labor to arrive at a sense of the truth.[9] Composers whose music emanates from any of the three ranges of the sixth center—wit, invention, or fantasy—are thinking mind composers. Most thinking mind composers will be either entertainers (lower 6), formalists (middle 6), or visionaries (upper 6).

The transition from one evolutionary phase to another is rarely smooth or abrupt. Gradually, the kind of music associated with the entertainer gives way to that of the formalist, which in turn gives way to that of the visionary.

Some musicians get comfortable in the entertainer, formalist, or visionary stage and never move beyond it. Others go through distinct stylistic periods, stamped with the characteristics of lower, middle, or upper 6. Still others evolve more sporadically, with sudden unexpected leaps to a higher level or temporary backsliding to a lower one. A formal inspiration is followed by a return to entertaining; a moment of vision by a return to questions of form or self-expression.

The true masters of composing from the thinking mind are those who can move fluently between expression, form, and vision, depending on the compositional needs of the moment; or who can combine all three of these modes at once. Tchaikovsky is an example of such a master, able to move between these levels of the thinking mind or combine them in a single piece. The same is true of many opera composers, such as Verdi.[10]

In jazz and jazz-rock fusion, the composing-performing duo Pat Metheny and Lyle Mays are such masters; in popular music, Elton John (b. 1947).

While such mastery might seem to be a worthwhile goal, it's only the beginning of what's possible for the composer dedicated to spiritual growth. As noted, there are ranges of consciousness beyond the thinking mind.

The thinking mind derives its sense of the truth from a systematic, rational perception of the world, synthesized through analysis: observation, supposition, inference, and the drawing of conclusions. Any form of *revealed* truth comes from a higher level of consciousness. Such truth carries with it a sense of authority that, according to Aurobindo, is usually absent from reason-based philosophical systems.

Charles says that when we've lost our connection to the soul as a means of providing trustworthy guidance in life, we have no *internal* authority to guide our behavior. Instead, we rely on external authority, or create rational systems of behavior to guide or justify our actions.

A number of twentieth-century composers have created rational systems to help them compose. The most influential of these is the twelve-tone system (also known as dodecaphonicism or serialism) invented by Schoenberg. I mentioned this system in chapter 3, in connection with my graduate studies at the University of Illinois. Rational compositional systems are products of the thinking mind. They're often used by composers who have lost the ability to justify what the next note should be, based on their internal authority: what the soul or supermind demands.

Thinking mind composers are able to access the expanded consciousness of the seventh center intentionally, though briefly—for example, when they want to create a moment of religious or noble feeling. Access to the cosmic consciousness of the eighth center happens by accident or not at all. Such access can only occur as a result of inspiration, when a composer has responded to the information-bearing waves of energy that originate from the supermind.

I suspect that Barber's Adagio for Strings was the result of such inspiration. Nothing in the rest of this composer's intelligent and moving output is anything like it. Barber was a thinking mind composer. He seems to have been most comfortable as a middle 6 formalist, although his music has more of the expressive fourth center in it than that of many of his contemporaries.

Composers who go beyond the thinking mind are able to access the higher centers more frequently and in a more sustained way. Over time, the seventh center supplants the sixth as the source of their music. If they continue to develop spiritually, the eighth center will become a constant source of inspiration.

We tend to revere the composers who have gone beyond the thinking mind as the paramount geniuses of Western music. In the yoga of listening, the idea is to expose ourselves as much as possible to the music of such composers—especially works that target the seventh and eighth centers.

Through immersion in such music, we may eventually learn how to replicate within ourselves the higher states of consciousness encoded in it. Our success will be measured by an increase in the frequency and spiritual intensity of our TMEs. If we're composers or performers, the next step is to charge our own creations, rehearsals, jam sessions, or public recitals with these higher states of consciousness, so that others may experience them as well.

I'm less familiar with the careers of jazz and rock composers and musicians. So, with one exception, I can provide examples of these higher levels of consciousness only from the ranks of classical composers. Also, some rock and jazz songs are jointly composed by all the members of a group or band, making it difficult to ascertain—for example, in the case of Yes—who, if anyone, in the band might be a musical adept.

The Higher Mind Composer

The first range of consciousness beyond the thinking mind is the higher mind, which Aurobindo defined as "a large clarity of the spirit."[11] Composers whose music continually emanates from the crisis point between the sixth and seventh centers (irrationality) or the lower range of the seventh center (the sublime, or fear of God) are higher mind composers.

The higher mind is "a luminous thought mind," which is made up "of Spirit-born conceptual knowledge." Here, there's no more "self-critical ratiocination," or "logical motion step by step towards a conclusion," or "deductions and inferences." The higher mind proceeds on the basis of "a system or totality of truth-seeking at a single view."

Beethoven achieved the level of higher mind in his late-period works, those composed after 1816. According to critic J. W. N. Sullivan, "Nowhere else in music are we made so aware, as here, of a state of consciousness surpassing our own."[12] Beethoven's late works often go beyond expression, form, and vision, to incorporate essential, though otherwise inexpressible, spiritual truths.

At this level of development, musical form begins to break down and recast itself organically. Complex, luminous, musical worlds are spun from the simplest musical ideas, as in Beethoven's String Quartets, Opp. 130–132, which are all based on the same four-note melodic fragment.

The reverent (middle 7) slow movement of the A Minor Quartet (Op. 132), called "Heiliger Dankgesang" ("Hymn of Thanksgiving"), is especially luminous and spiritually moving. Beethoven wrote it as a prayer of gratitude to God for recovery from a serious illness. The movement alternates between quiet, prayerful sections and those that demonstrate the higher level of life force available to Beethoven as a result of his recovery. In the yoga of listening, this would be an especially helpful piece for convalescents.

Higher mind composers tend to structure their music in terms of waves of accumulating and dissipating energy: the macrorhythmic structure that I described in chapter 14 as a quality of seventh center music. The higher mind also often has an obsessive, plodding intensity. For example, in the Diabelli Variations, Op. 120, Beethoven turned a silly waltz theme submitted to him by a publisher with the request that he compose a *single* variation on it into an hour-long tour of the whole spectrum of human nature, from the secular to the sacred, and beyond.

According to Aurobindo, the higher mind "seeks to purify through knowledge, to deliver through knowledge, to create by the innate power of knowledge."[13] That statement encapsulates the project of the Diabelli Variations, as it does all of Beethoven's late music.

Beethoven's higher mind music also includes his Ninth Symphony, which I discussed in chapter 14, two further string quartets (Opp. 127 and 135), and his late piano sonatas (Opp. 101, 106, and 109–111). The slow movement of the *Hammerklavier* Sonata (Op. 106) is one of the most profound meditations on the nature of human suffering that has ever been penned in Western music. Like Barber's Adagio for Strings, it achieves the distanced perspective and finely nuanced compassion of a bodhisattva, a characteristic of lower 8 music.

The radiant Benedictus of the Missa Solemnis (Op. 123), with its soaring violin solo, is the only example of middle 8 music (grace) that I know of in Beethoven's work.

Brahms was also a higher mind composer. Even though I've cited his *German Requiem* as an example of eighth center music, I know of no other instances of cosmic consciousness in Brahms's output. He seems to have been more comfortable with the seventh center's expanded consciousness, especially in the secular forms of sublimity (lower 7) and nobility (middle 7), although he, like Beethoven, also moved freely between the lower centers.

Bruckner, too, was a higher mind composer. His music is so thoroughly saturated with the expanded consciousness of the seventh center that it virtually excludes any of the lower centers.

A lot of Mahler's music targets the crisis point between centers six and seven. His source of inspiration was evolving from the thinking mind to the higher mind, but he didn't live long enough to complete this transitional process. I have more to say on Bruckner and Mahler in chapter 21.

One popular musician who may be working from the higher mind is the Irish-born, New-Age composer Enya. As I mentioned in chapter 4, Enya's music for the movie *The Lord of the Rings: The Fellowship of the Ring* provides an excellent example of what Cyril Scott called ethereal music. Perhaps he would have considered her a deva-inspired composer.

Almost every song I've heard by Enya originates in the seventh center. I used three examples of such songs to illustrate the levels of the seventh center in chapter 14. I find her music so heart-opening, radiant, and spiritually compelling that it has ruined me for any other New-Age music. I surveyed quite a bit of New-Age music by other composers while researching this book, but found nothing that I felt could stand up to it, which is why she's the only composer in this genre I've mentioned herein.[14]

Enya releases her albums after what, in the world of popular music, seems to be inordinate lengths of time—as long as five years, in one case. This suggests to me the plodding, yet intense, spiritual integrity of the higher mind composer.

Besides *Watermark*, which I've cited numerous times in this book, Enya's albums are *The Celts* (1987), originally the soundtrack for a television documentary; *Shepherd Moons* (1991), which won a Grammy Award in 1993 for Best New-Age Album; *The Memory of Trees* (1995); and *A Day Without Rain* (2000).[15]

The Illumined Mind Composer

Beyond the higher mind is the illumined mind, which Aurobindo described as "a Mind no longer of Thought, but of spiritual light." Composers whose music continually emanates from middle 7 (nobility or love of God) or upper 7 (ecstasy or praise of God) are illumined mind composers.

According to Aurobindo, the illumined mind involves a "luminous 'enthousiasmos' of inner force and power." This enthusiasm "replaces the comparatively slow and deliberate process of Higher Mind by a swift, sometimes a vehement, almost a violent impetus of rapid transformation." The illumined mind works on the basis of sudden, spontaneous, seerlike vision, rather than thought.[16]

Based on the speed of its composition and the strength and radiance of its religious feeling, I would say that Handel's *Messiah* is the product of an illumined mind composer. Handel moves easily between all levels of the seventh center. The radiant Hallelujah chorus is perhaps the best-known example of upper 7 (praise of God) in the entire history of Western music.

Mozart is also an example of an illumined mind composer. His compositional process surpassed the deliberative plodding of Beethoven's with its swiftness and vehemence. Mozart claimed that the ideas for his pieces would strike him at odd moments, when "travelling in a carriage, or walking after a good meal," or during a sleepless night. He would hum the themes that interested him in order to retain them better in memory.[17]

Over time, if not disturbed, Mozart would find that a whole piece, "though it be long," would stand "almost complete and finished in my mind." He could "survey it, like a fine picture or a beautiful statue, at a glance." Also, rather than hearing the parts in successive order in his imagination, he could hear them "all at once." Later, he would write down what he had heard in his creative reverie, which he called a "pleasing lively dream." The process was rapid, he claimed, and "rarely differs on paper from what it was in my imagination."[18]

The hallmarks of Mozart's music include not only the rapidity with which he composed, and the brilliant, surprising, yet inevitable sense of authority behind every phrase, but also the ease with which he was able to shift the dominant centers of his pieces throughout the continuum of human potential. He was equally at home in the passionate intensity of the third center; the pathos, yearning, and elation of the fourth; the exuberant sense of well-being of the fifth; the entertainment of lower 6 in his comic operas, the formal play of middle 6 in his concertos and symphonies, and the visionary upper 6 world of each of his operas as a whole; and the sublime lower 7 world of his Requiem and the middle to upper 7 celebration of life in the world from which his later music emanated.

Late in his life, Mozart created scores that were full of transcendental mirth, a spiritual laughter that catapulted him and his audience beyond the reach of emotional pain. Because most of his output is secular rather than religious, its rare instances of eighth center music show up in odd places—for example, in the comic opera *Die Zauberflöte* (*The Magic Flute*), K. 620.

Mozart wrote *The Magic Flute* as an expression of his belief in the mystical principles of the Masonic Order, into which he was initiated in 1784.[19] The one instance of eighth center music in this work is the radiant "March of the Priests" that opens Act II, an example of lower 8 compassion for humanity.

The rest of the opera resonates at the level of middle 7. On the one hand, middle 7 expresses love of God and the nobility of humankind—both Masonic ideals. On the other, as it shades into upper 7, it produces transcendental mirth, hence the comedic nature of the opera.

Because access to transcendental mirth lies high in the seventh center, it approaches and shares some of the characteristics of the compassion of lower 8. Thus we're deeply moved, even as we laugh, at Mozart's musical portrayal of the good-natured, though unspiritual, bird-catcher Papageno. His only interest in life appears to be finding a mate. Mozart juxtaposes Papageno's antics with the noble, spiritual resolve of the aristocratic Tamino, a candidate for initiation into the Masonic mysteries.

Another example of Mozart's eighth center music (middle 8 grace) appears in the beautiful late motet (choral composition for unaccompanied voices, usually on a sacred Latin text) entitled Ave Verum Corpus (Hail True Body), K. 618.

The glorious slow movement of the Clarinet Concerto in A Major, K. 622, is a rare instance of upper 8 music (union). Most clarinetists, however, seem not to be spiritually developed enough to bring out the full power of its healing radiance.

Mozart's 1787 opera *Don Giovanni*, K. 527, is a work of the higher mind. Thus Mozart's transition to the illumined mind must have taken place at some point during the last four years of his life. The closer the K. numbers that catalog Mozart's output come to 600 (his last work was the Requiem, K. 626), the greater the chance that the piece is a product of the illumined mind.

Schubert, too, by the end of his life, had achieved the status of illumined mind composer. His late work has not only the organic development of higher mind music, but also a luminous effortlessness like that of Mozart's. Like the Piano Trios, most of it is composed macrorhythmically.

A playlist of Schubert's works that express the illumined mind would include the String Quintet in C Major, D. 956; the Fantasy in C for violin and piano, D. 934; the Fantasy in F Minor for piano, four-hands, D. 940; the last three Piano Sonatas, in C Minor, A Major, and B-flat Major, D. 959–960; the Ninth Symphony in C Major (called *The Great*), D. 944; and the song cycles for voice and piano, *Die Winterreise* (*The Winter Journey*), D. 910, and *Schwanengesang* (*Swansongs*), D. 957.

Many of Schubert's late works derive solidly from middle 7, with few flights beyond it to upper 7 or any level of 8. I'm tempted to say his version of the illumined mind was somewhat less developed than Mozart's. Perhaps this was a result of their respective ages at their deaths: Schubert was 31, Mozart almost 36.

I have a theory that Schubert's unfinished Eighth Symphony, in B minor, D. 759, which consists of only two movements instead of the usual four, was never completed because the wave of inspiration behind it frightened the then twenty-five-year-old composer. That wave would have originated in what Aurobindo called the supermind. Somehow, during the remaining six years of his life, Schubert learned how to open himself up more fully to such waves of inspiration. Perhaps the Eighth Symphony marks Schubert's transition from thinking mind to higher mind.

The transition to illumined mind probably took place during the last year of Schubert's life. Thus any work with a Deutsch catalogue number in the high 800s and above would be a product of the illumined mind.

As I pointed out in chapter 15, the opening section of the Adagio of Schubert's Quintet in C is the most radiant music he ever wrote. My friend Pam, a pianist, author, and storyteller, responds strongly to another moment of radiance, of different character, in the first movement.

According to Pam, about two minutes into the movement, there's a moment "when time stops, dimensions shift." It's like "an intersection of universes" in which a single note causes the listener to "come out in a different landscape, like fairyland or a shamanic journey." Afterward, the music is like "a land under the lake where everything is luminous and alive."

Pam seems to be describing a shift between what Cyril Scott called the human and the ethereal elements in music. The emotional turbulence of the human element disappears and is replaced by a sense of nobility, spiritual tranquility, and happiness (middle 7).

For Pam, this effect became clear after many listenings. She was drawn to the music, but only after frequent exposure did she have a sense of "opening, more opening, and the magic that develops." Sometimes, in the yoga of listening, the magic of a TME develops incrementally, as a cumulative effect of becoming increasingly familiar with the music.

The Intuitive Mind Composer

Beyond the illumined mind is the intuitive mind, which involves what Aurobindo called "revelatory truth-seeing," "inspiration or truth-hearing," "truth-touch or immediate seizing of significance," and an "automatic discrimination of the orderly and exact relation of truth to truth."[20] Composers whose music continually emanates from the crisis point between centers seven and eight (disillusionment) or the lower range of the eighth center (compassion) are intuitive mind composers.

At the level of the intuitive mind, reason steps back and acts "as an observer or registrar." Its purpose is to understand and record the "luminous intimations, judgments and discriminations" of the supermind.[21] Such intuitions usually need to be translated into terms that ordinary consciousness can grasp. If reason becomes too involved in this translation process, intuitions from the supermind may lose their absolute sense of truth.

In yogic meditation, the highest truths emerge from a continual sense of self-transcending union, or identification, with the thing one wishes to understand. Intuition is a close second, a momentary flash of such identification and understanding.

By the end of his life, Wagner had achieved the status of intuitive mind composer. In his last opera, *Parsifal*, he was straddling the crisis point between centers seven and eight (disillusionment). He was attempting to rise above the ecstatic, world-transcending mirth (upper 7) of the illumined mind, which he expressed in *Die Meistersinger*, to achieve the compassion of lower 8.

Momentary flashes of self-transcendence occur in the radiant music that accompanies the Holy Grail ritual in Acts I and III of *Parsifal*. The opera's four-and-a-half-hour duration represents the enormous challenge of achieving the sense of union with the divine represented by the Grail.

Because Wagner's spiritual evolution can be traced from opera to opera, I go into more detail about his life and works in the next chapter.

The Overmind Composer

Beyond the intuitive mind is the overmind, which Aurobindo described as a "power of cosmic consciousness."[22] The overmind involves an egoless "sense of the universe in oneself or as oneself."[23] The rare composer whose music continually targets middle 8 (grace) and upper 8 (union) is an overmind composer.

At the level of the overmind, thought, as well as "feelings, emotions, sensations" seem to come into the mind from beyond, as if on "cosmic mind-waves." These waves have their source in the "cosmic immensity" of the supermind and seem to break over one's consciousness like oceanic waves.[24]

Palestrina is an overmind composer. As I pointed out in chapter 15, his *Pope Marcellus Mass* provides thirty minutes of exposure to the grace of middle 8. This music is among the most radiant I know. The grace waves it radiates can indeed wash over us like oceanic waves.

Another piece by Palestrina once induced a powerful TME in my friend Elizabeth. She was working on the stage crew for an annual holiday event called the Christmas Revels. Her mother had died two months earlier, and Elizabeth had found herself unable to cry in mourning during that entire period.

The Revels choir was rehearsing a brief motet by Palestrina called Sicut Cervus. The text of the motet is the first verse of Psalm 42: "As the deer longs for flowing streams, so longs my soul for thee, O Lord."

Even during rehearsal, Elizabeth was so deeply moved by the music that the tears of mourning for her mother were finally able to flow. When she played a recording of Sicut Cervus for me, I could hear that it was another example of eighth center music, emanating from the point where lower 8 (compassion) shades into middle 8 (grace).[25]

Afterward, Elizabeth told me that she wished choirs could go around to the beds of dying people and sing this motet. She felt that there could be no better way of letting them know that they are welcome and loved on the Other Side, just as we love them, in parting, on this one.

Bach is another overmind composer. To my knowledge, he never spoke about the sense of "the universe in oneself or as oneself" that Aurobindo described in connection with the overmind. Yet Bach was egoless in his devotion to serving God and humanity through the medium of music.

Bach's music ceaselessly showers listeners with life-enhancing, life-changing waves of goodness—a radiance that can easily lift a sensitive listener into the realm of self-transcendence. This seems to be true even in the most worldly of his scores—the Brandenburg Concertos or the Orchestral Suites, for example.

Bach's explicitly spiritual works, such as the B Minor Mass and the St. Matthew and St. John Passions, can be overwhelmingly intense. From the first note, listeners may have the sense of being summoned to participate in a multidimensional drama that began with the final days of Jesus and continues to transform the world.

Bach's last work, the *Art of Fugue*, a set of rigorous, highly formal contrapuntal compositions based on a single theme, could have been a merely intellectual exercise in the hands of most other composers. Instead it contains a life-changing radiance, although few performers are spiritually developed enough to bring out its full force.

My cellist friend Stephen once had a Bach-induced TME while listening to the *Art of Fugue.* He was driving along the back roads of western Connecticut on his way to a rehearsal when he heard the first piece of the *Art of Fugue* on the radio. The performer was the Russian pianist Tatiana Nikolayeva.

Stephen told me that by the time the pianist had completed the five-minute fugue he'd burst into tears, so deeply moved that he had to pull over to the side of the road until the wave of emotion passed. He bought the recording and played it for me, after having told me the story of how he'd discovered it. We listened to the first several cuts on the two-CD set, which were from other pieces. I could tell that he was disappointed that I was not responding to Nikolayeva's playing. But when we got to the first piece in the *Art of Fugue*, I burst into tears at exactly the same point he had.

I knew the music well from another recording, the one I used to study with, as described in chapter 3. But I'd never heard it played with such spiritual intensity, compounded of deep sensitivity to, and compassion for, human suffering, and a profound sense of truth. Clearly, Nikolayeva, too, was a musical adept.[26]

Not enough is known about the exact dates of composition of Bach's music for me to determine when he passed through each of the stages of development between thinking mind and overmind.

For those who, like me, are constantly searching for moments of self-transcendence in music, the two Passions are perhaps the best place to begin. They're among the most astonishing of Bach's works in their ability to pass effortlessly from the formal play (middle 6) of fugal writing to the visionary (upper 6) nature of the recitatives that carry forward the action; and from the many instances of the seventh center's love, fear, and praise of God to the lower 8 compassion of the chorales and the middle 8 grace of several quasi-angelic commentaries on the spiritual meaning of the action.

In the yoga of listening, Bach's Passions are the equivalent of the ancient yogic scriptures—pieces to go back to again and again for spiritual uplift, the building of faith, support in meditation, and ecstatic mystical insight. Like the yogic scriptures, their goal is to bring us ever closer to God.

Union with the Divine

Cyril Scott believed that César Franck was a musical adept, as I pointed out in chapter 4. During the ten-year period in which Franck was composing *Les Béatitudes*, he achieved the status of illumined mind composer, and may have been on his way to becoming an overmind composer. *Les Béatitudes* begins at the same point as Wagner's *Parsifal*, but it works its way up to upper 8 (union) on several occasions—a range of the eighth center that Wagner was never able to achieve.

The six-minute Prologue of *Les Béatitudes* begins at the crisis zone between upper 7 and lower 8 (spiritual disillusionment, but with strong overtones of compassion from lower 8). The eight movements that follow, ranging in length from ten to twenty minutes, each deal with one of the Beatitudes from Christ's Sermon on the Mount (Matthew 5:1–10).

The first movement ("Blessed Are the Poor in Spirit") begins with the passion of upper 3 and rises to the grace of middle 8 when Christ (sung by a baritone) intones the Beatitude.

The second movement ("Blessed Are the Meek") begins in the crisis zone between the seventh and eighth centers (disillusionment) and once again rises to middle 8 (grace) when Christ sings the Beatitude.

The third movement ("Blessed Are Those Who Mourn") begins in the crisis zone between centers 6 and 7. Although I've called this crisis zone the irrational, it also often serves composers who wish to portray spiritual anguish—not disillusionment, but doubt. The movement closes with a heavenly chorus that moves the music up to upper 8 (union).

The fourth movement ("Blessed Are Those Who Hunger and Thirst for Righteousness") begins with transcendental longing, the point between lower 7 fear of God and middle 7 love of God. It ends in lower 8 compassion.

The fifth movement ("Blessed Are the Pure in Heart") also begins with the devotion of middle 7 and ends with another heavenly chorus that carries the music up to upper 8 (union).

The sixth movement ("Blessed Are the Peacemakers") brings in the voice of Satan (a bass). It begins in the crisis zone between centers six and seven (the irrational), which is often used to portray evil or the forces of darkness. The movement ends in middle 7 (devotion or love of God). It's the only one in *Les Béatitudes* that doesn't make it up to the eighth center. The *yearning* for peace is so strong that the human element overpowers the divine.

One way to tell the difference between music of the seventh and eighth centers is by the amount of human yearning it contains. The music of the eighth center has passed beyond such yearning into peace.

The eighth and final movement of *Les Béatitudes* ("Blessed Are Those Who Are Persecuted for Righteousness' Sake") also begins with the voice of Satan, and the crisis point between centers six and seven. Over the course of twenty minutes, it eventually achieves the grace of middle 8, when Jesus sings, and the union of upper 8, with a final heavenly chorus.

Les Béatitudes deserves to be better known. Commentators, perhaps conductors as well, seem to be embarrassed by its libretto, which is seen as overly pious. Yet it provides the only opportunity I've encountered so far in the tradition of Western classical music of prolonged exposure to the full spectrum of the eighth center of the continuum of human potential.

In the yoga of listening, *Les Béatitudes* could serve as a reminder of the importance of aligning ourselves with the universal spiritual values represented by the Sermon on the Mount. Each movement represents the struggle to rise from the spiritual confusion of our ordinary lives in the world into the peace of union with the divine that comes by accepting and living from one of the Beatitudes.

I recommend listening to the two and a quarter hours of music in *Les*

Béatitudes in daily segments. Begin with the Prologue and First Beatitude. Then listen to each of the remaining Beatitudes on successive days. This divides the work up into ten- to twenty-minute portions.

Familiarize yourself with the text of each segment beforehand, but listen meditatively, rather than while reading the libretto. I suggest sitting or lying in a comfortable position, with eyes closed, and perhaps using headphones. This is music that may take a couple of hearings before you become aware of its life-changing spiritual power, and during which a TME is less likely to be spontaneous than the result of cumulative exposure.

20

Wagner the Seer

The operas of Wagner, with their enchanting story lines, gripping characters, scenic spectacles, and endlessly fascinating music, are among the few pieces of Western music that span the continuum of human potential from the first through the eighth centers. According to Thomas Mann, the great twentieth-century German writer and Nobel prize winner, Wagner "is one of those musicians who can persuade even the unmusical to listen to music."[1] Listeners who want to maximize their exposure to the continuum of human potential would do well to begin with Wagner's operas.

Yet Mann also said that Richard Wagner is among the "most complex" and "fascinating . . . phenomena in the history of art and intellect . . . because he offers the most profound challenge to one's conscience."[2]

According to British philosopher Bryan Magee, "people often describe themselves as feeling *guilty* about enjoying Wagner." Others dislike this music intensely: "[T]hey say that they feel as if Wagner is trying to impose himself on them forcibly, to subordinate their wills, to subjugate them."[3]

One of the ways in which the consciences of many post-World War II listeners have been challenged by the music of Wagner involves the manner in which his anti-Semitism got mixed up with the Nazis' attempt to eliminate the Jewish people from Europe. As Magee points out, "Many people nowadays write and talk as if Wagner provided a sort of sound-track for the Third Reich." Furthermore, "[t]his conception has become a cliché on film and television."[4]

Magee shoots down such misconceptions by pointing out that the only Nazi who enjoyed Wagner was Hitler himself. The number of performances of Wagner in Germany actually *declined* during the Nazi era. *Parsifal* was banned from the repertory on ideological grounds. Hitler's own favorite opera was not the *Ring* cycle (although that's the source for much of the bombastic music used in portrayals of the Third Reich in film and on television), but *Die Meistersinger.*

Although the Nazis came into power decades after his death, Wagner was indeed anti-Semitic. In an attempt to settle the question of conscience raised by this anti-Semitism, Magee quotes the great Wagner conductor Sir Georg Solti, himself a Jew:

> To me, anybody who can create such beauty, whether he be half-Jewish, anti-Semite, revolutionary, liberal, or royalist, is first and foremost a musical genius and will remain so as long as our civilization lasts.[5]

Wagner's intention in writing operas was threefold. First, he wanted to create a theater for the common people, similar to ancient Greek tragedies in the cathartic nature of their plots. Second, he wanted such a theater to be as universal in its representation of individual characters as the plays of Shakespeare. Third, he wanted his work to plumb the heights and depths of the human spirit through music as sublime and passionate as that of Beethoven.

The amazing thing is that Wagner so often succeeded in realizing this ambitious program, which reflected the shadowy side of human nature, as well as the noble, in order to represent the full range of our experience in the world.

Like Solti, we're often willing to forgive persons of genius for obnoxious personalities, so long as the works they've produced enlarge our experience of life. Wagner's music *does* enlarge our lives. It can provide a catharsis of negative emotions, such things as (to quote Bryan Magee) "incest wishes and unrestrained eroticism," as well as "hatred and malice, spite, anxiety, guilt, isolation, foreboding, concealed menace, the whole dark side of life."[6] But it can also connect us with a higher love.

As I've noted at several points in this book, Cyril Scott claimed that some portions of Wagner's operas portray a buddhic love that lies beyond even the human love for God. For Scott, one reason for the appearance of so-called "ugly emotions" in Wagner's operas is that "neither a dramatic nor a musical creation is possible without its due proportion of contrast."[7]

The side-by-side presence of the higher or "buddhic" emotions and the lower or "ugly" ones represents a spiritual struggle within the composer himself, as well as his desire to portray the full range of experience available to us: the complete continuum of human potential, from the purely physical—even bestial—to the most sublime or divine.

Wagner intended to start a religion in which art was the focal point, rather than the rituals and dogmas of Christianity or Buddhism. The temple of this new religion was to be the Bayreuth Festival Opera House, which was partially financed by the young King Ludwig II of Bavaria. *Parsifal*, with its amalgam of Christian (Holy Grail) and Buddhist (world-renouncing compassion, reincarnation) elements, would be this new religion's central "rite." The question of whether this religion was intended to appeal to universal spiritual needs or was merely an opportunity for personal self-aggrandizement remains open.

It seems unlikely that we'll ever see Wagner as anything but equivocal—and perhaps for good reason. Both his character and his music portray the full range of human potential with a much higher degree of honesty than many of the world's religions do. The latter often condemn the lower and exalt the higher aspects of human nature, but without finding a way to integrate and transcend them both. Wagner's message is that the creation and witnessing of great art can allow that integration and transcendence to occur.

According to Mann, in Wagner's music, we have a conjunction of "aesthetic and artistic motivation" with "social and ethical impulses and a concern for the morality of art." Together, these things generate "a cathartic process, a process of cleansing, purification and spiritualization," which takes place both in the work and in the man. Yet Wagner was also "intensely passionate, torn by dark and violent appetites for popular acclaim, power and pleasure."[8]

The process outlined by Mann sounds much like that described in the previous chapter, in which the contact with the supermind brings about a process of purging from the self everything that contradicts the truth of who one truly is. Thus the life of the artist may resemble that of the saint: the movement from ignorance and sin to enlightenment, undertaken with each new work, and perhaps within the life itself.

In Wagner's case, this movement can be traced in the operas. Each one represents a stage on the path from what Sri Aurobindo called the thinking mind to the higher, illumined, and intuitive minds.

I would now like to chart that development, opera by opera. For reasons of space, I can't go into much detail about each opera—just a few notes about the plot, and some mention of the portions of the music that seem to be the most worthwhile from a spiritual perspective, those that touch the seventh or eighth centers. With *Parsifal*, however, I provide a more detailed sketch of how Wagner uses the continuum of human potential to highlight important moments in the plot.

Der Fliegende Holländer (The Flying Dutchman)

For most people, Wagner's career as a composer begins with this, his fourth opera, completed in 1841. The first three, *Die Feen* (*The Fairies*), *Das Liebesverbot*,

(*Love's Prohibition*), and *Rienzi* are rarely performed, although recordings of them are currently available.

By this time, Wagner had developed into a full-fledged thinking mind composer, whose music originated from the visionary aspect of upper 6. The command center (the sixth) is strong in all of Wagner's music, which perhaps accounts for what some people experience as delightfully irresistible and others as dangerously controlling.

Wagner, like most composers, wants his listeners to experience everything he feels or wishes to express. He achieves this end by transmitting a musically encoded vision—in his case, a mythic world—that he has imagined down to the last detail. But, more than most composers, Wagner's project also involves the role of musical guru, or spiritual guide.

According to esotericist Corinne Heline, *The Flying Dutchman* has to do with the lesson of "How Good Overcomes Evil."[9] The captain of a ship named the *Flying Dutchman* has been cursed to roam the oceans of the world for having sworn, in the midst of a gale, that he would stick to his course, even if Hell should try to prevent him from doing so. The punishment for the sin of placing his own will before God's was that all ports would be closed to him. Once every seven years, he would be allowed to come ashore to seek redemption through the self-sacrificing love of an innocent woman. In the opera, this woman is Senta, who places the will of God before her own.

Much of the opera is melodramatic and conventional in style. Heline cites "Senta's Ballad," the highlight of Act II, Scene 1, as being of particular spiritual interest. It's saturated with the piety and devotion of the middle 7 love of God.

The Overture is upper 6 (visionary) music at its best. Wagner uses the command center to impel us to see, with inner vision, the rolling of the waves through which the damned phantom ship, the *Flying Dutchman*, reels—especially in the chromatic runs of the lower strings. As we shall see, these runs are not only an attempt to dramatize the movements of the ocean in sound, but also to illustrate a metaphysical principle, another function of upper 6 visionary music.

Toward the end of Act III, Scene 1, an encounter occurs between a ship full of Norwegian sailors and the ghostly crew of the *Flying Dutchman*. The former are full of good cheer, drinking merrily; the latter are apparently dead to the world. Gradually, however, the *Flying Dutchman*'s crew wakes up to make the run into shore to pick up their captain, who has been courting Senta.

Never has the battle between good and evil found a more exciting representation in music. The chromatic runs mentioned above now represent emotional turbulence, the spiritual seasickness of irrationality, the crisis point between the sixth and seventh centers.

Meanwhile, the Norwegian sailors keep calling out for their Helmsman. They want him to abandon his watch and join them in drinking. Acting in the role of spiritual guide and protector, he does not.

Back and forth the music goes between the roiling, downward-tending strains that represent spiritual death, and the upward-tending strains of the drinking song, with its constant invocation of the Helmsman, that represent spiritual life. By the end of the opera, the curse has been lifted from the Dutchman's ship because of Senta's willingness to sacrifice herself, out of love for him. The ship and its phantom crew sink, at last, to eternal rest.

The opera *The Flying Dutchman* represents the beginning of Wagner's transition from being a visionary, thinking mind composer to being a higher mind composer. The battle between good and evil in Act III is actually an inner struggle between the ego's tormenting doubt and irrational fear of death, represented by the crew of the ship the *Flying Dutchman*, and the upward pull of spiritual growth exerted by God and the soul, represented by the Helmsman.

The Helmsman triumphs. From this point forward, Wagner will listen to and act on the prompting of his intuition when he composes, instead of relying on the ego's desire for fame and fortune, which was the motivation for his previous brilliant, but conventional (thinking mind) opera *Rienzi*.

Tannhäuser

Wagner wrote *Tannhäuser* in 1843 to 1845 but revised the score extensively in 1860, after completing *Tristan und Isolde*. The opera as we know it is a hybrid of two different periods in Wagner's creative and spiritual life.

The portions of the opera that Wagner didn't change reflect a transition from the higher mind to the illumined mind—a transition that culminated in the composition of his next opera, *Lohengrin*. As we shall see, after completing *Lohengrin*, Wagner fell back from the illumined mind to the higher mind. Only with the completion of *Tristan*, fifteen years later, did he once again achieve the illumined mind.

Perhaps Wagner felt the need to tamper with *Tannhäuser* in order to bring the higher mind aspects of the score up to the level of the illumined mind. Most of these changes were made in the so-called Venusberg Music (or Bacchanal) that comprises the first two scenes of Act I.

In chapter 9, I mentioned the waves of desire associated with the Venusberg Music. While this music carries the pleasure-based imprint of the second center, the waves themselves are a seventh center phenomenon, indicating that Wagner was now composing in the macrorhythmic style typical of expanded consciousness.

There's a great deal of seventh center music in *Tannhäuser,* from all three ranges. Wagner is constantly playing the secular and religious aspects of this center off each other. Thus the heroic nobility of the song with which the title character tries to free himself from the clutches of Venus in the second scene of Act I—an instance of secular middle 7 music—reappears in Act II, Scene 4, opposed to a more piously tuned (religious middle 7) song about spiritual love by the character Wolfram von Eschenbach.

Similarly, a chorus of Pilgrims singing a purely devotional chorale (religious middle 7) contrasts effectively with the music of the noble court (secular middle 7), such as the orchestral interlude entitled Entry of the Noble Guests, toward the beginning of Act II. (This interlude eventually works itself up into an ecstasy of choral praise, thus accessing a secular version of upper 7.)

In Act III, Scene 1, Elizabeth, the love interest, sings a prayer full of transcendental longing, associated with the point where lower 7 fear of God shades into middle 7 love of God. Immediately afterwards, in Scene 2, comes Wolfram's "Song to the Evening Star," which is a secularized version of the same transcendental longing. Elizabeth sings to the Virgin. Wolfram sings to Elizabeth, whom he loves.

In the Finale of the opera, a chorus of younger pilgrims arrives from Rome carrying an omen that Tannhäuser, whose spiritual salvation has been in doubt from the beginning of the opera, has been saved. Here, Wagner treats us to a few minutes of middle 8 music, representing the grace of God—perhaps signaling that he has arrived at the higher plane of consciousness from which *Lohengrin* was composed: that of the illumined mind.

This passage is drowned out when the Pilgrims' theme returns, in the orchestra, in a blaze of glory, thereby dropping the music down into the religious ecstasy of upper 7.

Lohengrin

Thomas Mann called *Lohengrin* Wagner's "purest, noblest, and most beautiful achievement."[10] This opera, written between 1846 and 1848, when Wagner was in his early to mid-thirties, is a product of the illumined mind.

Lohengrin, the Knight of the Swan, has come from the mystical castle that houses the Holy Grail and the brotherhood that guards it. He becomes the spiritual guide of Elsa, the woman he loves, and who loves him in return. But she must never ask him about his true identity or origin. The forces of evil cause her to doubt him, and she asks the fatal question. Lohengrin tells her who he is and that he now must leave her. She dies as he departs for the Grail realm.

The story of *Lohengrin* can be interpreted in a number of ways, none of them necessarily excluding the others. On one level, it's a love story between a spiritually evolved man and a somewhat less evolved woman. On another, it's an allegory of the artist, coming from a world beyond with a divine message, only to be misunderstood and spurned by the public.

A third interpretive level is that put forward by Heline: Lohengrin is a nonphysical master teacher who has taken on physical form to lead Elsa forward in her spiritual development. The drama is an out-picturing of this inner process.

The opera can also be described, in Sri Aurobindo's terms, as an illustration of what happens when the supermind, as the source of all consciousness (represented by the Holy Grail and its realm), sends forth one of its waves of inspiration. Such a wave is intended to lift the recipient (Wagner, as well as Elsa) to a higher level of consciousness. This ascent takes place along the continuum of human potential.

I see *The Flying Dutchman* as Wagner's first higher mind opera. Because of its subject matter (the battle between good and evil), I identify it with the crisis point between the visionary upper sixth and sublime lower seventh centers. *Tannhäuser* represents a more advanced stage of this development. While still a higher mind opera, it rests solidly in the sublime, or fear of God, range of lower 7, corresponding with transcendental longing.

Lohengrin is Wagner's first achievement as an illumined mind composer. It fits squarely into the middle 7 range of devotion and love of God (or duty).

Unfortunately, Wagner wasn't able to sustain this level of inspiration from the supermind. When he began work on the *Ring* cycle, he lapsed back into the higher mind mode. Only with the completion of *Tristan*, nearly ten years later, did he resume his ascent toward the source of all consciousness and once again achieve the level of illumined mind.

Lohengrin is enjoyable and spiritually moving from beginning to end. So, with the exception of the Prelude, I won't list any highlights here.

Der Ring des Nibelungen

Wagner wrote the poem upon which he based his vast, fourteen-hour cycle of music dramas, *The Ring of the Nibelungs*, in 1851 to 1852. The completion of the music for the four operas of this cycle—*Das Rheingold* (*The Rhinegold*), *Die Walküre* (*The Valkyrie*), *Siegfried*, and *Götterdämerung* (*Twilight of the Gods*)—required nearly twenty-five years. During this period, Wagner also composed *Tristan* and *Die Meistersinger.*

Wagner originally conceived of the *Ring* cycle as a means of putting into practice some philosophical ideas he'd developed in a book called *Opera and*

Drama, written in 1850 to 1851. The words and music in the *Ring* were to reflect the theoretical system outlined in this book, as well as various socialist and revolutionary ideas that Wagner had written about elsewhere.

Attempting to systematize the compositional process seems to be a typical reaction of the ego to the intuitive promptings of the soul or supermind. The ego is afraid of being dissolved in that larger consciousness and seeks to control it. The result is spiritual backsliding.

Thus Wagner slipped from being an illumined mind composer back into being a higher mind composer. The *Ring* cycle represents a twenty-five-year battle between ego and soul for supremacy. The soul comes through in moments of illumined mind glory that are as wonderful as anything in *Lohengrin*. But the systematic laboring of the higher mind, for which the ego is responsible, tends to dominate.

Upon hearing a performance of *Die Walküre*, Scriabin wrote: "The intention is always more than the achievement. As in *Siegfried* there are two or three moments of enchantment and all the rest is frightfully boring."[11] Though for me, as for many others, there's nothing more enchanting than those "moments of enchantment," I've had a similar reaction to much of the music in the *Ring* cycle.

The reason for this alternation between enchantment and boredom lies in the struggle between Wagner's ego and the supermind, which results in a vacillation between the sources of Wagner's inspiration: the illumined mind, in the moments of enchantment; and the higher mind, in the long stretches of boredom. The products of the higher mind can seem boring to us because of their juxtaposition with those of the illumined mind, whose enchantments we instinctively prefer.

Heline adds an interesting esoteric note to our understanding of the *Ring* by suggesting that the gold of the Rhine, which is the root of so much suffering and tragedy throughout the cycle, represents cosmic wisdom. The dramatic conflicts that develop over its possession throughout the four operas reflect the selfish sin of attempting to appropriate this knowledge for oneself alone.

Wagner's own interpretation of the Rhinegold was more literal. He wanted to see the abolishment of the old economic order, in which money played such an important role, and to see it replaced by a revolutionary state, not unlike that envisioned by Karl Marx, in which all property would be owned in common.

Das Rheingold was written in 1853 to 1854. Its primary moment of enchantment is the Entry of the Gods into Valhalla at the end of Act III, an example of middle 7 nobility.

Die Walküre was written in 1854–1856. Its primary moments of enchantment are "The Ride of the Valkyries" at the beginning of Act III and Wotan's Farewell and the Magic Fire music at the end, when Wotan puts his daughter Brünnhilde to sleep behind a curtain of illusory fire.

"The Ride of the Valkyries" is perhaps Wagner's most misunderstood work. It sounds either terrifying and warlike (crisis zone between centers 6 and 7) or sublime (lower 7). In many performances, the martial elements tend to be so strongly emphasized—and the piece itself is so often used in war movies—that it's not surprising some people think of it as the theme song of Hitler and the Nazis.

Underneath this military patina, however, is an important spiritual message. Near-death experiencers have often described spiritual beings of light who come to their aid. So it is with the Valkyries: In Germanic mythology, they are the heroic female spiritual presences who act as guides in the transition to the Afterlife.

Siegfried was begun in 1856 to 1857, and completed during the period from 1864 to 1871, after a long break, during which Wagner composed *Tristan* and began *Die Meistersinger*. Two of its moments of enchantment are sometimes performed as stand-alone orchestral excerpts, Forest Murmurs (drawn from Act II), and the Siegfried Idyll (based on musical ideas from Act III). These are both upper 6 visionary evocations of landscape, with strong input from the fifth, or well-being center (specifically, lower 5, which often deals with the relaxed feelings connected with enjoyment of beautiful landscapes).

A third moment of enchantment occurs when the Magic Fire music returns, as Siegfried comes to awaken Brünnhilde from sleep, and they fall in love.

Götterdämmerung was written in 1869 to 1874. By this time, the battle between Wagner's ego and soul seems to have resolved itself. More of the illumined mind than the higher mind appears in this opera, so there are frequent moments of enchantment. These include the second part of the Prologue, which is a kind of mini-*Tristan*, enacted between Siegfried and Brünnhilde; two stand-alone orchestral excerpts: Dawn and Siegfried's Rhine Journey, which ends the Prologue, and Siegfried's Funeral March; and Brünnhilde's Immolation, which concludes Act III and the *Ring* cycle itself.

Throughout the *Ring* cycle, most of the moments of enchantment access some range of the seventh center, and include all but the eighth of the centers on the continuum of human potential. Many of the musical themes (called leitmotifs) that reference characters, objects, situations, or ideas have a sublime or noble element, and so touch the seventh center, though briefly. A few moments of eighth center compassion also break through here and there, in particular in Wotan's Farewell and Brünnhilde's Immolation.

Much of the *Ring*, however, is purely dramatic in nature, dealing with passions such as incest, greed, revenge, and so on. Long passages of the music take place in various ranges of the conflict-ridden third center. Even so, the macrorhythmic pattern of swells of accumulating and dissipating energy, typical of music composed from planes higher than the thinking mind, is present throughout the entire cycle.

Tristan und Isolde

Wagner composed *Tristan und Isolde* in the years 1856 to 1859. In chapter 9, I noted that Wagner intended the Prelude to represent the creation of the universe from the breath of desire. Thus the opera places a strong emphasis on the second, or pleasure, center.

Mann wrote that *Tristan* is "a thoroughly obscene work."[12] He claimed that "in its sensuous-suprasensuous passion, its lascivious desire for bed, it really is something for young people, at the age when the erotic is all-important."[13]

Certainly, the opera can be heard in that way. As I pointed out in chapter 11, Act II, Scene 2 provides an instance of the crisis point between the fourth and fifth centers, a specifically erotic delirium.

Yet Mann was not deaf to the opera's "unbounded spiritualized sensuality," which he felt had been "raised to a mystical order." Here, we have a "sensuality that will not be appeased by *any* gratification," except that of union in a mystical love-death.[14] Such mysticism has its basis in the seventh, or expanded consciousness, center.

According to Magee, *longing* is the keyword in *Tristan*.[15] But what sort of longing—desire (center 2), passion (center 3), love (center 4), or something more spiritual (center 7)?

The answer is: all of the above. As I pointed out in part 2, the lower centers of the continuum of human potential are usually active beneath the higher ones. Thus Wagner could write an opera infused with transcendental longing—a characteristic of the point where lower 7 shades into middle 7—and at the same time access versions of this longing that are more closely identified with the lower centers. The first chord of the Prelude, the famous *Tristan* chord, which saturates the entire opera, perfectly expresses this transcendental longing.

The first act of *Tristan* begins, as do all of the operas of the *Ring*, with the kind of plodding exposition that I associate with Wagner's ventures as a higher mind composer. About halfway through the third of its five scenes, however, it shifts onto the next higher plane, that of the illumined mind. Unlike the music dramas of the *Ring*, once *Tristan* has risen to this level, it's all enchantment—harrowing at times, but never boring. The Liebestod (Love-Death) music that comes at the end of the opera is one of Wagner's most thrilling musical creations—a portrayal of mystical and erotic ecstasy that leads us to the threshold of upper 7.

Die Meistersinger

Wagner wrote his one and only comedy, *Die Meistersinger* (*The Mastersingers*) in 1862 to 1867, after he'd finished *Tristan*, but before he'd completed the *Ring*. *Die Meistersinger* deals with the spiritual and mundane aspects of the arts of music and of love.

The transcendental longing of *Tristan* is gone from *Die Meistersinger*. It has been replaced by a healthier, life-affirming humor and compassion. As in much of the late music of Mozart, the humor itself is transcendental, full of the gentle irony that develops when we're able to look down upon human folly from the wiser perspective of the soul. For this reason, *Die Meistersinger* originates from a higher level on the continuum of human potential than *Tristan*: upper 7, or transcendental mirth.

The compositional technique of the opera is also on firmer ground than that of its predecessors, especially those of the *Ring* cycle. In *Die Meistersinger*, Wagner has completely mastered the use of leitmotifs. Not only do they each seem to be a perfect representation of the characters, situations, or ideas they portray, but also their appearances in the score, and the ingenious ways that they're contrapuntally combined with each other, have none of the frequent heavy-handedness of the *Ring* cycle.

Die Meistersinger is throughout a work of the illumined mind. It also shows signs of moving toward the next higher level, that of the intuitive mind—a transition that was completed fifteen years later, when Wagner finished his last music drama, *Parsifal*.

In the beginning, *Die Meistersinger* is about a young nobleman, Walther von Stolzing, who falls in love with Eva, the daughter of a Nuremberg goldsmith. She returns his love. But Eva's well-meaning father has complicated things by offering her hand in marriage as a prize for the best song in the yearly contest of a musical guild called the mastersingers. The guild's rules for composing such songs are extremely strict. They can only be mastered after years of rigorous apprenticeship. Naturally, the young nobleman fails in his first attempt to sing for the hand of his beloved.

As the opera progresses, however, the focus of attention shifts away from Walther to the elderly Hans Sachs, a cobbler and mastersinger. He, too, deeply loves Eva, despite the great difference in their ages. By the end of the opera, out of self-abnegating compassion, Hans Sachs manages to help Walther and Eva overcome the obstacles to their love.

This compassion, an expression of unconditional love, allows the music to access the lower eighth center. In a famous monologue in the third act, Hans Sachs bemoans the *Wahn* (folly or madness) of the world in the disillusioned tones of the crisis point between the seventh and eighth centers.

The musical highpoint of the opera is a quintet, also in the third act. Walther has received a master-song in a dream. Hans Sachs has helped him work it out and write it down. The two of them are joined by Eva, Sachs's apprentice David, and Eva's best friend Magdalene, who is also David's betrothed. Together, they honor a tradition of the mastersingers by "baptizing" the new song with a name.

While Walther's master-song is full of spiritual love, it contains too much longing to be an example of eighth center music. It's an instance of secular middle 7 music, in which the love expressed is both for a human being and for one's own soul, as projected onto her.

The quintet, however, is perhaps the highest example of eighth center, or cosmic-consciousness, music that Wagner ever wrote. It touches the point where the grace of middle 8 shades into the union of upper 8.

The last act of the opera contains music that accesses the crisis point between centers seven and eight, as well as the compassion of lower 8, and even opens into the middle to upper range of the eighth center. Thus it marks the beginning of Wagner's transition from being an illumined mind composer to being an intuitive mind composer.

Parsifal

Wagner's last opera, *Parsifal*, was composed between 1877 and 1882. It represents the culmination not only of his life's work as a composer, but also of his spiritual development.

As noted, according to Magee, *longing* is the keyword of *Tristan*.[16] Transcendental longing, as we've seen, is a characteristic of the point where middle 7 begins, a level associated with the transition to becoming an illumined mind composer. The dominant center of *Tristan* is middle 7.

Magee states that the keyword of *Die Meistersinger* is *Wahn*, an untranslatable German word that means not only "human folly" and "madness," but also "delusion and illusion."[17] These are characteristics of the crisis point between the seventh and eighth centers, which has to do with spiritual disillusionment.

As noted above, the dominant center in *Die Meistersinger* is middle to upper 7, or transcendental mirth. But the presence of disillusionment in the opera represents the beginning of Wagner's transition from illumined to intuitive mind composer.

According to Magee, *compassion* is the keyword of *Parsifal*. Compassion is a characteristic of lower 8 music, a level that I've associated with the intuitive mind composer. This is the level on the continuum of human potential from which *Parsifal* emanates. Because the opera expresses a movement from spiritual disillusionment to the compassion of selfless service, it represents the completion of Wagner's transition from illumined mind to intuitive mind composer.

Parsifal contains elements of both Christian and Buddhist mysticism. The Christian elements include the Holy Grail and the order of knights that protect it, as in *Lohengrin*. Temptations of the flesh, similar to those encountered in *Tannhäuser*, also appear, in Act II, in the form of the Flower Maidens and the Bosch-like Garden of Earthly Delights they inhabit, under the direction of an evil sorcerer by the name of Klingsor.

The fusion of Buddhist and Christian elements in the opera appears primarily in the character of Kundry, a woman cursed to reincarnate again and again because she committed the sin of laughing at Christ when he was carrying the cross to Golgotha for his crucifixion. Kundry spends half of her life serving the Grail and the other half under the domination of Klingsor.

At the beginning of the opera, the present keeper of the Grail, Amfortas, is suffering from a wound that won't heal, a result of his having succumbed to the erotic temptations of the Flower Maidens. The evil Klingsor was thus able to steal from Amfortas the magic spear that pierced the side of Christ on the cross and has wounded Amfortas with it. The Order of the Holy Grail is now dying for lack of spiritual nourishment, because Amfortas has become increasingly resistant to performing the rites of the Grail that keep the members of this order alive. Every time he performs these rites, the pain from his wound becomes intolerable.

Parsifal, the holy fool, stumbles upon the realm of the Grail as a youth. One of the knights, Gurnemanz, becomes his spiritual teacher and guide. Gurnemanz takes Parsifal to witness the unveiling of the Grail. Parsifal pledges himself to the task of recovering the magic spear that will heal the wound of Amfortas.

After overcoming the temptations of the Flower Maidens and Kundry in the second act, Parsifal battles Klingsor and regains the spear. In the third, he returns to the realm of the Grail, heals Amfortas, and becomes the next Keeper of the Grail. Kundry is redeemed in the process.

The Prelude to Act I begins with the solemnity and transcendental yearning of lower 7, which is immediately answered by the music that represents the revelation of the Grail later in the opera. Wagner calls this theme "love." It's repeated twice.

As in the Prelude to *Lohengrin*, the Grail music represents spiritual comfort and grace. It manifests itself directly from the soul, or from God, as an answer to the human yearning of the opening phrase. Therefore, it emanates from the transpersonal center, including both the compassion of lower, and the grace of middle, 8.

According to Wagner's program for the work, the second theme represents faith. It has the characteristics of praise and nobility that I associate with middle 7.

Because all is not well in the realm of the Grail, as the Prelude develops, the seventh center music is often shot through with a strong elegiac or lamenting element that emanates from the crisis point between centers seven and eight: the doubt of spiritual disillusionment. Such music recurs often throughout the opera.

At the point in Act I when Amfortas begins to sing, the passion of upper 3 enters the opera. This music symbolizes the King's unhealable wound and the unrestrained passion that threatens the stability of the Grail Order and its realm, as well as ours. No one from the Grail realm can come on special missions into our own world, as Lohengrin did, without the spiritual food provided by the Grail. Amfortas selfishly withholds this nourishment in order to ease his pain: His wound begins to bleed again whenever the Grail is revealed.

Toward the end of the act, and at a similar point in the third act, a scene transformation, from an outdoor forest to an indoor temple, occurs. According to Heline, the bells that accompany these scene changes are "astral bells," indicating that the characters in the opera are leaving the physical world and entering a higher spiritual plane.

The Grail ritual at the end of the first act returns the music to the seventh center, with a brief glimpse at middle 8 (grace) when the Grail itself is actually revealed. All three levels of the seventh center—solemnity and sublimity, nobility, praise and ecstasy—are present during this ceremony.

Parsifal's Grail music, to my ears, is not as enchanting as that in *Lohengrin*. But there may be a reason for its apparent weakness. As pointed out, all is not well in the realm of the Grail. The Grail's power has been diminished by spiritual disillusionment.

Act II is set in the environs of the evil sorcerer Klingsor's castle. Much of the music acts on various levels of the third center (tension, agitation, passion). The Prelude is a fine example of middle 3 agitation.

The entry of the Flower Maidens begins with conflict, but soon devolves into the sensual realm of middle 2 (pleasure), as they attempt to seduce

Parsifal. Kundry's temptation of Parsifal through love, however, is of a higher order than that through desire. For this, Wagner moves the music up to the bittersweet yearning of middle 4.

When conflict develops between Kundry and the pure Parsifal, who resists such temptation, Kundry's music falls into the passion of upper 3. Toward the end of the act, Parsifal rouses himself with a burst of heroic middle 7 music, reminding himself of his aims, and regains the magic spear. Klingsor's power is broken and his castle and pleasure garden are destroyed in a burst of third center intensity.

The Prelude to Act III brings us back to the realm of the Grail, with more music from the crisis point between centers seven and eight. This music illustrates how the power of the place has weakened even further, as a result of Amfortas withholding the spiritual nourishment of the Grail from his knights. Harmonic distortions of the faith theme from the Act I Prelude underline the fact that this is the music of spiritual disillusionment.

Shortly after the opening of Act III comes a section that is often played as an orchestral excerpt from the opera, without voices: the Karfreitagszauber (Good Friday Spell). Parsifal has arrived in the realm of the Grail on Good Friday. His task has been accomplished, but he's weary in heart and soul. He has just been given to drink from, and has bathed in, the waters of a holy spring. His strength has been replenished. His feelings of guilt over having taken so long to fulfill his goal of returning to the Grail realm with the magic spear have been washed away.

The Good Friday Spell begins with a burst of heroic middle 7 music (nobility). It continues through the portion of the opera in which Kundry is baptized by Parsifal, thereby absolving her from the sin that has kept her tied to lifetime after lifetime of suffering.

Just after this baptism, Parsifal's words have to do with the beauty and serenity of the landscape. Here, Wagner adds a dimension to the music that was not previously present in the opera: lower 5. Wagner has avoided the fifth, or well-being, center throughout the opera, to symbolize the weakening of the Grail realm. Only at the point when Parsifal, the new king of the realm, has arrived with the healing magic spear can the music of well-being at last make its appearance.

As before, "astral bells" again indicate a scene transformation from forest to temple. As before, the music rises to the seventh center and ranges through all three levels, from sublimity to ecstasy, with a brief moment of middle 8 grace when the Grail is revealed.

There are two differences between this portion of the opera and the end of Act I: The sixth center is strongly active, as Wagner combines the various leitmotifs that have represented characters, situations, objects, or ideas in the course of the opera; and the fifth center, which was absent from the first act, is now fully active, indicating that now all is well within the Grail realm.

By the end of the opera, which lasts four and a half hours, we feel that a healing process has taken place. We've healed and transcended the inner wounds of doubt and spiritual disillusionment and developed a closer relationship with the soul or supermind, represented by the Grail.

Listening to Wagner

Getting to know all ten of the Wagner operas described here is a huge investment in time and money, whether you purchase recordings of them or see them performed on stage or DVD. Before I began researching this book, I only knew a few excerpts that I heard years ago in a college music appreciation class and could barely recall. Because of the controversy surrounding Wagner as man and artist, I decided to proceed cautiously.

First I listened to two CDs of purely orchestral music selected from the thirty-five to forty hours of Wagner's mature output. Typically, such recordings include the Overtures or Preludes to each of the operas listed here, plus *Rienzi*, as well as the stand-alone excerpts, such as the Venusberg Music (or Bacchanal, usually performed with the Overture) from *Tannhäuser*; "The Ride of the Valkyries" from *Die Walküre*; Forest Murmurs and the Siegfried Idyll from *Siegfried*; Siegfried's Rhine Journey and Funeral March from *Götterdämmerung*; the Liebestod from *Tristan* (usually performed with the Prelude); and the Good Friday Spell from *Parsifal*.

I've mentioned a number of these excerpts in this book. If, in the yoga of listening, this is the only exposure you have to the music of Wagner, you'll have benefited greatly. Most of this music targets the upper 6 (visionary) center or above, and the Prelude to *Lohengrin* accesses middle 8 (grace).

From exposure to the orchestral music, I progressed to a two-CD set of highlights from the *Ring* cycle, which allowed me to deepen my familiarity with the nearly fifteen hours of music it contains. Sometimes it's possible with such a set, and even separately, to hear Wotan's Farewell from *Die Walküre*. This excerpt includes the Magic Fire music, which I've found to have an especially strong effect on the third-eye chakra (it's upper 6 visionary music). The music of the Farewell ranges through a number of centers, but is especially strong in the area of middle 7, when it expresses the spiritual dimension of Wotan's love for his favorite daughter, Brünnhilde.

A similarly moving excerpt is Brünnhilde's Immolation at the end of *Götterdämmerung*, in which she throws herself into Siegfried's funeral pyre in order to be joined with him forever. This ecstatic love-death music also expresses a higher love and targets the middle to upper range of the seventh center.

From here, I took on the whole of the *Ring* cycle. At this point, it was necessary to consult the librettos and other handy guidebooks to the musical and thematic richness of the *Ring* in order to orient myself. Rather than listen to each of the four operas in a single evening, which would have required from two to four hours, I divided them up into thirty- to forty-minute excerpts. That way I was able to bring my full attention to each listening session and the effects that the music has on the centers it targets.

My preference in listening to opera is to focus on the music rather than the words. I read the libretto beforehand. If you want to follow the libretto while you listen, you might want to go back to your favorite parts and listen again, with your eyes closed, to maximize the effects of the centers.

If you're seeing the opera in performance, the best way to maximize these effects is to give yourself completely to the combined experience of sound, words, and visuals. This will probably require some advance preparation, such as familiarizing yourself with the plot and libretto.

Much of the magic of such a performance can be lost if you don't know what's happening on stage and can't understand the words. Luckily, many opera houses these days are equipped with a captioning system that functions much like the subtitles on a filmed or televised version.

When you're ready to take the step of immersing yourself in Wagner's magical sound world by listening to an entire opera, if the *Ring* seems too intimidating, I recommend starting with *Lohengrin*.[18] As I mentioned, in the words of Thomas Mann, *Lohengrin* is Wagner's "purest, noblest, and most beautiful achievement."[19]

In the yoga of listening, the spiritual effects of exposing ourselves to complete Wagner operas are too numerous to be listed here, although I've hinted at some of them. Each work touches on most or all of the continuum of human potential and constantly shifts from center to center, depending on the dramatic needs of the moment.

If I had to encapsulate the spiritual lessons of Wagner's operas, however, it would go something like this. *The Flying Dutchman* helps us to right the inner disequilibrium, or battle between good and evil motivations, that results when we've lost touch with our souls. *Tannhäuser* does something similar, except the inner battle is between sensuality and spirituality instead of good and evil.

Lohengrin is about truing ourselves to our life purpose (represented by the Grail) with the help of the soul's inner guidance (represented by Lohengrin). It's also about the danger of losing contact with the soul if we allow ourselves to be swayed from this purpose by doubt or the malevolent influence of those who may be jealous of our success or happiness.

The *Ring* cycle is about how a world based on the corrupting influences of money, power, and selfish behavior can be redeemed—or destroyed and remade—on the basis of self-sacrifice and love.

Tristan is about our erotic and spiritual longing to overcome the many physical, personal, and social restrictions that stand in the way of achieving oneness of body and soul in a relationship of reciprocal love.

Die Meistersinger is about art, compassion, laughter, and love—especially the unconditional love expressed in selfless service—as antidotes to the folly or madness of the world.

Parsifal is about healing spiritual disillusionment. This healing, as in *Die Meistersinger*, takes place by means of compassion and selfless service, thereby opening the way for a closer relationship with the soul and God.

21

Celestial Symphonies:
Bruckner and Mahler

Wagner's music opened up new sound worlds that changed the course of musical history. His influence can be heard in the symphonies of Bruckner and Mahler, the tone poems of Strauss, the mysticism of Scriabin, and the impressionism of Debussy. Even the breakdown of tonality in twentieth-century music, as in the works of Schoenberg, had its roots in Wagner.

Wagner also had a profound influence on the spiritual development of later composers—in particular Bruckner and Mahler, who strived to bring the sublimity, ecstasy, and godlike grace they heard in his music into their own. Wagner showed Bruckner and Mahler that it was possible to compose music that expresses both longing for and union with the divine—music that affects the seventh and eighth centers on the continuum of human potential. The result was that each wrote a series of symphonies so rich in beauty and spiritually expansive that they deserve to be called celestial.

Anton Bruckner

One of the traditional yogic paths is called *bhakti*, the way of devotion. It has been described as "a passion for God" that "consumes all earthly passions." For the devotee, it's not merely "an undercurrent of joy which waters the depths of his heart in his own privacy, but a torrent that overflows the caverns of his heart into all his senses" resulting in "a spiritual intoxication of joy."[1]

When a composer allows himself to be taken over by such intoxication, the result may be a mystical masterpiece. The spiritual experience of the composer becomes a transcendent musical experience for the listener, in which the composer's longing for and love of the divine may be transmitted directly to us.

Although Anton Bruckner was a Catholic and not a yogi, his music is a perfect sonic expression of the bhakti yoga way of devotion: a "complete unconditional self-surrender to the Highest Being."[2] Bruckner's music encodes an ecstatic experience of the divine, capable of lifting susceptible listeners into self-transcending states of consciousness.

As I pointed out in chapter 19, Sri Aurobindo's supermind, the source of all consciousness, lies beyond the overmind, which correlates with the eighth center on the continuum of human potential. The overmind acts as a receiving station for the supermind. According to Satprem, a disciple of Aurobindo, the overmind is "the source of all creative and spiritual activity."[3]

Contact with the supermind, via the overmind, occurs "through anything that helps man surpass himself,"[4] such as Bruckner's intense spiritual devotion. Once this contact has been made, however briefly, *ideas* are no longer the source of one's art. Rather, "Vibrations, waves, or rhythms literally take possession of the seeker, invade him, *then*, as they come down, are clothed in words and ideas, or music, or colors" that "give a body to that first terribly compelling vibration."[5]

Such waves "come into consciousness with a sort of halo of eternity, which vibrates before and continues to vibrate long after."[6] This phrase expresses the feeling I have when I listen to the later symphonies of Bruckner.

These "self-sustained, self-luminous" vibrations usually break up into "spurts, thrusts, pulsations" when they move from the supermind, via the overmind, into lower planes or aspects of consciousness—the intuitive, illumined, and higher minds. Perhaps this breakdown process is responsible for the great waves of accumulating and dissipating energy that I sense in macrorhythmically composed music such as Bruckner's.

Such music progresses by means of huge accumulations of musical energy, through volume, dissonance, and sometimes speed, which are then allowed to dissipate and begin again. The result is a wavelike pattern of musical ebbs and flows that are built up and released over long stretches of time.

Music constructed in this way has the greatest potential for altering consciousness and producing TMEs. I've had more TMEs while listening to the music of Bruckner than I have with any other composer.

According to Satprem, "artists and creators generally have a sizable ego standing in their way,"[7] which may further break up the luminous waves of the supermind, rendering them virtually unrecognizable. In Bruckner, because of his lack of ego, they remain relatively pure. Page after page of his scores are filled with them.

Bruckner's music, especially in the first movements and adagios (slow movements) of his symphonies, provides a sustained exposure to these waves, as well as to the first through the seventh centers in the continuum of human potential. Averaging an hour in length, Bruckner's symphonies spend more than half of that time in the seventh center's state of expanded consciousness. I know of no other classical music that's so well suited to support prolonged states of meditation. The Sixth through the Ninth symphonies, in particular, make ideal auditory yantras for the yoga of listening.

The typical Bruckner symphony begins with a long first movement, in a moderate tempo, in four parts. The first part is an *exposition*, in which three themes of contrasting character are stated. The initial theme usually begins quietly and mysteriously, in lower 7. The second theme often has dancelike elements, and may bring the music down from its typical spiritual loftiness to lower or middle 5. The third theme is usually loud and stark, an example of lower 7 sublimity.

The exposition is followed by a *development* section, in which the themes are taken apart and recombined in various ways. Then comes a *recapitulation*, in which the themes are restated in forms that closely resemble those of the exposition. The movement comes to a close with a glorious *coda* (Italian for "tail") that usually rises from the nobility of middle 7 to the ecstasy of upper 7.

The second and third movements will be either a scherzo followed by an adagio or an adagio followed by a scherzo. The typical Bruckner adagio runs the gamut of religious feeling from piety (the point where lower shades into middle 7), through devotional love of God (middle 7), to glorification of God (where middle 7 shades into upper 7). The adagio usually involves a loud climax, about three quarters of the way through, that pushes the music into the ecstatic range of upper 7.

The scherzo takes the center down a notch but greatly ups the tempo. It's like a descent from the contemplative spiritual heights to the hubbub of the secular world, especially that of nature. The whole range of the sixth center is usually involved: the wit of lower 6, the elaborate formal play of middle 6, the visionary aspects of upper 6 (e. g., in the Scherzo of the Fourth Symphony, with its hunting calls), even the demonic force of the crisis point between centers six and seven. Sometimes the scherzo may reach as high as the sublimity of lower 7.

Bruckner scherzos always contain a contrasting middle section, called Trio, that is usually less dynamic. It frequently descends to lower 5: the tranquil sense of well-being that often arises in connection with contemplating the beauty of nature.

Bruckner finales begin with the formal play of middle 6. As in the first movement, three themes will usually be introduced, developed, and recapitulated, followed by a coda. Gradually, the music makes its way from the sixth center back up to the seventh. The finale ends, like the first movement, in the ecstasy of upper 7. Within the last few pages of the score, there's usually a climactic moment in which Bruckner superimposes the themes of each of the previous movements.

This pattern was so deeply ingrained in Bruckner's psyche that he departed from it in only two of his nine symphonies: the Fifth and the Eighth. The first movement of the Fifth Symphony begins with a slow introduction; the Finale begins with a restatement of the themes of the earlier movements, as in Beethoven's Ninth. The first movement of Bruckner's Eighth Symphony ends quietly, instead of with the usual progression from nobility to ecstasy.

The layout of Bruckner's symphonies is so uniform that a critic once quipped that he didn't write nine symphonies but one symphony nine times. The real joke is that Bruckner wrote *more* than nine symphonies more than once. He's the only composer on record who has written not only a Symphony Number Zero, but also a Symphony Number Double Zero. (These are both early productions that Bruckner didn't feel were good enough to authorize for public performance.)

Bruckner was often in doubt about the quality of his output and frequently revised it. There are three versions of the First Symphony, two of the Second, four of the Third, two different finales for the Fourth, and two versions of the Eighth. To make matters worse, the first editions of many of Bruckner's symphonies were often heavily revised by well-meaning friends to make them more "acceptable"—which meant louder, shorter, and more bombastically Wagnerian.

Scores that represented Bruckner's original intentions didn't become available until the 1930s. Perhaps that's why Cyril Scott's only reference to Bruckner in *Music: Its Secret Influence*, which first appeared in 1933, is so disparaging: "Yet that spate of composers who wrote in the Wagnerian style, minus Wagner's genius, have all been forgotten, save Bruckner, who can hardly be regarded as a great master."[8]

Bruckner's first three symphonies represent his thinking mind phase. The First and Second Symphonies are products of middle 6 formalism. The Third, written as a tribute to Wagner, begins his transition from middle 6 formalist to upper 6 visionary.[9]

The Fourth Symphony, subtitled *Romantic*, is among Bruckner's most-played works. The subtitle is not to be taken in the amorous sense—there's next to nothing about human love in any of Bruckner's works. Though he never took monastic vows, he was a lifelong celibate.

The Fourth is a visionary work (upper 6), in which Bruckner attempts to portray romantic landscapes, including a hunting scene in the Scherzo. But its emphasis on the romantic notion of the sublime also marks the beginning of Bruckner's transition from thinking mind to higher mind (lower 7) composer.

This transition was fully effected with the completion of Bruckner's Fifth Symphony in 1878. Much of the symphony deals with compositional problems of an intellectual nature—for example, how to incorporate an ambitious fugue into the Finale. The majority of the music expresses what Aurobindo called the thinking mind.

The coda of the Finale, however, is one of the most glorious musical apotheoses in all of Bruckner, if not of Western music—a genuine lifting up to God that carries the music from the formal play of middle 6 up to the ecstasy of upper 7.

Listening to the recording by Claudio Abbado and the Vienna Philharmonic, I once had a TME that I can only describe as a continual opening to the glory that is God. As each degree of this opening was achieved, I felt that no further glory could possibly be borne—and then there was more, on an even higher plane of spiritual intensity. The music seemed to portray the rising of kundalini to the extreme upper limits of the human capacity to sustain and survive samadhi (bliss).

Critics consider Bruckner's Sixth Symphony to be his weakest, but it's a personal favorite of mine. It follows the plan I've outlined. The Sixth is the first complete product of Bruckner's having attained the plane of higher mind. It's macrorhythmically composed throughout.

Prior to this symphony, Bruckner's work, like that of most of his contemporaries, expressed the restless motion of the thinking mind. Following the Sixth, his work expressed the more even motions of a focused, meditative consciousness. Only a conductor who knows how to bring out the macrorhythmic nature of such music is able to perform it successfully.

Critics may have based their negative judgment of Bruckner's Sixth on bad performances rather than its actual merits. The recording by Otto Klemperer and the New Philharmonia Orchestra leaves no doubt in my mind that the Sixth is Bruckner's first fully integrated masterpiece.[10]

Bruckner's Seventh Symphony was the only one for which he received public acclaim during his lifetime. It's perhaps the best piece for listeners who have never experienced Bruckner's music to get started with.

The opening theme touches the same center as the Prelude to Wagner's *Lohengrin*—the grace of middle 8. At this stage in Bruckner's development, he seems not to have known what to do with a melody so supremely beautiful. He just presents it and moves on. While this melody recurs in the recapitulation, there are no other moments of eighth center music in the rest of the symphony.

With the exception of two brief passages of lower 5 dancelike music, the remainder of the first movement runs the gamut of the seventh center, from the sublime lower 7 music of the third theme to the ecstatic upper 7 coda. This progression takes place, as I've described, in huge waves of sonic and emotional intensity that are constantly accumulating and dissipating.

The second movement follows the typical pattern of a Bruckner adagio, as I've outlined. It provides an excellent opportunity to experience the shades of difference between the lower and upper ends of middle 7. The main theme begins at the lower end, with piety; the second theme represents a much more passionate, yearning, devotional love of God.

The ecstatic (upper 7) climax comes about three quarters of the way through the movement, with a controversial cymbal crash and triangle roll—controversial because no one knows whether Bruckner or one of his admirers added it.

While working on this Adagio, Bruckner received word that Wagner had died. Bruckner revered Wagner, so he composed a brief musical epitaph for him toward the end of the movement, scored for the tenor tubas Wagner had invented for use in the *Ring* cycle. This is the only moment in the symphony that descends into the pathos of lower 4.

The Scherzo is also typical of the pattern outlined above. It seems to have the force—at times inimical, at others sublime—of a violent thunderstorm. The Trio (middle section) is a restful example of lower 5 music.

The Finale, too, follows the typical pattern of movement from the sixth to the seventh center, beginning with a scherzo-like playfulness (lower 6) and ending in the ecstasy of upper 7.[11]

After listening to the Seventh Symphony, I feel purified, as if the music had gently realigned my inner being with God. In the yoga of listening, it would be useful for anyone in need of such a realignment.

The Eighth Symphony (usually performed in its second version, of 1890) seems to be Bruckner's depiction of death and the Afterlife. The first movement is intended to represent the last moments of a dying man, including the terrifying trumpet call that summons him to judgment. Instead of ending in triumph, the movement closes with the man's final heartbeats dying away.

The second movement is a scherzo. I hear it as the soul's ecstatic flight toward God, as it revels in the magic and mystery of its freedom from the body. The Trio (middle section) sounds like the soul's arrival in some kind of self-imagined heaven, complete with harps (and noble middle 7 music).

The opening of the third movement has the glory of a spectacular sunrise. It seems to represent a dawning awareness that the true heaven isn't self-imagined but the actual experience of drawing ever closer to God.

This movement has a shape similar to that of the Adagio of the Seventh, including an ecstatic (upper 7) climax, and a composer-authorized cymbal crash and triangle roll. There's one major difference: The Adagio of the Seventh contains no eighth center music, but that of the Eighth Symphony does.

A ninety-second passage that accesses the grace of middle 8, like Wagner's vision of the Grail in *Lohengrin*, occurs about four and a half minutes into the movement and returns once, later on. In a good performance, the shift from the seventh center's supplicatory directedness toward God to the feeling of receiving a spine-tingling, radiant answer from the source of all life should be clearly audible.

The passage that immediately follows, which features a solo on the tenor tuba, shifts the music back to middle 7. It sounds like a moment of prayerful gratitude for this response from the Source.

The opening of the Finale has an almost apocalyptic intensity. Bruckner related it to the Cossacks galloping on horseback. To me, it sounds more like the four horsemen of the biblical Revelation come to announce the Day of Judgment (Revelation 6:1–7). The long coda is one of the most glorious passages in all of Bruckner—an apotheosis (lifting up to God) like that at the end of the Fifth Symphony.[12]

I've already mentioned the important role that Bruckner's Ninth Symphony played in my determination to become a composer. Bruckner was nearing the end of his life as he composed the work. The first movement sounds like a funeral march. It targets the solemn, mysterious, sublime range of lower 7. By the end, it has gradually worked itself into the ecstasy of upper 7.

The Scherzo may express Bruckner's fear of death. It's relentless and terrifying, a demonic scherzo touching the crisis point between the sixth and seventh centers. The Trio is lighter in tone, alternating passages that remind me of the flight-of-the-soul music in the Scherzo of the Eighth with others that seem to express a passionate yearning for God.

The slow movement is darker in mood than those of the Seventh and Eighth symphonies, expressing the progression from a fearful and doubt-tormented piety to inner peace.

Bruckner never finished the Finale. A performing version was prepared from his sketches in the early 1980s by William Carragan. Although I'm often disappointed by posthumous completions of a composer's unfinished pieces, Carragan's work is definitive.[13]

Toward the end of Carragan's version of the Finale is another of Bruckner's supremely beautiful eighth center melodies, once again touching on the grace of middle 8. The melody is chorale-like, features the solo trumpet, and is so startlingly weird and uplifting that a listener shouldn't have any trouble identifying it.

Bruckner began work on the Ninth in 1887 and died in 1896. During this nearly ten-year period, he attempted radical revisions of many of his earlier symphonies. Was he trying to raise them from their origins in the thinking mind to the plane of higher mind? Most critics don't consider these later versions to be improvements on the earlier ones. Bruckner must have sensed that the earlier versions were not right but didn't know how to improve them.

The Finale of the Ninth also gave Bruckner a great deal of difficulty, which is why he wasn't able to finish it before he died. Perhaps this difficulty had something to do with the labor-intensive aspect of being a higher mind composer. For Bruckner, the struggle was to find a way to incorporate that beautiful chorale melody—an inspirational gift from God or the supermind—into the flow of music that came from a different (and lower) plane of consciousness.

In addition to the nine symphonies, Bruckner also composed three musical settings of the Roman Catholic mass: in D Minor (1864), E Minor (1866), and F Minor (1868). All three works are worth knowing. Like the symphonies, they span the entire range of the seventh center. The Et Incarnatus Est of the Mass in F Minor is another example of eighth center music. Once again, it accesses the grace of middle 8.

In the yoga of listening, Bruckner's music can serve the purpose of leading us back to God, from awe, through praise and ecstasy, to grace.

Gustav Mahler

If Scott had known the original, rather than the bastardized, versions of Bruckner's symphonies, he might have recognized in them the spiritual qualities that he called ethereal. The human element is much reduced in Bruckner. There's little emotional turbulence (third center), no reference to romantic love (fourth center), and only a few passages of lighthearted dancelike music (fifth center).

The symphonies of Gustav Mahler, on the other hand, are full of human turbulence, love, dancelike music, and much more—including the ethereal element. Whereas Bruckner almost obsessively targeted the seventh center, Mahler ranged throughout the continuum of human potential, targeting every center but the eighth.

Bruckner seems to have had little in the way of professional or spiritual ambition, aside from the fact that he hoped to dedicate his Ninth Symphony to God, in the humble hope that He would accept it. Mahler, however, was quite spiritually and philosophically ambitious.

Mahler's Second Symphony was intended to chart the progress of the soul from death to resurrection. While I've described Bruckner's Eighth in similar terms, all we know about his intentions is that the first movement was to portray the final moments of a man on his deathbed. Mahler's program for his Second Symphony was more explicit.

The first movement of Mahler's Second is a funeral march for the symphony's deceased hero; the second a "pure and cloudless" memory of him, experienced by someone left behind; the third, the ceaseless whirl of life that threatens to engulf such memories; the fourth, the soul's desire to return to the primeval light of God; and the fifth, a choral plea to God for faith in the resurrection of the soul.[14]

Mahler's Third Symphony had an even more ambitious program. It was originally intended to have seven movements instead of the usual four. The symphony as a whole was to be called "A Midsummer Morning's Dream." Each movement was to have its own title, arranged in an ascending spiritual hierarchy: "Pan awakes" or "Summer marches in," intended to represent the inanimate aspects of nature; "What the flowers in the meadow tell me"; "What the animals in the forest tell me"; "What the night (or humanity) tells me"; "What the morning-bells (or angels) tell me"; "What love (or childhood) tells me"; and "What God tells me" or "The life divine."[15]

According to Mahler, the idea behind this grandiose work, which lasts about an hour and forty-five minutes, was that "Eternal love spins its web within us, over and above all else—as rays flow together into a focal point." The sixth movement was to be "a summary" of Mahler's "feelings towards all creatures, which develops not without deeply painful spiritual involvement, which, however, is gradually resolved into blissful confidence." The seventh was eventually dropped, and became the Finale of his Fourth Symphony.[16]

Mahler's Eighth Symphony was also highly ambitious. Part 1 employs an ancient Latin hymn: Veni Creator Spiritus (Come Holy—or Creative—Spirit). Part 2 is a setting of the transcendental last scene of Goethe's *Faust*, Part 2.

Mahler's letters are full of such spiritual ambition. About the Third Symphony, he writes: It "will be something the world has never heard before! In it Nature herself acquires a voice and tells secrets so profound that they are perhaps only glimpsed in dreams!"[17]

Mahler wanted to compose a celestial symphony. The program for the work, which Mahler eventually abandoned, is conceived as a set of "signposts and milestones" for the listener "on his journey—or rather, a map of the heavens, so that he can get a picture of the night sky with all its luminous worlds."[18] The awakening Pan of the first movement was intended to represent "the essential nature of All Things."[19] Mahler even had "an eery feeling" while composing the work's many movements, "as if it were not I who composed them."[20]

The spiritual hierarchy that Mahler referred to in his program for his Third Symphony is closely related to Cyril Scott's hierarchy of devas, which includes nature spirits at one end and angels at the other. Perhaps Scott would have identified Mahler's Third as an example of deva-inspired music.

About his Eighth Symphony, which is sometimes called *Symphony of a Thousand* because it includes a huge orchestra, many solo voices, and several choruses, Mahler wrote: "Try to imagine the whole universe beginning to ring and resound. These are no longer human voices, but planets and suns revolving."[21] I've already mentioned that the opening of the second movement of this work is a chorus of nature spirits.

Mahler began his career as a thinking mind composer. He constantly went to nonmusical sources, such as literature or art, for inspiration—a characteristic of the upper 6 visionary composer.

Mahler admits his dependence on words for musical ideas.[22] Besides a number of songs for voice and piano, and several orchestral song cycles—including *Das Lied von der Erde* (*The Song of the Earth*)—which is symphonic in scale, his Second, Third, Fourth, and Eighth Symphonies all employ the human voice in settings of various texts.

Mahler's First Symphony, which is all orchestral, was inspired by a novel called *Titan* by his favorite German romantic author, Jean Paul. The Third Symphony was inspired by Nietzsche's *Das Fröhliche Wissenschaft* (*The Gay Science*).

Other movements by Mahler take their inspiration from visual art or folklore. For example, the funeral march in the third movement of his First Symphony was inspired by a woodcut called "The Burial of the Huntsman" by Moritz von Schwind.[23] The second movement of the Fourth Symphony represents a violin-playing character from German folklore who leads away the soul after death.

The second and fourth movements of the Seventh Symphony, both entitled Nachtmusik (Serenade), also have a visionary aspect. They illustrate inner visions rather than works of art. The former seems to portray a fantastic nocturnal landscape full of imaginary beings; the latter a nocturnal love scene, in which a musician plays the mandolin before the window of his beloved.

In the yoga of listening, such visionary music, which targets the sixth center, can develop not only one's imagination, but also what esotericists call the third eye. As I pointed out in part 2, the third eye is responsible for inner or spiritual vision and clairvoyance.

But Mahler is more than a visionary composer. Many movements of his symphonies touch upon or dwell entirely within the crisis point between the sixth and seventh centers. This crisis point, irrationality, deals with portrayals of evil in music, as well as the ego's fear of death and the seemingly alien reality of the soul.

Music of this nature often shows up in Mahler's scherzos, which are frequently demonic. This is particularly true of the scherzos in the Second and Seventh Symphonies. In other scherzos, such as those of the Sixth and Ninth Symphonies, relatively innocent beginnings keep wandering off into fearful, nightmarishly whirling dances.

Mahler was obsessed with death. The First, Second, and Fifth Symphonies all contain funeral marches. The artistic hero of the Sixth is struck down by three hammer blows of fate in the Finale, which ends in a dirge played by the lower brass instruments. The unfinished Tenth Symphony contains two demonic scherzos, the second of which is marked "Death dances it with me." The fifth and final movement was intended to portray the funeral march of a New York fireman that Mahler witnessed shortly before he died.

Mahler's Ninth, too, is obsessed with death. At the climax of the first movement, the trombones are supposed to represent death knocking at the door. In college, I had a TME in connection with this movement. Although I was familiar with a recording by Leonard Bernstein and the New York Philharmonic, I was never able to figure out exactly when that climactic moment occurred.

But the first time I listened to the recording by Carlo Maria Giulini and the Chicago Symphony, lying on the floor in the dark with a friend, I had no doubt about when death came knocking. The trombones were so loud and terrifying that they knocked me right out of my body.

It wasn't a full experience of astral projection, just a sense of my astral body and my physical body being out of alignment with each other. I was unable to hear the music that came afterward, and I couldn't move, even when it was time to turn over the record. A few minutes later, I was able to sit up but couldn't talk. It took at least an hour before I felt completely normal again.

Another sign of music that targets the crisis zone between centers six and seven is spiritual anguish—the result of a desire for connection with the soul or God and fear that such a connection might be impossible: either one is damned to Hell, or God doesn't exist. Mahler's music is also full of moments like these—for example, the stormy second movement of the Fifth Symphony and the cynical first movement of *Das Lied von der Erde*.

Much of Mahler's music revolves around the transition between the sixth and seventh centers. Some passages or movements lean more toward the fantastic and visionary (upper 6), others toward the solemn and sublime (lower 7). The demonic scherzos, as well as the music of spiritual anguish, which can sometimes push itself to what seems like the limits of sanity, focus on the crisis point itself.

Mahler is more than a composer of the thinking mind, yet less than a composer of the higher mind. He was on his way from one level to the next, rising from the visionary, thinking mind signature of his first four symphonies to the sublime, higher mind signature of lower 7. But he either got stuck or didn't have enough time on Earth to complete the transition.

The ethereal aspect of Mahler's symphonies takes the form of seventh center epiphanies—sudden brief moments of exaltation, or illumination, that fade away like Maslow's peak experiences. I've found no eighth center music in Mahler's oeuvre. Though the Finale of the Fourth Symphony is supposed to represent paradise, Mahler intended it to be humorous—a child's naive vision (upper 6) of the Afterlife, rather than a depiction of the real thing.

Mahler frequently aims for the seventh center, but, because of emotional anguish, existential loneliness, and tormenting doubts about the reality of the soul and God, he ends up at the crisis point between the sixth and seventh centers. The resulting music is often cynical, mocking all spiritual aspirations, as in the Rondo Burlesque (third) movement of the Ninth Symphony or the Drinking Song that begins *Das Lied von der Erde.*

One of Mahler's seventh center epiphanies occurs in the slow third movement of the Fourth Symphony, when the main theme of the Finale is announced with a sudden, startling change of key. This epiphany targets the spiritual majesty of middle 7. Another occurs at the climax of the first movement of the unfinished Tenth Symphony, an adagio that was the last music Mahler completed before his death. This one targets the sublime range of lower 7.

Fuller exposures to the seventh center occur in the last two movements of the Second Symphony, which depict the soul's resurrection. They sweep from the sublime of lower 7 through the love of God of middle 7 to the sober (not quite ecstatic) praise of God of upper 7. The last movement ("What love tells me") of the Third Symphony is Mahler's most extended essay (nearly twenty-five minutes long) in the seventh center, much of it in middle 7.

My favorite spiritual moment in all of Mahler's work occurs at the opening of the second movement of the Eighth Symphony. While the first movement begins ambitiously, with upper 7 ecstatic praise of the Holy Spirit, it gets entangled in elaborate contrapuntal development, which pulls the music down into the formalism of middle 6. The upper 7 ecstasy returns as the movement closes.

The second movement begins with a representation of the sublime in nature (lower 7). This passage lasts only ten minutes, but it's the purest example of higher mind music in Mahler's oeuvre—perhaps a hint of what he would have achieved had he not died prematurely, just before his fifty-first birthday.

The last movement of Mahler's Ninth is another example of higher mind music. It seems a bit more labored than the opening of the second movement of the Eighth. We've already seen, in the case of Beethoven, that labor is often involved in bringing through the music of the higher mind.

The Ninth Symphony's last movement takes place entirely within the range of the seventh center. In chapter 14, I pointed out that this center has a Janus-like aspect. It looks either toward the soul and God, which is the case in Bruckner's music or back toward the world, seeing it from a higher perspective, which is the case in Mahler's.

The final Adagio of the Ninth is full of a heart-wrenching love for the world. He must have known that he would soon leave it. He'd already been diagnosed with the heart condition that would kill him less than two years after the symphony's completion.

In this adagio, there's also a lower 7 theme, introduced briefly in the contrabassoon, that hints at a sublime fear of God or the soul, a turning away from this world toward the next. This theme grows in importance throughout the movement, which ends with an ecstatic swell of praise (upper 7) that gradually fades away, leaving behind a hard-earned inner peace.

In terms of the yoga of listening, I turn to Mahler's music not only for spiritual contemplation but also for catharsis. All of the pain, doubt, frustration, rage, bitterness, agonizing doubts, and disillusionment of what it means to be human are there—as well as the intoxication of love, the beauty of the natural world (for example, in the slow movement of the Sixth Symphony, with its cow bells, intended to portray the Austrian mountain landscape in which Mahler often spent his summers), and the high spiritual aspirations.

Most concertgoers would probably rank Mahler above Bruckner in greatness. Mahler lived more deeply and expressed what it means to be human in ways that are familiar to us. He represents those of us who have all but lost faith in God and the soul because of scientific and technological advances and the resulting rise of the materialist worldview.

Bruckner, by comparison, is a monklike throwback to the Middle Ages. His music is almost entirely lacking in mundane love and joy. Yet the route toward oneness with God or the soul that was often closed to Mahler because of his doubt remained open to Bruckner. For this reason, I hear Bruckner's symphonies as more truly celestial.

Musical Lovemaking

Much of Mahler's output has the characteristic restlessness of music that originates in the sixth center or the thinking mind. This makes his music difficult to analyze in terms of the continuum of human potential—either because the dominant center is constantly shifting or because all centers from the first to the sixth are active in equal degree, sometimes at different levels of the orchestration.

The beautiful Adagietto of the Fifth Symphony is a notable exception. Centers one through four and six are active, the middle range of seven (nobility) shows up occasionally, but centers five and eight are absent. The second center's full range, from relaxation, through pleasure, to intoxication, is employed, lending the music a high degree of sensuality. The third center—from tension through agitation to passion—is also strong, adding sexual intensity to sensuality. The fourth, however, is the dominant center, mixing in the pathos, bittersweet yearning, and elation of love.

In contrast, the first and sixth centers operate in the background. The former provides just enough rhythmic interest to keep listeners from falling asleep; the latter lends the emotional expressiveness of the piece some coherence at the level of form.

The Adagietto is a musical analog of tender lovemaking. It puts us in touch with the sensual, sexual, emotional, and spiritual aspects of ourselves necessary to be fully present with a beloved partner. While this nine-minute movement could certainly be used as background music for lovemaking (and repeated as necessary), I recommend meditating on it with full attention, whether alone or with a partner.

In the yoga of listening, the idea is to immerse yourself as deeply as possible in the spiritual wisdom that the piece transmits. Doing so should allow that wisdom to be stored away and retrieved later. Whenever that wisdom may be required, try to replicate the feeling of the music in your body. This can be accomplished by inwardly reminding yourself of what the music sounds like, if you have a good memory for music, or by relistening to some or all of it.

During lovemaking, I've sometimes had the feeling of being *inside* Wagner's Prelude to *Tristan und Isolde* or that the music was inside me, guiding every buildup and release of tension, from the slight pressure of a caress, to the most tender or passionate kiss, and beyond these expressions of love to the great waves of intensity whose falling and rising eventually lead to an ecstatic sense of union. Similar energetic messages are encoded in the Adagietto of Mahler's Fifth.

In Tantra, sexual union with a partner represents the coming together of the Hindu gods Shiva and Shakti. Shiva represents the male principle, which is passive in Hindu mythology, and Shakti represents the female, which is active. When these two principles are joined, the kundalini is aroused and rises through the chakras from the base of the spine to the crown of the head. The result is an experience of ecstasy, perhaps also of enlightenment.

Some yogas advocate celibacy as a means of achieving enlightenment.

Bruckner represents this trend in music. Tantra, on the other hand, makes a place for pleasurable physical experience, including lovemaking, as a means of achieving enlightenment. In the yoga of listening, Wagner's Prelude to *Tristan und Isolde* and the Adagietto of Mahler's Fifth represent this trend.

22

The Would-Be Mystics:
Schoenberg, Berg, and Webern

At several points in this book, I've mentioned the twelve-tone system of composition, an atonal means of giving unity to a musical work. In this system, all twelve tones of the chromatic scale are arranged in a unique order, called a row, set, or series. This row can be played backwards, upside down, or in both ways at once. By means of transposition, it can begin on any note of the chromatic scale, yet still maintain its identity. Much twentieth-century music, especially that composed after 1950, was influenced by this system, which tends to reduce music to a series of mathematical manipulations.

By the time I attended graduate school in the early 1980s, the twelve-tone system had become firmly entrenched in academia. It was then called *total serialism*, because it had been extended into other musical dimensions, such as dynamics and tone colors, which were also arranged in strictly ordered (serial) progressions. In a required composition seminar, I had to generate a twelve-tone row and all of its permutations, as well as a mathematical formula that would allow me to determine, in advance, the placement of every pitch, rhythm, and musical event before I'd actually written a note.

The value of such a system for educators is undeniable. Unlike compositional inspiration—which comes from the soul—the twelve-tone method can be taught and evaluated with grades.

Unfortunately, the twelve-tone system tends to produce the cerebral music of the thinking mind, usually acting from middle 6 (formalism), without reference to any other center. Such music is proudly presented by academic composers as arrhythmic (no first center), nonsensual (no second), nondramatic (no third), unfeeling (no fourth), joyless (no fifth), and without spiritual trappings (no seventh or eighth center). It's the perfect sonic equivalent of science.

Strange to say, the inventor of the twelve-tone system, Arnold Schoenberg, was a would-be mystic.

Arnold Schoenberg

Schoenberg was a deeply spiritual man. Born into the Jewish faith, he converted to Lutheranism as a young man and back to Judaism in later life. At all times, he was fascinated with the writings of the seventeenth-century Swedish mystic Emanuel Swedenborg, who wrote detailed accounts of out-of-body-like visits to the Afterlife, including extensive conversations with the angels he encountered there.[1]

Schoenberg perceived himself as the prophet of a new age of music. He even composed an opera on the biblical subject of Moses and Aaron, in which he cast himself as Moses. He saw his laying down of the laws of the twelve-tone system and being reviled for doing so as similar to Moses's difficulties in getting the Hebrews to accept the Ten Commandments. The opera was never completed, for reasons I'll go into in a moment.

Shortly after inventing the twelve-tone system, Schoenberg boasted that it would guarantee the supremacy of German music for the next one hundred years. On the contrary, it seems to have driven away much of the audience for contemporary music—which, of course, is drawn to music for the things that the twelve-tone system eventually eliminated from it. As mystical composer Olivier Messiaen once said, Schoenberg "was not perhaps a great composer," but he was "at least, a great destroyer."[2]

During my two years in graduate school, I worked at the music library, which gave me access to the school's comprehensive record collection. Although I never cared for Schoenberg's music—it seemed too aggressive, too uncompromisingly harsh for my taste—I thought I would give it a fair hearing. I spent several months listening to his musical output in the order in which it was composed, smuggling the phonograph records out of the library, since they were noncirculating items for anyone but faculty, and returning them later.

I came away from all this listening with a respect for Schoenberg's integrity. He seemed to know what he was after. But I never wanted to hear most of this music again. Whenever I tried to give Schoenberg's music another chance, I ended up with a headache. I've learned that such headaches are the opposite of TMEs—indications that my soul doesn't want me to keep going in a certain direction.

While researching this book, I rediscovered Schoenberg's attempt to compose an oratorio about the Afterlife: *Die Jakobsleiter* (*Jacob's Ladder*). He began the piece in 1917, completing only the first half and the transition to the second. *Jacob's Ladder* is the first work in the history of Western music to present a non-Christian vision of the Afterlife.

Schoenberg wrote the text for *Jacob's Ladder.* In the first half, the Archangel Gabriel questions the souls of several people who have just passed on, in much the same way that contemporary near-death experiencers are questioned by a being of light. Each of those questioned represents a different level of spiritual development.

The music of the first half of *Jacob's Ladder* is merely interesting—it's limited to the formal invention of middle 6. Then comes a short orchestral interlude, intended to represent the transition to the Afterlife. In this interlude, Schoenberg had the revolutionary idea of instructing different parts of the orchestra to play slightly out of phase with each other, to represent the untying of the soul's bonds with earthly life. In the second half of the piece, which was never completed, the souls encountered in the first half were to prepare for future incarnations.

Schoenberg was unable to write the music for this part of *Jacob's Ladder* because it had to represent the nonphysical reality of heaven. The music of the first half was atonal, which sufficed for representing the transitional state between physical and nonphysical realities. But Schoenberg must have felt that neither tonality nor atonality would do for the music of heaven—and there were no other alternatives, as far as he could see.

Schoenberg encountered a similar difficulty in composing his opera *Moses und Aron*, in which the unfinished third act was to be "adequate to the idea of unity with God."[3] In the continuum of human potential, that would require music from the upper eighth center.

Schoenberg didn't know how to compose such music. Most composers don't—and no amount of tinkering with musico-mathematical systems is likely to produce it.

Schoenberg exemplifies the dilemma of many twentieth-century composers, beginning with Mahler: a desire to compose transcendental music that can't be realized because of fear of the soul or God, or debilitating doubt or lack of belief.

In order to compose at all, the ego takes control of the compositional process. It relies on rational systems, in the absence of methods of developing openness to, and trust of, the soul's musical guidance. The resulting music represents a narrowing of the continuum of human potential until it portrays nothing but the composer as pure mind—or *thinking* mind, in Sri Aurobindo's terminology.

Schoenberg's music has been shunned by all but the most progressive performers and audiences, such as those found in university settings. But a few of his pieces have made it into the concert repertoire, such as the early, ultra-Wagnerian oratorio *Gurrelieder* (*Songs of Gurre*), a last gasp of musical romanticism, and *Pierrot Lunaire* (*Moonstruck Pierrot*), Op. 21, an atonal masterpiece of musical and poetic surrealism, for speaking voice and an ensemble of five assorted instruments.

Only one of Schoenberg's compositions is at all popular, and even beloved: *Verklärte Nacht* (*Transfigured Night*), Op. 4, for string sextet (later arranged by Schoenberg for string orchestra). In *Music: The Keynote of Human Evolution*, Corinne Heline states that in this piece, Schoenberg "came close to parting" what she calls "the thin veil that divides the seen from the unseen."[4]

In *Transfigured Night*, for the only time in his life, Schoenberg achieved that rarest of musical accomplishments, the production of music that came directly from the soul or supermind. The resulting musical peak experience expresses a momentary oneness with a higher power—the upper 8 music that corresponds to union with God.

Perhaps Schoenberg's later career was an outcome of trying to repeat this moment of musical transcendence, in the only way he knew how: by making the soul bend to the will of his ego with the use of a musical system. The resulting music, like that of *Jacob's Ladder*, was often merely interesting—an expression of middle 6 invention.

I call Schoenberg a would-be mystic because, despite his apparent yearning to do so, he was never able to get beyond his starting point as a thinking mind composer. Even so, his spiritual masterpiece *Transfigured Night* has its uses in the yoga of listening, as we shall see at the end of this chapter.

Alban Berg

Alban Berg, a pupil and colleague of Schoenberg's, adopted the twelve-tone system in his own music. As with Schoenberg, I've listened to all of Berg's compositions in chronological order.

Berg's music is more emotionally direct in its appeal than Schoenberg's. Despite its high level of dissonance and constant experimentation with form and instrumental color, Berg's music maintains ties to the late-nineteenth-century post-romanticism of Mahler. In addition to the Violin Concerto mentioned in the first chapter of this book, Berg also composed two highly successful modernist operas, *Wozzeck* and *Lulu*.

Wozzeck, which premiered in 1925, is based on a play by an early-nineteenth-century German playwright by the name of Georg Büchner. It's a dark work about inhumane behavior—in the army, in relationships between men and women, and in society at large. A not very bright private by the name of Wozzeck is tormented by his superiors and betrayed by his common-law wife, who has a fling with a flashy drum major. Wozzeck goes insane, murders his mate, and drowns himself, leaving behind their young child.

Most of the music follows a typical twentieth-century pattern of targeting centers one through three (rhythm, sonority, dramatic intensity), plus six, including the formal (middle), visionary (upper), and crisis zone (irrationality) of the latter. There are a few moments of lower 4 (pathos), and none of centers five (well-being), seven (expanded consciousness), or eight (cosmic consciousness). As Corinne Heline says, this is

> a work of stark tragedy from beginning to end. None of the characters evinces the slightest humanitarian feeling toward one another, not even the children. Each is absorbed in his own selfish interests, utterly indifferent to the weal or woe of those about him.[5]

She comes to the conclusion that there is "nothing elevating or inspiring either in the story or in the music," which "expresses confusion of mind, darkness, turmoil, restless seeking and searching for something that is never found in the places where it is sought."[6]

The purpose of *Wozzeck* is not spiritual elevation but emotional catharsis. Berg had to serve in the army during World War I. From firsthand experience, he knew the horror he was writing about. His attempt to purge himself of this horror, through composing an opera about it, provides us, as members of the audience, with an opportunity to purge ourselves of the ways in which we, too, may have suffered at the hands of the less sensitive, or spiritually evolved, souls who surround us.

The character of Wozzeck is another example of what Charles calls a wayward reflection, someone who shows us a path that we don't want to take ourselves. "Yes, there is evil in the world," the opera seems to say, "but we mustn't allow ourselves to become victims of it in the way that Wozzeck does, by reacting passively, withdrawing into depression and repressed anger, and finally exploding in an act of violence that destroys both himself and what he loves.

For most operagoers, life is rarely that bad. We may even be in a position to do something about the kind of brutality that Wozzeck suffers from. Perhaps, through watching or listening to this opera, we may recognize the ways in which we pass on the torment we suffer at the hands of others and decide to change that behavior. Or we may become involved in changing the culturally held beliefs, attitudes, and behaviors that create the victim/victimizer dichotomy and produce universal social scapegoats such as Wozzeck. At the very least, we may be able to get on with our lives, consciously or unconsciously grateful that our own seemingly insurmountable problems are unlikely to lead to the dead end that Berg was warning us away from.

Cathartic works of art like *Wozzeck* can have any of these effects on an audience. While the means that produce them may seem to be anything but spiritual, such effects can be useful in the yoga of listening by realigning people with their own soul's growth.

Berg's other opera, *Lulu*, left unfinished when he died, but completed by another composer, was based on two plays by his contemporary Frank Wedekind, *Pandora's Box* and *Earth-Spirit*. *Lulu* has a cathartic effect similar to that of *Wozzeck* and uses the centers in much the same way. Its plot deals with the chaos created in the lives of a number of men of various ages, trades, and social standing by a mysterious, but sociopathic, beauty named Lulu.

When I studied the opera a number of years ago, I was as appalled by its apparent baseness as Heline was by *Wozzeck*. I couldn't imagine what Berg was trying to say with such a depressing and unspiritual plot. But one of my lucid-dreamlike adventures in consciousness helped me to understand the spiritual importance of cathartic works such as *Wozzeck* and *Lulu*. I found myself in a nonphysical reality in which the world's works for the stage exist in energetic form for the instruction of those who've passed on.

I saw opera houses in the form of an Egyptian temple, representing Verdi's *Aida*, and an Oriental pagoda, representing Puccini's *Madama Butterfly*, as well as a simpler one for Berg's *Lulu*. Upon entering the latter, I learned from a nonphysical Guide that here it was possible to enter the roles of any of the characters in Berg's opera and to experience what its events looked and felt like from that perspective.

The male characters in the opera, I was told, represented the ways in which men of all ages and walks of life can destroy themselves by means of an obsession with the youth and beauty of women. Lulu represented the self-destructiveness of a woman who allowed herself to be molded by what she believed the men in her life wanted her to be, rather than developing a personality of her own. The entire episode is described in my previous book, *The Unanswered Question.*[7]

Berg, like Schoenberg, was fascinated by Swedenborg, as well as by a novel called *Seraphita* by Honoré de Balzac, an early-nineteenth-century French author. *Seraphita* was based on Swedenborg's writings. At one point in his life, Berg planned to compose a Mahleresque symphony in four movements, in which the final movement would contain an excerpt from *Seraphita* sung by a boy soprano stationed in the performance hall's galley, to heighten the surreal effect. Schoenberg, too, had wanted to compose an operatic triptych based on this novel. Neither project came to fruition.

One biographer of Berg speaks of his "inclination to mysticism, which increased with advancing years."[8] This inclination is perhaps most noticeable in Berg's last completed work, the Violin Concerto that I described in chapter 1.

Although composed with the twelve-tone method, the Violin Concerto is Berg's most accessible work. Unlike many of his contemporaries, Berg didn't lose touch with emotional expression—especially pathos, or lower 4, which is especially appropriate in a piece about the untimely death of a beautiful and talented eighteen-year-old girl. Nor was he unable to summon up the zest for life represented by the fifth center: Waltz rhythms persist throughout much of the first movement of the two-movement concerto.

The beginning of the second movement falls into the typical twentieth-century pattern of centers one through three, plus six. But the pathos of lower 4 eventually makes an appearance, as well as the devotion of middle 7. The latter enters the music about halfway through the movement, when Berg introduces a quotation from a Bach chorale, which invokes a mood of prayerful resignation.[9]

The piece ends in a tranquil mood, achieved by reducing the music to centers one and two (rhythm and sonority), and emphasizing lower 2 (relaxation). As the second movement slows down, we're left with beautiful sounds that have been stripped of dramatic intensity (3), emotional expressiveness (4), and the lively tempos that convey a sense of well-being (5). Even the composer's fascination with the intellectual play of form (6) is attenuated in these tranquil moments, as the piece dissolves back into the simple musical ideas with which it began.

The TME that resulted from listening to this piece, described in chapter 1, may have been a result of its spanning so much of the continuum of human potential, like many masterpieces of a composer's late period. I find it significant, however, that to access the seventh center, Berg had to borrow a passage from Bach—as if he could no longer produce music from this center on his own.

Berg *was* capable of accessing the seventh center in his youth. His ability to do so is apparent in one of his loveliest early songs for voice and piano, "Über den Bergen" ("Over the Mountains"). This song, which lasts just less than two minutes, is one of the purest expressions of transcendental longing (lower to middle 7) that I've ever encountered.

Many of us feel as if we're living in exile from our real selves while we reside in physical reality. We long for the Other Side, represented in the poem by the other side of the mountains, "where happiness dwells." Yet, like the speaker in the poem, if we were to go over the mountains, we would come back in tears, forever yearning to return. Berg's song couldn't be a better example of music inspired by the soul.

What Berg learned from Schoenberg may have made him one of the twentieth century's great composers. But the cost, it seems to me, was the loss of the direct connection to the soul that he had as a young man when he composed this song.

I call Berg a would-be mystic because he, like Schoenberg, wanted to compose a transcendental music of the soul, but was unable to get beyond the thinking mind. His adherence to the twelve-tone system may have been responsible for this limitation.

In the yoga of listening, his operas *Wozzeck* and *Lulu* can each provide a powerful catharsis (third center) of the darker aspects of our nature, leaving more room for the spiritual and transcendent ones (seventh center) that may be developed through listening to other music. His Violin Concerto can help us grieve for loved ones who have died, as it moves from emotional agitation, through the consolation of prayer expressed in the Bach chorale it quotes, to the ending's tranquil quieting of the emotions in acquiescence.

Anton von Webern

The idea that Schoenberg's other famous pupil and colleague, Anton von Webern (1883–1945), was also a would-be mystic may come as a surprise to those familiar with twentieth-century music. He, too, was fascinated by Balzac's *Seraphita* and the writings of Swedenborg.

Webern's personal adaptation of the twelve-tone system invented by Schoenberg, which involved brevity, symmetry, and the serialization of musical elements other than pitch, became a springboard for the ultrarational approach to composing that prevailed after the Second World War. Because Webern was seen as the originator of this approach, references to his nature mysticism, his Swedenborgian belief in heaven, hell, and angels, and the overtly Christian texts he often chose to set have been downplayed in some of the biographies about him.

Webern loved the mountains. He took an active interest in botany and studied the tiny forms of plant life, lichens, and mosses present in alpine ecosystems. Much of his music is extremely brief, based on simple musical ideas that develop organically to create the whole composition. It's as if he were creating little organic life forms in music—or, in later years, when his methods tended increasingly toward the creation of formal symmetries, tiny crystals.

Webern saw nature in terms of Swedenborg's notion of correspondences, in which everything in the material world corresponds to something in the spiritual world. In Webern's belief, "the natural world with all that it contains exists and subsists from the spiritual world, and both worlds from the Divine Being."[10] Thus his music is a correspondence with both the natural world and the spiritual world.

Much of this music, however, is challenging for listeners, despite its brevity. In terms of the continuum of human potential, centers one (rhythm) and two (sonority) are active. Center three (intensity) has a tendency to drop out, so that the music is without dramatic tension. Centers four (expression) and five (well-being) are also generally absent. Middle 6 is particularly strong (formal play). Center seven, however, may show itself under certain conditions. Center eight is absent.

Webern's music presaged a gradual process of the elimination of all centers, other than the sixth, that continued throughout most of the twentieth century. By the 1960s, music was either ultrarational—to the point of expunging even rhythm and sonority, so that only purely mathematical relations determined its texture (center six alone), as in the music of American composer Milton Babbitt (b. 1916)—or completely nonrational, as in John Cage's chance-based music, which eliminated everything but pure sound, often in the form of literal noise (lower and middle 1).

Strange to say, many listeners are unable to determine a difference between chance-based music and ultrarational, or mathematically based, music. In both cases, as if the only center targeted were the first, the audience seems to be immersed in a sonic environment. This environment is often registered as noise, which the audience may ignore or only partially attend to, just as it would any randomly derived sonic environment experienced beyond the concert hall, in ordinary life.

The first time I heard a piece by Webern, I was in high school. I'd turned on the radio in the midst of a live performance of his aphoristic Five Pieces for Orchestra, Op. 10. I thought that I'd caught the orchestra warming up before the concertmaster had come on stage to tune them. I was surprised to discover that what I'd heard was a fully composed piece of music.

Years later, during the same period when I was listening to the oeuvres of Schoenberg and Berg, I made a similar attempt with that of Webern—and was unsuccessful. Although a recording of his complete works was available, and despite the brief durations of most of his pieces, I couldn't relate to this music. It was too spare and cerebral. Because of the attenuation of the third center (intensity), which more or less eliminated the possibility of dramatic contrast, Webern's music bored or made me drowsy.

I had a friend in college whose first hearing of Webern's music induced a TME that inspired him to begin composing. My drowsiness, however, had the opposite effect: It discouraged me from further exploration of Webern's work.

Since then, armed with an understanding of Webern's mystical proclivities and performances that did not seek to emphasize the rational (center six) over the mystical (center seven) elements in his music, I've come to appreciate his oeuvre as one might a collection of miniature, perfectly formed crystals.

I find it odd that Schoenberg, Berg, and Webern should have been so steeped in mysticism, yet at the same time should have been among the originators of the twentieth-century trend to eliminate everything from music but the intellectual element. All three were thinking mind composers who aspired to be more. Yet, at the level of the ego, they attempted to control the intuitive, inspirational, nonrational musical impulses of the soul.

Unlike Mahler, they were unable to begin the transition from thinking mind to higher mind. The result, not only in their own works, but also in those of the many later composers whom they inspired, was a wholly cerebral music, in which control was everything and the soul nothing. This is why I classify them as would-be mystics.

One piece of Webern's that has a direct appeal for many listeners is his arrangement of Bach's six-voice fugue (or Ricercare) from *The Musical Offering*, a piece that I first referred to in chapter 13. There, I described a TME it had once inspired, in which I found myself climbing around in the score as if on the bars of a jungle gym.

Webern developed a technique of orchestration that he called *Klangfarbenmelodie*, a means of passing a single melody from instrument to instrument so that its tone color (*Klangfarben*) was constantly changing. Bach never specified what instrument or ensemble should play his six-voice fugue. Many arrangements of it have been made. Webern's is the most imaginative and colorful.

A good performance of Webern's arrangement of Bach's Ricercare, taking cognizance of the macrorhythmic energy flow that Webern's dynamics bring out in the score, can be an eight-minute-long mystical experience, activating all of the centers from one through seven. The trick is to try to follow the fugue theme wending its way through the piece.

As I pointed out in chapter 13, in the yoga of listening, fugues provide a perfect analogy for the ways in which the spiritual themes of our lives, especially that of life purpose, are constantly weaving in and out of the texture of our moment-by-moment experience. Whenever I play on the piano, or listen to, a fugue by Bach, I follow the theme with this in mind. Doing so helps me develop the ability to see more clearly the spiritual themes that weave in and out of my own life.

A Musical Act of Compassion

In the yoga of listening, as in life itself, it's good for us to be reminded of the healing and self-transcending power of compassion and unconditional love. Schoenberg's *Transfigured Night* can provide just such a reminder. As I mentioned, the original version is for string sextet. The later arrangement for string orchestra, by the composer himself, greatly amplifies the piece's emotional intensity. This is the version that I prefer.

Transfigured Night was written as a musical realization of a poem by Schoenberg's contemporary Richard Dehmel. The poem tells the story of a couple who are engaged to be married. As they walk through a woods at night, the woman confesses that she's pregnant with another man's child, thinking that her fiancé will probably break off their engagement. In a surprising gesture of compassion and unconditional love, the man accepts her, despite her fallen state. He says that, once the child is born, he'll behave as if it had always been their own.

After this exchange, the man feels transfigured. The challenge of continuing to love this woman after her courageous revelation transforms him, her, the unborn child, and even the moonlit night itself.

The sextet version of *Transfigured Night* was not well received at its first hearing. One famous tirade against the piece claimed that it sounded as if the score of Wagner's *Tristan* had been smeared while the ink was still wet. Yet, when it's well performed (especially in the string orchestra version), the section in which the transfiguration occurs is a graphic depiction of what Maslow called the "unitive vision": a moment of radiance or illumination that corresponds to the upper eighth center on the continuum of human potential.

The music is restless (sixth center) and largely visionary (upper 6), as a result of its intention to portray the events of the poem upon which it's based. The transfiguration takes place in the fourth part of the poem (bar 229 in the score, a point which may have its own index number on a CD). The first, hymnlike phrase is middle 7 (nobility). The transfiguration occurs about two minutes later, and is quite brief. The music that follows the transfiguration is mostly middle or upper 4 (yearning or ecstatic love).

There's even a point at which the music expresses a fearful backlash against this moment of self-transcendence—exactly what we might expect from a real peak experience, in which the soul has broken through to us for a moment and the ego recoils. At this point, the lower half of the orchestra (or sextet) comes in playing *sul ponticello* (a special technique in which the bow plays very close to the bridge that holds the strings away from the body of the instrument), producing an eerie, icy, growl (crisis point between centers six and seven).

The transfiguration theme (upper 8) returns again in the final moments of the piece, like a blessing from above, bestowed not only on the remarkable couple depicted in Schoenberg's music, but also on ourselves as listeners. Its message is that any act of compassionate, unconditional love can bring about a feeling of self-transcendence, a peak experience, or a moment of unitive vision. This is how the soul, with a surge of life force, rewards us for such acts.

23

The Sometime Mystics: Busoni, Hindemith, Stravinsky, and Bartók

In calling Schoenberg, Berg, and Webern would-be mystics, I wanted to highlight the fact that they sought a relationship with the soul or God through their music. But the means they used—the twelve-tone system—made it difficult, if not impossible, for them to achieve this goal.

In the present chapter, I use the term *sometime mystics* to describe four composers with a different approach. These composers were sometimes able to access the seventh center (and in one case the eighth).

Many composers are mystics when it comes to their compositional process. Even my ultrarational teacher and composer of computer music at the University of Illinois, Herbert Brün (1918–2000), felt the need to extinguish the electric lamps and fill his study with lit candles to put himself in the right mood to compose. But when it comes to accessing the mystical realms of the seventh and eighth centers, the results vary widely.

Some composers have an active interest in spirituality, which manifests itself in a fascination with either the traditional objects of religious devotion or the occult. When such a composer is capable of communicating something of this fascination—which can amount to an obsession, as with Scriabin and Messiaen—through music, then I consider him an achieved mystic, rather than a would-be or sometime mystic. Such a composer attempts to render the soul's growth or transform the radiance of God into sound.

Ferruccio Busoni

When experiencing emotional turmoil in college, I often went to the music library and listened to the seven-minute Symphonia that acts as a prelude to *Doktor Faust*, an opera by the early-twentieth-century composer Ferruccio Busoni (1866–1924). I never had a dramatic TME in connection with this work, but the cumulative effect of frequent listenings resulted in my leaving the music library feeling centered and serene.

Despite its brevity, this Symphonia expresses a range of spiritual issues, from the torment of doubt (the crisis point between centers six and seven) to the magic and mystery of spring (the sublime, lower 7); from the redeeming power of unconditional love (middle 7) to the promise of grace (middle 8). Grace manifests itself in the form of two phrases of a soft, medieval-sounding chorale that emerge from a tonally ambiguous haze—as if the clouds of doubt were parting to reveal, for a moment, the elusive call of the Source to come back into alignment with it. I would listen to the piece until I felt that I'd reestablished that alignment within myself.

Busoni, though baptized as a Catholic, "was at heart an atheist," but had "a lifelong interest in mysticism and oriental philosophy."[1] *Doktor Faust*, left unfinished at the composer's death, was completed by one of his students. It's a mystical retelling of the Faust legend, based on medieval puppet plays rather than the more famous later version by Goethe. Busoni's late masterwork finds a place for the entire spectrum of what it means to be human, from the first to the eighth center.

The second Prologue, in which Faust uses a magic book given him by three mysterious students, is one of the most convincing portrayals of the occult in opera. Faust conjures up six different spirits, each of them operating at a different speed, from that of the sand passing through the hourglass, to a falling leaf, a brook, a bullet, a tempest, and finally, just after Faust has stepped out of his protective magic circle, Mephistopheles, who moves as quickly as the thoughts of man. The chorale that represents grace in the Symphonia returns in this Prologue, punctuating each clause of the soul-binding contract that Mephistopheles places before Faust with chilling irony.

Another high point of the opera is a visionary (upper 6) tour de force in the second scene, in which, under the baleful influence of Mephistopheles, Faust inadvertently incites a riot in a tavern filled with students. The students divide into groups of Catholics and Protestants. The Catholics sing a Te Deum (an ancient Latin hymn of praise to God) at the same time as the Protestants sing Martin Luther's well-known chorale "A Mighty Fortress Is Our God."

The opera ends with Faust losing his soul to Mephistopheles, but not before he has used his magic to bequeath his life to his own dead child. The latter rises up as a naked youth bearing a flowering branch and strides confidently back to a nearby village. This youth represents the eternal soul of humankind, always striving to grow beyond the errors of past generations.

I know of no other music by Busoni in which the mystical element is as apparent as in *Doktor Faust*. This is why I've classified him as a sometime mystic. Like Schoenberg, he was visited by an inspiration that resulted in a few moments of eighth center music—and never again. But unlike Schoenberg, this visitation did not result in an attempt to control his compositional process with a rigid system based in the thinking mind.

In the yoga of listening, the middle 8 music of grace in the Symphonia from *Doktor Faust* could be useful as a means of realigning ourselves with the soul whenever we've gotten off the path of realizing its plans for our growth. Grace is the feeling of inner peace that comes when we're finally able to give up our resistance to those plans. At the close of the Symphonia, the chorus keeps singing the word *pax* (peace). Inner peace is what I experienced as a result of listening to this music over and over again when I was in college.

Paul Hindemith

I referred to Hindemith in chapter 2 in connection with the type of TME in which a composer sees the whole terrain of an unwritten piece as if illuminated by a lightning bolt of inspiration. Hindemith was a man of deep faith. His music, at least that composed in the mid-1930s and 1940s, accesses the seventh center at times. But, like Schoenberg, Hindemith developed a system of musical composition that prevented his soul from coming through in his music during the last twenty or so years of his life—even though this system was based in tonality, rather than the atonality of Schoenberg. Hindemith produced no late masterworks as the result of an ongoing process of spiritual evolution.

In college, I often listened to Hindemith's Suite from *Noblissima Visione* (*Most Noble Vision*), a 1938 ballet based on the life of Saint Francis, for the same reason as I listened to Busoni's Symphonia: to calm myself during times of inner turmoil. Hindemith's Suite consists of three movements, the first two of which are divided into two parts.

The first part of the first movement portrays Saint Francis in meditation. It's full of peace, devotion, nobility, and middle 7 love of God. The second part, Rondo, represents the symbolic wedding of Saint Francis to Poverty. The music is solemn (lower 7), as befits a holy mystery. As with Busoni's Symphonia, I never had a dramatic TME in connection with this movement. But listening to it again and again was profoundly centering.

The first part of the second movement, March, contains music from a scene of the ballet in which the young Saint Francis tries to associate himself with a merry band of mercenary warriors and eventually leaves them in disgust. (The order of movements in the Suite is not chronological, as in the ballet.) This movement is essentially a scherzo (lower 6), but it takes a twist in the demonic direction in the fugue of its center section (crisis point between centers six and seven). The scherzo-like march returns, briefly, to round out this part of the movement.

The second part of the second movement, Pastorale, comes from the portion of the ballet in which three ladies appear to Saint Francis—Chastity, Obedience, and Poverty—and he recognizes his calling to the life of a monk. It begins with the solemnity of lower 7 and ends with a brief passage in middle 7, which represents yearning for God.

The third movement, entitled Passacaglia, is based on an ancient Latin hymn of praise to the creator: Incipiunt Laudes Creaturarum (All Creatures Begin to Praise). A passacaglia is a variation form that uses the same brief tune over and over again, as the composer carries it from instrument to instrument through the entire range of the orchestra.

The tune is stated first in the brasses. Gradually, Hindemith adds fresh harmonic and melodic ideas. The latter appear above or below the tune, weaving around it an ever-thickening tapestry of sound. In terms of centers, the movement begins in middle 7 (love of God); ascends to upper 7 (praise of God); drops, in a softer middle section, back to lower 7 (awe of God); and moves again through middle 7 to end in the ecstasy of upper 7. This gradual undulation within the seventh center is a macrorhythmic wave.

Pure mysticism, such as that in the Suite from *Noblissima Visione*, appears in no other piece by Hindemith—not even in his more famous 1934 Symphony, *Mathis der Maler* (*Matthias the Painter*), which includes much seventh center music. The three movements of this symphony depict the three panels of the Isenheim Altarpiece, a triptych by the medieval German painter Matthias Grünewald.

Hindemith was planning to write an opera on the life of this painter. The symphony provided him with an opportunity to sketch out some major dramatic points. The first movement is called Angel Concert (the angels are singing to the Virgin as she holds the Christ child on her lap); the second, the Entombment (of Christ); and the third, the Temptation of Saint Anthony.

The Angel Concert movement begins with a slow introduction, which taps into the solemnity and mystery of lower 7. The faster section that follows this introduction, however, is much more like a traditional symphony than an angelic concert. Its primary center is middle 6 (invention). The seventh center hasn't entirely disappeared. But, as is usual with music focused primarily in the sixth center, other centers come and go without displacing it, including the seventh.

The second movement's Entombment is more clearly centered in the solemnity and mystery of lower 7. The third movement, which in the usual symphonic pattern would be a scherzo, is a hellish vision that corresponds to the crisis point between centers six and seven, an example of the demonic scherzo, full of tormenting doubt on a Mahlerian scale. It ends with the nobility of secular middle 7.

Hindemith was a brash experimenter at the beginning of his career. Midway through life, however, he invented a new, tonally based musical system, which he hoped would supplant Schoenberg's. So obsessed was Hindemith with the notion of becoming a musical savior that he revised some of his early music, and composed all of his later music, according to this new system.

It's difficult, if not impossible, to court the soul in music by means of a compositional system. Though Hindemith's system is easier on the ears than Schoenberg's, it produced music with a dreary sameness about it, a dry academic sound. Little of the large-scale music composed by this system after Hindemith's most popular piece, the *Symphonic Metamorphoses on Themes of Carl Maria von Weber*, of 1943, is any longer played.

Although Hindemith was capable of creating entire compositions that targeted the seventh center, he never went beyond being a thinking mind composer. For this reason, I call him a sometime mystic.

In the yoga of listening, however, the *Noblissima Visione* Suite could be a useful reminder of the importance of devotion (middle 7) and praise (upper 7) in our spiritual development. Like the symphonies of Bruckner, it expounds a Christian musical equivalent of bhakti yoga, the yoga of love, devotion, and service to God.

Igor Stravinsky

Stravinsky, too, was a man of deep faith. Yet he composed only a handful of works that expressed this faith, including the famous *Symphony of Psalms*. To my ear, these works don't contain anything like the magic and mystery of his early works. Nor, despite his extremely long life, did he compose any late masterworks that spanned the entire continuum of human potential. Toward the end of his life, he, like Schoenberg, went twelve-tone.

I've already mentioned Stravinsky in chapter 13, in connection with his early upper 6 visionary masterpieces: *The Firebird* (1910), *Petrouchka* (1911), and *The Rite of Spring* (1913). Each of these works is soul-inspired, although

Petrouchka contains no seventh center music and *The Rite of Spring* does not touch this center for more than a few moments at a time.

Within a few years of the completion of *The Rite of Spring*, however, something happened to Stravinsky that caused him to rely more on the ego than the soul as the source of his musical ideas. The turning point occurred between 1917 and 1918. In 1917, Stravinsky completed his ballet *Chant du rossignol* (*Song of the Nightingale*). About halfway through the piece, the soul that animated the music disappeared, never to appear again in any later composition.

Significantly, in 1918, Stravinsky completed *L'histoire du Soldat* (*The Soldier's Tale*), the first of his so-called neoclassical pieces. This miniature stage work, composed for seven instruments, dancers, and a narrator, tells the Faustian story of a soldier who gives up his violin (and his soul) to the devil in exchange for a book that will supposedly reveal how to achieve wealth and happiness.

The plot of this piece represents Stravinsky's own dilemma: He gave up his soul-inspired music (represented by the violin), not to the devil, but to the ego. The result was that he slipped from being a visionary upper 6 composer into being a middle 6 formalist.

Stravinsky composed according to the formalist neoclassical style for several decades. With *The Rite of Spring*, he'd inadvertently set the pattern of much twentieth-century music: centers one (rhythm), two (sonority), three (intensity), and six (intellect) are active; centers four (expression) and five (well-being) are suppressed; and centers seven and eight are absent. The neoclassical style allowed Stravinsky to restore centers four and five, but not seven, to his music.

As I mentioned, toward the end of his life, Stravinsky adopted the twelve-tone system, producing music that had a certain rhythmic (first center), sensual (second center), and intellectual (sixth center) appeal, but which was too abstract for most audiences to enjoy.

Stravinsky's slippage from upper to middle 6 is the reverse of the pattern that prevails when a composer develops along the continuum of human potential. Such a composer grows constantly, reaching into the upper centers until his music is composed from the expanded consciousness of the seventh center instead of the intellectual control of the sixth, at which point he has become a higher mind composer.

Stravinsky claimed, with respect to *Le Sacre du printemps* (*The Rite of Spring*), that "I had only my ear to help me. I heard and wrote what I heard. I am the vessel through which *Le Sacre* passed."[2]

Not only did this piece change the history of music, setting the pattern of centers that would prevail for much of the twentieth century, but also its violence seemed to presage the First World War, which broke out a year after its premiere. (Perhaps Cyril Scott would have seen a "secret" cause-and-effect influence here.)

My theory is that Stravinsky was frightened of once again becoming such a vessel. After *The Song of the Nightingale*, he took the safer route of allowing his ego to control the compositional process instead of his soul. He adhered to ever more rigid compositional schematta as his life progressed, finally ending in serialism.

Stravinsky wrote one sacred work widely considered to be a masterpiece, the *Symphony of Psalms* (1930), a deep expression of religious faith. It accesses the seventh center, but the sense of expanded consciousness that usually accompanies music from this center is attenuated. The sixth center's formalist tendencies are too strong, a sign of the fear of the soul that was the cause of Stravinsky's having turned away from his brilliant, visionary early style toward a drier, academic one.

What Sri Aurobindo said about poetry also applies to music:

> The intellect is an absurdly overactive part of the nature; it always thinks that nothing can be well done unless it puts its finger into the pie and therefore it instinctively interferes with the inspiration, blocks half or more of it and labours to substitute its own inferior and toilsome productions for the true speech and rhythm that ought to have come.[3]

For me, the "true speech and rhythm" is present in the pre-1917 masterworks of Stravinsky. Afterward, although I know that many people would disagree with me, I hear nothing but "inferior and toilsome productions." Stravinsky's later works may not be *intellectually* inferior—far from it. They're often the epitome of musical wit. But they don't speak to me with the voice of the soul, which is my criterion for greatness in music. For this reason, I think of Stravinsky as a sometime mystic.

In the yoga of listening, Stravinsky's three great ballets, *The Firebird*, *Petrouchka*, and *The Rite of Spring*, provide excellent opportunities for awakening the visionary aspect of the sixth center, which esotericists call the third eye. As I pointed out in chapter 13, the visionary element is especially powerful in *The Firebird*, which ascends from the sixth to the seventh center, thereby moving from an opening of the third eye directly into expanded consciousness.

Béla Bartók

In his twenties, Bartók was a self-professed atheist. Though he may not have believed in God or the soul, his music is full of mystical moments, like brief peak experiences. By the end of his life, he was composing late masterworks that contain the entire range of human experience. These late masterworks are as spiritual as anything in Beethoven's late period. That spirituality, however, is secular in nature, like Maslow's.

I've loved Bartók's music since I first discovered it in high school. I will never forget the TME that resulted from my first hearing of his Music for Strings, Percussion, and Celesta.

It was the summer between my sophomore and junior years. I had just gotten back from a summer music camp, in which a violinist friend had introduced me to Bartók's Concerto for Orchestra. I hadn't known what to make of that piece, but became curious enough about Bartók's music to buy an LP of the Music for Strings. On a warm, sunny, late afternoon in my bedroom, which was shaded by a woods in back of the house, I lay down on the floor with my head between the loudspeakers to listen to my new record. Although my eyes were closed, I was aware of the slight changes in light in the room caused by the swaying of the trees outside my window.

My TME occurred in the middle of the third movement. The strings began to build up a haze of trills. The room suddenly seemed much brighter, as if infused with a radiance greater than that of the sun outside my window, bright enough for the change to be perceived through my closed eyelids. Some of the upper strings began sliding from one note to the next in a spooky way. I was transfixed, unable to move.

Then an icy, eerie, inhumanly beautiful melody started to sound in the violins. My bedroom seemed to be filled with a fearsome, radiant presence like that of an angel. I was afraid to open my eyes lest I actually see this presence. But I was also paralyzed; I couldn't have opened my eyes in any case.

After the movement ended—it's about seven minutes long—my altered state gradually dissolved. By the end of the final movement, whose lively dancelike music I barely registered, the sense of presence was gone, the radiance had gradually diminished, and I was able to move and open my eyes again.

Scott would probably have classified my TME as deva-inspired. Bartók was very close to nature. His music was often inspired by bird and insect calls as well as folklore.

Scott spoke not only of nature-spirit devas, but also of "Lesser National Devas," associated with the development of the world's peoples, especially folklore.[4] If what I'd sensed was an angel, then perhaps the seraphic quality of deva inspiration was present in this passage. The music certainly had the ecstasy and grandeur without human emotion that Scott associated with the highest range of deva music.

I doubt that Bartók would have had an angelic visitation in mind when composing the third movement of his Music for Strings. He once said, "[I]f I ever crossed myself, it would signify 'In the name of Nature, Art and Science.'"[5]

In Scott's terms, however, he could have been an unconscious medium for such music.

I believe that what occurred during this TME was a direct inner revelation of my own soul. My soul wanted to make a strong impression on me, similar to that which occurred in connection with my first live hearing of Saint-Saëns's *Danse Macabre* when I was in elementary school, as described in chapter 2. As a result of this TME, which had the force of a conversion experience, Bartók became an important influence on my music, and remains so to this day.

Bartók had this to say about his aims as a composer:

> My own idea, however—of which I have been fully conscious since I found myself as a composer—is the brotherhood of people, brotherhood in spite of all wars and conflicts. I try—to the best of my ability—to serve this idea in my music; therefore I don't reject any influence, be it Slovakian, Rumanian, Arabic or from any other source. The source must only be clean, fresh and healthy![6]

Perhaps it was this sense of a "clean, fresh and healthy" source that my soul wanted me to note and learn from in Bartók's music.

During his lifetime and afterward, Bartók's music was often disparaged as "eclectic." Rather than seeing this eclectic quality as a fault, I take it to mean that Bartók was dedicated to realizing as much of the continuum of human potential in music as he could. He never suppressed the fourth (expressive) and fifth (well-being) centers, as so many of his contemporaries did.

Moments that touch the seventh center are relatively rare in Bartók's work but all the more trenchant for that. They seem to be a musical embodiment of Maslow's transitory peak experiences.

The passage in Music for Strings that I mentioned is an example of such a peak experience, corresponding to the lower 7 sense of the sublime. I can think of no better musical illustration of Rilke's idea that "beauty is the beginning of terror"—an awe-inspiring sense of the soul's presence.

An example of middle 7 nobility appears in Bartók's 1911 opera *Bluebeard's Castle*. In this castle, seven locked doors hide some aspect of the protagonist Bluebeard's character. Behind the fifth of these doors lies the magnificence of his worldly power, his extensive properties, which the music illustrates with a grandiose chorale.

Usually, Bartók is a formalist composer. His primary focus is middle 6 (formal play), but he's able to activate all of the centers below that one, either successively, or at once. His music has the constant intellectual restlessness of all sixth center music.

Toward the end of his life, perhaps as a result of his belief in the importance of organically developing form, Bartók's primary center shifted upward, into the domain of the seventh, allowing him to create some late masterworks: the Fifth and Sixth string quartets, the Concerto for Orchestra, and the Third Piano Concerto. Bartók had achieved the level of consciousness development that Aurobindo called higher mind.

Of these works, the Fifth Quartet is probably the most challenging for many listeners because of its high level of dissonance. It's notable for the presence of the seventh center in the hushed chorales of the second movement.

The Sixth Quartet was written just before Bartók was forced into exile in America by the worsening political situation in Hungary on the eve of the Second World War. It's a profoundly resigned yet moving work.

Though Bartók was not yet confronted by the imminence of his own death as he composed this quartet, he was leaving behind all that he loved about his homeland. Despite the small ensemble it employs, the work has the emotional and spiritual impact of compositions such as Mahler's Ninth, which are retrospective looks at the world, from the vantage point of the seventh center Witness, as one is poised to leave it.

There's no eighth center music in Bartók's oeuvre, perhaps because of his apparent lack of belief in a deity or ultimate source for all of creation. But the human is fully developed in it, especially in the Concerto for Orchestra. The ecstatic (upper 7) conclusion of this work is surprising, given the fact that Bartók was acutely ill when he began it.

Bartók's illness had not yet been diagnosed as the leukemia that would kill him within a couple of years. The disease apparently went into remission while he worked on the Concerto for Orchestra, so that he felt he'd returned to radiant health by the time he'd completed it.

Here is an instance of what Charles means when he says that the soul provides us with an increased amount of life force when we're fulfilling our life purpose. Bartók had been so stricken with grief over leaving his homeland, and so overwhelmed by the intensity and foreignness of New York City, where he began his self-imposed exile in America, that he'd been unable to compose until the commission for the Concerto for Orchestra came through. He believed that writing the piece healed him.

The Third Piano Concerto is perhaps a lesser work than the Concerto for Orchestra. It was written for Bartók's wife, as a birthday present, and to let her know that *he* knew he was dying. The piece is strong on center four. It contains a great deal of heart-opening love. The fifth center is also frequently present, perhaps as a spilling over of the well-being that resulted from completing the Concerto for Orchestra, or an expression of hope for its return, since

Bartók's health began to fail once again while he worked on the piece. The Third Piano Concerto was the last thing he completed (except for the orchestration of the last seventeen measures, which were accomplished by one of his colleagues) before he died.

The central movement is the most significant. It's marked, for the first time in Bartók's music, Adagio Religioso. The music of this movement is related to the middle 7 "Hymn of Thanksgiving" in Beethoven's String Quartet in A Minor, Op. 132.

Beethoven had written this piece to thank the deity for his convalescence from an illness. Perhaps Bartók was doing something similar, or imploring whatever forces he believed had been responsible for his earlier remission from illness for another return to health. The opening and concluding sections of this tripartite movement are the most extended passages of seventh center music in Bartók's oeuvre.

Another significant feature of the concerto's second movement is its fast center section, which is intended to evoke the sounds of a summer evening, full of insect noises and bird calls. Such music, a result of Bartók's love of nature, targets the visionary aspect of upper 6.

As in the Concerto for Orchestra, the finale of the Third Piano Concerto is full of gusto (fifth center), as well as brains and wit (sixth center). It concludes with a few radiant moments of seventh center ecstasy.

By the time of his death, Bartók seems to have completed the transition from thinking mind to higher mind composer. But he didn't have the opportunity to consolidate what he'd learned in the process, producing works that were entirely composed from the seventh center, or to develop beyond that point. For this reason, I call him a sometime mystic.

A Healing Journey

In the yoga of listening, Bartók's Concerto for Orchestra is the perfect remedy for anyone suffering from depression, illness, or the effects of physical, emotional, or spiritual exhaustion. Perhaps because of Bartók's precarious health and the apparently miraculous healing that came about as he worked on it, the Concerto for Orchestra is more directly about the fluctuations of life force—its rising and falling at the instigation of the soul—than any other music I'm familiar with.

The work begins with a slow introduction that originates in lower 7, with a sense of mystery, awe, the sublime. The subsequent faster music has the restlessness and extreme changeability of mood of sixth center music, although it frequently touches on the sense of tragedy and passion of upper 3.

Occasional brass fanfares bring out the nobility of middle 7. The dominant center, however, is middle 6 (formal play and invention).

The second movement, called "Game of Pairs," is like a symphonic scherzo. It adds in the wit of lower 6, by means of duets between the first- and second-chair players of each section of the winds. A brass chorale in the middle section once again brings in middle 7.

The third movement dwells in the emotional depths of depression, including emotional anguish and the fear of death. Thus the music emanates from the crisis zone between centers six and seven, although its dominant center is the pathos of lower 4. As in much of Bartók's music, there are momentary peak experiences—flashes of the seventh center that amount to glimpses of the soul.

The fourth movement, called "Interrupted Intermezzo," is by turns playful and poignant, the former relating to lower 6, the latter to the bittersweet yearning of middle 4—a melody so full of heart-opening human love that I consider it to be one of the most beautiful moments in all of twentieth-century music.

This movement takes a hilarious turn when Bartók parodies a passage from the Seventh Symphony of Dimitri Shostakovich, which was often played on the radio while Bartók was composing the piece, complete with imitations of laughter in the woodwinds at the inanity of Shostakovich's music, which Bartók couldn't stand. That's the "interruption" mentioned in the title of the movement.

Much of the Finale appeals to exuberance of upper 5, although there's also a great deal of intellectual and formal play (sixth center) in this movement, including the least academic, most good-humored fugue you'll ever hear. The end of the piece carries it from the nobility of middle 7 to the ecstasy of upper 7 in a rush of notes that always seems to pull me up by the hair—an almost physical sensation of the opening of the crown chakra.

The macrorhythmic waves of rising and falling energy that are typical of seventh center music are especially audible in this movement. Although I haven't mentioned moments in which the first or second centers were targeted by themselves, they're constantly present throughout the piece. Thus Bartók's Concerto for Orchestra touches on the entire continuum of human potential, with the exception of the eighth chakra, as he journeys from the depths of depression to the healing ecstasy of union with the soul, carrying the listener along in his wake.

24

The Achieved Mystics: Scriabin and Messiaen

We've seen examples of twentieth-century composers who wanted to be mystics but didn't know how to attune themselves to the soul as the source of musical inspiration. They turned instead to ego-based mathematical processes in order to compose. We've also seen examples of twentieth-century composers who may or may not have wanted to be mystics but were sometimes able to attune themselves to the voice of the soul.

Now let's look at the work of two twentieth-century composers whose approach to composing was largely soul-based. Both of these composers are *achieved* mystics because their primary motivation was to express transcendent states of consciousness through music, with the hope of inspiring such states in listeners.

Alexander Scriabin

Scriabin was one of the few composers in the history of Western music with an intimate knowledge of esoteric traditions and a desire to express this knowledge through music. According to his brother-in-law, Boris de Schloezer, Scriabin believed himself to be a missionary "of superior powers" who was "sent to earth to reveal the secret truth in its various aspects for the benefit of humanity." He was to be "a custodian and restorer of ancient wisdom."[1]

I noted previously that, as composers develop, the center from which their music emanates may rise. Although Scriabin is capable of sustained passages of upper 7 music, his primary center seems to be lower 7, the sublime. This makes him, like Beethoven and Bruckner, a higher mind composer.

Schloezer made the insightful remark that all of Scriabin's later large-scale works, especially the piano sonatas

> are built according to a uniform succession of states: languor, longing, impetuous striving, dance, ecstasy, and transfiguration. This outline is basically simple; it is built on a series of upswings, with each successive wave rising higher and higher toward a final effort, liberation, and ecstasy.[2]

Music that emanates from the seventh center tends to be constructed macrorhythmically, that is, in terms of the accumulation and dissipation of energy. Schloezer's description of Scriabin's music, in terms of "a series of upswings" and "successive" waves, matches my definition of macrorhythmically composed music. It also implies that Scriabin's music traverses the range of the seventh center, from sublime to ecstatic.

The other centers are not absent. The second center shows up in the lush and sensual harmonies. The fourth center appears as pathetic, bittersweet, or elated sensations of love. The sixth center is also active: Scriabin's music is rigorous in formal construction (middle 6), and visionary (upper 6) in its attempt to picture such things as physical and spiritual lovemaking, as in the *Poem of Ecstasy.*

The dramatic intensity of the third center comes and goes in Scriabin's music. The fifth center, having to do with well-being, is frequently absent. This perhaps explains why Scriabin's music can sometimes sound cloying, decadent, or unhealthy.

Scriabin's desire to create a piece of music, the *Mysterium*, that would end the world may be an indication of how much he wanted to be liberated from it. This desire expresses itself in his music as the attenuation of the fifth center, resulting in a psychic signature that I call transcendental longing (1, 2, 4, 6, and lower to middle 7). When the fifth center does show up, however briefly, the music becomes dancelike.

Schloezer said that in Scriabin's music there are two "contrasting elements." One is "tender, caressing, erotic; the other, turbulent, winged, luminous." Scriabin's "creative imagination" could best be summed up in the image of "the dancing Shiva of Hindu statuary, which creates and destroys worlds without end or beginning."[3]

In the tradition of Tantra, these two "contrasting elements" are Shiva and Shakti. Shakti, as the active principle, is "turbulent, winged, luminous," while

Shiva, as the passive, is "tender, caressing, erotic." Scriabin, perhaps without knowing it consciously, seems to have expressed the union of Shiva and Shakti in music—the result of which, in Tantra, is not merely sexual pleasure, but the awakening of the kundalini and spiritual transcendence.

Schloezer divided Scriabin's music into two periods, early and late, lying on either side of the 1902–1903 composition of the Fourth Piano Sonata, Op. 30—although many works produced after that date revert to the earlier style.[4] The earlier music is more emotional and reflects the thinking mind; the later is overtly spiritual and reflects the higher mind.

The Poem of Ecstasy, Op. 54, is one of Scriabin's mystical masterpieces. It begins in the visionary realm of upper 6, as a musical depiction of a poem by the composer himself. Gradually, it moves through an erotically charged sense of transcendental longing (lower to middle 7). The climax of the piece is a glorious example of the self-transcending ecstasy of upper 7, as well as a musical illustration of sexual and spiritual orgasm, both personal and universal, like the union of Tantric devotees embodying the embrace of Shiva and Shakti.

Prometheus, the Poem of Fire, Op. 60, is Scriabin's other mystical masterpiece. It involves a concerto-like solo piano part, a wordless chorus wearing white robes, a full orchestra, and a *tastiera per luce* ("light keyboard"), which is intended to suffuse the concert hall with various colors of light as the piece progresses.

This multimedia work, completed in 1910, was clearly ahead of its time. The technology necessary to fulfill Scriabin's intentions—one imagines lasers rather than mere colored gels—wouldn't become available for more than fifty years.

Prometheus begins in the magic and mystery of lower 7 and ends in the ecstasy of upper 7. One writer has called it "two symphonies to be played concurrently," "one of music, the other of light."[5] Scriabin hoped that such a combination would "act as 'a powerful psychological resonator for the listener.'"[6]

Other major mystical works of Scriabin include the Fifth through the Tenth piano sonatas. Listeners interested in maximizing their exposure to the seventh center, and its concomitant expanded consciousness, might want to explore them.

Scriabin especially liked the Seventh Sonata, Op. 64, passages of which he described as "pure" and "holy." He called it his *White Mass* Sonata.[7]

The harmonies and melodies of the Eighth Sonata, Op. 66, according to Scriabin, are derived from five melodic fragments announced in the first five measures. He intended these fragments to represent the five elements of yogic philosophy: "earth, air, fire, water, and the mystic ether."[8] The combination of themes in the compositional process would provide a mystical parallel to the creation of the material world from these elements.

A friend of Scriabin's, finding the music of his Ninth Sonata, Op. 68, to be dark and foreboding, gave it the title *Black Mass*. Throughout his life, the composer was plagued with accusations of dabbling in Satanism, based on the titles of pieces such as the "Satanic Poem," for piano, Op. 36, or this *Black Mass* Sonata. Schloezer responded to such accusations as follows:

> True art can never produce a depressing or debilitating influence on the soul; even melancholy, sad, and mournful works of art invariably introduce into the psyche an element of reconciliation, unity, and harmony, as if purifying it. This is the catharsis of Aristotle, which saves the soul from an ominous, lurking, menacing chaos.[9]

Thus, according to Schloezer, Scriabin's most terrifying music is intended to exorcise the forces of darkness, which for Scriabin possessed "an objective existence." The composer "compels" these forces "to assume an image of divinity, thus divesting them of malevolent power and elevating them to a superior state of being."[10] Music of this nature may begin in the crisis point between the sixth and seventh centers (irrationality), but it ends in the transcendent ecstasy of upper 7.

Scriabin described the Tenth Sonata, Op. 70, which is my favorite, as "a sonata of insects. Insects are born from the sun . . . they are the sun's kisses."[11] Perhaps he was thinking of the multihued iridescence of certain beetles. The sonata closes in a radiant halo of trills—a quiet, blissful, inwardly turned ecstasy perhaps akin to the yogic notion of samadhi. This is yet another example of Scriabin's penchant for ending his major works in upper 7.

Scriabin's output also included a large number of lesser, often Chopinesque, works for the piano: preludes, etudes, mazurkas, poems, pieces, and so on. Most of these miniatures are less than five minutes in duration. Only those composed in the last few years of Scriabin's life—with opus numbers beginning in the high fifties and ending with his last completed work, the Preludes, Op. 74—consistently make reference to the seventh center. Because the sonatas provide more prolonged periods of exposure to this center, I recommend them over the lesser works.

Now we come to what was, without a doubt, Scriabin's most ambitious work, the *Mysterium*. The strange thing about it is that, according to Schloezer, the *Mysterium* "was never put on paper, was never even begun, and never existed except conceptually."[12]

The *Mysterium* was to involve all of the arts, thousands of performers and spectators, and a full week for its complete performance, not to mention years of prior training for the participants. It would also end the world and usher in a new age of spiritual evolution for humanity. Scriabin came no closer to realizing this apocalyptic conception than creating a jumble of sketches for what he called the *Acte préalable* (*Prefatory Action*), which was to prepare the world for the *Mysterium*.

Here is a description of the *Prefatory Action*, assembled from numerous remarks made by Scriabin in letters and conversations recalled by his contemporaries:

> Bells suspended from clouds in the sky would summon spectators from all over the world. The performance was to take place in a half-temple built in India. A reflecting pool of water would complete the divinity of the half-circle stage. Spectators would sit in tiers across the water. Those in the balconies would be the least spiritually advanced. The seating was strictly graded, ranking radially from the center of the stage, where Scriabin would sit at the piano, surrounded by hosts of instruments, singers, dancers. The entire group was to be permeated continually with movement, and costumed speakers reciting the text in processions and parades would form parts of the action. The choreography would include glances, looks, eye motions, touches of the hands, odors of both pleasant perfumes and acrid smokes, frankincense and myrrh. Pillars of incense would form part of the scenery. Lights, fires, and constantly changing lighting effects would pervade the cast and audience, each to number in the thousands.[13]

Scriabin was setting himself up as a musical guru. He even bought land in India near the Himalayas as a possible location for this rock-concert-like extravaganza.

The *Mysterium* was to be more of the same, lasting for seven days, and leading, through ecstasy, to the death of humanity and its transfiguration onto a higher plane. For this reason, Scriabin's enemies referred to *Prefatory Action* as the "Safe Mysterium."[14]

Scriabin's premature death, at forty-three, from sepsis that started with a carbuncle on his lip, has long been an object of speculation by esotericists. Cyril Scott felt that it was a result of his having attempted to channel deva-inspired music without the proper guidance or training. I've also heard a persistent rumor that Scriabin was "offed" by the superior nonphysical beings who guide the spiritual evolution of the planet because he might indeed have been capable of destroying the world with his *Mysterium*.

In reading his biography, I came to the conclusion that such conceptions of the spiritual reasons for Scriabin's premature death have little to do with reality. He was barely able to make a living as a composer or pianist and had an estranged wife who refused to divorce him and four children (two of whom died while Scriabin was alive) to support. Meanwhile, he was living with another woman by whom he had three more children. It wasn't the devas that wore him out, but his family and financial situation.

If Scriabin's charisma had increased to the point of his recruiting people to fulfill his dream of the *Mysterium*, like a guru, the powers that guide the spiritual evolution of the planet might indeed have been anxious to get him out of the way. Scriabin could have led his followers away from their own souls' growth in order to support his, behavior that the higher spiritual powers would not have supported.

I doubt that any decision on the part of these powers to get rid of Scriabin would have been based on the potential danger of his music. The apocalyptic idea behind *Mysterium* belongs to the crisis point between the eighth center and the higher levels of spiritual evolution that take place in nonphysical reality. As I pointed out in chapter 15, the music of this crisis point, translation, can't be realized in sound.

The history of Scriabin's "Safe Mysterium," the *Prefatory Action*, was not closed by the composer's death in 1915. There was to be another chapter that Cyril Scott would probably have delighted in.

In the late 1970s, I discovered that a Russian composer by the name of Alexander Nemtin (1936–1999) had attempted to complete part of Scriabin's *Prefatory Action* from the sketches left behind by the composer at his death.

The record company that issued the first recording of this piece placed a photograph of the clean-shaven Nemtin next to one of the bearded Scriabin in the liner notes. There was an eerie resemblance in the structure of the two faces. Although it was never stated explicitly, the implication was that Nemtin was the reincarnation of Scriabin, who had come back to finish his last great work.

By the time I began researching this book, I no longer owned that recording. But I was amazed to find out that Nemtin had continued working to realize the rest of Scriabin's ambitions for the *Prefatory Action*, newly released on CD as *Preparation for the Final Mystery*. In twenty-five years of work, Nemtin had produced more than two and a half hours of music from a mere fifty-four pages of musical sketches by Scriabin.[15]

If such a determination to finish what Scriabin had left behind wasn't a case of reincarnation, perhaps it could be called a case of possession—if not by Scriabin himself, then by the music. Thomas Mann once said, in connection with Wagner, that "the driving ambition" behind a work of art "belongs not to the artist but to the work itself, which aspires to be much greater than he ever dared to hope (or feared), and which imposes its will on him."[16] Certainly, it seems as if Scriabin's *Prefatory Action*—or the process configuration behind it— had imposed its will on Nemtin.

Preparation for the Final Mystery provides one of the most prolonged opportunities for exposure to the consciousness-expanding properties of the seventh center in the history of Western music. If you like Scriabin's twenty-three-minute *Prometheus*, then simply multiply its length by seven and you've got the duration of *Preparation for the Final Mystery*.

The usefulness of Scriabin's music for the yoga of listening lies in how it opens us up to the expanded consciousness of the seventh center. It's full of transcendental longing for union with the divine, which can motivate us inwardly to prepare ourselves for such a union.

Scriabin's approach is like that of Feuerstein's "verticalist" yoga traditions: "in, up, and out."[17] Here, the "in" refers to listening to the music, and the "up, and out" to the potential effects of exposure to the seventh center. This exposure is meted out in smaller doses in the piano sonatas, and larger ones in *The Poem of Ecstasy* and *Prometheus, the Poem of Fire.*

Preparation for the Final Mystery may be too much of a good thing for a single listening session. I found myself feeling ungrounded after exposing myself to this music for longer than a half-hour per session.

One potential problem with the verticalist approach to music is that prolonged exposure to transcendental longing can promote an eagerness to leave the body and the physical world behind. When such an approach is balanced, as in Tantra, with practices that *increase* our willingness to be present in the body and on the planet, we're less likely to want to destroy ourselves, or yearn for an apocalyptic end of the world, in order to achieve that union.

Scriabin's *The Poem of Ecstasy* is a perfect expression of this Tantric approach. It links the desire to transcend the body and the world to the physical and spiritual expression of love, demonstrating that union with the divine can be achieved here and now, through union with a beloved human partner.

Olivier Messiaen

Another achieved mystic concerned with transcendental longing, human and divine love, and apocalyptic visions was the twentieth-century French composer Olivier Messiaen. Unlike Scriabin, who took his inspiration from esoteric teachings, Messiaen drew from the mysteries of the Catholic Church, as well as the love depicted in "the greatest myth of human love, that of Tristan and Isolde."[18] Messiaen considered human love "a pale reflection . . . of the only true love, Divine love."[19]

A further component of Messiaen's music is "a profound love of nature, in which it's possible to 'lose oneself'" as if it were "a kind of nirvana." Messiaen considered nature "a marvellous teacher,"[20] which led him to the study of bird-song. He traveled all over the world with a tape recorder to capture the songs of exotic birds, which he would then transcribe in musical notation and weave into his compositions. For him, birds were the earthly choristers of God.

Messiaen's output was huge, both in terms of the number of pieces he created and their size. Many of his compositions take an hour or more to perform. They tend to be noisy, in terms of both volume and dissonance. Indeed, Stravinsky once said that Messiaen's "main interest often seems to be in piling up decibels as though he were jealous of the sonic boom."[21]

There are many instances of music from all three ranges of the seventh center in Messiaen's oeuvre, as well as a number of radiant examples of music from the eighth center. However, in the work of no other mystical composer is this statement by Sri Aurobindo more true:

> When any real effect is produced, it is not because of [the artist's] beating and hammering, but because an inspiration slips down between the raising of the hammer and the falling and gets in under cover of the beastly noise.[22]

The works that Messiaen produced during the period from the late 1920s to the late 1940s are the most accessible and enjoyable. These include a number of pieces for organ: *Le banquet céleste* (*The Celestial Banquet*); *Apparition de l'église éternelle* (*Apparition of the Church Eternal*); *La Nativité du Seigneur* (*The Nativity of Our Lord*); and *Les corps glorieux* (*The Glorious Bodies*). The long fourth movement of the latter, "Combat de la mort et de la vie" ("Battle of Death and Life"), contrasts a terrifying depiction of death, and the fear it inspires (crisis point between centers six and seven), with an upper 8 depiction of eternal life, or union with God.

The following piano works from the same period are also of interest: *Visions de l'Amen*, for two pianos, and *Vignt regards sur l'Infant-Jésus* (*Twenty Meditations on the Infant Jesus*), for solo piano. The latter is a gargantuan work, lasting nearly two hours in performance. It makes almost inhuman demands on both listeners and the pianist. There are wonderful moments, but also much "beastly noise."

Visions de l'Amen, on the other hand, is one of the few pieces by Messiaen likely to appeal to listeners from beginning to end. It includes musical visions of the Creation, angels, saints, birds, stars, the rings of Saturn, the Crucifixion, and the Last Judgment. Though loud at times, the noise is usually more jubilant (upper 7 ecstasy) than beastly.

Of Messiaen's orchestral works from this period, I've already mentioned *L'Ascension*, whose final movement is an example of upper 8 music. The first movement of this piece is a fine example of middle 7 grandeur and love of God. The other two movements are visionary (upper 6) portrayals of theological ideas.

The *Turangalîla-symphonie*, also from this period, is one of the masterworks of mid-twentieth-century music. The word *Turangalîla* comes from Sanskrit and means the divine play of time (in the form of rhythm and movement) in the cosmos, including both creation and destruction and "the spiritual-physical union of love."[23]

Turangalîla-symphonie contains an unearthly "theme of love," scored with an eerie early electronic instrument called the *ondes martenot*.[24] In the first of the piece's ten movements, this theme seems to be buried in all the "beastly noise" of time. But, like a diamond from the matrix of surrounding stone, it gradually emerges from movement to movement.

The sixth movement, called "Jardin du sommeil d'amour" ("Garden of Love's Sleep"), could be a sequel to Scriabin's *The Poem of Ecstasy*. Here, the theme of love depicts the sleep of a pair of lovers after they've experienced physical and spiritual union. But in the eighth movement, the theme of love begins to sound less like human love (fourth center) or love of God (seventh center), and more like divine love itself (middle to upper eighth center).

In the Finale, which begins with the ecstasy of upper 7, Messiaen tries to build up enough musical energy (kundalini?) to catapult the music from upper 7 into the eighth center. I have yet to hear a performance that brings out the full effect of the eighth center at this point, overwhelming as the music may already be in intensity and volume.[25]

Another piece that I enjoy from Messiaen's most accessible period is called *Trois petites liturgies de la Présence Divine* (*Three Small Liturgies of the Divine Presence*). This is a choral work, with a spiritual text by Messiaen himself. It's scored for female voices, with big solo parts for the piano and the *ondes martenot*, as well as celesta, vibraphone, percussion, and strings.

This is Messiaen's only full-length work (lasting just over twenty minutes) that accesses the seventh center and above from start to finish. I'm especially fond of the third movement, which, like the Finale of *Turangalîla-symphonie*, begins in the ecstasy of upper 7 and catapults itself into the eighth center (the section for solo voice and strings). Here again, I have yet to find a performance that brings out the full effect of the eighth center—that overwhelming sense of having to change one's life after being exposed to the divine presence.

After 1950, Messiaen became involved in technical experimentation. He was among the first composers to develop Webern's use of the twelve-tone system into total serialism. His attempts at birdsong notation also became increasingly complex.

I've listened to all of Messiaen's major works from this point until his death in 1992. But, like much music of the last half of the twentieth century, these works involve a gradual stripping away of centers on the continuum of human potential. The fourth, fifth, and eighth centers were the first to disappear, followed by the third and seventh. In much of this music, only the first, second, and sixth centers are active.

Judging by the music Messiaen wrote in the 1930s and 1940s, he could have been a perfect "deva exponent," to use Scott's term. His work was inspired by nature, in the form of birdsong, as well as by both seraphic (seventh center) and buddhic (eighth center) love. But, as in the case of Schoenberg, he ended up confining his music to the sixth center, becoming more mathematical and less mystical.

Two works of the composer's last years bring back some of the splendor and humanity of his pre-1950 music: *Éclairs sur l'au-delà* (*Illuminations of the Beyond*), Messiaen's last completed work; and the *Concert à quatre* (*Concerto for Four*), which he was working on when he died, and whose last movement his wife completed.

The fifth and eleventh movements of *Illuminations* may be examples of middle and upper 8 music, respectively. I'm not sure, because the performers on my recording may have been unable to bring through this aspect of the music.

In the *Concert à quatre*, the joy and exuberance of the fifth center and the wit of lower 6 come forward, after having been silenced by Messiaen's more serious theological and experimental concerns for more than forty years.

Messiaen began his career as an upper 6 (visionary) composer, one whose music came from what Sri Aurobindo called the thinking mind. During his most productive and accessible period, from the late 1920s to the late 1940s, his level rose to lower 7, making him a higher mind composer. This is the period when he was able to access the seventh center more or less constantly, and at times the rarely achievable eighth. The many masterful movements and works of this period are those of an achieved mystic.

After 1950, however, either Messiaen's avant-garde technical preoccupations submerged the voice of the soul or God in his music or he reverted to being a thinking mind composer. The seventh center showed up less frequently and the eighth disappeared. What was left was a formalistic tendency (middle 6) and a visionary penchant to depict theological concepts in music (upper 6). At the end of his life, the soul seems to have reemerged, in Messiaen's final works, indicating that he was once again composing from the higher mind.

If, in the yoga of listening, the purpose of Scriabin's music is to open us up to the expanded consciousness of the seventh center, that of Messiaen's best music is to prepare us for and propel us into the cosmic consciousness of the eighth.

A Musical Ascent into Heaven

Messiaen's most popular piece is his *Quatour pour la Fin du Temps* (*Quartet for the End of Time*), for violin, clarinet, cello, and piano. The work was composed early in the Second World War, while Messiaen, having been captured by the Germans, was interned in a concentration camp in Silesia (at that time part of Germany, now in Poland).

Messiaen was lucky that the commanding officer in charge of the camp was a music lover. He arranged for the composer to have music paper. Legend has it that the piece was premiered in the camp, before "an audience of 5000 fellow-prisoners," on inadequate instruments—the cello had only three, instead of the usual four, strings, and the piano was an old upright whose keys stuck in the extreme cold.[26]

Messiaen's *Quartet* is dedicated to the rainbow-haloed angel who appears during the Apocalypse to announce the end of Time (Revelation 10:1–7).

The magnitude and horror of the Second World War may have had something to do with Messiaen's turning to Revelation for inspiration. Esotericists have sometimes compared Hitler to the Antichrist, whose appearance on the world scene was supposed to trigger the Apocalypse.

The eight movements of the *Quartet for the End of Time* depict a musical ascent into heaven. This ascent begins at dawn, on Earth (first movement), and passes through transcendental longing and spiritual desolation (second and third movements). After a playful break from such weighty concerns (fourth movement), the longing for God becomes increasingly passionate (fifth movement). An angelic dance of wrath and ecstasy breaks out, in anticipation of the end of time and the world (sixth movement); after which our longing for God becomes tangled up in the rainbows of the apocalyptic angel who announces the end of Time (seventh movement). At last, we're gradually lifted toward heaven from such longing, to experience a sense of redemption by, and oneness with, God (eighth movement).

The psychic signatures of the eight movements of the *Quartet* are unusually stable, providing a rare opportunity to observe how a composer uses various combinations of centers to create the effects he desires.

I recommend listening to this work, which is nearly fifty minutes long, one movement at a time. First, read my description of the movement's psychic signature; then lie back and let the combination of centers it targets wash over you. Later, try listening to the entire work in one sitting, allowing it to take you along on its gradual ascent into heaven. In terms of the yoga of listening, it not only evokes our transcendental longing for union with the divine, but also satisfies that longing with a musical depiction of God's grace.

The first movement of the *Quartet for the End of Time* is entitled "Liturgie de cristal" ("Crystal Liturgy"). As a visionary portrayal of the dawn chorus of birdsong, imitated in the violin (nightingale) and clarinet (blackbird), its predominant center is upper 6. We're on Earth at the beginning of a new day.

As with most Western music, centers one (rhythm) and two (sonority) are present. Center three (intensity) is attenuated, to bring out the calmness of the dawn. There's no drama, no fluctuation of volume or dissonance. Center four (expression) is also attenuated. The melodies, like birdsong, are without most human emotion.

Center five (well-being), however, is present in the joy of the birdsong. This center often comes forward when the composer wants to depict the feelings of well-being inspired by a landscape in music. Centers seven (expanded consciousness) and eight (cosmic consciousness) are absent.

The second movement is called "Vocalise, pour l'Ange qui annonce la fin du Temps" ("Vocalise for the Angel Who Announces the End of Time"). The predominant center in the brief opening and closing sections of the movement is upper 6, a visionary portrayal of the apocalyptic angel announcing the end of Time. The music is violent and dramatic, in the typical pattern of much twentieth-century music: centers one, two, three, and six are active; four, five, seven, and eight absent.

The majority of the movement is taken up with the vocalise, an expressive songlike melody played by the violin and cello.[27] Here, the dominant center is seven: The music targets the point where lower 7 fear of God shades into middle 7 love of God.

The big change in this section is that center four (expression) has come forward, although in a subordinate role. While the piece is about human feeling, these feelings have little to do with the love of one human being for another, but rather our longing for God.

Centers one, two, and six are active, and eight is absent. Centers three and five have dropped out. This pattern (1, 2, 4, 6, 7, with 4 strong and 7 dominant) is the typical signature of transcendental longing. This longing appears in several other movements of the *Quartet*.

Messiaen described the piano chords that accompany the vocalise as "faraway chimes" intended to represent "the impalpable harmonies of heaven."[28] As I mentioned in chapter 15, I once heard chimes like these in one of my adventures in consciousness, in which I was told that they represent the nearly inaudible call of the Source to align ourselves and journey toward oneness with it.[29]

The third movement, a long solo for clarinet, is called "Abîme des oiseaux" ("Abyss of the Birds"). According to Messiaen, the abyss of the title is the world of time. He feels that we're imprisoned within this world, called "fallen" in Catholic belief, as if in an abyss. But we have the joyful song of the birds to console us, symbolizing "our yearning for light, stars, rainbows and jubilant voices."[30]

The predominant mood of the movement involves a combination of lower 4 pathos, and lower 7 fear of God, creating a sense of spiritual desolation—a more dejected version of the transcendental longing of the second movement. In the central section, with its imitation of birdsong, this spiritual desolation fades out, and the joy of middle 5 breaks through.

Throughout, center one is present, since there is rhythm, but two is attenuated, since there is no harmony but that implied by the melody. Center three comes through at the intense climax of the movement, just before the music returns to the spiritual desolation of the beginning. As with most Western music, center six is constantly active, determining the formal shape of the music.

The fourth movement is called "Intermède" ("Interlude"). In this exuberant, scherzo-like movement, the predominant center is middle 6 (invention), with a dash of wit (lower 6), and exuberance (upper 5). Life in the world involves not merely transcendental longing and spiritual desolation, but also humor and joyful play.

The fifth movement, entitled "Louange à l'Eternité de Jésus" ("Praise of the Eternity of Jesus"), is for cello and piano. The predominant center is lower to middle 7. Centers one, two, three, four, and six are active below it; centers five and eight are absent. Here again we have the mood of transcendental longing for union with the divine, with an added element of passion contributed by the third center. The use of third center passion in a supportive role is like adding shadow effects to a drawing to make the subject more three-dimensional and lifelike.

The sixth movement is called "Danse de la fureur, pour les sept trompettes" ("Dance of Wrath, for the Seven Trumpets"). The seven trumpets of the title once again come from Revelation (seventh through eleventh chapters), in which they announce the Day of Judgment (hence the "wrath" of the title).

This movement portrays an ecstatic, though wrathful, angelic dance. The dominant center is upper 7 (ecstasy). The other centers are also active, with a few hints of middle 8 (grace) appearing from time to time. Only center two is attenuated: Because the four instruments play in unison or octaves throughout, there's no harmony except that implied by the melody.

The movement is a tour de force of rhythmic ingenuity and intensity, so centers one and three are particularly strong, with the latter bringing forward the wrath of the title. Yet there's also exuberance, contributed by the fifth center. Only in the ecstasy of upper 7, it seems, can both wrath and exuberance be fused into a single emotion.

In the center section of this movement, the clarinet, doubled by the piano, gets to play the role of angelic trumpeter, obstinately repeating a three-note pattern. This is an upper 6 visionary move on the part of the composer.

There are also a few odd passages of softer music that may represent the divine love behind all of this apocalyptic fury. They add the hints of middle 8 grace that I mentioned above.

The seventh movement is entitled "Fouillis d'arcs-en-ciel, pour l'Ange qui annonce la fin du Temps" ("Tangle of Rainbows, for the Angel Who Announces the End of Time"). It's comprised of two contrasting kinds of music that alternate with each other.

The first employs centers one, two, three, four, six, and seven, in the same pattern of passionate transcendental longing that I noted in the fifth movement. Instruments are added each time this music appears, allowing it to expand into the lower 7 and middle 7 ranges, rather than simply marking the point between them. It becomes both more sublime and mysterious and more full of devotional longing and love.

The angel who announces the end of time makes another appearance in the more violent music of the contrasting sections, which have the same pattern as the opening and closing of the second movement: Centers one, two, three, and six are active; centers four, five, seven, and eight are attenuated or absent. These sections of the movement, based on the principle of theme and variations, are more developmental than visionary. Thus the predominant center is middle 6 (formal play), rather than upper 6.

The eighth, and final, movement, entitled "Louange à l'Immortalité de Jésus" ("Praise for the Immortality of Jesus"), is for violin and piano. This is an example of middle 8 music (grace). Although the other centers are active, they're subordinated to this one. The slow pace and even rhythm create the metarhythmic sense of timelessness that's characteristic of this center.

Here, the violinist must be careful not to fall into the trap of simply making beautiful sounds (second center), playing with great expression (fourth center), or playing in a pious or prayerlike fashion (middle 7). The music demands both mastery and transcendence of these qualities.

Messiaen said that he intended this movement to represent the human aspect of Jesus, raised up to immortality. As the melody rises, it depicts "the ascension of man towards God, of the Son of God towards his Father, of the creature become divine towards Paradise."[31]

In the continuum of human potential, the eighth center represents the fully realized human being—one who, in Charles's terms, is at one with the soul. While music that accesses the upper range of the eighth center can indeed depict the feeling of oneness that we call Paradise, the eighth movement of Messiaen's *Quartet* doesn't go that far. It depicts the ascent *from* grace, the level of spiritual development in which all conflicts and resistances to the soul's (or God's) master plan for our growth are resolved, *toward* that higher level of oneness (upper 8).

For me, one sign of Messiaen's being an achieved mystic is that the cosmic consciousness of the eighth center—absent from most Western music, as it is from most of the movements of the *Quartet for the End of Time*—is wonderfully present in the last. Here, the transcendental longing of the earlier movements is fulfilled, as we arrive at the goal of both Catholic and yogic mysticism: union with the divine.

25

The Evolving Mystics:
Stockhausen and Rautavaara

In the informal schema that I've developed for describing the music of the twentieth century in spiritual terms, the would-be mystics are composers who are fascinated by the mystical aspects of music but who attempt to control the compositional process with a rigid, often mathematical, system. Doing so confines their music to the level of the thinking mind.

Composers of this type usually lose the ability to express transcendent states in their music, such as the expanded consciousness of the seventh center and the cosmic consciousness of the eighth. Their egos have blocked their ability to access the soul or supermind for musical inspiration.

The sometime mystics are composers who may or may not be fascinated by the mystical aspects of music. Occasionally, whether intentionally or not, they're able to compose passages or pieces that access the seventh or eighth centers.

Composers of this type are more open to inspiration from the soul or supermind. But this openness may disappear as a result of fear of the soul, especially if they develop a rigid compositional system. Some composers of this type, like Bartók, may make the transition from thinking mind to higher mind.

The achieved mystics are composers who are not only deeply committed to developing the mystical or religious aspects of their music, but also regularly able to access the seventh and eighth centers. They're open to inspiration from the soul or supermind, which guides their compositional process. But, like Messiaen, they may lose their connection with the divine source of their music if they adopt an overly intellectual compositional system.

Composers of this type have left the thinking mind behind but may not have progressed beyond the higher mind. Scriabin, Messiaen, and Bruckner are all higher mind composers of this type. Mahler was on his way to becoming an achieved mystic but didn't live long enough to complete the transition from thinking to higher mind.

In the present chapter, I introduce the concept of *evolving* mystics. These are the composers who are committed to expressing mystical or religious ideas in their music, can access the seventh and eighth centers freely, receive inspiration from the soul or supermind, and have progressed to or beyond the level of higher mind.

Like Wagner, such composers are evolving toward oneness with the source of all life, passing through the levels of higher, illumined, and intuitive mind, on their way to composing from the overmind. Their music is a record of that journey, a series of progressive initiations that can guide us on our own spiritual paths.

The evolving mystics are the great musical teachers in the yoga of listening. When we meditate upon the works of such composers, in the words of David Tame, "the energies and states of consciousness necessary for spiritual attainment and initiation are transferred to us."[1]

Has the twentieth century produced any evolving musical mystics? At various points in my listening career, I've believed so. For example, I've always been deeply moved by the music of Swiss composer Frank Martin (1890–1974), whose Mass for Double Choir is a masterpiece of twentieth-century sacred music. Some of his instrumental music, such as the Petite Symphonie Concertante, end in a blaze of radiance. Martin may have been a higher mind composer. Toward the end of his life, however, like many composers of his generation, he adopted the twelve-tone system.

At one time, I had my eye on the American composer George Crumb as a possible evolving mystic. He produced a series of mystical masterworks in the 1970s, including *Black Angels*, *Vox Balanae*, the two volumes of pieces for amplified piano called *Makrokosmos*, and *Music for a Summer Evening*, each of which I've mentioned at some point in this book. But I've found nothing he has written since then to be as compelling, and he seems to compose fewer pieces with each passing year. Crumb may have achieved the level of higher mind, but he seems to have lost touch with the source of his inspiration.

Joseph Schwantner is another American composer I might once have nominated for the role of evolving mystic. He, like Crumb, produced a series of mystical masterpieces, including *Sparrows*, *Magabunda* (*Witchnomad*), and *Aftertones of Infinity*, an orchestral piece for which he won the Pulitzer Prize in

1979. Subsequently, he began to repeat himself rather than evolve. Schwantner may been a visionary thinking mind composer who got stuck on his way to becoming a higher mind composer.

The Estonian composer Ärvo Pärt, whose *Cantus in Memory of Benjamin Britten* I mentioned in chapter 1, is another possible candidate for the status of evolving mystic. I believe him at least to be a higher mind composer, based on the few pieces of his that I know. But I would need to familiarize myself more thoroughly with his work to determine whether he has evolved beyond that point.

In the yoga of listening, Pärt's composition *Fratres*, which exists in arrangements for a wide variety of instrumental ensembles, makes an excellent focus for meditation. It's an example of lower 7 music, a solemn and ceremonial approach to the divine, about eleven minutes in length.

An American composer named Morten Lauridsen (b. 1943) has also come to my attention as a possible evolving mystic whose music I intend to look into more fully. I've been spiritually moved by his sacred choral compositions *Lux Aeterna* (*Eternal Light*) and *O Magnum Mysterium* (*O Great Mystery*), and have enjoyed a number of secular works, also for chorus, such as *Les Chansons de Roses* (*Songs of Roses*), based on French poems by my favorite poet, Rainer Maria Rilke.

The two living composers that I consider most likely to be evolving mystics are Karlheinz Stockhausen (b. 1929), from Germany, and Einojuhani Rautavaara (b. 1929), from Finland.

Karlheinz Stockhausen

Stockhausen was a pioneer of electronic music in the 1950s. He was a student of Messiaen and one of the first composers to extend the principles of serialism beyond pitch to include other components of a musical work, from rhythm to expression (articulation, volume, and timbre) to form. The resulting compositional method came to be called total serialism. If this were Stockhausen's only contribution to music, I would have to classify him as a thinking mind composer.

Stockhausen's experiments with cutting, splicing, and looping electronic tape led to an early wave of popularity. He became a top earner for Deutsche Gramophon in the category of contemporary classical music, surpassed only by Stravinsky. He was even honored with two "Greatest Hits" albums.

The Beatles acknowledged Stockhausen's influence on pop culture by including his photograph in the collage on the cover of *Sgt. Pepper's Lonely Hearts Club Band*. The composer's fame eventually declined, however, due to "a very personal religious-spiritual conception of music"[2]—in other words, his mysticism. Stockhausen claims to have come from a more advanced technological and musical civilization connected with the star Sirius, where he "completed [his] musical education."[3]

Stockhausen's musical and spiritual education has indeed been diverse. He began life as a Catholic and was later attracted to Buddhism, the Mayan and Aztec cultures, and the music and theatrical performances of the Indonesian island of Bali. The Hindu and Moslem religions have also influenced his work, as well as his 1971 discovery of *The Urantia Book*, a New-Age scripture channeled from extraterrestrials between 1928 and 1935. Sri Aurobindo and Hazrat Inayat Khan were also important influences.

Stockhausen believes in reincarnation and claims that his interest in different cultures reflects his past lives. He also believes that life on other planets may have evolved to the point of producing musical cultures that may be superior to ours. He looks forward to contact and exchange with such cultures and has even included shortwave radios in some compositions, hoping that he might receive not only terrestrial transmissions, but also extraterrestrial ones.

Stockhausen, like Scriabin, believes that his music contains "new vibrations" that may transmit "laws of the universe." Stockhausen also feels that his music reflects both "the sufferings of sensory existence" and "the transcendental life of the spirit," or "the beast and the angel in man." His dream is that some aspects of his music might "transport us to worlds far removed from our planet."[4]

In the mid-1970s, Stockhausen embarked on an ambitious project called *Licht* (*Light*) that dwarfs Wagner's achievement in the four-night *Ring* cycle and Scriabin's plans for a seven-night *Mysterium* intended to end the world as we know it. *Licht* is a series of seven operas, each of which takes its name from a day of the week.

These operas use both traditional (often amplified) instruments, synthesizers, and computer-generated music. Only three singing characters are involved: the archangel Michael, the fallen angel Lucifer, and the progenitrix of humankind, Eve.

Licht's opposition of Michael and Lucifer has its origins in *The Urantia Book*. In the opera series, Lucifer symbolizes "dissenting intellect" and Michael "affirmative spirituality."[5] The electronics, as in many of Stockhausen's other pieces, represent a "transcendental reality."[6]

Each of *Licht*'s three singing characters is associated with an instrument and its player, as well as a dancer, whose repertoire of movements and gestures is carefully notated in the score. Like Wagner, Stockhausen wrote his own texts for *Licht*. His hope was that his use of wordplay, archetypal situations, and transcendental characters would act directly on the consciousness of his audience and alter it.

Stockhausen states, "Music is mathematics, the mathematics of listening, mathematics for the ears."[7] He has invented a method of what he calls "super-formula" composition, which determines the length of each opera, as well as that of individual sections, and the musical pitches and rhythms to be employed.

Little of *Licht* is presently available on commercially produced CD. I would be interested to hear whether Stockhausen's method of super-formula composition allows him to access the seventh and eighth centers. As we've seen, compositional systems can often prevent the creation of music of the soul.

Stockhausen, like Wagner, likes to design impressive stage spectacles that go beyond what has ever been attempted in opera. *Mittwoch* (*Wednesday*), for example, employs a "helicopter quartet." Each member of a string quartet is supposed to fly aboard a separate helicopter, while the sounds and sights of their journeys are relayed to video screens and loudspeakers in the concert hall.

Also like Wagner, Stockhausen is always seeking to improve the conditions at contemporary opera houses:

> I want a chorus of excellent young people, who know how to sing from memory, and who know how to move about, and who are prepared to rehearse in separate sections, and I want them arranged in such a way that the stage looks better than the paintings of William Blake. Create for me earthy roads in the form of a spiral, a sky made of light alone.[8]

To encourage such improvements, Stockhausen has established a summer music program for young people, in which they come to the Bavarian village of Kürten—where he lives in a hexagonal house of his own design in the forest—to learn to perform and analyze his music under ideal conditions. This is Stockhausen's version of Wagner's Bayreuth Festival, where the world premieres of new works are often undertaken by master teachers who've devoted their musical careers to the exact realization of the Master's extremely demanding scores.

Not since Bach has Germany seen such an intergenerational musical cottage industry as Stockhausen's. The highly prolific composer is simultaneously engaged in salvaging the deteriorating tapes of his earliest electronic compositions, creating new works, supervising the performances and analysis of his music during the summer music program, involving himself with other performances and festivals of his music throughout the world, producing deluxe editions of his scores with his own publishing house, and overseeing an "offi-cial" mail-order CD series of his compositions. Several of Stockhausen's chil-dren are also musicians: a trumpeter (Markus), a pianist (daughter Majella), and a composer (Simon), whom he considers to be his successor.

According to *The New Grove Dictionary of Music and Musicians*, 2nd edition, Stockhausen sees his work

> not as messianic revelation, but as patient steps towards his own spir-itual evolution, which also, perhaps more importantly, may facilitate the passage of willing listeners to similar goals.[9]

One piece by Stockhausen that perhaps could facilitate the spiritual evolu-tion of willing listeners is *Stimmung*, composed in 1968.[10] The German title has a multitude of meanings, including *tuning, mood, frame of mind*, and *impres-sion*. Stockhausen wrote the piece after a visit to the ancient ruins of Mexico in which he tried to enter the frame of mind of the Aztecs, Maya, and other peoples who constructed them.

Stimmung requires six solo voices, three female and three male. The text is a collage of syllables, vowels, and words from many languages, including the names of the days of the week in German and English, and of gods from many of the world's religious traditions, including ancient Egyptian and Greek, Aztec, Hindu, Native American, and Australian Aboriginal. There are also two erotic poems in German by Stockhausen himself.

Perhaps the most unusual thing about *Stimmung* is the singing technique. Try singing the vowel sound *oo* (as in *moo*) on a single low pitch, with lips tightly pursed, then gradually transform the vowel sound to *ee* (as in *we*) with-out changing the pitch. Do this several times. If you listen carefully, you'll hear an interesting halo of sounds above the pitch that you're singing. As you move from the first vowel to the second, this halo of what are called *harmonics* will gradually change, creating the illusion of a melody hovering over the pitch you're singing, which is called the *fundamental*.

Stimmung is the first fully notated piece in the history of Western music to be based on this technique, which is found throughout the world in cer-tain kinds of chanting. Listening to the melodies and harmonies created by the harmonics shifting above their fundamentals is fascinating, even mes-merizing.

In the yoga of listening, *Stimmung* is an excellent piece to meditate to. Besides targeting the expanded consciousness of the seventh center, it could be used to develop three aspects of traditional yogic meditation. First, because it's based on just six of the twelve notes of the chromatic scale, its harmonic and melodic language is somewhat restricted. Listening to seventy minutes of such music is an exercise in what the yogis call sense restraint.

Second, *Stimmung* can help develop what the yogis call one-pointedness of mind. The trick is to keep bringing the focus of the mind back to the music.

Third, the constant repetition of words, syllables, and vowel sounds is similar to the chanting practices of mantra yoga. The "magic names" of the gods, as Stockhausen calls them, serve to reinforce the sacred or mantric intentions of the piece.

The first time I listened to *Stimmung*, while lying on the couch and using headphones, I went into a deep state of meditation that lasted about twenty minutes. I was unaware of my body, and found myself continually pulled deeper and deeper into the peculiar sonic universe of the piece. Certain sound combinations vibrated in my head in ways that seemed delightful, ecstatic, even luminous. Gradually, I became more and more aware of the subtle melodies created by the harmonics.

After that first twenty minutes, however, I began to become impatient, wanted to move around, couldn't keep my mind consistently focused on the music. Rather than considering the piece boring or monotonous, however, I saw it as a challenge similar to the one I encountered in high school when I began listening to Bruckner's slow-moving compositions. The trick would be for me to keep working on one-pointedness of mind until I was able to get through the whole of *Stimmung* without distraction. Doing so could perhaps lead to TMEs as ecstatic as those I've had while listening to Bruckner.

Einojuhani Rautavaara

Rautavaara began his career composing in the 1950s neoclassical style that prevailed in Finland after the Second World War. After studies in America, Austria, and Cologne, he went the way of most composers of his generation: In 1957, he adopted the twelve-tone method of composition.

Something in him instinctively recoiled against this rational, mathematical approach to composition, because he immediately began to subvert it. His Third Symphony, completed in 1960, though based on a twelve-tone row, harks back to Bruckner. Rautavaara even quotes the opening horn-call of the latter's Fourth Symphony. Yet Rautavaara's own Fourth Symphony, called *Arabescata* (1962), was composed in accord with strict serialist principles.

In 1968, ten years after his adoption of serialism, Rautavaara was planning a new piece for orchestra based on James Joyce's experimental novel *Finnegans Wake*, in which all of the characters are asleep and dreaming, and the story is told in a mumbled, only partially intelligible, dream language. The work would be serialist in structure, with many musico-literary references to the two opening paragraphs of Joyce's novel.

According to the composer, something strange happened after he'd written about fifty bars of the piece:

> The music no longer agreed to submit to becoming literary symbols. It was emancipated. It refused to obey me, it showed a complete disrespect for Joyce and any plans I might have had for it.[11]

The result was *Anadyomene* (*Adoration of Aphrodite*), a twelve-minute work that, in Rautavaara's words, had "wrenched itself free (and liberated me) from the serial straitjacket and quasi-scientific thinking" about music. Ever since that time, Rautavaara has allowed his music to develop organically, letting each piece determine its own form.

Anadyomene is romantic in breadth and gesture, yet modern in sonority. Like much of Bruckner, it accesses the lower (sublime) and middle (noble) range of the seventh center. Also, as in Bruckner, the piece is macrorhythmically composed throughout, in great accumulating and dissipating waves of sound.

The sudden shift in direction in Rautavaara's work that occurred while he was composing *Anadyomene* represents the beginning of his movement from thinking mind to higher mind composer. The needs of a deeper layer of Rautavaara's being had asserted themselves: what Charles calls the soul, and Sri Aurobindo, the supermind.

Composers choose hyperrational methods of composing because their egos are afraid of the soul. They want to control every aspect of a musical composition to make sure that the soul has no way of asserting its needs. The ego is terrified when it's confronted by what feels like a foreign and superior spiritual force, the soul or supermind.

Twentieth-century civilization, with its scientific and materialist beliefs, has alienated many people from the soul. As the century progressed, the result was music that gradually lost all but its intellectual (sixth center) appeal.

In Rautavaara's next work, the First Piano Concerto of 1969, it's as if all the soul-based energy, or life force, that had been repressed during his ten years as a serialist came rushing through him. I know of no other piece like it in the history of Western music. It's the musical equivalent of a kundalini awakening that has exuberantly broken through all internal obstructions and opened each center on the continuum of human potential, from the first through the upper, ecstatic, range of the seventh, touching even the eighth for the briefest of moments in its final movement.

This moment of lower to middle 8 music is an odd chorale-like gesture in which the horns predominate. It goes by so quickly that it might be missed by someone who doesn't know Rautavaara's music well. Similar gestures of longer duration, which makes them easier to identify, occur in some of his later works.

The dominant center in the first movement is middle 7 (nobility, grandeur). In most of the second movement, it's lower 7, just at the point where it turns into the middle range (devotion). After a dramatic solo cadenza that represents the crisis point between the sixth and seventh centers (irrationality), and which draws heavily on the intensity of the third center, the brief final movement takes off from the upper 5 exuberance of Gershwin-like jazz into the mystical ecstasy of upper 7.

The First Piano Concerto is a piece that I go back to again and again, constantly amazed by its brilliance and spiritual depth. But it's not as well known as the 1972 work *Cantus Arcticus*, subtitled *Concerto for Birds and Orchestra*. This is Rautavaara's most frequently performed orchestral piece. *Cantus Arcticus* is no less amazing than the Piano Concerto, although for different reasons.

The birdsongs were taped in the Arctic Circle; hence the title of the piece. They were electronically enhanced for playback in the concert hall, rather than meticulously notated for orchestral instruments, as were Messiaen's.

Rautavaara says that, in the first movement, entitled "The Marsh," the entry of the string instruments "might be interpreted as the voice and mood of a person walking in the wilds."[12] The predominant center is the seventh: lower 7 for the sublimity of nature, and middle 7 for the human love of nature.

The middle movement, "Melancholy," is a rare, fully realized example of lower 8 (compassion) music, much like Barber's Adagio for Strings. Here, the melancholy mood of the person walking in the wilds seems to be elevated and consoled by his presence amid the beauties of nature.[13]

The third, and final, movement of *Cantus Arcticus*, "Swans Migrating," is my favorite. The honking swans are heard throughout. As the piece progresses, it seems as if their numbers are constantly increasing. Once again, as in the first movement, the beginning targets lower 7, which soon rises, with the strings and brass, to the sweeping grandeur of middle 7.

I always feel not merely uplifted by this music, but also lifted up, as if I were flying with the swans. In the yoga of listening, this movement could serve as a focal point for those interested in developing astral projection skills. It invokes feelings similar to those I've experienced in astral flights over a physical landscape.

Chief among Rautavaara's compositions are those in his Angel Series. This series began in 1978 with the composition of a twenty-minute orchestral tone poem called *Angels and Visitations*. Other works in the series include a Concerto for Double Bass and Orchestra, subtitled *Angel of Dusk* (1980); a work for brass ensemble entitled *Playgrounds for Angels* (1981); and the Seventh Symphony, subtitled *Angel of Light* (1994–1995).

The composer says that the angels in these works

> didn't come from fairytales or religious kitsch, but from the conviction that other realities exist beyond those we are normally aware of, entirely different forms of consciousness. From this alien reality, creatures rise up which could be called angels. They may bear some resemblance to the visions of William Blake, and are certainly related to Rainer Maria Rilke's awe-inspiring figures of holy dread.[14]

At this point in his narrative, Rautavaara quotes the opening lines of the first of Rilke's *Duino Elegies* (see chapter 14, p. 186 for my translation of these lines). Rilke's description of angels as both beautiful and terrifying brought back a nightmarish, dreamlike "vision" from Rautavaara's childhood, which occurred around the time that he was seven or eight years of age:

> Again and again in my dreams, an enormous, grey, powerful, silent creature would approach me and clasp me in its arms so that I feared its mighty presence would suffocate me. I struggled for dear life—as one is supposed to wrestle with an angel—until I awoke. The figure came back night after night, and I spent the days fearing its return. Finally, after dozens of these battles, I learned to surrender, to throw myself into the creature, to become part of it, and after a while the nocturnal visits ended.[15]

The piece inspired by this recollection, *Angels and Visitations*, is one of my favorites. It runs the gamut from the visionary (upper 6) desire to illustrate this angelic visitation in music to lower 8 compassion and middle 8 grace, in what the composer calls a "Palestrina-like violin texture."[16] (In chapter 15, I pointed out that Palestrina, in his Pope Marcellus Mass, created an unusually extended period of exposure to the middle range of the eighth center.)

Angels and Visitations also touches on the crisis point between the sixth and seventh centers, with music that "sounds like a riotous pack of demons."[17] Such music represents the blind terror of the time- and space-bound ego at the alienness of the soul, or any other nonphysical being that resides outside of space and time, such as an angel. There are also moments of the sublime (lower 7) that correspond to Rilke's idea that beauty is the beginning of terror, and moments of nobility, glory, or grandeur (middle 7).

The composer claims that his angel-based music gives "expression to powerful, contradictory, archetypal associations."[18] It's not intended to be a musical narrative of angelic visitations to the composer. Even so, I recognize in this piece the emotional tenor of my own "angelic" visitations, as recorded in *Otherwhere*:

> On several occasions I've been awakened in the middle of the night by a nonphysical entity standing at the foot of my bed. This being appears to be shrouded entirely in black. A hood obscures its face. A bright light surrounds the entity, like the sun's corona during a total eclipse. The entity grasps my big toe and gently shakes my foot until I awaken. It then takes me on a journey into nonphysical reality.[19]

I discuss the most recent work in Rautavaara's Angel Series at the end of the chapter.

Another favorite of mine is the eight-minute orchestral work *Apotheosis*, originally the last movement of Rautavaara's Sixth Symphony. That symphony, subtitled *Vincentiana*, was based on themes from the composer's opera about the painter Vincent van Gogh. The symphony included a part for synthesizer that was supposed to represent the strange world of van Gogh's paintings. *Apotheosis* was revised so that it could be performed without the synthesizer and stand alone.

Listening to the one available recording of *Apotheosis*,[20] I felt as if the music had placed me in a closer than usual relationship with the cosmic normative balance. The music seemed to be radiating a gentle, yet irresistible, sense of goodness, to which I had to conform. I was being lifted up toward oneness with this higher power. The music even expressed the painfulness of a spiritual opening that, like an encounter with Rilke's angel, goes beyond one's capacity to embrace or endure it.

Not all of Rautavaara's work is likely to appeal to the listener who is hoping to achieve transcendent musical experiences. Some of it is serial or experimental; some even sounds like movie music, according to his harsher critics. But I have yet to encounter in the music of any other living composer such a sense of closeness to the soul or God as I do in the best of Rautavaara.

For decades, composers and critics have been exposed to music that has stripped away every center but the intellectual sixth on the continuum of human potential. At the same time, that continuum has been kept alive in our consciousness by composers for film. Rautavaara has been gradually adding back the sensuous, dramatic, emotional, joyful, and spiritual qualities of music that the serialists and avant-gardists of the latter half of the twentieth century eliminated, so it makes sense to compare his music to that for films.

Some of the passages that sound like film music may not be the fault of the composer. I suspect that most conductors and orchestras don't yet know how to reveal the full glory of Rautavaara's music.

I often find myself dissatisfied with one of his pieces until I discover another recording that unexpectedly reveals new dimensions and depth. What sounds like the sublimity of lower 7 in one recording could reveal itself as the compassion of lower 8 in another, as I discovered in comparing two recordings of the second movement of the *Cantus Arcticus*.

There may come a time when more of Rautavaara's music becomes capable of producing life-changing transcendent musical experiences than is presently the case. Bringing out such musical revelations, as in the case of Bruckner's symphonies, will require conductors of great spiritual sensitivity.

Rautavaara began his career as an upper 6 (visionary) thinking mind composer. During his serial period, he descended into the formalism of middle 6. Formal play has continued to be an important part of his compositional process, but once he shook off the "straitjacket" of serialism, Rautavaara's best music, like Bruckner's, began to emanate from the lower 7 range, making him a higher mind composer.

In becoming acquainted with Rautavaara's work from the 1990s, I've begun to suspect that the originating center has continued to rise. Rautavaara may now be composing from middle 7, from which so many of the late masterpieces of Western music have derived. This would make him an illumined mind composer. His Eighth Symphony, completed in 1999 and subtitled *The Journey*, is such a late masterpiece, spanning the continuum of human potential from the first through the middle of the seventh center.

The Essential Rautavaara is an excellent introduction to this composer's music.[21] It contains *Cantus Arcticus*, the third movement of the Seventh Symphony (*Angel of Light*), and the whole of the First Piano Concerto.

The recording also includes two delightful early pieces, from Rautavaara's pre-serialist days, *The Fiddlers* and *Requiem for Our Time*, and a tone poem from 1995 entitled *Isle of Bliss*. The latter focuses on the exuberance of upper 5, the bittersweet yearning of middle 4, and the transcendental longing of lower to middle 7.

Rautavaara is a masterful writer for chorus. He has produced much sacred choral music, as well as settings of poems by twentieth-century literary favorites such as Rilke and Federico García Lorca. His *Vigilia* of 1972, written to accompany the all-night vigil celebrated by the Orthodox Church in honor of Saint John the Baptist, is one of the great sacred choral works of the last half of the last century.[22]

Another piece by Rautavaara that I enjoy is *True & False Unicorn*, based on an English text by the California beat poet and experimental filmmaker James Broughton. It's an allegory of the artist's role in society.

The premise of the poem is that the characters depicted in a medieval tapestry come to life and speak about the unicorn, which is its chief feature. These characters include the unicorn himself, the lion on the British coat of arms, "Sigmund of Vienna" (Freud, of course), a virgin, the Queen of Byzantium, Queen Victoria, Big Black Sambo, and several constellations of the zodiac.

The poem reflects, with surrealistic irony, on the artist's archetypal quest for identity. The unicorn is painfully aware of the dangers of getting caught up in his own myth (especially his preference for the world of the imagination over that of everyday life), as well as in the projections of others, who want to see him as an object of lust or romantic desire, a victim of self-delusion, a spiritual savior, a wayward child who needs to be tamed, and a threat to the social order.

True unicorns are the artists who discover themselves through following their unique vision of the world. This vision is symbolized by the single horn growing out of the unicorn's forehead. In the yogic tradition, this is where the sixth chakra, or third eye, is. False unicorns are the artists who lose themselves in their own myths or the projections of others.

The music ranges from the energetic lower 7 sublimity of section 1 down to the middle 1 interest of section 12, and back up to an apotheosis of middle 7 nobility in the final section. It's a wonderfully surreal, even humorous, work, completely unpredictable. I especially love the collage of national anthems, including that of the United Kingdom, France, Austria, and the United States, sung piously (middle 7) to completely ridiculous words, with jazz riffs between verses (lower 6 humor), in section 9.

Rautavaara has composed both human and ethereal music, to use Cyril Scott's terms. The latter might have linked Rautavaara's *Cantus Arcticus* to the lower devic realm of nature spirits and his Angel Series to the upper seraphic realm. Rautavaara's music, such as *Apotheosis*, also contains moments of apparent illumination that seem to go beyond the devic plane, drawing upon what Scott called the buddhic.

We've already seen that Scott's deva-inspired music accesses the seventh center in the continuum of human potential and that buddhic music accesses the eighth. Scott might have recognized in Rautavaara a worthy addition to his list of deva-inspired composers—perhaps representing the next evolutionary step beyond Scriabin, who never got past composing from the higher mind. As noted, since the 1990s, Rautavaara seems to have been composing from the illumined mind.

Whether or not Rautavaara would agree with the term *deva-inspired*, or with my model of the continuum of human potential, I consider him to be in the forefront of the last century's spiritual composers. I honor his willingness to listen within himself, regardless of prevailing musical fashions, to what his own music wants to be—whether it comes from his unconscious, as he sees it, or the soul, God, or supermind.

For me, Rautavaara has become, like Bruckner, a spiritual teacher. But he's something more than the monklike Bruckner was: a fully realized human being, for whom the process of musical composition has provided a means of self-actualization, and whose succession of works records the journey on that most spiritual of paths.

Angel of Light

While researching Rautavaara, I found this anonymous review (on Amazon.com) of Rautavaara's Seventh Symphony, *Angel of Light*, composed in 1994 to 1995:

> My reaction to the third movement of this astounding work was unlike any I've ever had. I could feel my mind growing to perceive this wondrous music. I could not move—I couldn't do anything save listen. It was one of the most incredible experiences of my life.

Clearly, this reviewer had a TME, including a sense of expanding consciousness and loss of awareness of the body—just what I would expect from music that touches the eighth center.

A second reviewer, identifying himself only as a professional conductor, called Rautavaara's symphony a "revelation" and "catharsis." He went on to say, "The spiritual power of this symphony has completely changed my philosophy on the meaning of music, and music in our time." That's another effect that I've noticed about eighth center music: After listening to it, in the words of Rilke, "You must change your life."

The first and last movements of the Seventh Symphony exemplify Rautavaara's characteristic mix of lower (sublime) and middle 7 (nobility) music. The second movement, an often shrill scherzo reminiscent of Prokofiev or Shostakovich, runs the gamut from the humor of lower 6 to the quasi-Mahlerian sarcasm and psychic pain of the crisis point between the sixth and seventh centers.

The radiant third movement, entitled in Italian "Come un sogno" ("Like a Dream"), is an example of eighth center music. The dominant center lies between the lower range of compassion and the middle range of grace. The music exudes a serenity beyond all human feeling—what Scott would have called seraphic, if not buddhic love.

About two thirds of the way through the movement, this serenity becomes clouded. It's as if someone experiencing samadhi (bliss) in meditation—or the angel of the title—has temporarily fallen back into the realm of human emotion, and then recovers her serenity just in time.[23]

The first time I played this movement of *Angel of Light* for my composer friend Ruth, she remarked that it "sounds like home." She didn't mean her apartment in Boston but the nonphysical home of the soul.

In the yoga of listening, this ten-minute exposure to the eighth center can put us in touch with the source of all life, helping us to feel more at home in ourselves and the world. I listen to it often, either to stabilize my state of consciousness if I'm experiencing emotional turmoil or to remind myself of the inner peace that's the goal of yogic practice: a sense of oneness with the Source.

Finale

26

Achieving Transcendent Musical Experiences

The goal of the yoga of listening is for listeners, performers, and composers to achieve transcendental musical experiences (TMEs). In part 1, "Music and the Soul," I defined TMEs as musical experiences in which one's relationship with some aspect of life, whether physical, emotional, intellectual, or spiritual, has been immeasurably enriched or enhanced. I gave many examples of TMEs, explained how they arise from fluctuations of life force produced by the soul, and related them to the ancient yogic ideas of kundalini energy and the chakras, or psychic energy centers of the body.

In part 2, "The Yoga of Listening," I developed a spiritual practice that allows listeners, performers, and composers to achieve TMEs through meditative listening to music. I generated a continuum of human potential, pointing out how listening to different types of music can enable our physical, emotional, intellectual, and spiritual growth. I also provided examples of music that targets each of the eight centers along this continuum and explained how such music can be used in the yoga of listening to achieve therapeutic, developmental, integrative, and transcendent goals.

In part 3, "Music of the Soul," I explained how composers and performers can become spiritual teachers for us. Through the yogic practice of transmission, the wisdom encoded in their music can be passed on to us as listeners, thereby enhancing our capacity for TMEs. I demonstrated how the transcendental stages of consciousness defined by Sri Aurobindo—higher mind, illumined mind, intuitive mind, and overmind—have shown up in the works of some of the greatest composers of Western classical music. These composers have gone beyond the usual source of music in the thinking mind to produce a genuine music of the soul.

Throughout the book, I've provided exercises in the yoga of listening, pointing out pieces that seem likely to induce TMEs and providing information about the spiritual wisdom encoded therein. Now I would like to offer some practical advice on how listeners, performers, and composers can achieve their own TMEs.

Achieving TMEs as Listeners

My friend Jennifer, a psychotherapist, had a TME when attending a concert by Libana, an a capella women's choral group that celebrates the musical history and traditions of women. The evening of the concert coincided with a lunar eclipse.

The concert was held at a small church more than an hour by car from Boston. The audience filled the nave and spilled out into the foyer. Many audience members stood outside to watch the eclipse until the concert started.

A member of Libana introduced the evening, welcoming both the audience and the eclipse. She announced that the group would begin the program with a song dedicated to the period of darkness at new moon when new ideas, plans, and inspirations are born. She said that the eclipse represented the "dark of the moon" in a different but meaningful way.

Jennifer felt a "surge of excitement" when she heard this announcement. She was hoping that Libana would open with this song, because it had "personal meaning" for her. She had loved the song when she first heard it, and when she and her husband were on vacation she had sung it at night while they were "driving in an open jeep along roads filled with the scent of tropical jungle."

Jennifer reports that when the women's voices of Libana came together in the song, "I was filled with happiness, gratitude, appreciation, and poignancy. My feelings melded and peaked, and I was moved to tears. I was grateful to the women of Libana for singing together for twenty-five years, for their commitment to music, nature, and women's musical tradition, for their strength, connection, and the love they emanated, and for the clarity of their voices, which filled the hall and myself.

"I felt their music reach out to the audience and bring us together. During that song, for the rest of the concert, and afterward, in the cold air where the moon shone again brightly, I was transported, filled, connected to myself and the world."

Jennifer has described an ideal set of inner and outer conditions for creating a TME as a listener. Among the outer conditions are the live concert, a large audience, a favorite group and song, and a special occasion (the eclipse). Among the inner conditions are a sense of excitement, personal associations with the music, and an open heart created through gratitude and appreciation for the group and the music.

I've often found that TMEs occur when a trigger or catalyst brings such inner and outer conditions together, creating a state of consciousness that I call *inner equals outer.* In this state, the listener feels a coincidence, synchronicity, or congruence between her internal and external realities. The sense of connectedness that Jennifer describes in her TME is often a result of this state of inner equals outer. In her case, the trigger was the resonance between the external eclipse, the song about the dark of the moon, and her internal associations with that song.

The state of inner equals outer has the four characteristics of a mystical experience described by William James. First, it's ineffable, in that it can't be easily described in words.

Second, it's noetic, in that it contains an element of illumination or wisdom that allows inner experience to be interpreted in the light of outer experience and vice versa—each seems to represent or be symbolic of the other. Such a state of knowledge, in James's words, seems "full of significance and importance."[1]

Third, the state of inner equals outer is transient. Jennifer enjoyed the sense of connectedness to the world that resulted from it during the concert and for a while afterward, by the light of the moon. Although she didn't include this information in her narrative, at some point, of course, she returned to her ordinary state of consciousness.

Finally, the state of inner equals outer is achieved passively, rather than as an act of will, although it may be preceded by physical or spiritual practices intended to facilitate it. Jennifer was ideally prepared for her TME. She was familiar with Libana's music and the song about the dark of the moon. She had made the effort to get to the concert, driving more than an hour to get there. She was in an excited, grateful, receptive mood.

Charles says that the state of inner equals outer occurs when we're feeling connected and at one with our souls. According to Charles, "Symbols are a means consciousness uses to monitor its own development." Thus, everything that we experience in our lives on Earth is in some way symbolic of our spiritual growth. When we're able to perceive that symbolism, we're seeing our lives from the soul's perspective.

When seeing things from the soul's perspective, we may weep, as Jennifer did during her TME. As I explained in chapter 3, being moved to tears is a sign that we've experienced a great truth about ourselves or the world. The soul uses our tears to highlight this fact.

Jennifer also speaks of the love that emanated from the performers, as well as their commitment to women's music and nature. She was speaking about the values represented by the women of Libana and their music.

As I pointed out in chapter 16, when people who share the same values come together, their energy fields open up and meld with each other, creating a value field. In such a value field, we feel safer, more deeply connected, and perhaps even one with each other.

Jennifer was experiencing such a value field when she said that the music of Libana reached out to the audience members and brought them together. The creation of a value field is in part the responsibility of the performers, but to enjoy the spiritual opening that such a field can produce, one must be receptive to it, as Jennifer was to the values expressed by Libana. Gratitude and appreciation for performers, composers, and the values they represent can create such receptivity.

From Jennifer's TME, it may be possible to derive a blueprint for achieving TMEs as listeners. First, we should follow our pleasure.

As the playwright George Bernard Shaw says, "You use a glass mirror to see your face: you use works of art to see your soul." The music that we love is an outpicturing of our souls. It shows us who we are in that moment or who we could become, how much of the continuum of human potential we've realized or are drawn to realize. In the case of music that touches the crisis points between the centers, it shows us wayward reflections to avoid becoming.

Second, we should choose with care the composers and performers who will be our spiritual teachers. The best spiritual teachers in music are those who reflect our highest values and possibilities for physical, emotional, intellectual, and spiritual growth.

Third, we should make ourselves ideally receptive to these values, both by living them and by frequent exposure to the favorite music of our chosen teachers. If possible, we should attend live concerts that involve our teachers or their music. We can then open ourselves to the value field that results from being with others who share our values, including our love for our spiritual teachers and their music.

A sense of gratitude and appreciation for the composers and performers involved and for their values can make us more receptive to this value field and the feeling of oneness with other audience members that it induces. Sometimes this oneness manifests itself as joy or ecstasy, at others as a solemn sense of being in the presence of the sacred. In either case, it can help us overcome our feelings of loneliness and separation from the rest of humanity.

Finally, in all that we do, we should try to see the soul's perspective on things. We should notice the fluctuations in life force that indicate when we're realizing the soul's master plan and when we're not.

Increases in life-force flow indicate that we're on the soul's path. Such increases are accompanied by feelings of satisfaction, happiness, even ecstasy. Declines in life-force flow indicate that we're off the soul's path. Such declines are accompanied by feelings of dissatisfaction, unhappiness, even depression.

We should keep our eyes open for symbols that can help us monitor our development. I've learned from years of interpreting my dreams that many events in waking life can be interpreted symbolically as well. The practice of doing so keeps me alert to coincidences and synchronicities, which are often triggers for the state of inner equals outer. As a result of this practice, when listening to music that perfectly matches my inner state, I'm more susceptible to TMEs, a sense of oneness with my soul, and the tears of truth that often accompany the state of inner equals outer.

Achieving TMEs as Performers

My friend George, who plays oboe with the Virginia Symphony, has been studying yogic breathing techniques for several years. Once when the orchestra was playing Brahms's Second Symphony in concert, he began practicing yogic breathing on stage, when he wasn't playing.

George's yoga teacher had taught him that a complete breath begins in the pelvis and ends at the palate. During the concert, he had a TME as a result of breathing in this way. George experienced a sense of timelessness, that the energy of the music was carrying him along. He didn't have to think about the points when he had to begin playing again.

George felt fully present. The music seemed to be playing itself through his body. It was easy to fit into the fabric of the orchestral sound, with perfect intonation, rhythmic ease, a sense of "locking in" with other players. He says that he was "letting the music play me and relaying that to the audience."

George's TME, like Jennifer's, also involves the state of inner equals outer. In George's case, the flow of the breath, an internal experience, became equated with the external flow of the music around him.

The blueprint for achieving TMEs as performers, both in ourselves and in the audience, includes all of the elements of the blueprint for listeners. All performers of music were listeners first, and listening to music constantly reinforces their dedication to the art.

While yogic breathing during a performance may be one way of achieving TMEs as performers, an appropriately spiritual attitude is also necessary.

Indian classical musician Ravi Shankar once said that the first step in creating transcendent musical experiences in ourselves and an audience is for performers to "shut out the world" and "go down deep within" themselves.[2] Even the process of warming up and tuning their instruments can allow them to access the deep state of concentration, almost like meditation, that underlies and supports the best performances, those most likely to create TMEs.

Shankar wrote of stepping "onto the threshold" of the *raga*, or piece of music to be played, as if it were a sacred state of consciousness, or temple in sound. Performers who wish to create TMEs in themselves and others should approach the works they play "with feelings of humility, reverence and awe."[3]

In the tradition of classical Indian music, a raga is conceived as a godlike, living spiritual presence. According to Shankar,

> a *raga* is like a living person, and to establish that intimate oneness between music and musician, one must proceed slowly. And when that oneness is achieved, it is the most exhilarating and ecstatic moment, like the supreme heights of the art of love or worship.[4]

In Western music, the blueprint for achieving TMEs as performers requires meditation on what the composer is saying. Performers should attempt to achieve a sense of oneness with the composer by becoming aware of the piece's process configuration and the energy transformations and wisdom encoded within it.

Here, too, the result can be ecstatic, a TME that lets the performer know that a merging of minds has occurred between composer and performer. As I pointed out in chapter 16, such a merging of minds is possible even when the composer has long since died. In performance, in the words of esotericist Geoffrey Hodson, "an instant rapport" can be established with the composer, whether alive or dead, because his music contains "a measure of his egoic life and consciousness."[5]

Yogic practitioners believe that they continue to be guided by gurus who have passed on. As noted above, such guidance takes place telepathically through the sixth, or command, center. That center is active in all Western music, encoding within it the telepathic commands of the composer for performers and listeners to feel, think, or see as he or she does.

Once the merging of minds has taken place between composer and performer, the yogic act of transmission can take place. The energy transformations encoded in the music—the physical, emotional, intellectual, and spiritual wisdom that it contains—may be transmitted from the composer, as guru, through the performer to a receptive audience.

When music is improvised, as in the genres of jazz and classical Indian music, this transmission occurs directly from performer to listener. How would jazz differ if the modes and chord changes it employs were considered as living, sacred beings, like ragas?

When the music is composed, the composer is the sacred being. The performers become vehicles for passing on the wisdom contained in this music, while allowing themselves to be transformed in the process. For this transmission to take place, the performers' attitude must be one of humble devotion, rather than aggressive self-assertion.

Shankar described the TME that links performer and audience as follows:

> In these miraculous moments, when I am so much aware of the great power surging within me and all around me, sympathetic and sensitive listeners are feeling the same emotions. It is a strange mixture of all the intense emotions—pathos, joy, peace, spirituality, eroticism, all flowing together. It is like feeling God.[6]

Pathos, joy, peace, spirituality, and eroticism are points on the continuum of human potential. When the centers they represent are fully active, the result may be a TME for performers and audience members alike. One of the common descriptions of such a peak experience is a sense of union with God.

The continuum of human potential can be used to enhance any performance. Most performers attempt to project either the feeling (fourth center) or the form (sixth center) of a piece. The better performers, of course, project both feeling *and* form. But the best possible performance is one in which *all* of the centers that the composer has targeted are fully functional. Such performances are the most likely to induce TMEs in an audience.

Performers can add the first center (arousal) to the blueprint for achieving TMEs in themselves and an audience by playing the rhythms of a piece as accurately, naturally, and fully coordinated with the rest of the ensemble as possible. A slight pulse at the beginning of each measure often raises the level of arousal produced by this center from mere interest to entrained fascination.

To add the second center (desire) to this blueprint, performers should love the sounds they're producing and those that surround them. Our culture has trouble giving itself permission to experience sensual enjoyment. So, many performers play expressively and intelligently but are unable to project a sensual enjoyment that would greatly increase the power of their playing.

The greatest sensual pleasure in both performers and audience derives from chords that are in tune and properly balanced. Some performers approach the intonation and voicing of chords intellectually, but such things may best be accomplished through sensual enjoyment. An intention to maximize pleasure at the sensual level should naturally lead performers to deeper listening and more or less automatic adjustments of pitch and volume.

To add the third center (intensity) to the blueprint for achieving TMEs, performers should develop a sensitivity to the inner drama of every phrase they play. This inner drama shows itself in the constant interplay of tension and release through fluctuating levels of volume and dissonance.

Most composers mark the large-scale fluctuations of volume in their music to underline the formal and dramatic aspects of the piece. But even the smallest musical motifs have their own shape, in terms of rising and falling volume and level of dissonance—a pattern of implied tension and release. By knowing where each note fits in that pattern, and playing it as naturally and unselfconsciously as possible, performers can add as much brilliance and dramatic fullness to the music as the play of light and darkness does to the subjects of Renaissance paintings—even when the third center, like the first two, is operating in the background.

The expressive qualities that the fourth center lends to music need little comment here. So much music has been written to open the heart center—to express a composer's feelings and transmit them to an audience—that it's the focus of much musical training.

Playing from the heart center becomes a problem only when it's overdone. When this center is targeted at the expense of others that may be active in a piece, the result can seem mawkish or shallow—especially if the performers have prioritized the fourth center over the sixth through ignoring the formal aspects of the piece.

The fifth center is not always active in a piece of music. It's usually absent from pieces that express pathos, yearning, transcendental longing, or, as with Wagner's *Parsifal*, a profound state of emotional and spiritual unrest. Knowing how to suppress it in performance may be just as important as knowing how to add it in.

When this center is dominant, tempo will determine the degree of well-being expressed in the music. It's important for performers to know how to distinguish the proper tempos of lower, middle, and upper 5, and not to drag or rush them.

The fifth center is also involved in the moral aspects of music. The genre or style of such music is an encoded message (and if there are lyrics, often a blatant one) about what feels good, and why, as well as the sense of belonging that comes from surrounding ourselves with others who think and feel in similar ways.

In most classical music, the feel-good group that performers and listeners are invited to join in this way is the brotherhood or sisterhood of humanity, which makes it relatively harmless. Other genres and styles may encourage membership in more questionable in-groups, often involving the crisis points between centers.

It's a good idea for performers to select what they transmit to their audiences with care. Music that targets the crisis points between centers should only be used for educational purposes, as lessons in what to avoid as we realize within ourselves the continuum of human potential.

A disturbing development in music education over the last few decades has been an increasing emphasis on virtuosic instrumental technique, often at the expense of other aspects of music, especially the spiritual. The focus is on playing faster and more perfectly, but not necessarily more expressively, to impress audiences and potential employers.

Virtuosity has always been a part of professional music-making. It can express exuberance, the highest level of the well-being center, but only if it's not overdone. The musical exhibitionism of the crisis point between centers five and six can be as much a result of a performer's choosing a tempo that's too fast for a genuine feeling of exuberance to come through as of the composer's intent. In either case, the failure lies in focusing more on the attempt to impress an audience than on communicating something meaningful about the continuum of human potential.

Much musical training goes into bringing out the formal dimension, or sixth center aspects, of music. I admire performers who play expressively and think like composers.

Purely intellectual performances often seem arid. But an *intelligent* one, which uses the analytic abilities of the sixth center to realize everything that's present in the music, from rhythm to sonority, dramatic intensity to expressive nuance, well-being to wit, formal inventiveness, and visionary flights of fancy, is immensely satisfying, and more likely to create TMEs in an audience. So much music is composed from the sixth center that such intelligence can hardly go wrong, as long as the seventh and eighth centers aren't present, or are touched only briefly.

Playing seventh center music in order to induce TMEs in performers and listeners requires an ability to capture the luminous waves of energy encoded in it—the macrorhythmic waves. Most performers aren't aware of the existence of such waves, which permeate the work of composers who have achieved states of consciousness beyond the thinking mind. The best way for performers to learn how to bring out these waves is to listen to performances in which they're realized, such as the music of Yes described in chapter 18, and the Odeon Trio's recording of Schubert's two Piano Trios, mentioned in chapter 19.

The problem of playing eighth center music in order to induce TMEs seems to be one of recognition, which may require a higher than average level of spiritual development in performers and listeners. For example, I recently heard a recording of the Sixth Brandenburg Concerto of Bach and was surprised to discover that the second movement is an instance of lower 8 compassion. In other performances I've heard of this familiar piece, the second movement was merely heartfelt and pretty.[7]

Frequent exposure to eighth center music, such as that listed in this book, should help performers identify it more easily, and learn how to realize its TME-inducing qualities in concert.

Finally, performers interested in inducing TMEs in themselves and an audience should learn how to create a value field. They must become aware of their values, live them with dedication and passion, and communicate them as deeply as possible through their playing.

The highest values to live by and bring through in one's playing are those that Maslow called the B-values, which include

truth, beauty, goodness, perfection, fairness, simplicity, necessity, consistency, richness, wholeness, transcendence, self-sufficiency, uniqueness, effortlessness, significance, playfulness, humor, and immersion in process.[8]

Achieving TMEs as Composers

My friend Ruth, the composer for film and television to whom I've referred several times in this book, recently finished scoring a piece for a museum exhibition about jellyfish and saving the oceans. The music was supposed to "hold the space" for museum-goers walking through the exhibition.

Before she got the commission for the piece, Ruth had been vacationing in the Arizona desert. In meditation, she received the message "Write their song." Whose song? she wondered. Her inner guidance told her: "The creatures of the ocean." She thought, "That's a strange message to receive in the desert." But when she returned to Boston, she was contacted about the museum gig. The "creatures of the ocean" turned out to be jellyfish.

While working on the piece, Ruth had a number of TMEs. She experienced the love and beauty of the ocean creatures she was writing about. At times, she felt that the "vibration of love within the music" was so powerful that it "could pop out the windows" in her studio. "A keen sense of connectedness with the universe" developed as she worked, a sense of "the pure light and friendship that connects everything."

The score had a number of "earth-level parameters." It was being written for an exhibition, so it had to fit "certain logistical guidelines," including mood, instrumentation, and length.

Halfway through completing the project, Ruth received the following information while meditating:

> At the most subtle and powerful levels of inner light, this gives permission to all who come into the vibration of the music to be free. You have been given this work so that the music is free to roam throughout space and heal all who walk through the exhibit. The sea creatures bring their song to you, of life, of light, of healing. You are to be the bridge.[9]

When I interviewed her, Ruth didn't identify the source of this inner guidance. Cyril Scott, however, might point to Ruth as an example of a deva-inspired composer, the characteristics of which include a sensitivity to nature, becoming a conduit for the healing power of love, working for the benefit of humankind and all of life, and establishing a musical bridge between the human, natural, and ethereal realms.

How can those of us who write music become such bridges and serve humanity in a similar way? By attempting to achieve TMEs as composers, as Ruth has done, and transmitting the spiritual wisdom thereby attained to performers and audiences.

The blueprint for achieving TMEs as composers includes the advice I've given to both listeners and performers. Most composers have come to composition after first having been listeners and performers. Some enrich their compositional process by continuing to perform and listen to the music of others.

Sufi musician and mystic Hazrat Inayat Khan claimed that "music excels religion, for music raises the soul of man even higher than the so-called external forms of religion."[10] For this reason, Inayat Khan called music "the most exalted of the arts," and said that "the work of the composer of music is no less than the work of a saint."[11]

According to Inayat Khan, more than compositional technique is required to achieve this saintly work: "The composer needs tenderness of heart, eyes open to all beauty, the conception of what is beautiful, the true perception of sound and rhythm, and its expression in human nature."[12] In other words, composers need to understand, live, and write from the continuum of human potential. Only then can they create their "own world in sound and rhythm."[13]

Such work should not be "a labour," but "a joy of the highest order." Therefore, composers should not write out of a sense of obligation but when the "heart is singing," the "soul is dancing," and the "whole being is vibrating harmony."[14]

In order to create a mood suitable for composition, composers should, like Ravi Shankar, "shut out the world" and "go down deep within" themselves.[15] They should approach the soul, as the source of their music, as Shankar approaches the playing of a raga, "with feelings of humility, reverence and awe."[16]

The soul, like a raga, is a sacred being. When creating music, composers should approach the soul as if stepping "onto the threshold" of a sacred state of consciousness, in the hope of producing a temple in sound.

Composers should create art in service to humanity, rather than their egos, keeping their minds clear of vanity, pride, or the desire to impress. Meanwhile, they must develop, harmonize, and integrate each center in the continuum of human potential in their life and work.

Listening to music that targets the seventh and eighth centers can teach them how to compose such music. Paying attention to the rise and fall of energy levels in the seventh center's macrorhythmically composed music can attune them to the luminous waves sent out by Sri Aurobindo's supermind, or what I call the cosmic normative balance. Such waves may then be easier to capture in their own music. By attempting to render them with ever greater clarity, composers may begin ascending the ladder of consciousness from thinking mind to the higher mind and beyond.

Aurobindo said that the approach to the supermind must be initiated from above. No musical system, or attempt on the part of the ego to control the compositional process, as we've seen in the case of several twentieth-century composers, will lead a composer to the music of cosmic consciousness. As with any mystical experience, composers can only prepare themselves to receive eighth center music, hoping for the act of grace that will allow it to come through.

The key to creating music of the soul is inner listening, which can only be achieved by letting go of compositional systems and the mind's ideas about what a piece should be and where it should go. In an interview, Einojuhani Rautavaara said that it's not the task of composers "to be the maker of the music, its mother." The composer's task "is to be the midwife who helps the music to live on its own terms."[17]

My friend Ruth is one of the best inner listeners I know. She listens to inner guidance that tells her what her next project will be even before she's contacted by potential employers. She listens as the music takes shape within her and while she attempts to translate or realize this internal shape in sound.

Whether the source of her music is the soul, God, the supermind, the cosmic normative balance, angelic devas, or the nature spirits of sea creatures such as jellyfish hardly matters. The only important thing is that she keeps listening and translating both the sound and the inner guidance that provides her with instruction in how to proceed. While she works, the result of such inner listening is the love and connectedness of a more or less continual, window-popping TME.

A Soundtrack for Changing Your Life

I first mentioned my friend Carl, another good inner listener, in chapter 2, in connection with TMEs induced by Vaughan Williams's *The Lark Ascending*. Carl's most intense TMEs have been the result of composing his own music. He feels the urge to do so during "life's greatest turning points of spiritual growth," making albums when he needs access to "a life-organizing, elevated state of consciousness."

Unlike Ruth and me, Carl has no academic musical training. He's a computer programmer. He composes by ear using multitracking recording technology, including a tape recorder that allows him to record a number of musical tracks singly and reproduce them simultaneously; and a Kurzweil synthesizer capable of producing a wide variety of instrumental sounds, as well as recording and reproducing up to sixteen musical tracks. While composing, Carl feels that he is "self-reprogramming." His music resonates with deeper sides of himself that need to come to the surface, giving them permission to do so.

Carl's compositional process involves working out the melodic and rhythmic details of a particular track through playing it on Kurzweil's keyboard, recording it, and then having the synthesizer play it back to him. Once he has "laid down a track" in this way, a "new self comes in from the underside of my consciousness," producing another melody that stands on its own, yet harmonizes with the first one. This process repeats itself until what Carl calls a "synergistic whole" has emerged.

Composing such multipart music is a "great thrill" for Carl. As different aspects of himself come out in this process, each self contributing a melody, what emerges is counterpoint-oriented, yet capable of inducing a trance. Like world music, his songs might include an African rhythm track, a Celtic flute sound, and instruments associated with other cultures and eras.

Carl claims that his songs put him in touch with archetypal aspects of himself or past lives, including a seventeenth-century European composer, an African drummer, and a Celtic minstrel. These selves work together as he composes.

The synergistic wholes created in this way may sound chaotic to other people, he says. But they resonate deeply whenever he listens to them, inducing TMEs in which mystical ecstasy develops from "having a multifaceted experience of my own soul."

Carl calls this practice of composing and listening to his own music "creating a soundtrack for changing my life." One such soundtrack, produced after his first marriage failed and he lost his job, allowed him to reorganize his priorities. While listening to this soundtrack, Carl felt a tremendous sense of "self-love and destiny," which gave him the courage to find a new job, new friends, a new love relationship, and a spiritual community that supported his growth.

During this period, Carl walked around the Boston area listening to his self-composed music on a Walkman. He was amazed by the number of coincidences and synchronicities he perceived. By composing his own music, he had externalized his inmost self. Then, by listening to the result, he was reinternalizing it. This practice induced TMEs in which his inner and outer realities became ever more congruent, a more or less continual experience of the state that I call inner equals outer.

Carl speaks of the "joy of birthing a song as a living thing," a "startling" process in which the whole is clearly greater than the sum of its parts—a "manifestation of the soul." Listening to his self-composed music, he says, is like listening to the spiritual advice and comfort of "a guiding friend." When he does so, he feels both centered in himself and at the center of the universe.

Years have passed since Carl created this particular soundtrack for changing his life. When he listens to it now, he vividly recalls the transitional period that produced it. Sometimes he has a TME in which he cries with "spiritual tears," the sort I've referred to as a message from the soul that one has experienced some great truth. Listening to old self-created soundtracks allows Carl to feel "more connected and whole across time and space," rather than having his "usual fragmented daily feeling."

The music we surround ourselves with often becomes so deeply associated with events occurring at that time that it can indeed become a soundtrack for our lives. We may only become aware of our favorite songs and pieces *as* a soundtrack when we hear them years later and they summon up memories of the period when we listened to them so often.

When we come up with a playlist of our favorite music and make a tape or CD of it to accompany us on our daily round—as my friend Deanna has done with the songs of Led Zeppelin, as described in chapter 17—we're somewhat more consciously creating a soundtrack for our lives. If we've stored favorite CDs on our computers or downloaded MP3 files of beloved songs from the Internet, then we have a huge hard drive memory bank from which to create such soundtracks.

With the appropriate software, we can link up our favorite tunes in all sorts of intentional or unexpected ways, giving us the capacity to create an infinite number of possible soundtracks for our lives. If we want to create a soundtrack for *changing* our lives, however, we don't necessarily have to become composers like my friend Carl. All we need is the yoga of listening.

Throughout this book, I've recommended songs or pieces of music that target the centers in the continuum of human potential in specific ways. I've done so in part to help you identify what music sounds like when a particular center is dominant.

Most people can feel such distinctions intuitively. By describing the levels and centers of the continuum of human potential, I've provided a vocabulary that can help you develop this intuitive sense and make use of it more consciously.

Through applying what you've learned from listening to the musical examples in the chapters on the centers, you should be able to determine the dominant center of much music that I haven't mentioned. Developing this skill can provide you with a new way of sorting the songs or pieces in your music collection and creating tapes, CDs, or computer-organized playlists that you can use as soundtracks to change your life.

I've said that the yoga of listening can serve any of four purposes: therapeutic, developmental, integrative, or transcendent. If you want to change your life by healing emotional wounds or depression, the therapeutic aspect of the yoga of listening might help. Create a tape, CD, or playlist of fourth center music that opens the heart or fifth center music that increases well-being. If you want to release pent-up frustration or anger, listen to music that expresses conflict by targeting the third center, such as opera.

If you want to change your life by developing yourself in new ways, determine which centers on the continuum of human potential you're comfortable with and which are less familiar or unknown. Then create a tape, CD, or playlist that exposes you to the less familiar centers.

If you're interested in reawakening your sense of presence in the body, then listen to music that targets the physical/sensing centers, one (arousal) and two (desire). If you're interested in opening yourself up to a wider range of emotional expression, then listen to music that targets the emotional/feeling centers, three (intensity) and four (expression).

If you want to expand your mental capacities, listen to music that targets the intellectual/thinking centers, five (well-being) and six (command). Remember that fifth center music works on lifestyle issues and the moral sense. Witty music that targets lower 6 develops the sense of humor. Formal music that targets middle 6 is good for developing analytic abilities. Visionary music that targets upper 6 is helpful for developing the imagination and opening the third eye.

If you're interested in developing your psychic abilities, listen to music that targets the spiritual/intuiting centers, seven (expanded consciousness) and eight (cosmic consciousness). Music that targets these centers may be less familiar than that which targets many of the others, so I've given many examples of seventh and eighth center music in this book, along with indications of the purposes it can serve in changing your life.

If you want to change your life by integrating the continuum of human potential into a working whole, bringing the centers into alignment with each other and harmonizing them, then listen to music that targets as much of the continuum of potential as possible, such as the operas of Wagner.

If you're interested in changing your life by creating experiences of self-transcendence, listen to music that brings you closer to your soul, especially that of the seventh and eighth centers. Frequent exposure to the luminous waves of macrorhythmically composed seventh center music, or the source of those waves in the supermind or cosmic normative balance, as encoded in metarhythmically composed eighth center music, should help you achieve TMEs more frequently.

The more I listen to seventh and eighth center music, the deeper my experience of expanded and cosmic consciousness becomes. But I can't listen to such music all day, every day—only occasionally, in a state of meditation, as a spiritual practice, with plenty of time between exposures to think about and integrate the effects of such listening. Between these periods of meditation, I work on aligning my life ever more deeply with the soul's master plan and the cosmic normative balance, the source of all consciousness.

I mentioned the musical NDE of cartoonist Arthur E. Yensen in chapter 15. He said, "Sometimes now when I listen to the best of earth-music I notice a slight resemblance to heaven-music as if the composer were consciously, or unconsciously, trying to imitate it."[18]

The music heard in NDEs is a representation of the harmony that exists within the cosmic normative balance. On our side of the boundary between life and death, the closer a composer approaches the soul or God, the more likely it is that his or her music will express something of the harmony that Yensen called heaven-music. One purpose of TMEs may be to help us recognize these moments of heaven-music, and to align ourselves with the high harmony they represent, to bring us into a right relationship with the cosmic normative balance.

If, as the e-mail correspondent I quoted in chapter 16 implied, "Norm" is the only composer, then it seems that the ultimate purpose of composing, performing, and listening to music is to get as close to "Norm" as possible. The yoga of listening is one way to achieve this goal.

I believe that the yoga of listening is as capable of leading listeners, performers, and composers to experiences of self-transcendence or enlightenment as traditional yogic practices are. I hope that it might also help people discover for themselves, here on Earth, the high harmony of heaven-music—that of the seventh and eighth centers on the continuum of human potential.

When I first felt the call to become a composer—to write music that moved me as deeply as the celestial symphonies of Bruckner do—there was nothing but the music itself to guide me. This is the book I wish had existed then, to point the way toward how to compose, perform, and listen to the music of the soul. May it be an aid to composers, performers, and listeners who find themselves on a similar path, showing them how to achieve self-transcendence through music, and supporting them in enabling the transcendent musical experiences of others.

Now, using the continuum of human potential and the yoga of listening, I invite you to create a soundtrack for changing your life. Compose it, perform it, make tapes, CDs, and playlists of it. Listen to this soundtrack again and again. Meditate on it until you've achieved the state of inner equals outer. Enjoy and learn from the resulting TMEs. In this way, the art of music becomes a mirror, enabling you to see your soul.

Notes

Preface

1. Cyril Scott, *Music: Its Secret Influence Throughout the Ages*, rev. ed., 1958, reprint (New York: Samuel Weiser, 1981), p. 142.

2. For more information on who Charles is and how he came into my life, as well as examples and overviews of his teachings, please visit my website: www.kurtleland.com.

3. Scott, *Music*, p. 98.

4. Abraham H. Maslow, *The Farther Reaches of Human Nature*, reprint, 1971 (New York: Penguin Compass, 1993), p. 186.

5. Hazrat Inayat Khan, *The Mysticism of Sound and Music: The Sufi Teaching of Hazrat Inayat Khan*, rev. ed. (Boston: Shambhala, 1996), p. 245.

Acknowledgments

1. For information on the Borromeo Quartet, including the option to download recordings of live performances by the group, please visit their website: www.borromeo quartet.org.

Chapter 1

1. The works of many composers from the eighteenth century to the early twentieth century are identified by opus numbers. The word *opus* (abbreviated as *op.*) means "work" in Latin. This form of identification was a convenient way for publishers, performers, and the listening public to distinguish between different works in the same genre and key. For example, three of Beethoven's sixteen string quartets are in the key of F major. These are identified as: Opus 18, No. 1 (six of Beethoven's early quartets were published together as Opus 18, so each of them also received a separate number within that opus); Opus 59, No. 1 (three of his middle period quartets were published together as Opus 59); and Opus 135 (which stands alone). Sometimes opus numbers reflect the approximate order in which a composer's works were written, more often the order in which they were published. They can also be useful, as in Beethoven's case, for figuring out whether a piece was composed early or late in a composer's life.

2. Opus numbers aren't the only way to distinguish between the works of a particular composer. Much of Schubert's music was unpublished at the time of his death, at the age of thirty-one. A man by the name of Otto Erich Deutsch compiled an extensive

catalogue of Schubert's works, listing them in approximate order of composition. Any mention of a piece by Schubert is likely to contain a D. number, short for "Deutsch listing." Once again, as with opus numbers, such listings help to differentiate between pieces in the same genre and key. In this case, however, Schubert wrote only one of his fifteen string quartets in the key of A minor.

3. William James, *The Varieties of Religious Experience: A Study in Human Nature*, 1902, reprint (New York: Random House, 1994), p. 414.

4. Ibid., p. 415.

5. Newman Flower, *George Frideric Handel: His Personality and His Times*, rev. ed., 1959, reprint (London: Panther Books, 1972), p. 272.

6. Paul Hindemith, *A Composer's World: Horizons and Limitations*, 1952, reprint (Gloucester, Mass.: Peter Smith, 1969), pp. 70–71.

7. Ibid., p. 71.

8. Lane Arye, *Unintentional Music: Releasing Your Deepest Creativity* (Charlottesville, Va.: Hampton Roads, 2001), p. 182.

Chapter 2

1. Edith Hamilton and Huntington Cairns, eds., *The Collected Dialogues of Plato, Including the Letters* (Princeton, N.J.: Princeton University Press, 1961), p. 1175 (Timaeus 47c–e).

2. Paul McKay, "Mapping the Musical Brain," *Ottawa Citizen* (November 18, 2002); published on the Web at www.enchantedear.com.

3. Ibid.

4. Ibid.

5. Anthony Storr, *Music and the Mind* (New York: Ballantine Books, 1992), p. 176.

6. Robert Jourdain, *Music, the Brain, and Ecstasy: How Music Captures Our Imagination* (New York: Avon Books, 1998), p. 331.

7. Ibid.

8. Ibid.

9. Maslow, *Farther Reaches*, p. 47.

10. Ibid., p. 184.

11. Ibid., p. 170.

12. David Tame, *The Secret Power of Music: The Transformation of Self and Society through Musical Energy* (Rochester, Vt.: Destiny Books, 1984), pp. 20–21.

13. Amy Clampitt, *Predecessors, Et Cetera: Essays* (Ann Arbor, Mich.: University of Michigan Press, 1991), p. 103.

14. Ibid.

15. Maslow, *Farther Reaches*, pp. 308–309.

16. Ibid., p. 328.

17. Ibid., p. 46.

18. Ibid., p. 265.

19. Abraham H. Maslow, *Religions, Values, and Peak-Experiences*, 1964, reprint (New York: Penguin Compass, 1994), pp. xv–xvi. Italics in original.

20. Ibid., p. xvi.

21. Maslow, *Farther Reaches*, p. 183.

22. Storr, p. 187.

23. Ibid., p. 186.

Chapter 3

1. Scott, *Music*, p. 40.

2. Ibid., p. 29.

3. Ibid., pp. 30–31.

4. David Tame, *Beethoven and the Spiritual Path* (Wheaton, Ill.: Theosophical Publishing House, 1994), p. 75.

5. Scott's and Tame's notion of a spiritual hierarchy that guides the evolution of humankind seems to parallel information that I've received in out-of-body experiences, as recorded in my book *Otherwhere*, concerning what I call Overseers and Facilitators. Like Scott's Great White Lodge, the Council of Overseers also commissions great works of art, such as poetry and paintings, to further their mission. The Great White Lodge and the Council of Overseers seem to be so similar in function that they may just be two ways of describing the same kind of nonphysical being. See chapter 18 of *Otherwhere* for more information on the Council of Overseers.

6. Tame, *Beethoven*, p. 76.

7. Scott, *Music*, p. 87, note.

8. Hamilton and Cairns, p. 666 (Republic 424c).

9. Scott, *Music*, p. 82.

10. Ibid., p. 103. This assertion seems even more questionable to me when I consider that Strauss's own program for the work cast himself, as composer, in the role of hero and his critics, rather than another country, in the role of enemies.

11. Scott, *Music*, p. 142.

12. Ibid., p. 200.

13. Ibid.

14. Ibid., p. 201.

15. Ibid., p. 202.

16. In both *Otherwhere* and *The Unanswered Question*, I noted a tendency for people to represent nonphysical beings to themselves as if they were physical. It seems possible to me that my composer friend may be in touch with nonphysical beings who present themselves—or are perceived by her—as space aliens in *this* reality, so that she can relate to them more easily.

17. Scott, *Music*, p. 202.

18. Ibid.

Chapter 4

1. Scott, *Music*, p. 119.

2. Ibid, p. 122.

3. Ibid., p. 134.

4. Ibid., p. 98.

5. Ibid.

6. Ibid., p. 199.

7. Periodically, in these notes, I cite specific recordings that may be of particular interest to my readers. The one in question here is Cyril Scott, *Chamber Music*, The London Quartet (Dutton 7116). There seems to be little standardization of record company catalog numbers. I've drawn the numbers used in these notes from the CDs themselves or from www.towerrecords.com.

8. Cyril Scott, *Bone of Contention: Life Story and Confessions* (New York: Arco, 1969), p. 84.

9. Scott, *Music*, pp. 124, 127.

10. Ibid., p. 128.

11. A new recording of Scott's Second Piano Concerto, as well as his Third Symphony (subtitled *The Muses*) and a symphonic poem called *Neptune*—all mature works, written after Scott had published *Music: Its Secret Influence*—was released as this book was in production. Beautifully performed by the BBC Philharmonic, with Howard

Shelley at the piano and Martyn Brabbins conducting, this recording (Chandos 10211) has received an Editor's Choice award from the influential classical music magazine *Gramophone.* It demonstrates what an intelligent and imaginative composer Scott was, but without illuminating the connection between his music and his spiritual beliefs— especially the question of what he meant by deva music.

12. Scott, *Music*, pp. 128.

13. Ibid., p. 129.

14. Ibid., pp. 128–129.

15. Ibid., p. 128.

16. Ibid., p. 121.

17. Ibid., p. 120.

18. Ibid., p. 123.

19. Ibid., p. 122.

20. Ibid., p. 98.

21. Ernest Newman, *The Wagner Operas*, 1949, reprint (Princeton, N.J.: Princeton University Press, 1991), p. 127.

22. Scott, *Music*, p. 98.

23. Ibid., p. 134.

24. Ibid., p. 132.

25. Enya, *Watermark* (Geffen 24233).

26. Billie Holiday, *Lady Day: The Best of Billie Holiday* (Columbia/Legacy 85979).

27. The soundtrack has been released as *Lord of the Rings: The Fellowship of the Ring* (Reprise 48110).

28. John McLaughlin, *The Inner Mounting Flame*, The Mahavishnu Orchestra (Columbia/Legacy 65523).

29. Madonna, *The Immaculate Collection* (Sire 26440).

Chapter 5

1. Eknath Easwaran, *The Bhagavad Gita for Daily Living*, Vol. 1, *The End of Sorrow* (Tomales, Calif.: Nilgiri Press, 1975), p. 291.

2. Hamilton and Cairns, p. 1175 (Timaeus 47c–e).

3. Georg Feuerstein, *Tantra: The Path of Ecstasy* (Boston: Shambhala, 1998), p. xv.

4. The sources for this synthesis are M. P. Pandit, ed., *Sri Aurobindo on the Tantra* (Pondicherry, India: Dipti Publications, 1967); and Swami Satyananda Saraswati, *Kundalini Tantra*, 1984, reprint (Munger, Bihar, India: Yoga Publications Trust, 2001).

5. The kundalini effects listed in this and the following six paragraphs have been paraphrased from Swami Vishnu Tirtha, "Signs of an Awakened Kundalini," in John White, ed., *Kundalini, Evolution and Enlightenment*, rev. ed. (New York: Paragon House, 1990), pp. 94–97.

6. M. S. S. Singh Khalsa, "Exploring the Myths and Misconceptions of Kundalini," in John White, ed., *Kundalini, Evolution and Enlightenment*, rev. ed. (New York: Paragon House, 1990), p. 144.

7. Gopi Krishna, "The Phenomenon of Kundalini," in John White, ed., *Kundalini, Evolution and Enlightenment*, rev. ed. (New York: Paragon House, 1990), p. 229.

8. John White, "Some Possibilities for Further Kundalini Research," in John White, ed., *Kundalini, Evolution and Enlightenment*, rev. ed. (New York: Paragon House, 1990), pp. 355–356.

9. Khalsa, in White, p. 137.

10. Flower, p. 272.

11. Halsey Stevens, *The Life and Music of Béla Bartók*, rev. ed. (New York: Oxford University Press, 1964), p. 253.

12. Feuerstein, *Tantra*, p. 264.

13. Swami Sivananda Radha, "Kundalini: An Overview," in John White, ed., *Kundalini, Evolution and Enlightenment*, rev. ed. (New York: Paragon House, 1990), p. 56.

14. Gopi Krishna, in White, p. 231.

15. Lee Sannella, "Kundalini: Classical and Clinical," in John White, ed., *Kundalini, Evolution and Enlightenment*, rev. ed. (New York: Paragon House, 1990), p. 313.

16. For a personal account of kundalini awakening by a former English professor at a midwestern university, see Dorothy Walters, *Unmasking the Rose: A Record of Kundalini Initiation* (Charlottesville, Va.: Hampton Roads, 2002).

17. Swami Satyananda, p. 39.

18. Georg Feuerstein, Ph.D., *The Shambhala Encyclopedia of Yoga* (Boston, Shambhala, 1997), s.v. "mantra."

19. Ibid.

20. Pandit, p. 38.

21. Faubion Bowers, *Scriabin: A Biography*, 2d rev. ed., 2 vols. in one (New York: Dover Publications, 1996), vol. 2, pp. 70–71.

22. Feuerstein, *Tantra*, p. 191.

23. Alice Bailey, "Ordered Meditation and Loving Service," in John White, ed., *Kundalini, Evolution and Enlightenment*, rev. ed. (New York: Paragon House, 1990), p. 460.

24. Stephen Cope, *Yoga and the Quest for the True Self* (New York: Bantam, 1999), pp. 263–264.

25. Bruckner's Eighth Symphony exists in two versions. I was listening to the second version, of 1890.

Chapter 6

1. Khan, p. 44.

2. Ken Wilber, "Are the Chakras Real?" in John White, ed., *Kundalini, Evolution and Enlightenment*, rev. ed. (New York: Paragon House, 1990), p. 121.

3. Feuerstein, *Tantra*, p. 149.

4. Swami Satyananda, pp. 363–365.

5. Swami Radha in White, p. 48.

6. Swami Rama, "The Awakening of Kundalini," in John White, ed., *Kundalini, Evolution and Enlightenment*, rev. ed. (New York: Paragon House, 1990), p. 30.

7. Swami Satyananda, p. 22.

8. Swami Rama in White, p. 30.

9. Hamilton and Cairns, p. 1175 (Timaeus 47c–e).

10. Carl G. Jung, "Approach to the Unconscious," in Carl G. Jung, ed., *Man and His Symbols* (Garden City, N.Y.: Doubleday, 1964), p. 61. Please note that though I'm borrowing these terms from Jungian psychology, my definitions of them are not identical to Jung's.

11. Georg Feuerstein, *The Yoga Tradition: Its History, Literature, Philosophy and Practice*, 2d ed. (Prescott, Ariz.: Hohm Press, 2001), p. 355.

12. Vasant V. Merchant, "Sri Aurobindo, the Tantra and Kundalini," in John White, ed., *Kundalini, Evolution and Enlightenment*, rev. ed. (New York: Paragon House, 1990), p. 90.

13. Ibid., p. 89.

14. Charles has borrowed the concepts of both the Shadow and the Anima or Animus from the dream psychology of Jung.

15. Further information on the eight dream characters, or components of the psyche, and how to use them to interpret dreams, appears on my website (www.kurtleland.com) as a series of articles called "A Crash Course in Dream Interpretation."

16. Pandit, p. 15.
17. Ibid., p. 17.

Chapter 7

1. Swami Satyananda, p. 39.
2. Khan, p. 106.
3. Ibid., p. 77.
4. Ibid., p. 52.
5. Ibid., p. 65.
6. Ibid., p. 101.
7. Ibid., p. 100.
8. Ibid., p. 103.
9. Ibid., p. 77.
10. Pandit, p. 16.
11. Swami Satyananda, p. 122.
12. Swami Rama in White, p. 30.
13. Maslow, *Farther Reaches*, p. 265.
14. Khan, p. 8.
15. Ibid., p. 161.
16. Ibid., p. 8.
17. Ibid., p. 161.
18. Satprem, *Sri Aurobindo, or the Adventure of Consciousness*, trans. Michael Danino, 4th ed. (New Delhi, India: The Mother's Institute of Research, 2000), p. 214.
19. Sri Aurobindo Ghose, *The Future Evolution of Man: The Divine Life on Earth*, ed. P. B. Saint-Hilaire, reprint (Twin Lakes, Wis.: Lotus Press, 2002), p. 131.
20. Ibid., p. 111.
21. Swami Saraswati, p. 117.
22. Peter Michael Hamel, *Through Music to the Self: How to Experience and Appreciate Music Anew*, trans. Peter Lemesurier (Boulder, Colo: Shambhala, 1979), p. 63. Patekar's rules were originally published in English, in a concert program, but were translated into German for Hamel's book, then back into English for the English edition of that book.
23. Ibid., p. 64.
24. Khan, p. 64.
25. Hamel, p. 64.
26. Khan, p. 98.
27. Hamel, p. 64.
28. Maslow, *Farther Reaches*, p. 62.
29. Hamel, p. 64.
30. Ibid.

Chapter 8

1. Khan, p. 151.
2. Ibid.
3. W. A. Mathieu, *The Listening Book: Discovering Your Own Music* (Boston: Shambhala, 1991), p. 3.
4. Igor Stravinsky and Robert Craft, *Themes and Episodes* (New York: Knopf, 1966), p. 19.
5. Mathieu, p. 18.
6. Ibid., p. 15.
7. Ibid., p. xii.
8. Ibid., p. 26.

9. Ibid., p. 22.

10. Ibid.

11. Khan, p. 151.

12. Ibid., p. 76.

13. Doudou N'Diaye Rose, *Djabote* (EMI/Virgin 8394702).

14. For more information on the patented Hemi-Sync sound technology developed by the late Robert Monroe, please visit the website of the Monroe Institute: www.monroeinstitute.org.

Chapter 9

1. The Dave Brubeck Quartet, *Time Out* (Columbia/Legacy 65122).

2. Newman, p. 208.

3. Brian Eno, *Ambient 1: Music for Airports* (EG Records 17).

4. Philip Glass quoted in Joseph Machlis, *Introduction to Contemporary Music*, 2d ed. (New York: Norton, 1979), p. 552.

5. Roger Nichols, *Ravel Remembered* (New York: Norton, 1988), p. 50.

Chapter 10

1. Robertson Davies, *The Lyre of Orpheus* (New York: Viking, 1989), p. 147.

2. All the examples from Stravinsky's *The Rite of Spring* given in this chapter are "pure" specimens of the levels given. For the entire duration of the section, Stravinsky holds to the level in question. There are no pure examples of middle 3 agitation in *The Rite of Spring*. Stravinsky makes frequent use of this level, but moves through it too quickly for me to point to any one section as a good demonstration of what middle 3 sounds like.

3. Pat Metheny, *Imaginary Day* (Warner Brothers 46821).

Chapter 11

1. Feuerstein, *Tantra*, p. 155.

2. Ibid., p. 156.

3. Swami Satyananda, p. 163.

4. Ibid., p. 166.

5. Billy Joel, *An Innocent Man* (Columbia 69389).

6. Khan, p. 100.

7. Madonna, *The Immaculate Collection* (Sire 26440). All the Madonna songs cited in this chapter are from this album.

8. Billie Holiday, *Lady Day: The Best of Billie Holiday* (Columbia/Legacy 85979). All the Billie Holiday songs cited in this chapter come from this compilation. For convenience, when I cite jazz standards (as well as the compositions or improvisations based on them) in the text of a chapter and the playlist at the end, I attribute them to the artist rather than the original composer.

9. Also available on Miles Davis, *The Essential Miles Davis* (Columbia/Legacy 85475). All the Miles Davis selections cited in this chapter, and many in subsequent chapters, are from this compilation. A number of jazz composers and arrangers have contributed to this two-CD set. For convenience, when the composition or arrangement is by someone other than Davis, I refer to a Miles Davis "rendition" in the text of a chapter and attribute it to him in the playlist at the end.

10. Also available on John Coltrane, *The Very Best of John Coltrane* (Rhino 79778).

11. Also available on *The Beatles: 1962–1966* (Capitol 97036).

12. "Michelle," *The Beatles: 1962–1966* (Capitol 97036); "Something," *The Beatles: 1967–1970* (Capitol 97039).

13. Cyndi Lauper, *She's So Unusual* (Legacy 62169).

14. Khan, p. 125.

15. These sections start at the words "Maybe this won't last very long" and "I had second thoughts at the start."

16. U2, *War* (Island 811148); U2, *Rattle and Hum* (Island 842299).

17. See Dante's *Inferno*, Canto V, 73–140.

18. The timings I'm using here come from my recording of the work, in which the National Symphony Orchestra is conducted by Antal Dorati (London 443003). These timings may vary from performance to performance. Luckily, the changes from one level to the next in this piece are sufficiently well defined that, even without my timings, it should be possible for an attentive listener to grasp the points I'm making here.

Chapter 12

1. For more information on the concept of life purpose, see Kurt Leland, *Menus for Impulsive Living: A Revolutionary Approach to Organizing and Energizing Your Life* (New York: Doubleday, 1989), pp. 11–16.

2. Ravi Shankar, *My Music, My Life* (New York: Simon and Schuster, 1968), p. 26. *Scherzo* is a term from Western music, referring to the often lighthearted second or third movement of a four-movement symphony. The word itself means "joke" or "jest" in Italian. We'll encounter the term again, with reference to the sixth center, in the next chapter.

3. Bob Marley, *Rastaman Vibration* (Island Records 548897).

4. The Beatles, *Sgt. Pepper's Lonely Hearts Club Band* (Capitol 46442).

5. The Beatles, *Abbey Road* (Capitol 46446).

6. All the Madonna songs cited in this chapter are from Madonna, *The Immaculate Collection* (Sire 26440).

7. All the Hendrix songs cited in this chapter are from Jimi Hendrix, *Live at Woodstock* (MCA 11987).

8. All the Miles Davis examples cited in this chapter are from Miles Davis, *The Essential Miles Davis* (Columbia/Legacy 85475).

9. Mozart's music is usually referred to with a K. number. The K. stands for Köchel, the man who first catalogued Mozart's music—in much the same way that, as I pointed out in a note to chapter 1, D. stands for Deutsch, the cataloguer of Schubert's music.

10. Nickel Creek, *Nickel Creek* (Sugar Hill 3909).

11. The sung portions of the song, which use words such as *wishes*, *dreaming*, and *enchanted*, target upper 6, the visionary aspect of the sixth center, also appropriate for imagining what a new love might be like.

12. Nickel Creek, *This Side* (Sugar Hill 3941).

13. The Police, *Regatta de Blanc* (A&M 3312).

14. John Coltrane, *The Major Works of John Coltrane* (Impulse 2113).

15. Joachim-Ernst Berendt, *The Jazz Book: From Ragtime to Fusion and Beyond*, revised by Günther Huesmann, trans. H. and B. Bredigkeit, Dan Morgenstern, and Tim Nevill, 6th ed. (Brooklyn, N.Y.: Lawrence Hill Books, 1992), pp. 118–119.

16. Ibid., p. 117.

17. Ibid.

18. Ibid.

19. Berendt, p. 130.

Chapter 13

1. Feuerstein, *Tantra*, p. 153. Italics in original.

2. Pandit, pp. 23–24.

3. Satyananda, p. 129.

4. Davies, p. 2.

5. With the exception of songs from *Abbey Road*, discussed later, all of the songs cited in this chapter are available on *The Beatles: 1962–1966*, (Capitol 97036) or *The Beatles: 1967–1970* (Capitol 97039).

6. All Jimi Henrix songs mentioned in this chapter are from Jimi Hendrix, *Live at Woodstock* (MCA 11987).

7. Madonna, *The Immaculate Collection* (Sire 26440).

8. Bobby McFerrin, *The Voice* (Elektra 60366).

9. John Coltrane, *The Very Best of John Coltrane* (Rhino 79778).

10. James, p. 414.

11. Miles Davis, *The Essential Miles Davis* (Columbia/Legacy 85475).

12. Oregon, *Winter Light* (Vanguard 79350).

13. The Beatles, *Abbey Road* (Capitol 46446).

14. In chapter 4, I mentioned the soundtrack of Peter Jackson's film *The Lord of the Rings: The Fellowship of the Ring*. I used the section "Concerning Hobbits" as an example of human realm music. The music shifts swiftly between emotions, as quickly as the camera moves from one scene to another. Such changes are a characteristic of music in which the sixth center is dominant. Though this music has its origin in upper 6, since it's an auditory equivalent of the camera, it also touches the fourth center in the moments when we're to feel Bilbo's nostalgia for the village life he's leaving behind, and the fifth in the dance-like sections.

The other section of the film that I cited, "The Council of Elrond," is an example of ethereal realm music. Here, the dominant center is the seventh, especially the sublime (lower) and noble (middle) ranges of this center. This track ends with a return to the human realm music of the hobbits.

15. Miles Davis, *Sketches of Spain* (Columbia/Legacy 65142).

16. John McLaughlin, *The Inner Mounting Flame*, The Mahavishnu Orchestra (Columbia/Legacy 65523).

17. Scott, *Music*, p. 128.

18. King Crimson, *In the Court of the Crimson King* (Caroline 1502).

19. Genesis, *Wind and Wuthering* (Atco 82690).

20. Todd Rundgren, *Initiation* (Rhino 70866).

21. Yes, *Tales from Topographic Oceans* (Atlantic 82683).

22. Nirvana, *Nevermind* (David Geffen Company 24425).

Chapter 14

1. Swami Satyananda, p. 186.

2. Jourdain, p. 134.

3. Satprem, p. 205.

4. Ibid. Italics in original.

5. Newman, p. 208.

6. Ibid.

7. John McLaughlin, *The Inner Mounting Flame*, The Mahavishnu Orchestra (Columbia/Legacy 65523). In terms to be explained later, this piece begins with the spiritual devotion of middle 7, rises to the ecstasy of upper 7, then returns to the devotion of middle 7.

8. My recording of this antiphon is Hildegard von Bingen, *Celestial Light*, Tapestry (Telarc 80456). It also includes a modern sacred composition by American composer Robert Kyr (b. 1952) that targets the seventh center.

9. This and other tunes by Enya cited in this chapter are from Enya, *Watermark* (Geffen 24233).

10. Rainer Maria Rilke, "The First Elegy," *Duino Elegies*, trans. Kurt Leland, as first published in *The Unanswered Question: Death, Near-Death, and the Afterlife* (Charlottesville, Va: Hampton Roads, 2002), p. 129.

11. *Webster's New International Dictionary*, 2d ed., s.v. "sublime."

12. John Coltrane, *A Love Supreme* (Impulse GRD 155).

13. Led Zeppelin, *Physical Graffiti* (Swan Song 92442).

14. This and the other Dead Can Dance tune cited in this chapter are from Dead Can Dance, *Into the Labyrinth* (4AD 45384).

15. Maslow, *Farther Reaches*, p. 265.

16. Also available on *The Essential Miles Davis* (Columbia/Legacy 85475).

17. Led Zeppelin, *Led Zeppelin IV* (Atlantic 82638).

18. Also available on *The Essential Miles Davis.*

19. Also available on *The Beatles: 1967–1970* (Capitol 97039).

20. Also available on *The Essential Miles Davis.*

21. Billie Holiday, *Lady Day: The Essential Billie Holiday* (Columbia/Legacy 85979).

Chapter 15

1. For more information on Swedenborg, near-death experiences, and the cosmic normative balance, see Leland, *The Unanswered Question*, pp. 285–289, and chapters 27 and 29.

2. Arthur E. Yensen, *I Saw Heaven*, 6th ed. (Parma, Idaho 1979), p. 16.

3. *Samuel Barber/Thomas Schippers* (Sony Classical MHK 62837).

4. Brahms, *Ein Deutsches Requiem*, Op. 45, The Berlin Philharmonic, conducted by Claudio Abbado (Deutsche Gramophon 437517).

5. Enya, *A Day Without Rain* (Warner Brothers 47426).

6. Wagner, *Orchestral Music*, The MET Orchestra, conducted by James Levine (Deutsche Gramophon 447764); Wagner, *Lohengrin* (complete opera), The Vienna Philharmonic, conducted by Claudio Abbado (Deutsche Gramophon 437808).

7. The Tallis Scholars, *The Best of the Renaissance* (Philips 462862).

8. Yes, *Relayer* (Atlantic 82664).

9. Fauré, *Requiem*, conducted by Philippe Herreweghe (Harmonia Mundi HMC 901771).

10. The full account of this adventure in consciousness is posted on my website: www.kurtleland.com. Click on the OBE-Log tab, then go to AC 221. This number stands for my 221st adventure in consciousness.

11. Kurt Leland, *Otherwhere: A Field Guide to Nonphysical Reality for the Out-of-Body Traveler* (Charlottesville, Va.: Hampton Roads, 2001), pp. 5–6.

12. Messiaen, *Turangalîla Symphony*, conducted by Antoni Wit (Naxos 8554478/9).

13. Brian Eno and Robert Fripp, *Evening Star* (Editions EEGCD 3).

14. Satyananda, p. 120.

15. The String Quintet in C may be one of Schubert's best-loved, worst-played works. I recommend the recording by the Melos Quartet with Wolfgang Boettcher (Harmonia Mundi HMA 1951494), in which the eighth center characteristics of the Adagio are clearly audible.

Chapter 16

1. Shankar, p. 17.

2. Ibid., pp. 26–27.

3. Ibid., p. 27.

4. Sourindro Mohun Tagore, *Universal History of Music Compiled from Diverse Sources Together with Various Original Notes on Hindu Music*, 1896, reprint (Delhi, India: Mittal Publications, 1989), Appendix, p. iv. Italics in original.

5. Boris de Schloezer, *Scriabin: Artist and Mystic*, trans. Nicolas Slonimsky (Berkeley, Calif.: University of California Press, 1987), p. 85.

6. Ibid., p. 86.

7. Ibid., p. 87.

8. Cyril Scott, *The Philosophy of Modernism (In Its Connection with Music)* (London: Kegan, Paul, Trench, Trubner, 1917), pp. 106–107.

9. Kenneth Peacock, "Synaesthetic Perception: Alexander Scriabin's Color Hearing," *Music Perception* 2 (1985), p. 496.

10. Claude Samuel, *Conversations with Olivier Messiaen*, trans. Felix Aprahamian (London: Stainer and Bell, 1976), p. 14.

11. Ibid., p. 19.

12. Ibid.

13. Geoffrey Hodson, *Music Forms: Superphysical Effects of Music Clairvoyantly Observed* (Adyar, Madras, India: Theosophical Publishing House, 1976), p. 18.

14. Ibid., pp. 18–19.

15. Ibid., p. 19.

16. Ibid.

17. Annie Besant and C. W. Leadbeater, *Thought-Forms*, 1901, abridged reprint (Wheaton, Ill.: Theosophical Publishing House, 1969), p. 67.

18. Ibid., p. 74.

19. Ibid., p. 69.

20. Tame, *Secret Power*, p. 21.

21. Ibid., p. 20.

22. Hodson, p. 18.

23. Ibid.

24. Disney, *Aladdin: The Original Soundtrack* (Disney 860717).

25. Hamel, p. 64.

26. Eberhard Weber, *Silent Feet* (ECM 1107).

27. Hodson, p. 19.

28. Actually, the bass has been acting from the expressive fourth center from the beginning of the piece. In this analysis, I've tended to focus on the ways in which the centers develop in the piano, because it's generally in the foreground.

Chapter 17

1. Hodson, pp. 18–19.

2. Ibid., p. 19.

3. Quoted in Berendt, *Jazz*, p. 133.

4. Feuerstein, *Tantra*, pp. 124–125.

5. Ibid., p. 124.

6. Ibid.

7. Ibid., p. 125.

8. Joachim-Ernst Berendt, *Nada Brahma (The World Is Sound): Music and the Landscape of Consciousness*, trans. Helmut Bredigkeit (Rochester, Vt.: Destiny Books, 1987), p. 156.

9. Feuerstein, *Encyclopedia*, s.v. "yantra."

10. Ibid., s.v. "mantra."

11. Feuerstein, *Tantra*, p. 191.

12. Berendt, *Nada Brahma*, p. 38.

13. Ibid., p. 42.

14. Feuerstein, *Tantra*, p. 25.

15. Ibid., p. 48.

16. Ibid., p. 265.
17. Ibid., pp, 18–19.
18. Led Zeppelin, *Physical Graffiti* (Swan Song 92442).
19. Led Zeppelin, *Led Zeppelin IV* (Atlantic 82638).
20. Led Zeppelin, *Led Zeppelin II* (Atlantic 82633).
21. Led Zeppelin, *Houses of the Holy* (Atlantic 82639).
22. Berendt, *Jazz*, p. 435.
23. Liner notes to John Coltrane, *A Love Supreme* (Impulse GRD 155), p. 10.

Chapter 18
1. Scott, *Music*, p. 142.
2. Tame, *Beethoven*, p. 93.
3. Ibid., p. 144.
4. Ibid., pp. 151–152.
5. Tame, *Secret Power*, p. 81.
6. Feuerstein, *Yoga Tradition*, p. xxix.
7. Khan, p. 245.
8. Ibid., p. 82.
9. Ibid., p. 102.
10. Ibid., p. 7.
11. Ghose, p. 83.
12. Tame, *Secret Power*, pp. 200–201.
13. Ghose, p. 88.
14. Tame, *Secret Power*, p. 79. Italics his.
15. Tony Williams, *Wilderness* (ARK21 810083).
16. Ibid., p. 115.
17. This quality comes through strongly in the performance of Beethoven's Violin Concerto by Yehudi Menuhin and the New Philharmonia Orchestra under Otto Klemperer. There are several currently available CDs of this performance on different labels.
18. This quality comes through strongly in a recording of Beethoven's *Pastoral* Symphony by Claudio Abbado and the Berlin Philharmonic, released in 2000 (Deutsche Gramophon 471489).
19. Yes, *Close to the Edge* (Atlantic 82666).
20. Scott, *Music*, pp. 135–136.
21. Yes, *The Yes Album* (Atlantic 82665).
22. Yes, *Going for the One* (Atlantic 82670).
23. Yes, *Tales from Topographic Oceans* (Atlantic 82683); Todd Rundgren, *Initiation* (Rhino 70866).
24. Mathieu, p. 14.
25. Yes, *Relayer* (Atlantic 82664).

Chapter 19
1. Schubert, *Piano Trios Nos. 1 & 2*, The Odeon Trio (Capriccio 10387).
2. Ghose, p. 75.
3. Ibid., p. 73.
4. Ibid., p. 79.
5. W. Y. Evans-Wentz, ed., *Tibet's Great Yogi Milarepa: A Biography from the Tibetan*, 2d ed., 1951, reprint (New York: Oxford University Press, 1969), p. 96 (note).
6. Ibid., p. 282.

7. Berendt, *Nada Brahma*, pp. 133–134.

8. Ghose, p. 85.

9. Ibid., p. 80.

10. I've already mentioned the presence of third center intensity in Verdi's *Aida*, and that the final love duet targets the heart-opening fourth center. There is also much seventh center music in *Aida*, including the famous Triumphal March (Act II, Scene 2), which targets middle 7 nobility. Other examples of seventh center music occur in connection with the scenes involving Egyptian priests and temple rites. Verdi's intention is for us to feel, think, see as he does, so the dominant center throughout *Aida* is the sixth. Even the moments of seventh center music are used as auditory equivalents of the visual scene and action, whereas Wagner composes directly from the seventh center, as we shall see.

11. Ghose, p. 85.

12. J. W. N. Sullivan, *Beethoven: His Spiritual Development* (New York: Vintage, 1960), p. 117.

13. Ghose, p. 86.

14. If you would like a useful introduction to the genre of New-Age music, see Henk N. Werkhoven, *The International Guide to New Age Music: A Comprehensive Guide to the Vast and Varied Artists and Recordings of New Age Music*, trans. Galen Yates Beach and Nynke Doetjes (New York: Billboard Books, 1998).

15. Enya, *The Celts* (Reprise 45681); *Shepherd Moons* (Reprise 26775); *The Memory of Trees* (Reprise 46106); *A Day Without Rain* (Warner Brothers 47426).

16. Ghose, p. 87.

17. Brewster Ghiselin, *The Creative Process: A Symposium* (Berkeley, Calif.: University of California Press, 1952), p. 34. Ghiselin notes that the authenticity of this letter "remains in doubt."

18. Ibid., pp. 34–35.

19. The principles of Freemasonry were important enough to Mozart that he wrote a number of cantatas for solo voice, chorus, and piano based on Masonic texts. This music would be virtually unknown were it not for a 1966 recording, still available on CD, of Mozart's *Complete Masonic Music* (VoxBox CDX 5055). While the performances on this recording are more earnest than inspirational, the existence of this music indicates that Mozart was far more spiritual than popular belief, based on the movie *Amadeus*, has portrayed him to be.

20. Ghose, p. 90.

21. Ibid.

22. Ibid., p. 91.

23. Ibid., p. 92.

24. Ibid., p. 91.

25. My friend Elizabeth wasn't happy with the recording of Sicut Cervus that she played for me, saying that it had none of the power of the Revels choir's live performance. The piece's eighth center qualities may not come through in a poor performance. I prefer the performance by Musica Contexta: Palestrina, *Music for Holy Saturday* (Chandos Chaconne Series 0679), in which the eighth center qualities in this motet are clearly audible.

26. Bach, *Die Kunst der Fuge* (*The Art of Fugue*), Tatiana Nikolayeva (Hyperion 66631). Nikolayeva's recording of Bach's Goldberg Variations (Hyperion 66589) is also a revelation: the slow, minor-key variation (No. 25), for example, raises the level of the music from the middle 4 pathos of most performances to the godlike compassion of lower 8.

Chapter 20

1. Thomas Mann, *Pro and Contra Wagner*, trans. Allan Blunden (Chicago: University of Chicago Press, 1985), p. 108.

2. Ibid. p. 198.

3. Bryan Magee, *The Tristan Chord: Wagner and Philosophy* (New York: Henry Holt, 2001), p. 274.

4. Ibid., p. 365.

5. Ibid., p. 357.

6. Bryan Magee, *Aspects of Wagner*, 2d ed., rev. and enl. (Oxford, England: Oxford University Press, 1988), p. 43.

7. Scott, *Music*, p. 99.

8. Mann, pp. 176–177.

9. Corinne Heline, *Esoteric Music Based on the Seership of Richard Wagner*, rev. ed., 1953 reprint (La Canada, Calif.: New Age Press, 1974), p. 12.

10. Mann, p. 104.

11. Bowers, vol. 2, p. 22.

12. Mann, p. 67.

13. Ibid., p. 83.

14. Ibid., p. 130.

15. Magee, *Tristan*, p. 215.

16. Ibid.

17. Ibid.

18. While the singing is arguably better on some other presently available recordings of *Lohengrin*, I prefer the one by Claudio Abbado and the Vienna Philharmonic (Deutsche Gramophon 447764). The orchestral playing perfectly captures the macrorhythmic structure of the work—its constant swells of accumulating and dissipating energy. I've come to think of such swells as typical of music composed by intuitive as opposed to purely intellectual means. As noted in chapter 14, these macrorhythmic swells are a hallmark of seventh center music.

19. Mann, p. 104.

Chapter 21

1. Surendra Nath Dasgupta quoted in Georg Feuerstein, *The Shambhala Guide to Yoga* (Boston: Shambhala, 1996), p. 22.

2. Ibid., Inder Pal Sachdev quoted.

3. Satprem, p. 214.

4. Ibid., p. 211.

5. Ibid., p. 215. Italics in original.

6. Ibid.

7. Ibid., p. 214.

8. Scott, *Music*, p. 137. Because of the confusion of editions and versions of Bruckner's symphonies, those who wish to become familiar with recordings of the composer's works need to know what they're getting into. A few historic recordings of the bastardized first editions (either by the Schalk brothers or Ferdinand Löwe) are still on the market. These should be avoided.

The critical edition of Bruckner's works has gone through three publishing phases. Under the first editor, Robert Hass, the symphonies were supposedly restored to represent Bruckner's original intentions. Hass, however, tampered with a few of them. He included passages from Bruckner's numerous revisions of some scores that he believed were aesthetically superior to those of the composer's last authorized version. Some critics felt that his choices were genuine improvements; the purists were appalled.

The second editor of the critical edition, Leopold Nowak, removed all of Hass's emendations, but may have been overzealous in his crusade to purge the scores of every manuscript change not in Bruckner's own hand or clearly authorized by him. The recent revision of the Nowak edition by William Carragan has sought to address this problem.

Most recordings of Bruckner symphonies are clearly labeled as representing the Hass, Nowak, or Nowak revised by Carragan editions. Most listeners may not be able to tell the difference between these editions. The changes are much less noticeable than those made by Bruckner himself in the various versions of the symphonies. Being a composer myself, however, I prefer the Nowak or the revised Carragan editions: I want to hear what Bruckner originally intended.

For the Bruckner enthusiast, recordings of all the alternative versions and movements of the first three symphonies, as well as the Fourth and the Eighth (and the Zero and Double-Zero symphonies), are currently available on Teldec, as conducted by Eliahu Inbal, and on Naxos, as conducted by George Tintner. These valuable series, however, are not recommended for neophytes.

9. Of the symphonies that exist in several versions, the First and Third are the most potentially problematic for the Bruckner neophyte. The First exists in a "Linz" version of 1865–1866 and a "Vienna" version of 1890–1891, each named after the city in which it was completed. The Third is performed in a version of 1877 and one of 1888–1889. In both cases, the earlier version seems to be the more characteristic. The 1877 version of the Second Symphony seems to be that preferred in performance.

10. Bruckner, *Symphonie No. 6*, The New Philharmonia Orchestra, conducted by Otto Klemperer (EMI Classics CDM 567037).

11. My favorite recording of Bruckner's Seventh, by Claudio Abbado and the Vienna Philharmonic (Deutsche Gramophon 437518) is unfortunately out of print. Abbado is one of the few contemporary conductors I'm aware of who is sensitive to the macrorhythmic structure of seventh center music—and always brings it out.

12. Unfortunately, I can't recommend a recording of Bruckner's Eighth. Abbado hasn't released one. None of the those I've heard so far have quite mastered the macrorhythmic dimension of the piece.

13. I highly recommend the recording of the four-movement version of Bruckner's Ninth Symphony by Yoav Talmi and the Oslo Philharmonic (Chandos 7051). The recording includes not only a solid performance of the first three movements, as well as Carragan's completion of the Finale, but also renderings of the sketches themselves, which Bruckner had written out in great detail. Thus it's possible to hear how much of Carragan's completion is authentic Bruckner (about 72 percent).

14. Gustav Mahler, *Selected Letters*, ed. Knud Martner, trans. Eithne Wilkins, Ernst Kaiser, and Bill Hopkins (New York: Farrar, Straus, Giroux, 1979), p. 180.

15. Ibid., pp. 163–164, 188.

16. Ibid., pp. 164–165.

17. Ibid., p. 190.

18. Ibid., pp. 179–180.

19. Ibid., p. 190.

20. Ibid.

21. Ibid., p. 294.

22. Ibid., p. 212.

23. Ibid., p. 177.

Chapter 22

1. For further information on Swedenborg's journeys to the Afterlife, see chapters 27 and 29 of my book *The Unanswered Question.*

2. Samuel, p. 116.

3. *The New Grove Dictionary of Music and Musicians*, 2d ed. s.v. "Schoenberg, Arnold."

4. Corinne Heline, *Music: The Keynote of Human Evolution*, rev. ed. (Santa Monica, Calif.: New Age Bible and Philosophy Center, 1994), p. 127.

5. Ibid., p. 132.

6. Ibid.

7. Leland, *The Unanswered Question*, pp. 184–196.

8. Hans F. Redlich, *Alban Berg: The Man and His Music* (New York: Abelard-Schuman, 1957).

9. The name of the chorale that Berg quotes is "Est ist genug" ("It is enough").

10. Letter cited in Julian Johnson, *Webern and the Transformation of Nature* (New York: Cambridge University Press, 1999), p. 34.

Chapter 23

1. *The New Grove Dictionary*, 2d ed., s.v. "Busoni, Ferruccio."

2. Igor Stravinsky and Robert Craft, *Expositions and Developments* (Garden City, N.Y.: Doubleday, 1962), p. 169.

3. Satprem, p. 281.

4. Scott, *Music*, p. 101.

5. János Demény, ed., *Béla Bartók Letters* (New York: St. Martin's, 1971), p. 82.

6. Ibid., p. 201.

Chapter 24

1. Schloezer, p. 218.

2. Ibid., p. 97.

3. Ibid., p. 332.

4. Ibid., p. 317.

5. Peacock, p. 503.

6. Ibid., p, 483 (quoted from an unpublished letter).

7. Bowers, vol. 2, p. 231.

8. Ibid., p. 244.

9. Schloezer, pp. 256–257.

10. Ibid., p. 248.

11. Bowers, vol. 2, p. 245.

12. Schloezer, p. 160.

13. Bowers, vol. 2, p. 253.

14. Ibid.

15. Scriabin, *Preparation for the Final Mystery*, realized by Alexander Nemtin, conducted by Vladimir Ashkenazy (London/Decca 466329).

16. Mann, p. 184.

17. Feuerstein, *Yoga Tradition*, p. xxix.

18. Samuel, pp. 2–3.

19. Ibid., p. 7.

20. Ibid., p. 12.

21. Stravinsky, *Themes and Episodes*, p. 199.

22. Satprem, p. 281.

23. Malcolm Hayes, "Instrumental and Choral Works to 1948," in Peter Hill, ed., *The Messiaen Companion* (Portland, Ore.: Amadeus Press, 1995), p. 191.

24. *Ondes* means "waves," referring to the ability of this instrument to slide from one pitch to another in an effortless, wavelike manner. Martenot is the surname of the inventor of the instrument.

25. For those new to Messiaen or contemporary music, I recommend choosing a recording of *Turangalîla-symphonie* with a longer rather than a shorter duration. Most recordings take up only one CD and end up sounding like an assault (too much musical information delivered too quickly). The one on Naxos (8554478/9), by Antoni Wit and the Polish National Radio Symphony Orchestra, extends to a second CD and also includes *L'Ascension*. It's perhaps the most accessible introduction to the piece.

26. Hayes in Hill, p. 180.

27. A *vocalise* is a song without words, usually sung on a neutral syllable like *Ah* or *Oo*.

28. Liner notes, by the composer, from a CD of *Quatour pour la fin du temps* (Erato 91708), p. 14.

29. As noted in Chapter 15, note 10, the account of this adventure in consciousness is posted on my website: www.kurtleland.com. Click on the OOB-Log tab, then go to AC 221.

30. Liner notes to *Quatour pour la fin du temps*, p. 14.

31. Ibid., p. 17.

Chapter 25

1. Tame, *Beethoven*, p. 76.

2. *The New Grove Dictionary*, 2d ed., s.v. "Stockhausen, Karlheinz."

3. Mya Tannenbaum, *Conversation with Stockhausen*, trans. David Butchart (Oxford: Clarendon Press, 1987), pp. 34–35.

4. Robin Marconie, *The Works of Karlheinz Stockhausen*, 2d ed. (Oxford: Clarendon Press, 1990), pp. v–vi.

5. *The New Grove Dictionary*, 2d ed., s.v. "Stockhausen, Karlheinz."

6. Tannenbaum, p. 247.

7. Ibid., p. 84.

8. Ibid., p. 67.

9. *The New Grove Dictionary*, 2nd ed., s.v. "Stockhausen, Karlheinz."

10. Karlheinz Stockhausen, *Stimmung*, Singcircle (Hyperion 66115).

11. Liner notes, by the composer, to a CD featuring Rautavaara's *Anadyomene* (Ondine 921), p. 4.

12. Liner notes, by the composer, to a CD featuring Rautavaara's *Cantus Arcticus* (Naxos 8554147), p. 2.

13. The lower 8 quality of this music is more noticeable on the Naxos recording by Hannu Lintu and the Royal Scottish National Orchestra than on the Ondine recording by Max Pommer and the Leipzig Radio Symphony Orchestra. In the recording by Osmo Vänskä and the Lahti Symphony Orchestra (BIS 301038), the taped birdcalls are too loud, reducing the orchestra to an accompanying role. The piece comes off as an avant-garde experiment, in which the seventh and eighth centers don't come through at all.

14. Liner notes, by the composer, to a CD featuring Rautavaara's *Angels and Visitations* (Ondine 881), p. 5.

15. Liner notes to *Angels and Visitations* (Ondine 881), p. 5.

16. Ibid., p. 7.

17. Ibid.

18. Ibid.

19. Leland, *Otherwhere*, p. 44.

20. This recording of *Apotheosis* is paired with Tchaikovsky's Sixth Symphony, the *Pathétique* (Ondine 1002).

21. *The Essential Rautavaara* (Ondine 989).

22. *Vigilia* (Ondine 910).

23. Three recordings of the Seventh Symphony are presently available: by Hannu Koivula and the Royal Scottish National Orchestra (Naxos 8555814); by Leif Segerstam and the Helsinki Philharmonic Orchestra (Ondine 869); and by Osmo Vänskä and the Lahti Symphony Orchestra (BIS 301038). I prefer the last-named recording for its richness, depth, and cohesiveness.

Chapter 26

1. James, p. 415.

2. Shankar, p. 57.

3. Ibid.

4. Ibid.

5. Hodson, pp. 18–19.

6. Ibid., pp. 57–58.

7. Bach, Brandenburg Concertos, Helmuth Rilling, The Oregon Bach Festival Chamber Orchestra (Hänssler 92.126).

8. Maslow, *Farther*, pp. 308–309.

9. Private communication.

10. Khan, p. 4.

11. Ibid., p. 101.

12. Ibid.

13. Ibid.

14. Ibid.

15. Shankar, p. 57.

16. Ibid.

17. Pekka Hako, "Einojuhani Rautavaara, 70: Music Has a Will of Its Own," trans. Susan Sinisalo, *Nordic Sounds* (1998, No. 3), p. 18.

18. Yensen, p. 16.

Bibliography of Works Cited

Arye, Lane. *Unintentional Music: Releasing Your Deepest Creativity.* Charlottesville, Va.: Hampton Roads, 2001.

Bailey, Alice. "Ordered Meditation and Loving Service." In White, John, ed. *Kundalini, Evolution and Enlightenment.* Rev. ed. New York: Paragon House, 1990, pp. 459–461.

Berendt, Joachim-Ernst. *The Jazz Book: From Ragtime to Fusion and Beyond.* Revised by Günther Huesmann. Trans. H. and B. Bredigkeit, Dan Morgenstern, and Tim Nevill. 6th ed.. Brooklyn, N.Y.: Lawrence Hill Books, 1992.

———. *Nada Brahma (The World Is Sound): Music and the Landscape of Consciousness.* Trans. Helmut Bredigkeit. Rochester, Vt.: Destiny Books, 1987.

Besant, Annie, and C. W. Leadbeater. *Thought-Forms.* 1901. Abridged reprint. Wheaton, Ill.: Theosophical Publishing House, 1969.

Bowers, Faubion. *Scriabin: A Biography.* 2d rev. ed., 2 vols. in one. New York: Dover Publications, 1996.

Clampitt, Amy. *Predecessors, Et Cetera: Essays.* Ann Arbor, Mich.: University of Michigan Press, 1991.

Cope, Stephen. *Yoga and the Quest for the True Self.* New York: Bantam, 1999.

Davies, Robertson. *The Lyre of Orpheus.* New York: Viking, 1989.

Demény, János, ed. *Béla Bartók Letters.* New York: St. Martin's, 1971.

Easwaran, Eknath. *The Bhagavad Gita for Daily Living.* Vol. 1, *The End of Sorrow.* Tomales, Calif.: Nilgiri Press, 1975.

Evans-Wentz, W. Y., ed. *Tibet's Great Yogi Milarepa: A Biography from the Tibetan.* 2d ed., 1951. Reprint. New York: Oxford University Press: 1969.

Feuerstein, Georg, Ph.D. *The Shambhala Encyclopedia of Yoga.* Boston: Shambhala, 1997.

———. *The Shambhala Guide to Yoga.* Boston: Shambhala, 1996.

———. *Tantra: The Path of Ecstasy.* Boston: Shambhala, 1998.

———. *The Yoga Tradition: Its History, Literature, Philosophy and Practice.* 2d ed. Prescott, Ariz.: Hohm Press, 2001.

Flower, Newman. *George Frideric Handel: His Personality and His Times.* Rev. ed., 1959. Reprint. London: Panther Books, 1972.

Ghiselin, Brewster. *The Creative Process: A Symposium.* Berkeley, Calif.: University of California Press, 1954.

Ghose, Sri Aurobindo. *The Future Evolution of Man: The Divine Life upon Earth.* Ed. P. B. Saint-Hilaire. Reprint. Twin Lakes, Wis.: Lotus Press, 2003.

Hako, Paka. "Einojuhani Rautavaara, 70: Music Has a Will of Its Own." Trans. Susan Sinisalo. *Nordic Sounds* (1998, No. 3), pp. 18–21.

Hamel, Peter Michael. *Through Music to the Self: How to Experience and Appreciate Music Anew.* Trans. Peter Lemesurier. Boulder, Colo.: Shambhala, 1979.

Hamilton, Edith, and Huntington Cairns, eds. *The Collected Dialogues of Plato, Including the Letters.* Princeton, N.J.: Princeton University Press, 1961.

Hayes, Malcolm. "Instrumental and Choral Works to 1948." In Peter Hill, ed. *The Messiaen Companion.* Portland, Ore.: Amadeus Press, 1995, pp. 157–200.

Heline, Corinne. *Esoteric Music Based on the Seership of Richard Wagner.* Rev. ed. 1953. Reprint. La Canada, Calif: New Age Press, 1974.

———. *Music: The Keynote of Human Evolution.* Rev. ed. Santa Monica, Calif.: New Age Bible and Philosophy Center, 1994.

Hindemith, Paul. *A Composer's World: Horizons and Limitations.* 1952. Reprint. Gloucester, Mass.: Peter Smith, 1969.

Hodson, Geoffrey. *Music Forms: Superphysical Effects of Music Clairvoyantly Observed.* Adyar, Madras, India: Theosophical Publishing House, 1976.

James, William. *The Varieties of Religious Experience: A Study in Human Nature.* 1902. Reprint. New York: Random House, 1994.

Johnson, Julian. *Webern and the Transformation of Nature.* Cambridge, England: Cambridge University Press, 1999.

Jourdain, Robert. *Music, the Brain, and Ecstasy: How Music Captures Our Imagination.* New York: Avon Books, 1998.

Jung, Carl G. "Approach to the Unconscious." In Jung, Carl G., ed. *Man and His Symbols.* Garden City, N.Y.: Doubleday, 1964, pp. 18–103.

Khalsa, M. S. S. Singh. "Exploring the Myths and Misconceptions of Kundalini." In John White, ed. *Kundalini, Evolution and Enlightenment.* Rev. ed. New York: Paragon House, 1990, pp. 132–147.

Khan, Hazrat Inayat. *The Mysticism of Sound and Music: The Sufi Teaching of Hazrat Inayat Khan.* Rev. ed. Boston: Shambhala, 1996.

Krishna, Gopi. "The Phenomenon of Kundalini." In John White, ed. *Kundalini, Evolution and Enlightenment.* Rev. ed. New York: Paragon House, 1990, pp. 221–253.

Leland, Kurt. *Menus for Impulsive Living: A Revolutionary Approach to Organizing and Energizing Your Life.* New York: Doubleday, 1989.

———. *Otherwhere: A Field Guide to Nonphysical Reality for the Out-of-Body Traveler.* Charlottesville, Va.: Hampton Roads, 2001.

———. *The Unanswered Question: Death, Near-Death, and the Afterlife.* Charlottesville, Va.: Hampton Roads, 2002.

Machlis, Joseph. *Introduction to Contemporary Music.* 2d ed. New York: Norton, 1979.

McKay, Paul. "Mapping the Musical Brain." *Ottawa Citizen* (November 18, 2002). Published on the Web at www.enchantedear.com.

Magee, Bryan. *Aspects of Wagner.* 2d ed., rev. and enl. Oxford, England: Oxford University Press, 1988.

———. *The Tristan Chord: Wagner and Philosophy.* New York: Henry Holt, 2001.

Mahler, Gustav. *Selected Letters.* Ed. Knud Martner. Trans. Eithne Wilkins, Ernst Kaiser, and Bill Hopkins. New York: Farrar, Straus, Giroux, 1979.

Mann, Thomas. *Pro and Contra Wagner.* Trans. Allan Blunden. Chicago: University of Chicago Press, 1985.

Marconie, Robin. *The Works of Karlheinz Stockhausen.* 2d ed. Oxford: Clarendon Press, 1990.

Maslow, Abraham H. *The Farther Reaches of Human Nature.* 1971. Reprint. New York: Penguin Compass, 1993.

———. *Religions, Values, and Peak-Experiences.* 1964. Reprint. New York: Penguin Compass, 1994.

Mathieu, W. A. *The Listening Book: Discovering Your Own Music.* Boston: Shambhala, 1991.

Merchant, Vasant V. "Sri Aurobindo, the Tantra and Kundalini." In John White, ed. *Kundalini, Evolution and Enlightenment.* Rev. ed. New York: Paragon House, 1990, pp. 76–93.

Newman, Ernest. *The Wagner Operas.* 1949. Reprint. Princeton, N.J.: Princeton University Press, 1991.

Nichols, Roger. *Ravel Remembered.* New York: Norton, 1988.

Pandit, M. P., ed. *Sri Aurobindo on the Tantra.* Pondicherry, India: Dipti Publications, 1967.

Peacock, Kenneth. "Synaesthetic Perception: Alexander Scriabin's Color Hearing." *Music Perception* 2 (1985), pp. 483–505.

Radha, Swami Sivananda. "Kundalini: An Overview." In John White, ed. *Kundalini, Evolution and Enlightenment.* Rev. ed. New York: Paragon House, 1990, pp. 48–60.

Rama, Swami. "The Awakening of Kundalini." In John White, ed. *Kundalini, Evolution and Enlightenment.* Rev. ed. New York: Paragon House, 1990, pp. 27–47.

Redlich, H. F. *Alban Berg: The Man and His Music.* New York: Abelard-Schuman, 1957.

Samuel, Claude. *Conversations with Olivier Messiaen.* Trans. Felix Aprahamian. London: Stainer and Bell, 1976.

Sannella, Lee. "Kundalini: Classical and Clinical." In John White, ed. *Kundalini, Evolution and Enlightenment.* Rev. ed. New York: Paragon House, 1990, pp. 306-315.

Saraswati, Swami Satyananda. *Kundalini Tantra.* 1984. Reprint. Munger, Bihar, India: Yoga Publications Trust, 2001.

Satprem. *Sri Aurobindo, or the Adventure of Consciousness.* Trans. Michael Danino. 4th ed. New Delhi, India: The Mother's Institute of Research, 2000.

Schloezer, Boris de. *Scriabin: Artist and Mystic.* Trans. Nicolas Slonimsky. Berkeley, Calif.: University of California Press, 1987.

Scott, Cyril. *Bone of Contention: Life Story and Confessions.* New York: Arco, 1969.

———. *Music: Its Secret Influence Throughout the Ages.* Rev. ed., 1958. Reprint. New York: Samuel Weiser, 1981.

———. *The Philosophy of Modernism (In Its Connection with Music).* London: Kegan, Paul, Trench, Trübner, 1917.

Shankar, Ravi. *My Music, My Life.* New York: Simon and Schuster, 1968.

Stevens, Halsey. *The Life and Music of Béla Bartók.* Rev. ed. New York: Oxford University Press, 1964.

Storr, Anthony. *Music and the Mind.* New York: Ballantine Books, 1992.

Stravinsky, Igor, and Robert Craft. *Expositions and Developments.* Garden City, N.Y.: Doubleday, 1962.

———. *Themes and Episodes.* New York: Knopf, 1966.

Sullivan, J. W. N. *Beethoven: His Spiritual Development.* New York: Vintage, 1960.

Tagore, Sourindro Mohun. *Universal History of Music Complied from Diverse Sources Together with Various Original Notes on Hindu Music.* 1896. Reprint. Delhi, India: Mittal Publications, 1989.

Tame, David. *Beethoven and the Spiritual Path.* Wheaton, Ill.: Theosophical Publishing House, 1994.

———. *The Secret Power of Music: The Transformation of Self and Society through Musical Energy.* Rochester, Vermont: Destiny Books, 1984.

Tannenbaum, Mya. *Conversations with Stockhausen.* Trans. David Butchart. Oxford: Clarendon Press, 1987.

Tirtha, Swami Vishnu. "Signs of an Awakened Kundalini." In John White, ed. *Kundalini, Evolution and Enlightenment.* Rev. ed. New York: Paragon House, 1990, pp. 94–97.

Walters, Dorothy. *Unmasking the Rose: A Record of Kundalini Initiation.* Charlottesville, Va.: Hampton Roads, 2002.

Werkhoven, Henk N. *The International Guide to New Age Music: A Comprehensive Guide to the Vast and Varied Artists and Recordings of New Age Music.* Trans. Galen Yates Beach and Nynke Doetjes. New York: Billboard Books, 1998.

White, John, "Some Possibilities for Further Kundalini Research." In John White, ed. *Kundalini, Evolution and Enlightenment.* Rev. ed. New York: Paragon House, 1990, pp. 348–359.

Wilber, Ken. "Are the Chakras Real?" In John White, ed. *Kundalini, Evolution and Enlightenment.* Rev. ed. New York: Paragon House, 1990, pp. 120–131.

Yensen, Arthur E. *I Saw Heaven.* 6th ed. Parma, Idaho: N.p., 1979.

Index

About the Author

Kurt Leland is an award-winning poet, composer, professional psychic, and author of *Menus for Impulsive Living: A Revolutionary Approach to Organizing and Energizing Your Life* (Doubleday, 1989), *Otherwhere: A Field Guide to Nonphysical Reality for the Out-of-Body Traveler* (Hampton Roads, 2001), and *The Unanswered Question: Death, Near-Death, and the Afterlife* (Hampton Roads, 2002). He received his master's degree in music composition from the University of Illinois. Since 1984, Leland has maintained a consulting practice in the Boston area called Spiritual Orienteering, whose purpose is to help people develop and maintain a soul-based approach to the challenges and opportunities of life. He is the winner of several poetry awards and was featured in 1996 in *The Top 100 Psychics in America*. He lives near Boston, Massachusetts. He may be contacted at: www.kurtleland.com.

Hampton Roads Publishing Company

. . . for the evolving human spirit

Hampton Roads Publishing Company
publishes books on a variety of subjects,
including metaphysics, health,
visionary fiction, and other related topics.

For a copy of our latest catalog, call toll-free
(800) 766-8009, or send your name and address to:

Hampton Roads Publishing Company, Inc.
1125 Stoney Ridge Road
Charlottesville, VA 22902

e-mail: hrpc@hrpub.com
www.hrpub.com